THE
SLOW
COOK BOOK

THE SLOW COOK BOOK

HEATHER WHINNEY

LONDON, NEW YORK, MUNICH,
MELBOURNE, and DELHI

Photography Stuart West
Recipe Editor Emma Callery

DK UK
Editor Shashwati Tia Sarkar
Senior Art Editor Sara Robin
Managing Editor Dawn Henderson
Managing Art Editor Christine Keilty
Senior Jackets Creative Nicola Powling
Production Editor Tony Phipps
Senior Production Controller Alice Sykes
Creative Technical Support Sonia Charbonnier

DK INDIA
Senior Editor Chitra Subramanyam
Art Editor Heema Sabharwal
Assistant Editor Tina Jindal
Managing Editor Glenda Fernandes
Managing Art Editor Navidita Thapa
DTP Manager Sunil Sharma
DTP Operator Sourabh Challariya

First published in Great Britain in 2011
by Dorling Kindersley Limited
80 Strand, London WC2R 0RL

Penguin Group (UK)
2 4 6 8 10 9 7 5 3 1
001 – 180673 – September/2011

A CIP catalogue record for this book is available
from the British Library.

ISBN 978-1-4053-6782-0

Printed and bound by Tien Wah Press, Singapore

Discover more at
www.dk.com

Contents

Note:
All the recipes in this book are written for the medium
size range of slow cookers, from a minimum of 3.5 litres
to 5 litres capacity. Allowances should be made for the
differences within this size range; depending on the
internal volume of your slow cooker, liquid quantities
may need to be adjusted to ensure the food is covered
where necessary.

Foreword

I am generally not a fan of kitchen gadgets, but I have to admit to being a convert to the slow cooker. The thrifty cook in me is thoroughly excited by using the cheaper cuts of meat and beans and pulses that are so suited to slow cooking, while the ease of throwing a collection of ingredients into a pot and letting them do their own thing for hours is enormously attractive – so little effort is needed, but the rewards are great.

Our attitude towards food and cooking is changing. We seem to have a stronger desire to make home-cooked food that nourishes us and our family, as well as reining in our spending. Slow cooking is perfect for meeting this need – it suits every level of cook, especially the novice, as it is a style of cooking that doesn't rely heavily on precision. It's one of the most forgiving cooking techniques, requiring little time or skill from the cook. Moreover, by its very nature, slow cooking isn't an extravagant way to cook. By choosing value cuts and seasonal produce we naturally spend less, and the running costs of a slow cooker are minimal, little more than running a low watt light bulb, consequently conserving energy.

The great benefits of the slow cooker lie in its convenience and versatility. To be able to simply "set and forget" the slow cooker has enormous advantages for our hectic lives – it can sit day or night unattended. It ticks all the boxes for such a wide range of people: those cooking for one, large families, busy mums, and it's ideal for entertaining as it makes dinner party cooking a breeze. I didn't at first realise the potential of the slow cooker; as well as casseroles and stews, it can be used to cook whole joints of meat, delicate risottos, and delicious soups. It can also be used as a water bath or bain-marie for puddings and desserts, from mousses to steamed sponges.

The practical nature of slow cooking greatly appeals to me. It lends itself to cooking in large batches, and I love being able to cook up something delicious to serve one day and perhaps freeze for another. It is extremely satisfying to know there is the option of leftovers, thus relieving that sometimes niggling pressure of knowing what we are going to cook for dinner the next night. Of course it requires some planning, as does all cooking, but through this it also reduces food waste, which I feel passionately about. Again, the thrifty cook in me rearing its head!

Although we always think of simmering pots of meat and vegetables when slow cooking is mentioned, I think it is fair to say that the slow cooker isn't just for cold winter days. In fact, it is ideal in summer, for maybe a curry or ribs, when you don't want the heat of the cooker on all day. I've tried to reflect this throughout the book so you can always find inspiration as you dip in and out throughout the seasons. To me, Creole Fish and Corn Stew or Squid Stew would be just as welcome served up on a warm summer's evening with a hunk of crusty bread and some cold rosé wine as the Stuffed Lamb, Greek Style would be on a fresh spring day.

This book contains more than 200 recipes for slow cooking. It includes a mixture of world cuisines, features many classics, and offers some new adventurous flavour combinations. Chapters cover Soups and Broths; Stews; Casseroles, Cassoulets, and Meatballs; Tagines; Curries; Chillies and Gumbos; Pot Roasts and Ribs; Risottos, Pilafs, and Paellas; and a Pudding chapter that includes favourites such as rice pudding and crème caramel.

Step-by-step photographs take you through the types of slow cooking from stewing to poaching as well as the principles of slow cooking, such as browning ingredients and reducing sauces. A comprehensive list is also given for the slow cook's storecupboard, as a well-stocked larder is a great asset; once you have this, you need shop for little else but the perishables.

I hope this book inspires you to experiment with slow cooking. Let your imagination conjure up the thought of Beef and Anchovy Stew, the beef nestling in a mixture of heady red wine and robust herbs, cooked to perfection until it melts in your mouth; or a slow-cooked pork dish such as Belly Pork and Prunes cooked with earthy celeriac and sage, and simmered slowly in a little wine until the pork falls apart at the touch of your fork. Just the thought of it makes you want to head off into the kitchen and reach for your apron!

Heather Whinney

Techniques

Slow cooking is ideal for many households, from the time-poor cook's to the frugal one's. Food can be left unattended, less expensive ingredients can be used, and it delivers a nutritious meal at the end of the day.

Why slow cook?

Slow cooking is a method of cooking food slowly, as the name suggests, but not all food that is cooked slowly can be defined as "slow cook". To "slow cook" means that ingredients are cooked for a long time at a low heat, in a cooking pot with a fitted lid, and either covered or partially covered in liquid. Stews, casseroles, and pot roasts are all examples of slow cook dishes, and all are satisfyingly simple to make.

Prep and forget

Any cooking involves a certain amount of preparation, but with slow cooking this is kept to a minimum, as practically all the labour takes place early on in the cooking process. Once the food is in the cooking pot, it can be left to its own devices, requiring minimal attention from you. However, planning your meals and organizing your shopping list is essential – it will enable you to assemble a dish effortlessly.

Maximize flavour

When left to slow cook, ingredients "marry" together and the flavours intensify. When meat is slow cooked, the gelatine is extracted from the meat and bones, which results in a rich, concentrated sauce; it is this exchange of flavours between the meat and sauce that gives slow cooking its wonderful rich but mellow taste. Aromatic vegetables and spices such as cloves, cinnamon, and star anise are great to use as their distinct flavours are not lost when slow cooked.

Be thrifty

Slow cooking makes economic sense as it works best using cheaper cuts of meat that have high bone and fat content, and inexpensive staples such as beans and lentils. It is also easy to cook large quantities at once, creating leftovers for another day or to freeze. Slow cooking is also an opportunity to be creative and make meals out of very little – long, gentle cooking will turn the remnants of your refrigerator or storecupboard into a feast.

Tips for success

Choosing the right equipment and using your ingredients with a little know-how will help you achieve great results from slow cooking.

For traditional slow cooking, choose a thick-walled flameproof casserole that holds the heat well, such as a cast-iron one or an enamelled cast-iron one. Ensure it has a well fitting lid and can be used on the hob or in the oven. Cast-iron casseroles can be heavy, so choose one with two easy-to-hold handles. Pick a size to suit your requirements: as a rule of thumb, food should only reduce down to about three-quarters of the pot's volume once cooked from full.

Moroccan tagines, cone-shaped earthenware cooking pots with tall lids, are apt for slow cooking. They are designed to return condensation back into the dish to keep the food moist. For versatility, choose one that can be used on the hob (with a diffuser) and the oven.

For maximum flavour, brown the meat at the start of cooking, and soften aromatic vegetables such as onions and garlic by sautéing.

Be careful not to over season; salty flavours become concentrated with slow cooking. Season lightly initially, then adjust at the end of cooking if needed.

Peppercorns and seeds, such as cumin, coriander, and fennel, are best crushed before adding to the pot so they release their flavour slowly.

Woody herbs, such as rosemary and thyme, are robust enough to add at the beginning of cooking; add delicate herbs, such as parsley, towards the end of cooking, or stir into the finished dish.

Always add delicate ingredients that don't need much cooking, such as fish and seafood, towards the end of the cooking time.

If topping up the liquid during cooking, add hot liquid to prevent lowering the cooking temperature.

Clockwise from top left: slow cooking lends itself to soothing soups (Pumpkin and ginger soup p86), fresh and light risottos (Risotto primavera p302), hearty casseroles (Osso bucco p162), and summer ribs (Pork ribs Oriental p294).

With so many slow cookers on the market it is important that you choose one to suit your needs. There are certain variables, both in terms of design and price, but slow cookers generally operate on similar principles.

How to use your slow cooker

A slow cooker consists of a sturdy, heatproof outer casing and an inner cooking pot into which the food is placed. The outer casing is made of either stainless steel or aluminium and is where the heating element and controls are housed. The inner cooking pot is usually removable. The lid on a slow cooker fits snugly so that heat cannot escape. The condensation that occurs during the slow, low-heat cooking process gathers around the lip of the pot and creates a water seal. The condensation is then released back into the pot and it is this that keeps the food moist. The combination of a long cooking time and the steam that is created within the pot destroys any bacteria, making it a safe cooking method. It is important to resist the temptation to open the lid to look – this will release heat and break the water seal and you will need to add a further 20 minutes to the cooking time.

Choosing the right shape and size

Slow cookers come in a range of sizes, but small machines start from 1.5 litres (2¾ pints), which is suitable for 1–2 people; a medium-sized 3.5-litre (6-pint) cooker is great for 4 people; for 6 people or more, choose a 5-litre (8¾-pint) model or larger. However, bigger isn't necessarily better unless you are catering for large numbers or wish to batch cook – you need to half-fill a slow cooker for optimum performance, and accommodate it on your kitchen worktop, so choose wisely. Slow cookers can be either round or oval in shape; the choice is down to personal preference. Casseroles, chillies, and curries are all perfect for round cookers but an oval one is preferable if you wish to cook whole joints of meat or chickens, and fit in pudding basins or ramekins. The removable inner cooking pots are usually ceramic, but they are also available in cast-aluminium. Ceramic pots are easiest to wash and clean, retain the heat well, and can be served straight to the table. Cast-aluminium pots are lighter and allow you to brown food in them first before cooking. Always choose a slow cooker with a recognised safety mark.

Adapting recipes for the slow cooker

You can easily adapt conventional recipes for the slow cooker. Firstly, find a recipe in this book that is similar in style and has similar ingredients, such as the meat cuts, beans, or vegetables. From this you can ascertain the length of cooking time needed. If you are at all worried, leave it to cook for longer – a slow cooker won't boil dry. Secondly, adjust the ingredient quantities to ensure they will all fit in the pot. Finally, as a general guide, halve the liquid in your recipe. This is because the liquid doesn't evaporate in the slow cooker as it does with other methods. You can always top it up if needed, or if you do find yourself with too much, remove the lid and cook on High until the excess liquid has evaporated away. When adapting recipes, bear the following in mind:

The recipe must contain some liquid if going into the slow cooker.

Make sure all frozen ingredients are thawed and meats are thoroughly defrosted before cooking.

If a recipe calls for milk, cream, or soured cream, only add this for the last 30 minutes of cooking. For best results, stir in cream just before serving.

You may need to reduce spices and herbs as their flavour becomes concentrated in the slow cooker.

GENERAL GUIDE TO COOKING TIMES

The table below indicates preferred cooking times, but refer to your manufacturer's instructions.

	Low	High
Meat stews and casseroles	6–8 hours	3–4 hours
Pot roasts	6–8 hours	3–4 hours
Whole chickens	6–8 hours	3–4 hours
Ribs	6–8 hours	n/a
Dried beans	6–8 hours	3–4 hours
Steamed puddings	n/a	3–4 hours

Using the slow cooker

Slow cookers are more efficient than traditional ovens and can help to reduce your fuel bill as they use minimum electricity – often only as much as a low watt light bulb. The vast majority of slow cookers have only 2 or 3 heat settings, making them very easy to use. For best results, the slow cooker should be at least half full but no more than two-thirds full when cooking.

Lid—glass lids allow you to check the food without breaking the water seal.

Inner cooking pot— usually removable to make cleaning easier.

Heat controls—often a simple dial. Some allow you to program the cooking time.

Outer casing—contains the electrical parts. Wipe it with a damp cloth to clean it.

HEAT SETTINGS

The various slow cooker models have different functions for heat settings, but as a rule they all have Low and High. Some also have Auto, Warm, or even Medium settings. Preheating the slow cooker before use raises the temperature of the pot before adding the food. The necessity of doing this differs for each slow cooker so it is advisable to read the manufacturer's instructions for your model.

Low: This is the lowest temperature you can cook at and is ideal for leaving food throughout the day or overnight. It is the best setting for cheaper cuts of meat. Cooking times for Low vary between 6–12 hours. The food will cook at around 100°C (200°F).

High: This setting is around 150°C (300°F), and in general the food cooks between 3–6 hours. As a rule of thumb, the High setting takes half as long as the Low one, so 1 hour on High setting equals 2 hours on Low.

Auto: This setting starts cooking the food on High for 1 hour then reduces it to the Low temperature for the remainder of the cooking time.

Keep warm: This holds the food at a lower temperature than Low to keep it at an ideal heat for serving. Many cookers switch to this setting automatically once the food is cooked. However, do not leave the food standing in the cooker keeping warm for longer than 1–2 hours.

There are various types of slow cooking method, which you can do traditionally or in the slow cooker. Poaching involves gentle simmering in water, braising is excellent for sealing in flavour before long cooking, stewing produces wonderful sauces where the ingredients have melded together, and pot roasting is ideal for cooking whole joints of meat.

Types of slow cooking

Poaching

The ingredients are immersed in water, then simmered very gently. This is good for both delicate meats, such as fish or chicken breast, and dense or tough meats, such as silverside of beef; a clean, silky texture is achieved. A fitted lid is essential for keeping the moisture in the pan. Never attempt to rush poaching – hard boiling dries out meat. The traditional method (shown with chicken) is described here, but if using a slow cooker, simplify it by adding the meat, water, and any flavourings to the pot at the beginning.

1 Use enough cold water to cover the meat, then bring the water to the boil. Add a pinch of salt and the meat. Reduce the heat and bring back to a gentle simmer, cover the pan with the lid, and poach for 30 minutes.

2 Add vegetables to flavour the stock, such as artichokes, carrots, broad beans, and any other green vegetables you want to include – maybe shredded cabbage or runner beans – and cook for 5–10 minutes until they are tender.

3 To test the chicken for doneness, pierce the thigh to the bone – if the juices run clear it is done, if they are red it is not. Tip the bird slightly as you lift it out of the pan so that the hot stock in its cavity runs back into the pan.

Braising

This technique combines both dry heat and moist heat cooking. The meat, poultry, or vegetables are first seared in hot fat and then cooked slowly in a pan with minimal liquid, just enough to cover. Searing helps to keep the meat succulent. The meat is cut into slightly larger pieces than for stewing. Slightly more expensive cuts can be used for braising, although this technique works just as well with cheap cuts. Braising suits cuts such as brisket, shanks, and oxtail very well. The traditional method steps are shown below, but the process is the same for the slow cooker up to step 3; after the alcohol has evaporated, transfer everything to the slow cooker, pour over the stock, and cook on either setting.

1 Heat the oil in a frying pan over a medium-high heat and brown the meat. Let the pieces sit for about 5 minutes until brown underneath, then turn them and cook the other side for another 5 minutes. Remove with a slotted spoon and set aside.

2 Add a mixture of aromatic vegetables, such as carrots, onions, celery, and leeks, stir well with a spatula to collect the meat residue, then cook until the vegetables are browned. Add flavourings, such as thyme, bay leaves, and garlic, and continue to cook for a few minutes more.

3 Put the meat and vegetables in a flameproof casserole, pour in some wine, and boil over a high heat until nearly evaporated. Add enough stock to cover the meat. Bring to a simmer, cover with the lid, and cook in the oven on a low heat until the meat is tender.

Stewing

Here the ingredients are simmered fully covered in stock or water, and sometimes wine. This is great for tougher cuts as the connective tissue and fat break down while cooking, releasing gelatinous juices and making the meat tender. For a slow cooker, transfer everything to the slow cooker at the end of step 3.

1 Cut the meat into large bite-sized pieces and toss in flour, if you wish (this will help to thicken the stew later). Sear the meat in hot fat and cook for about 5–8 minutes until browned on all sides. Remove and set aside.

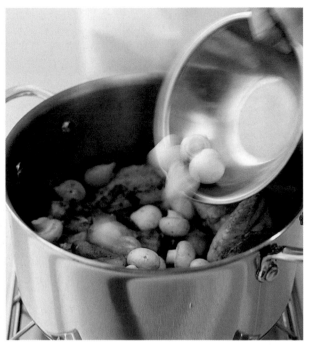

2 Add a selection of vegetables and cook for 5 minutes until golden. Remove and set aside. Deglaze the pan with a little stock or wine and return the meat and vegetables with any sturdy herbs, such as rosemary.

3 Pour in any remaining wine and enough stock to cover the contents of the pan completely. Raise the heat and bring to the boil.

4 Reduce the heat to bring to a gentle simmer and cover with the lid. Cook in the oven on a low heat for a few hours, until the meat is tender.

Pot roasting

This is essentially a braised dish that uses a whole joint of meat, usually of a tougher cut. Liquid is used to barely cover the meat, and vegetables and herbs are added to the pot. A pot roast is cooked in a covered pot on a low heat in the oven or slow cooker for several hours, until the meat is fork tender. The whole joint is usually browned first as this improves the flavour of the finished dish. If using a slow cooker, transfer everything to the slow cooker at the end of step 2, pour over the stock, and cook on auto/low.

1 Heat 2 tbsp of oil in a flameproof casserole until very hot. Add the meat (it should sizzle) and brown it well on all sides. Remove the casserole from the heat, take out the meat, and discard all but 2 tbsp of fat from the casserole.

2 Return the meat to the casserole and add vegetables and herbs of your choice. Pour in some wine and cook on the hob for a few minutes so that the alcohol evaporates.

3 Pour in the stock and stir well. Cook for about 3 hours in a low oven, turning the meat 3 or 4 times, and topping up with more stock if too much liquid evaporates.

Keeping a good storecupboard makes any style of cooking easier, but it can really come into its own if you are slow cooking. It reduces the need to plan too far ahead so you can cook spontaneously and decrease your shopping trips. The storecupboard shouldn't be just a place to keep half-open packs and half-used jars; when it is organized well with staple ingredients, you can create meals with only a few fresh additions.

The slow cooking storecupboard

Flavourings

Pastes, seasonings, and oils contribute vital flavour – a spoonful of Thai curry paste or a dab of French mustard can determine the cuisine of your dish in an instant. Use honeys to adjust the sweetness of a marinade. Both olive oil and sunflower oil are versatile enough to be used at high and low temperatures.

- Tomato purée
- Thai curry paste – red and green
- Assorted mustards
- Black peppercorns – whole and crushed
- Sea salt
- Honey
- Olive oil
- Sunflower oil

Canned and jarred ingredients

An assortment of cans and jars is indispensible for slow cooking. Tomatoes form the base of many stews and ragù dishes, while coconut milk is useful for curries and soups. Choose full-fat varieties of coconut milk, though, as low-fat versions can split on cooking. Canned sweetcorn and jarred olives are a great way to add vegetables when you have none in the fridge.

- Tomatoes
- Sun-dried tomatoes
- Coconut milk
- Dried mushrooms
- Anchovies
- Sweetcorn
- Pulses
- Olives
- Capers

Grains and pasta

Store a range of pasta shapes and sizes so you can add them to soups or casseroles. They are good for late additions to the pot or to serve as accompaniments, as are noodles. Grains such as rice, pearl barley, or farro will happily simmer slowly on a low heat.

- Rice – basmati, white, and brown
- Risotto rice – arborio or carnaroli
- Pearl barley and farro
- Dried pasta
- Dried noodles – rice and egg

Crushed black peppercorns

Dried mushrooms

Dried pasta

Sauces and stocks

A good selection of sauces and stocks gives you countless options. Use sauces for marinades or for adjusting flavour at the end of cooking. Vinegars can be used to deglaze after browning, adding richness and depth to your dish. While fresh stock is preferable, powdered stock, or bouillon, is an essential item to keep in the storecupboard if you like to cook without planning too far ahead. Be careful with seasoning, however, when you use powdered stocks – they often contain added salt so taste your dish first before adding any extra seasoning.

- Soy sauce
- Fish sauce
- Tabasco sauce
- Worcestershire sauce
- Flavoured vinegars – white wine, red wine, and cider
- Balsamic vinegar
- Rice wine vinegar
- Powdered stock (bouillon) – vegetable, chicken, and beef

Beans and pulses

All beans and pulses are ideal for slow cooking. They retain their shape and texture if cooked for a long time and they are a good way of adding bulk and protein to a dish. They also keep indefinitely, so there is no fear of them spoiling. Plan ahead, as most pulses need soaking overnight, except lentils, which just need rinsing well. The older the pulses, the longer they will need soaking. For general soaking and cooking times, see page 37.

- Kidney beans
- Cannellini beans
- Haricot beans
- Butterbeans
- Black beans
- Black-eyed beans
- Adzuki beans
- Borlotti beans
- Flageolet beans
- Pinto beans
- Chickpeas
- Yellow and green split peas
- Red lentils
- Puy lentils

Spices and dried herbs

Herbs and spices play an important role in slow cooking, especially if cooking cheaper cuts of meat, as they can transform a simple dish into something special. It is always advisable to taste at the end of cooking and adjust herbs and spices as necessary.

- Allspice
- Cinnamon – ground and sticks
- Coriander seeds
- Cumin – ground and seeds
- Caraway seeds
- Cardamom pods
- Chili flakes
- Cayenne pepper
- Cloves – ground
- Curry powder
- Fennel seeds
- Ginger – ground
- Juniper berries
- Mustard seeds
- Nutmeg – whole
- Paprika
- Saffron threads
- Star anise
- Turmeric
- Dried oregano

Star anise

Kidney beans

Red wine vinegar

As with any cooking, good ingredients will produce good results, but this doesn't necessarily mean choosing expensive ingredients. Slow cooking enables you to make the best possible food with whatever is available, whether it's a collection of humble root vegetables, a cheap meat cut, or some fresh seafood. All it requires is time and care so it can be cooked to perfection.

Choosing and using ingredients

Vegetables

As a rule, the harder, tougher vegetables respond best to slow cooking as it turns them deliciously sweet and tender. The more delicate vegetables should be added to the pot later so they don't fall apart while cooking.

Gem squash
This small squash is sweeter than the rest of the pumpkin family, with orange flesh inside the tough green skin. Peel using a potato peeler and add to stews or curries.

Pumpkin
These are usually more fibrous and watery than other squash. If sold in pieces, use within a few days as the flesh is more perishable once cut.

Butternut squash
A common variety of winter squash with a smooth, dense flesh, which is sweet and nutty. It will keep for a few weeks in a cool place. Good with lentils or coconut milk-based dishes.

Acorn squash
A mild-flavoured squash, slightly sweet, with firm, yellow-orange flesh. To prepare, cut in half, scoop out the seeds, then cut into quarters. Peel and cut to the size you require.

Carrot
Use either finely diced and
sautéed with celery and onion
to form a flavour base, or sliced
to add colour and sweetness.

Turnip
The familiar top-shaped turnip is usually
purple fading to white at the root. When
small, the flavour is sweet and delicate.

Parsnip
The flavour of this creamy beige root
has hints of parsley and carrot, but
with a slight sweetness and nuttiness.
Use the scrubbed peel with other
vegetable trimmings to make a winter
vegetable stock.

Beetroot
The firm, juicy flesh of beetroot has
an earthy, sweet flavour. It is best
cooked with other red vegetables, or
those that will absorb the seeping
crimson juices.

Celeriac
Celery root, or celeriac, has a thick,
rough skin that conceals a crisp white
flesh. It has a refreshing, slightly herbal
flavour, combining the tastes of parsley
and parsnip with celery.

Shallot
They look like miniature onions, but shallots have a sweet, flowery flavour that does not overwhelm, and forms a rich flavour base for numerous sauces.

Garlic
Sauté garlic briefly at the beginning of a dish to add a layer of flavour; never cook until browned or it will taste bitter.

Brown onion
The workhorse of the kitchen, the pungent brown onion is used in numerous savoury dishes, raw, fried, braised, stewed, boiled, or roasted.

Sweet red onion
The juicy crimson and white flesh is noticeably sweet, although pungent when raw. Slow cooking caramelizes the juices and mellows the flavour.

Potato
Choose waxy potatoes if you want them to hold their shape, or floury ones if you want them to dissolve and thicken the sauce.

Sweet potato
These have softer flesh than potatoes so will cook far quicker; add them to slow cooked dishes as a late addition. The taste is sweet, rather like squash.

New potato
Firm, with waxy flesh, these often don't need peeling and can be added to a dish whole. Use in summer casseroles.

Savoy cabbage
The attractively crinkled leaves are more loosely wrapped round the head than those of other cabbages and are more full-bodied in flavour.

Celery
A kitchen staple, celery makes a great base for casseroles and stews, along with carrot and onion. Trim the base and pull away any stringy bits.

Red cabbage
Offering beautiful, vibrant colour, red cabbage is sweeter than white, but the leaves are tougher, so they take longer to cook.

Curly kale
Exceptionally nutritious, the leaves have a rich, meaty flavour and robust texture. Kale will hold together quite well when slow cooked, or it can be added at the end.

Fennel
With its sweet, warm aniseed flavour and crisp texture, fennel makes a great vegetable for slow cooking. Either chop finely and sauté first with onion, or roughly chop and add to the pot. The flavour is subtler when cooked.

Poultry

The term "poultry" covers domesticated birds, including chicken, turkey, goose, guineafowl and duck (farmed duck is classified as game). This most versatile of meats works with most flavours and cooking methods. Whole birds or portions with the bone left in are ideal for slow cooking.

Whole chicken leg
Comprises the thigh and drumstick. A leg joint is good for slow cooking as the meat remains tender and juicy. Perfect for classics such as Coq au vin.

Chicken thigh
Sold skin on or off, bone-in, or boneless. Best with bone in for slow cooking as it keeps the meat tender and the taste is superior. When deboned, they are excellent stuffed and rolled up. Thighs are better than breast for slow cooking.

Whole chicken
These are perfect for poaching in flavoured liquid. The flesh becomes tender, moist, and silky and falls off the bone effortlessly. The bones can then be used for stock. Choose free range chicken, if you can, for ethical reasons and taste.

Whole duck
It is better to joint these for slow cooking as they can be fatty. Ducks have a rich, dense meat that is best teamed with citrus fruits or spices that will cut through the fattiness of the meat.

Duck leg
These have a superb flavour and rich dark meat. They take longer to cook than breast meat and have a little more sinew, but this makes them an incredibly tasty choice for slow cooking. Prick or slash the layer of skin and fat before browning in a pan.

Pork

Almost all pork cuts are suitable for slow cooking, but the cheaper, fattier varieties are the best as they provide the tastiest sauce. They go well with acidic-flavoured fruits, woody herbs, earthy vegetables, and lentils.

Pork leg
These are very lean so need careful cooking to prevent them from drying out. To cook as an escalope, leg steaks are beaten out very thinly.

Spare ribs
Trimmed ribs are sold as a rack or individually cut. Indivual ribs are easier to fit into a pot.

Rolled leg joint
Cuts from the lower leg, where the muscles are tougher, are suited to slow cooking. Pork leg meat can be bought cut into bite-sized pieces.

Belly slices
This is a fatty cut from the underside of the belly. Buy in whole pieces or slices. Slow cooking transforms it into tender meat. Goes well with Asian spices, hearty vegetables, or pulses.

Hock
The hock is the joint near the foot and is sometimes called pork knuckle. It is a cheap cut with lots of flavour that requires long and slow cooking.

Beef

There are many beef cuts suited to long slow cooking. These come from the forequarters and are less expensive than the leaner cuts. Choose beef that is a good, dark red colour, which has preferably been hung for 21 days. Beef responds well to marinating, as it adds depth of flavour to the finished dish and will tenderize the meat.

Minced beef
Forequarter (second grade) mince can be quite fatty but has good flavour. Minced shin needs the longest cooking. Steak mince from the back or leg is the leanest and most tender.

Diced braising steak
Usually lean chuck, blade, or flank. Often sold minced. Braise, casserole, or stew.

Shin of beef
Cut from the foreleg, it needs careful trimming. Dice and use for stews and casseroles.

Oxtail
The tail is sold in chunks. The bones enrich sauces with their marrow. Stew, braise, or use in soup.

Brisket
Cut from the underside behind the front leg. Brisket needs long slow cooking because it has a lot of connective tissue, but has great flavour.

Lamb

As with all the best meats for slow cooking, the well-exercised parts of the animal make the choicest cuts. The high fat content in lamb meat makes it ideal for the slow cooker or casserole; slow cooking renders the meat meltingly tender and adds lots of flavour. Team lamb with sweet vegetables such as peas or fresh herbs such as mint, as these flavours cut through the fatty richness.

Minced lamb
This can be quite fatty and will add flavour and succulence to a dish. However, too much fat can make it greasy. Leg or shin will yield the leanest mince.

Neck fillet
Derived from the tender eye of the neck muscles, this cut of lamb is versatile and responds well to both high-heat quick cooking and long slow cooking. Cut into bite-sized pieces, or stuff it and cook it whole.

Shank
Slow, moist cooking is required to turn the sinews in the shank into a succulent jelly. Allow one shank per person. Foreleg shanks are slimmer than those from the back leg.

Half leg
This is a prime cut, but requires long slow cooking. It can be cooked bone in or bone out. It has more flavour when cooked with the bone in, as the meat becomes fork tender and falls away from the bone.

Fish

As a rule, fish is added towards the end of slow cooking as its delicate flesh needs only minimal time to cook. It adds a distinctive flavour to a slowly simmered sauce. Always choose sustainable fish.

Halibut
Noted for its dense, firm, and low-fat white fillets, which have a mild taste. It is best served grilled or pan-fried with a flavoured butter.

Tuna
Rich and full of flavour, tuna is robust enough to add to a slow cooked dish. Choose steaks that are fairly thick and try searing them first for extra flavour.

Salmon
The flesh is firm, moist, and oily with a rich flavour. Choose chunky pieces and cut to a uniform size to add to the pot. Delicious added to a fish soup or stew.

Monkfish
With its dense texture, this is quite a "meaty" fish. It is a good choice for slow cooking as it won't fall apart easily. Monkfish has mildly flavoured, slightly chewy, white flesh.

Swordfish
These meaty steaks have a similar texture to tuna and are ideal for using as a late addition to the pot.

Cod
This fish has white, chunky flakes with a delicate flavour. It needs very little cooking before the flesh is ready and turns opaque. If overcooked, cod will disintegrate and become chewy.

Haddock
This has a delicate, creamy, sweet flavour, similar to cod, and can be used instead of cod in recipes. Its delicate flesh needs only minimal cooking; add to the pot for a short time once the sauce is cooked.

Seafood

As with fish, seafood needs to be added late as it requires very little cooking. Seafood adds much flavour, texture, and protein to a dish and can transform an everyday sauce into a memorable meal.

Octopus

Slow cooking turns the meat tender and moist; undercooked, it can be chewy. You can buy it prepared or frozen, but be sure to defrost it thoroughly before adding to the pot. It is particularly good with a tomato-based sauce.

Squid

This requires either "fast flash" cooking or slow cooking in a simmering sauce to become tender. Like octopus, it is good in a tomato sauce. It has a mellow flavour so can take punchy sauces.

Clams

These have a delicate, sweet flavour with a texture similar to mussels. They need very little cooking and will steam open in minutes when added to a simmering sauce. A hearty, full-flavoured sauce makes a good accompaniment. Discard any clams that don't open after cooking.

Prawns

Add prawns at the end of cooking as they will become tough and chewy if overcooked. The cooking time is dependent on their size. The shells make a tasty stock.

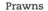

Mussels

They taste slightly salty, with an intense flavour of the sea. Add them to a dish late to prevent overcooking, which results in a rubbery texture. Once all the shells are open they are ready to eat.

Most vegetables are suited to slow cooking, although some need longer cooking than others. Knowing how to prepare vegetables correctly saves time and is key to a successful dish.

Preparing vegetables

Peeling and chopping garlic

1 Place each garlic clove flat on a cutting board. Place the flat of a large knife blade on top and pound it with the heel of your hand.

2 Discard the skin and cut off the ends of each clove. Slice the clove into slivers lengthways, then cut across into tiny chunks. Collect the pieces into a pile and chop again for finer pieces.

Peeling and dicing onions

1 Cut the onion in half and peel it, leaving the root to hold the layers together. Make a few slices into the onion, but not through the root.

2 With the tip of your knife, slice down through the layers of onion vertically, cutting as close to the root as possible.

3 Cut across the vertical slices to produce an even dice. Use the root to hold the onion steady, then discard it when all the onion is diced.

Skinning and deseeding tomatoes

1 Remove the green stem, score an "X" in the skin of each tomato at the base, then immerse it in a pan of boiling water for 20 seconds, or until the skin loosens.

2 Using a slotted spoon, remove the tomato from the pan of boiling water and place it into a bowl of iced water to cool.

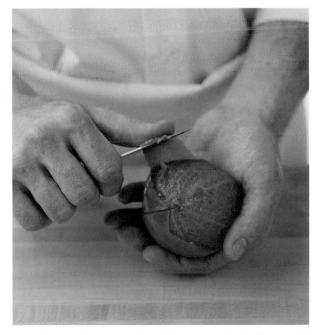

3 When cool enough to handle, use a paring knife to peel away the loosened skin.

4 Cut each tomato in half and gently squeeze out the seeds over a bowl. Discard the seeds.

Roasting and peeling peppers

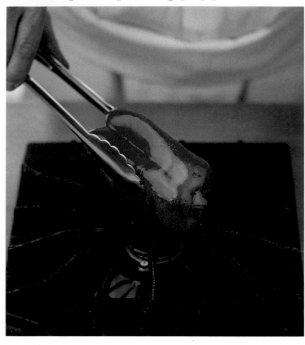

1 Using tongs, hold each pepper over an open flame to char the skin. Rotate the pepper to char it evenly.

2 Put the peppers into a plastic bag and seal tightly. Set the bag aside and allow the skins to loosen.

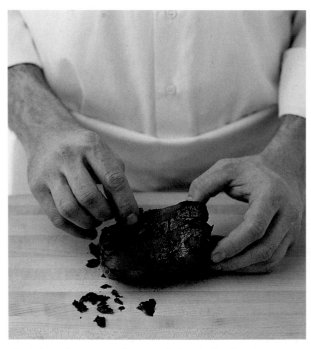

3 When the peppers have cooled completely, use your fingers to peel away the charred skin.

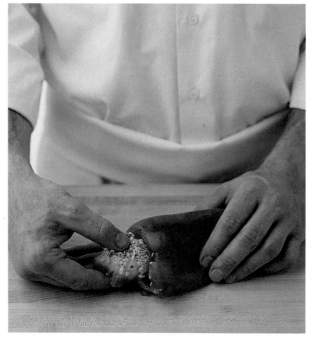

4 Pull off the stalk, keeping the core attached. Discard seeds and slice the flesh into strips, or roughly chop.

Coring and shredding cabbage

1 Hold the head of cabbage firmly on the cutting board and use a sharp knife to cut it in half, straight through the stalk end.

2 Cut the halves again through the stalk lengthways and slice out the core from each quarter.

3 Working with each quarter at a time, place the wedge cut-side down. Cut across the cabbage to shred it finely.

Trimming greens

1 Discard all limp and discoloured leaves. Slice each leaf along both sides of the centre rib, then remove it and discard.

2 Working with a few leaves at a time, roll them loosely into a bunch. Cut across the roll to the desired width, making strips.

Peeling squashes

1 Holding the squash firmly, use a chef's knife to cut it lengthways in half, working from the stalk to the core.

2 Using a spoon, remove the seeds and fibres from each squash half and discard them.

3 Use a vegetable peeler or knife to remove the skin. Cut into pieces, then into chunks, or slice as required.

Rehydrating mushrooms

1 To rehydrate dried mushrooms, place the mushrooms – either wild or cultivated – into a bowl of hot water. Allow them to soak for at least 15 minutes.

2 Remove the mushrooms from the soaking liquid using a slotted spoon. If you plan to use the soaking liquid in your recipe, strain the liquid through a fine sieve, coffee filter, or muslin to remove any sand or grit.

Herbs and spices are essential for adding aroma and flavour to a slow-cooked dish. Experience will teach you which spices to use with which foods, so use them sparingly at first. Add woody herbs, such as thyme and bay, at the beginning of slow cooking, but delicate ones, such as parsley and mint, are best added at the end as they can lose their potency. Chillies, on the other hand, can intensify on slow cooking.

Using herbs and spices

Making a bouquet garni

This is a bundle of herbs used to flavour a sauce. For a classic combination, tie sprigs of thyme and parsley and a bay leaf together. You could also include sage or rosemary.

Deseeding and cutting chillies

Slice chillies in half lengthways then scrape out the seeds (this will reduce their heat, so leave if you wish). Slice or chop finely; wearing plastic gloves is a good idea.

Dry-roasting spices

To dry-roast spices such as cloves, cinnamon, and star anise, place them in an oven preheated to 160°C (325°F/Gas 3), or fry them in a dry pan until lightly browned.

Frying spices in oil

When spices are fried until lightly coloured, their flavour gets trapped in the oil. This is called tempering. The oil is used along with the spices at the start or end of cooking.

The hard exteriors of dried pulses need long simmering to soften, making them a natural choice for slow cooking. The basic preparation of pulses is simple – sort, rinse, soak if needed, and simmer. They can then be used for different dishes, including favourites from around the world such as Boston baked beans from the US, the fragrant dahls of the Indian subcontinent, or Spain's grand meat and vegetable stew *Cocido*.

Preparing pulses

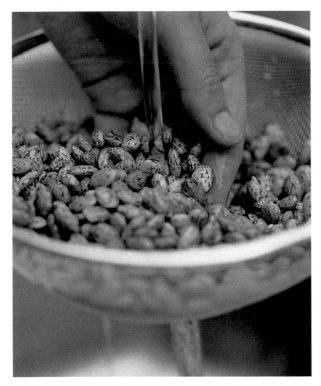

Sorting and rinsing

Whatever kind of pulse you're using, whether beans, lentils, whole peas, or split peas, start by sorting and rinsing them. Place the pulses in a colander and carefully pick out any damaged or broken ones, and any foreign material such as husks, pieces of grit, or tiny pebbles. Then rinse the pulses well under cold running water. Rinsing is essential for removing excess dust and dirt from the pulses.

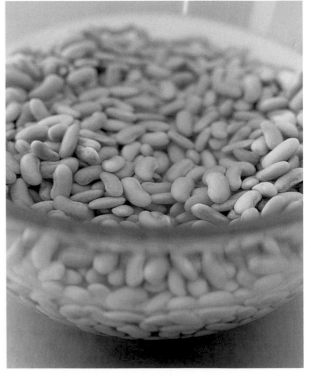

Soaking

Apart from lentils and split peas, all pulses need to be soaked for at least 8 hours, and preferably overnight (you will find that old pulses need soaking for longer, so it is best to plan to leave them overnight). Soaking enables pulses to cook more quickly and evenly. Place them in a bowl, add three times their volume of cold water, then cover and place in the refrigerator. When you are ready to cook, drain the pulses and discard the soaking water.

Boiling

Drain the soaked pulses, then place them in a large pan along with any flavourings. Pour in four times their volume of cold water and add 1 tbsp of vegetable oil to stop them sticking. Bring rapidly to the boil, and boil hard for 10 minutes, skimming away any foam with a slotted spoon. (Some pulses, such as kidney beans, contain toxins that are destroyed by this initial 10 minutes of hard boiling.) Lower the heat, part-cover with a lid, and simmer until tender, or transfer to the slow cooker to cook.

Adding flavour

The flavour of pulses can be rather bland, so it's usually a good idea to add some aromatics. A bouquet garni or a sprig of herbs will do the trick: bay leaf, parsley, rosemary, or thyme all work well. A pinch of cumin, coriander, chilli, or caraway is another option, but you can also pop a carrot into the pan, or an onion studded with cloves. Alternatively, you can cook pulses in a well-flavoured stock, but never season it with salt – it will prevent them from softening.

SOAKING AND COOKING TIMES

Use the following soaking times to prepare pulses for both the slow cooker and for traditional cooking. The cooking times given are general guides for the stove; for the slow cooker, allow 6–8 hours on Low or 3–4 hours on High.

Type of pulse	Soaking time	Approximate cooking time
Adzuki beans	overnight	40–45 mins
Black beans	overnight	1 hr
Black-eyed peas	overnight	1–1½ hrs
Borlotti beans	overnight	1–1½ hrs
Butter beans	overnight	1–1½ hrs
Cannellini beans	overnight	1–1½ hrs
Chickpeas	overnight	2–3 hrs
Flageolet beans	overnight	1½ hrs
Haricot beans	overnight	1–1½ hrs
Lentils (split)	not required	25 mins
Lentils (whole)	not required	45 mins
Pinto beans	overnight	1–1½ hrs
Kidney beans	boil hard for 10 mins, then soak for 4 hrs	1–1½ hrs
Split peas	not required	45 mins

Versatile poultry works well with all types of slow cooking. The following techniques show you how to truss a bird for pot roasting, debone it, and portion it for stews and casseroles.

Preparing poultry

Trussing

This technique can appear quite fiddly but once mastered, it only takes minutes to do. Trussing a bird before cooking allows it to hold its shape perfectly. It also helps cook it evenly, without overcooking any of the bony parts first. A poussin is shown here, but this works on other birds, too.

1 Season the insides of the bird with salt and pepper. Holding the bird breast-side down on a clean work surface, tuck the neck skin under the bird, and fold the wings over it.

2 Turn the bird over and pass a length of string under the tail end of the bird; tie a secure knot over the leg joints. Bring the strings along the sides of the body, between the breast and the legs, and loop them around the legs.

3 Turn the bird over so it is breast-side down again and tie the strings tightly under the body. Bring both ends of the string down between the sides of the body and the insides of the wings.

4 Tie the wing bones at the neck opening so they are tucked securely under the body. After cooking, cut the string to remove it.

Deboning poultry

If you prefer boneless meat, leg pieces (shown here) are better for slow cooking than the leaner breast meat. You may also wish to remove the bone to stuff the meat. Use a good, sharp knife and a series of shallow cuts to free the bone while preserving all the flesh. You can save the bones for stock.

1 To debone a drumstick, start in the middle and insert the tip of your knife until you locate the bone. Slice along the bone in both directions to expose it fully.

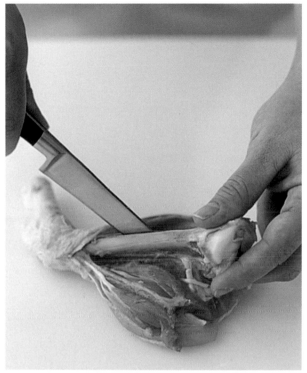

2 Open the flesh and cut neatly around the bone using short strokes to free it completely from the flesh. Discard the bone, or use it to flavour stock.

3 To debone a thigh, place the thigh skin-side down on a cutting board. Using a small, sharp knife, cut away the flesh to expose the thigh bone.

4 Cut an incision through the flesh, following the contour of the exposed bone. Cut around the bone to free it from the flesh. Discard the bone or use it for stock.

Jointing a chicken

This is a good skill to learn as it is often more economical to buy a whole chicken and joint it yourself than to buy expensive chicken pieces. The leftover bones and carcass can be used to make stock or soup. This jointing technique can be used for all poultry.

1 First, remove the wishbone. Using a sharp knife, scrape the flesh away from the wishbone, then use your fingers to twist and lift it free.

2 Place the bird breast-side up onto a cutting board. Cut down and through the thigh joint to separate the leg from the rest of the body.

3 Bend the leg back to dislodge the leg joint. When the ball is free from the socket, you will hear a pop.

4 Cut any meat or skin still attached to the body. Repeat to remove the other leg. Each leg can be divided into a thigh and a drumstick.

5 Fully extend one wing, then use sharp poultry shears to cut off the winglet at the middle joint. Repeat to remove the other winglet.

6 Grasp the backbone with your hands and break it from the crown (the 2 breasts and wings on the bone).

7 Using poultry shears, cut the lower end of the backbone from the remaining body.

8 Starting at the neck, cut all the way through the backbone to separate the breasts. The bird is now in 4 pieces.

9 Use the poultry shears to cut each breast in half diagonally, producing one breast and one wing. Repeat to separate the other breast.

10 Cut each leg through the knee joint, above the drumstick that connects to the thigh, to separate. Now, there is one drumstick and one thigh. Repeat to separate the other leg.

11 The chicken is now cut into 8 pieces. Leg and thigh pieces are the choicest cuts for slow cooking, although breast pieces can work well when left on the bone for stewing. The wings contain juicy meat that is excellent for pot roasting.

Many cooks lack confidence when it comes to preparing fish, but all you need is the correct kit and a little know-how. An essential tool is a filleting knife, which is slightly flexible with a long blade. This makes it easy to remove the skin from fish and cut through the bones. Always buy good quality fresh fish and buy seafood on the day you will cook it. Clean seafood carefully so that nothing unwanted goes into the pot.

Preparing fish and seafood

Scaling and trimming fish

1 Lay the fish on top of a clean work surface. Holding the fish by the tail, scrape the scales off with a fish scaler or the blade of a chef's knife, using strokes towards the head.

2 Once the fish is descaled, use kitchen scissors to remove the dorsal (back) fin, the belly fins, and the two fins on either side of the head.

Filleting and skinning a fish

1 Don't scale a fish if you plan to skin it. To fillet, gut the fish through the stomach, then cut into the head at an angle, just behind the gills, until you reach the backbone. Move to the top side of the backbone and, starting near the gills, cut down the length of one side of the backbone.

2 Turn over, and repeat the cut on the other side of the backbone. Place the fillet skin-side down onto a clean work surface. Insert a filleting knife into the flesh of the fish near the tail end. Turn the blade at an angle almost parallel to the skin and cut off the flesh, while holding the skin taut.

Preparing mussels

1 Discard any mussels that are broken or wide open. In the sink, scrub the mussels under cold, running water. Rinse away grit or sand and remove any barnacles with a small, sharp knife.

2 To remove the "beard", pinch the dark, stringy piece between your fingers, pull it away from the mussel, and discard. If a mussel is not tightly closed, tap it to check it is fresh; if it doesn't close when you tap it, discard it.

Peeling and deveining prawns

1 Remove the head and legs by pulling them off with your fingers, then peel away the shells. Save the shells for stock, if you like.

2 Using the tip of a paring knife or cocktail stick, hook the vein where the head was and gently pull it away from the body.

Slow cooking provides a convenient one-pot cooking method, but with most dishes there are a few stages of cooking that are needed first, such as marinating, browning the meat, or sautéing vegetables. Each of these techniques adds depth of flavour to the finished dish. Deglazing during cooking is vital for enhancing the taste of your sauce, while reducing and thickening are great troubleshooting techniques for thin sauces.

Essential recipe techniques

Marinating

A marinade is a mixture that meat or fish is steeped in before cooking, and should be made up of acidic ingredients such as wine, citrus juice or vinegar, and salt. Soaking the meat is called marinating, a process that tenderizes and enhances flavour in tougher, cheaper cuts. Trim the meat before marinating and cut it to the required size. Natural yogurt can also be used as a marinade and is a common tenderizer for chicken, turkey, or seafood, although it can be used for red meat as well. Spices, herbs, and aromatic vegetables such as garlic, onion, and ginger are often included in marinades to add extra flavour. Make sure the meat is immersed in the marinade, then leave it in the refrigerator to marinate for 4–12 hours.

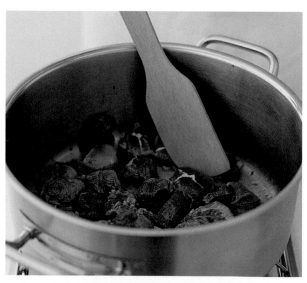

Browning

This technique caramelizes the natural sugars that are in meat and turns it a rich golden colour. Browning adds flavour and depth to your dish, so it is well worth doing at the beginning of the recipe before adding the meat to the other ingredients. Season the meat and add it to a little hot oil or butter in a pan and cook at a medium-high heat. Leave the meat to cook undisturbed for a few minutes. You will know it is ready when it comes away from the bottom of the pan easily. When the underside is golden, turn and cook the other side. Remove the meat and set it aside while you prepare the rest of the ingredients. You could dust the meat in seasoned flour before browning, as it is a good way to help thicken the consistency of the sauce.

Sautéing

This requires high heat and a good heavy-based pan. Sautéing vegetables enables their natural water content to evaporate, thus concentrating their flavour. Heat some oil or butter, add the vegetables to the pan, and cook until they start to caramelize and soften. This takes no longer than around 5–8 minutes, depending on the vegetables you are cooking. Move them around the pan to prevent burning. Always cook the hardest vegetables first as these will take longer. Don't overcrowd the pan or the vegetables will sweat rather than sauté.

Deglazing

The sauce is all-important as it can make or break the finished dish. Pan sauces and gravies are made from deglazed caramelized juices released from roasted or fried meat, poultry, and vegetables. In slow cooking, this technique is used often after browning and sautéing. Remove the food from the pan and spoon off excess fat, then deglaze the caramelized juices by adding stock, water, or wine. Stir to loosen the particles and incorporate them into the liquid. Reduce and finish as required. Making a sauce like this gives a richness and depth of flavour that cannot be achieved just by simmering ingredients.

Reducing and thickening

When a sauce is too thin, it can be either reduced or thickened to improve its flavour and texture. Reducing decreases the sauce's volume through evaporation and intensifies its flavour. To reduce, cook in an uncovered pan over a high heat, stirring occasionally. Add stock and bring back to boil, then boil, uncovered, for about 20 minutes to reduce again by half, regularly skimming off any impurities. Thickening gives sauces extra body and consistency. There are different ways to do this. A simple method is to dissolve cornflour in water and add the mixture to the simmering dish. You could also add a roux – a mixture of flour and water – stirring it into the simmering sauce and cooking to prevent it from turning the sauce lumpy.

Using your slow cooker is a simple and efficient way to make stock – the liquid won't evaporate and boil dry, so you can leave it unattended. Save the carcass or bones from poultry, meat, or fish when preparing a dish, then add them to the slow cooker with water and flavourings and leave it to simmer overnight. Stock freezes well, so if you are not using it straight away, let it cool and freeze it for up to 1 month.

Making stock in the slow cooker

Vegetable stock

1 Save scraps, peelings, stalks, tops, and ends from vegetables such as onion, carrot, celery, leek, and fennel to use as the base of your stock.

2 Add the vegetable scraps to the slow cooker. You can also add any herbs you may have, such as parsley stalks and a bay leaf, along with a few black peppercorns and a pinch of salt.

3 Boil enough water to cover all the ingredients, then pour this into the slow cooker. Cover with the lid, and cook on auto/low for 6–8 hours. Skim the stock halfway through the cooking time, if needed. Strain the stock and allow to cool before storing in the refrigerator or freezer.

Meat stock

1 Add a chicken carcass or beef bones to the slow cooker with a handful of raw vegetables such as carrot tops, celery, and onion.

2 Add some black peppercorns and a pinch of salt to the slow cooker, along with herbs such as parsley or a bay leaf, if you wish.

3 Boil enough water to cover all the ingredients, then pour this into the slow cooker. Cover with the lid, and cook on auto/low for 6–8 hours. Skim the stock halfway through the cooking time, if needed. Strain the stock and allow to cool before storing in the refrigerator or freezer.

Fish stock

1 Ask your fishmonger for some fish heads, or use leftovers from another dish. Choose white fish such as sea bass or haddock, but avoid oily fish as their stonger flavour will taint the stock.

2 Add the fish scraps to the slow cooker along with some fresh herbs, such as thyme, and some fennel scraps or onion.

3 Pour over enough boiling water to cover all the ingredients, cover with the lid, and cook on auto/low for 6–8 hours. Skim the stock halfway through the cooking time, if needed. Strain the stock and allow to cool before storing in the refrigerator or freezer.

Fish stock

Skimming stock

When making stock, quite often a layer of frothy "scum" will appear on the surface. To skim it off, use a ladle or a metal spoon to scoop it away and then discard it. You may find you need to do this a few times during cooking. Meat and fish stocks are most likely to need skimming.

Straining stock

Once the stock has finished cooking, strain it straight away; don't leave it sitting. To strain the stock, turn the slow cooker off then lift out the inner pot. Carefully strain the stock liquid into a jug or bowl through a fine nylon mesh sieve, or you could line a sieve with muslin. It is easiest to do this a ladleful at a time. Discard any bones, carcass, and vegetables used and leave the stock to cool.

Adding dumplings, a cobbler topping, or breadcrumbs to a stew or casserole can make a dish inviting, more filling, and substantial. All are easy to prepare while your dish is simmering; simply add them to the pot to get a complete one-pot meal without any additional cooking.

Extras and toppings

Suet dumplings

1 The secret to light and fluffy dumplings lies in handling the dough as little as possible. Add 150g (5½oz) shredded suet (either regular or vegetarian) and 150g (5½oz) self-raising flour to a bowl and mix together with your hands. Season well with salt and pepper.

2 If you wish, some extra flavourings could be added to the mixture at this point, such as 30g (1oz) freshly grated Parmesan cheese, 1 tsp mustard or horseradish, or 1–2 tsp fresh chopped herbs such as parsley, thyme, and rosemary. Mix any flavourings into the dry ingredients.

3 Make a well in the middle of the flour mixture and slowly drizzle in cold water a little at a time. Mix with your hands until the mixture starts to come together and leaves the sides of the bowl easily.

4 Turn out onto a lightly floured board and roll into a sausage shape. Form into 6 large or 12 small dumplings (they will double in size as they cook). For the slow cooker, add the dumplings in for the last 45–60 minutes of cooking. For the traditional method, add them to the casserole for the last 30 minutes of cooking. They should be just immersed in the liquid and covered with a lid.

Non-suet dumplings

1 This recipe uses butter instead of suet to make a light, moist version of the dumpling. Add 100g (3½oz) white breadcrumbs, 100g (3½oz) self-raising flour, and 140g (5oz) butter to a food processor and whiz into a crumb mixture. You could also add some extra flavourings to the food processor, if you like, such as freshly grated Parmesan cheese, mustard or horseradish, or fresh chopped herbs like parsley, thyme, and rosemary.

2 Add 2 eggs to the food processor and season with salt and pepper. Whiz again until the mixture comes together as a moist dough.

3 Turn the dough out onto a lightly floured board and roll into 6 large or 12 small balls (keep in mind that the dumplings will double in size as they cook). For the slow cooker, add the dumplings to the pot for the last 45–60 minutes of cooking. For the traditional method, add the dumplings to the casserole for the last 30 minutes of cooking. They should be just immersed in the liquid and covered with a lid.

Vegetable casserole (p168) with herby suet dumplings

Artichokes, beans, and peas (p298) with breadcrumbs stirred through

Breadcrumbs

1 Using a food processor, whiz 2 slices of torn bread into coarse crumbs. Add any flavourings of your choice, such as herbs or grated cheese, and whiz again. If your recipe calls for fresh breadcrumbs, then they can be used at this stage. For the slow cooker, lightly toast the breadcrumbs in a dry frying pan; sprinkle over, or carefully fold into, the finished dish. For the traditional method, sprinkle into the casserole and cook in the oven for the last 30 minutes of cooking; remove the lid for the last 10 minutes, or until the topping is golden.

2 For fine, golden breadcrumbs, spread them onto a baking tray and put in the oven at 200°C (400°F/ Gas 6) for about 10 minutes until golden. Remove, tip back into the food processor, and whiz again until fine. You can add any flavourings at this time, if you wish, such as fresh herbs or grated cheese. Use to top the dish for the last hour of cooking for both the slow cooker and for the traditional method.

3 If you are not using the breadcrumbs immediately, they can be frozen for up to 3 months. They don't require defrosting before use.

Cobblers

1 A cobbler topping is a small savoury scone that makes a wholesome and filling dish. Use them to top chicken, beef, lamb, or vegetable stews and casseroles. Put 200g (/oz) sifted self-raising flour and salt and pepper in a bowl and mix together. Add any flavourings, such as grated cheese, chopped sun-dried tomatoes or olives, or ground walnuts to the dry ingredients, if you wish.

2 Cut 100g (3½oz) butter into cubes and rub it into the ingredients in the bowl with your fingertips until the mixture resembles breadcrumbs. Add 2 lightly beaten eggs and mix until the dough comes together, then add 4 tbsp milk a little at a time, mixing until it becomes a soft dough.

3 Turn the dough out onto a lightly floured board and roll out so it is fairly thick. Using a 2.5cm (1in) metal cutter, cut out 6 rounds. For the slow cooker, add the cobblers to the top of the dish for the last hour of cooking. For the traditional method, add the cobblers to the top of the casserole, brush the tops with the milk, and cook in the oven, uncovered, for the last 30–45 minutes of cooking.

Recipe choosers

Vegetarian

Provençal vegetable soup p68
🕐 Slow cooker 8 hrs or 4 hrs; Traditional method 1 hr

SOUPS
Ribollita p80
🕐 Slow cooker 5–6 hrs or 3–4 hrs;
Traditional method 1¼ hrs

Borscht p81
🕐 Slow cooker 6–8 hrs or 3–4 hrs;
Traditional method 1½ hrs

Minestrone p89
🕐 Slow cooker 6–8 hrs;
Traditional method 1¾ hrs

Cannellini bean, garlic, and mushroom soup p98
🕐 Slow cooker 4 hrs;
Traditional method 50 mins

Spanish pepper and tomato soup p99
🕐 Slow cooker 8 hrs or 3 hrs;
Traditional method 1¼–1½ hrs

MAINS
Sweet and sour pumpkin stew p129
🕐 Slow cooker 8 hrs or 4 hrs;
Traditional method 1 hr

Ratatouille p166
🕐 Slow cooker 4–5 hrs or 2–3 hrs;
Traditional method 1¼ hrs

Pumpkin and ginger soup p86
🕐 Slow cooker 8 hrs or 4 hrs;
Traditional method 1 hr

Risotto primavera p302
🕐 Slow cooker 1½–2 hrs;
Traditional method 1 hr

Aubergine massaman curry p228
🕐 Slow cooker 8 hrs or 3–4 hrs;
Traditional method 1 hr

Jamaican corn stew p126
🕐 Slow cooker 6–8 hrs or 3–4 hrs; **Traditional method** 1½–2 hrs

Vegetable casserole with dumplings p168
🕐 Slow cooker 6–8 hrs or 4 hrs; **Traditional method** 1¼ hrs

Courgette, herb, and lemon tagine p199
🕐 Slow cooker 2–3 hrs;
Traditional method 45–55 mins

Chickpea, tomato, and herb tagine p219
🕐 Slow cooker 6–8 hrs or 3–4 hrs;
Traditional method 1¼ hrs

Sri Lankan coconut pumpkin curry p226
🕐 Slow cooker 3–4 hrs,
Traditional method 1¼ hrs

Malaysian mango curry p227
🕐 Slow cooker 3–4 hrs,
Traditional method 1 hr

Cauliflower curry p238
🕐 Slow cooker 8 hrs or 4 hrs;
Traditional method 1 hr

Paneer and sweet pepper curry p243
🕐 Slow cooker 5–6 hrs or 3–4 hrs;
Traditional method 1 hr

Asparagus and Taleggio risotto p322
🕐 Slow cooker 1–1¼ hrs;
Traditional method 45–55 mins

Vegetable biryani p325
🕐 Slow cooker 2–3 hrs;
Traditional method 1¼ hrs

SIDES
Red cabbage with cider p138
🕐 Slow cooker 8 hrs or 4 hrs;
Traditional method 1–1½ hrs

Red lentil dahl p244
🕐 Slow cooker 8 hrs or 4 hrs;
Traditional method 1¼ hrs

Rice and peas p326
🕐 Slow cooker 2–3 hrs;
Traditional method 45 mins

Thai coconut rice p327
🕐 Slow cooker 2½–3 hrs;
Traditional method 40 mins

Fish and seafood

Prawn laksa p100
🕐 Slow cooker 6–8 hrs; **Traditional method** 1½ hrs

SOUPS
Japanese-style fish broth p84
🕐 Slow cooker 3 hrs;
Traditional method 1 hr

New England chowder p90
🕐 Slow cooker 2–3 hrs;
Traditional method 55–60 mins

Shellfish soup p91
🕐 Slow cooker 6–8 hrs or 3–4 hrs;
Traditional method 1¼ hrs

MAINS
Pork and clam cataplana p106
🕐 Slow cooker 6–8 hrs or 3–4 hrs;
Traditional method 2¼–2½ hrs

Salt cod braised with vegetables p111
🕐 Slow cooker 6–8 hrs or 3–4 hrs;
Traditional method 40 mins

Rich fish soup p82
🕐 Slow cooker 8 hrs or 4 hrs; **Traditional method** 1 hr

Red mullet with Middle Eastern spices p212
🕐 Slow cooker 3–4 hrs;
Traditional method 1½ hrs

Creole fish and corn stew p270
🕐 Slow cooker 3–4 hrs; Traditional method 1¼ hrs

Monkfish and green chilli stew p132
🕐 Slow cooker 6–8 hrs or 3–4 hrs;
Traditional method 1¼ hrs

Squid stew p133
🕐 Slow cooker 6–8 hrs or 3–4 hrs;
Traditional method 1¼–1¾ hrs

Bouillabaise p134
🕐 Slow cooker 2–3 hrs;
Traditional method 45 mins

Monkfish and white wine stew p140
🕐 Slow cooker 2–3 hrs;
Traditional method 40–45 mins

Fish tagine p211
🕐 Slow cooker 4–5 hrs;
Traditional method 1¼–1½ hrs

Prawn makhani p230
🕐 Slow cooker 4–5 hrs or 3–4 hrs;
Traditional method 40 mins

Kenyan fish curry p237
🕐 Slow cooker 6–8 hrs or 3–4 hrs;
Traditional method 45 mins

Prawn dhansak p242
🕐 Slow cooker 6–8 hrs or 3–4 hrs;
Traditional method 50 mins

Prawn and okra gumbo p253
🕐 Slow cooker 6–8 hrs or 3–4 hrs;
Traditional method 1¼ hrs

Paella p316
🕐 Slow cooker 2¾ hrs;
Traditional method 1 hr

Risotto with mussels p323
🕐 Slow cooker 1 hr;
Traditional method 45–55 mins

Prawn risotto p324
🕐 Slow cooker 2–3 hrs;
Traditional method 50 mins

Seafood stew p130
🕐 Slow cooker 3–4 hrs; Traditional method 1½ hrs

Poultry

Mustard chicken casserole p190
🕐 Slow cooker 6–8 hrs or 3–4 hrs; Traditional method 1¾ hrs

SOUPS
Chunky chicken soup p75
🕐 Slow cooker 6–8 hrs or 4 hrs;
Traditional method 1½ hrs

Malaysian chicken soup p92
🕐 Slow cooker 6–8 hrs or 3–4 hrs;
Traditional method 40–50 mins

Chicken broth with celeriac and orange p95
🕐 Slow cooker 8 hrs or 4 hrs;
Traditional method 1 hr

MAINS
Chicken and beer stew p116
🕐 Slow cooker 6–8 hrs or 3–4 hrs;
Traditional method 1 hr

American Brunswick stew p125
🕐 Slow cooker 6–8 hrs;
Traditional method 2–2½ hrs

Coq au vin p161
🕐 Slow cooker 6–8 hrs or 3–4 hrs;
Traditional method 1½–1¾ hrs

Chicken fricassée p165
🕐 Slow cooker 5–6 hrs or 3–4 hrs;
Traditional method 1 hr

French-style duck and lentils p176
🕐 Slow cooker 4½–5 hrs;
Traditional method 3¾ hrs

Duck legs with cabbage, pine nuts, and raisins p136
🕐 Slow cooker 6 hrs or 3–4 hrs;
Traditional method 2½ hrs

Hunter's chicken stew p114
🕐 Slow cooker 5–6 hrs or 3–4 hrs;
Traditional method 45–60 mins

Chicken and green olive tagine p196
🕐 Slow cooker 6–8 hrs or 3–4 hrs;
Traditional method 2 hrs

Chicken cobbler p177
🕐 Slow cooker 6–8 hrs or 4 hrs;
Traditional method 2¼ hrs

Turkey and cranberry casserole p182
🕐 Slow cooker 6–8 hrs or 4 hrs;
Traditional method 1¼–1¾ hrs

Duck with turnips and apricots p186
🕐 Slow cooker 6–8 hrs or 3–4 hrs;
Traditional method 1½–2 hrs

Chicken paprika with dumplings p193
🕐 Slow cooker 6–8 hrs or 3–4 hrs;
Traditional method 1½ hrs

Chicken with olives and peppers p198
🕐 Slow cooker 6–8 hrs or 3–4 hrs;
Traditional method 1½ hrs

Chicken and orange tagine p206
🕐 Slow cooker 6–8 hrs or 3–4 hrs;
Traditional method 1¾ hrs

Chicken, aubergine, and tomato tagine p215
🕐 Slow cooker 6–8 hrs or 3–4 hrs;
Traditional method 1¼ hrs

Chicken tikka masala p233
🕐 Slow cooker 4–5 hrs or 2–3 hrs;
Traditional method 50 mins

Pot roast chicken with turnips and fennel p284
🕐 Slow cooker 8 hrs or 4 hrs;
Traditional method 2–2½ hrs

Poussins with plums and cabbage p286
🕐 Slow cooker 6–8 hrs;
Traditional method 1¾ hrs

Arroz con pollo p317
🕐 Slow cooker 3–3½ hrs;
Traditional method 45 mins

Turkey mole p250
🕐 Slow cooker 6–8 hrs or 3–4 hrs; Traditional method 1¼–1¾ hrs

Duck curry p240
🕐 Slow cooker 8 hrs;
Traditional method 2 hrs

Chicken jambalaya p264
🕐 Slow cooker 2–3 hrs;
Traditional method 1½ hrs

Pork

Pea, ham, and potato soup p78
🕐 Slow cooker 16 hrs or 8 hrs; Traditional method 2 hrs

SOUPS
Pistou soup p88
🕐 Slow cooker 6–8 hrs or 3–4 hrs;
Traditional method 1¾ hrs

MAINS
Pork and clam cataplana p106
🕐 Slow cooker 6–8 hrs or 3–4 hrs;
Traditional method 2¼–2½ hrs

Pork goulash p135
🕐 Slow cooker 6–8 hrs or 3–4 hrs;
Traditional method 1 hr

Stuffed pork noisettes p150
🕐 Slow cooker 6–8 hrs or 3–4 hrs;
Traditional method 2 hrs

Feijoada p174
🕐 Slow cooker 6–8 hrs or 3–4 hrs;
Traditional method 1¾ hrs

Spanish lentils p175
🕐 Slow cooker 5–6 hrs or 3–4 hrs;
Traditional method 1 hr

Pork with red cabbage, pears, and ginger p183
🕐 Slow cooker 8 hrs or 4 hrs;
Traditional method 1¾ hrs

Lentil and Toulouse sausage casserole p156
🕐 Slow cooker 6–8 hrs;
Traditional method 1¾ hrs

Pot roast smoked ham p282
🕐 Slow cooker 16 hrs or 8 hrs;
Traditional method 3¼ hrs

Belly pork and prunes p178
🕐 Slow cooker 8 hrs;
Traditional method 3–3½ hrs

Pork ribs Oriental p294
🕐 Slow cooker 8 hrs; **Traditional method** 2–2½ hrs

Red lentil and spicy sausage hotpot p189
🕐 Slow cooker 6–8 hrs or 4 hrs;
Traditional method 1¾ hrs

Pork vindaloo p232
🕐 Slow cooker 6–8 hrs or 3–4 hrs;
Traditional method 1 hr

Chilean pork and beans p263
🕐 Slow cooker 6–8 hrs;
Traditional method 3–3½ hrs

Sausage chilli pot p266
🕐 Slow cooker 6–8 hrs or 3–4 hrs;
Traditional method 1¾ hrs

Ribs in a chilli and ginger tomato sauce p285
🕐 Slow cooker 6–8 hrs;
Traditional method 2–3 hrs

Spicy pork with cabbage and caraway seeds p291
🕐 Slow cooker 6–8 hrs;
Traditional method 2½ hrs

Belly pork and squash p292
🕐 Slow cooker 8 hrs;
Traditional method 2¼–2¾ hrs

Spicy devilled pork ribs p296
🕐 Slow cooker 6–8 hrs;
Traditional method 2–2½ hrs

Pork with rice and tomatoes p306
🕐 Slow cooker 1–1½ hrs;
Traditional method 1 hr

Hoppin' John p310
🕐 Slow cooker 6–8 hrs;
Traditional method 3–3½ hrs

Sausage and mixed pepper savoury rice p312
🕐 Slow cooker 2–3 hrs;
Traditional method 1 hr

Squash, sausage, and pecorino risotto p318
🕐 Slow cooker 1½–2 hrs;
Traditional method 50–60 mins

Beef

Vietnamese beef soup p96
🕐 Slow cooker 8 hrs or 4 hrs; Traditional method 1¼ hrs

SOUPS
Oxtail soup with nutmeg and star anise p74
🕐 Slow cooker 8 hrs;
Traditional method 2¾–3¼ hrs

Beef mulligatawny soup p94
🕐 Slow cooker 8 hrs or 4 hrs;
Traditional method 1½ hrs

MAINS
Beef with barley and mushrooms p110
🕐 Slow cooker 6–8 hrs or 3–4 hrs;
Traditional method 2¼–2½ hrs

Asian beef and bok choy p113
🕐 Slow cooker 6–8 hrs;
Traditional method 2¼–2¾ hrs

Italian beef braised in red wine p117
🕐 Slow cooker 6–8 hrs;
Traditional method 2¼–3¼ hrs

Peppery Tuscan beef p118
🕐 Slow cooker 8 hrs;
Traditional method 2–2½ hrs

Greek stifado p122
🕐 Slow cooker 8 hrs;
Traditional method 2¼ hrs

Shredded beef in barbecue sauce p274
🕐 Slow cooker 8 hrs;
Traditional method 3¼ hrs

Beef and greens p142
🕐 Slow cooker 6–8 hrs;
Traditional method 1¾ hrs

Beef pot roast p278
🕐 Slow cooker 8 hrs;
Traditional method 2½ hrs

Osso bucco p162
🕐 Slow cooker 6–8 hrs or 4 hrs; **Traditional method** 1¾–2¼ hrs

Braised oxtail with star anise p146
🕐 Slow cooker 8 hrs; **Traditional method** 3¼ hrs

Beef and anchovy stew p145
🕐 Slow cooker 6–8 hrs;
Traditional method 2¼–2¾ hrs

Provençal daube of beef p149
🕐 Slow cooker 6–8 hrs or 3–4 hrs;
Traditional method 3½–4 hrs

Beef stew with Stilton dumplings p151
🕐 Slow cooker 8 hrs or 4 hrs;
Traditional method 2¾ hrs

Boeuf bourguignon p160
🕐 Slow cooker 6–8 hrs;
Traditional method 2½ hrs

Beef carbonnade p170
🕐 Slow cooker 8 hrs or 4 hrs;
Traditional method 3¼ hrs

Mexican meatballs p180
🕐 Slow cooker 6–8 hrs;
Traditional method 1¾–2¼ hrs

Cumin beef tagine p210
🕐 Slow cooker 6–8 hrs or 3–4 hrs;
Traditional method 2½ hrs

Cardamom and ginger beef curry p224
🕐 Slow cooker 5–6 hrs or 3–4 hrs;
Traditional method 2–2¼ hrs

Beef rendang p225
🕐 Slow cooker 6–8 hrs,
Traditional method 3¾–4¼ hrs

Hot and fiery chilli with beer p256
🕐 Slow cooker 6–8 hrs or 3–4 hrs;
Traditional method 1¾ hrs

Beef chilli mole p262
🕐 Slow cooker 6–8 hrs;
Traditional method 2¼–2¾ hrs

Slow-cooked beef p272
🕐 Slow cooker 6–8 hrs;
Traditional method 2¼ hrs

Pot au feu p281
🕐 Slow cooker 6–8 hrs;
Traditional method 3½–4 hrs

Lamb

Lamb mince and squash with green chillies p258
🕑 Slow cooker 8 hrs;
Traditional method 1½–2 hrs

Lamb with artichokes, broad beans, and dill p152
🕑 Slow cooker 6–8 hrs or 3–4 hrs;
Traditional method 1¾ hrs

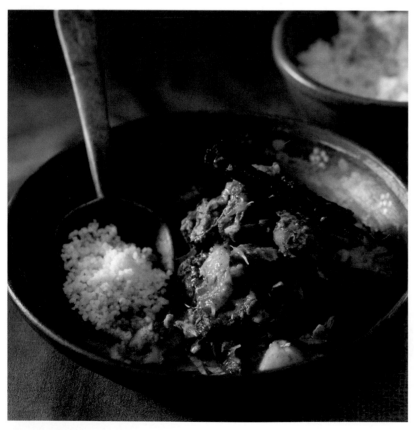

Slow-cooked lamb with orange and chestnuts p208
🕑 Slow cooker 6–8 hrs; Traditional method 2¼ hrs

SOUPS

Moroccan harira soup p72
🕑 Slow cooker 8 hrs;
Traditional method 2 hrs

MAINS

Fruity lamb shanks p123
🕑 Slow cooker 8 hrs;
Traditional method 3¼–3¾ hrs

Lamb ratatouille p141
🕑 Slow cooker 6–8 hrs or 3–4 hrs;
Traditional method 2–2¼ hrs

Smoky aubergine and lamb stew p144
🕑 Slow cooker 6–8 hrs;
Traditional method 1¾ hrs

French braised lamb p148
🕑 Slow cooker 6–8 hrs or 3–4 hrs;
Traditional method 2–2½ hrs

Navarin of lamb p164
🕑 Slow cooker 6–8 hrs or 3–4 hrs;
Traditional method 2 hrs

Lamb shanks with harissa and shallots p171
🕑 Slow cooker 6–8 hrs or 4–5 hrs;
Traditional method 2¼–2¾ hrs

Lamb chops champvallon p181
🕑 Slow cooker 6–8 hrs;
Traditional method 2¼ hrs

Lebanese meatballs p187
🕑 Slow cooker 6–8 hrs or 3–4 hrs;
Traditional method 1 hr

Lamb meatballs in a tomato sauce p188
🕑 Slow cooker 6–8 hrs or 3 hrs;
Traditional method 2½ hrs

Fiery lamb and chutney tagine p203
🕑 Slow cooker 6–8 hrs or 3–4 hrs;
Traditional method 1½ hrs

Lamb tagine with walnuts and figs p207
🕐 Slow cooker 6–8 hrs or 3–4 hrs;
Traditional method 1¾–2¼ hrs

Braised lamb with lemon and peas p214
🕐 Slow cooker 6–8 hrs or 3–4 hrs;
Traditional method 1¼ hrs

Turkish lamb and lemon p218
🕐 Slow cooker 6–8 hrs or 3–4 hrs;
Traditional method 1¼–1¾ hrs

Lamb dhansak p231
🕐 Slow cooker 6–8 hrs or 3–4 hrs;
Traditional method 2 hrs

Lamb korma p247
🕐 Slow cooker 5–6 hrs or 3–4 hrs;
Traditional method 2½–3 hrs

Sweet and sour lamb p297
🕐 Slow cooker 6–8 hrs;
Traditional method 2 hrs

Saffron and lamb biryani p305
🕐 Slow cooker 6–8 hrs or 3–4 hrs;
Traditional method 1¾ hrs

Provençal lamb daube with olives p184
🕐 Slow cooker 6–8 hrs; Traditional method 3¾–4¼ hrs

Stuffed lamb, Greek style p120
🕐 Slow cooker 8 hrs;
Traditional method 2¼–2¾ hrs

Turkish lamb and pomegranate pilaf p308
🕐 Slow cooker 2–3 hrs;
Traditional method 1 hr

Lamb with parsley, tomato, and breadcrumbs p288
🕐 Slow cooker 8 hrs;
Traditional method 3¼ hrs

Healthy

SOUPS

Asian chicken and prawn broth with ginger and coriander p70
🕐 Slow cooker 2–2½ hrs;
Traditional method 1 hr

Chunky chicken soup p75
🕐 Slow cooker 6–8 hrs or 4 hrs;
Traditional method 1½ hrs

Beef broth with Parmesan dumplings p76
🕐 Slow cooker 6–8 hrs;
Traditional method 2½ hrs

MAINS

Braised pork in soy and cinnamon p112
🕐 Slow cooker 6–8 hrs or 4 hrs;
Traditional method 2¼–2½ hrs

Mixed mushroom stew p128
🕐 Slow cooker 3–4 hrs;
Traditional method 1 hr

Sweet and sour pumpkin stew p129
🕐 Slow cooker 8 hrs or 4 hrs;
Traditional method 1 hr

Malaysian chicken soup p92
🕐 Slow cooker 6–8 hrs or 3–4 hrs; **Traditional method** 40–50 mins

Middle Eastern chickpea stew p216
🕐 Slow cooker 6–8 hrs or 3–4 hrs;
Traditional method 1¼ hrs

Ham hock with red cabbage p108
🕐 Slow cooker 12–16 hrs;
Traditional method 3 hrs

Pumpkin and parsnip cassoulet p172
🕐 Slow cooker 8 hrs or 4 hrs;
Traditional method 1¾ hrs

Brazilian black bean and pumpkin stew p104
🕐 Slow cooker 6–8 hrs;
Traditional method 2½–3 hrs

Mixed vegetable tagine p204
🕐 Slow cooker 3 hrs;
Traditional method 50 mins

Karahi chicken p222
🕐 Slow cooker 6 hrs or 3 hrs;
Traditional method 1 hr

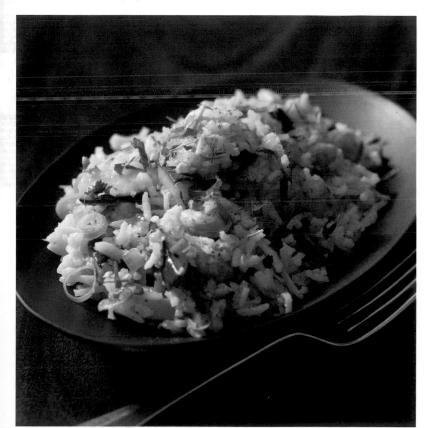

Cashew and courgette rice p320
🕐 Slow cooker 2–2½ hrs; **Traditional method** 40 mins

Ginger and okra curry p245
🕐 Slow cooker 8 hrs or 4 hrs;
Traditional method 1¼ hrs

Spicy turkey and sweetcorn p268
🕐 Slow cooker 6–8 hrs;
Traditional method 1¼ hrs

Hot chilli and beans p269
🕐 Slow cooker 8 hrs or 4 hrs;
Traditional method 1 hr

SIDES
Red cabbage with cider p138
🕐 Slow cooker 8 hrs or 4 hrs;
Traditional method 1–1½ hrs

Middle Eastern lentils and peppers p200
🕐 Slow cooker 1½–2 hrs;
Traditional method 45 mins

Vegetable sambar p234
🕐 Slow cooker 4–6 hrs or 2–3 hrs;
Traditional method 50 mins

Red lentil dahl p244
🕐 Slow cooker 8 hrs or 4 hrs;
Traditional method 1¼ hrs

Soups & broths

This soup is just as good in summer made with fresh tomatoes and basil pesto stirred through it, as it is in winter with added canned beans to bulk it out. It is excellent for freezing.

Provençal vegetable soup

SERVES 4–6 **FREEZE** UP TO 3 MONTHS

1 tbsp olive oil
1 onion, finely chopped
salt and freshly ground black pepper
3 garlic cloves, finely chopped
2 celery sticks, finely chopped
2 carrots, peeled and roughly chopped
sprig of tarragon, leaves finely chopped
2 sprigs of rosemary

400g can tomatoes, blended until smooth
900ml (1½ pints) hot vegetable stock, for
 both methods
3 potatoes, peeled and chopped
 into bite-sized pieces
325g (11oz) green dwarf beans or French or fine green
 beans, trimmed and chopped into bite-sized pieces
30g (1oz) Parmesan cheese, grated (optional)

in the slow cooker PREP 15 MINS COOK 10 MINS PRECOOKING;
AUTO/LOW 8 HRS OR **HIGH** 4 HRS

1 Preheat the slow cooker, if required. Heat the oil in a large heavy-based pan over a medium heat, add the onion, and cook for 3–4 minutes until soft. Season with salt and pepper, then stir through the garlic and celery and cook for a further 5 minutes or until the celery is soft.

2 Stir in the carrots, tarragon, and rosemary and cook for a minute before transferring everything to the slow cooker. Stir in the puréed tomatoes and stock and cook on auto/low for 8 hours or on high for 4 hours. Add the potatoes for the last 15 minutes of cooking.

3 When the potatoes are soft, add the beans and cook for 10 minutes, or until they are cooked but retain a bite. Taste and season, remove the rosemary, and ladle into warmed large shallow bowls. Sprinkle over the Parmesan, if using, and serve with some crusty French bread.

traditional method PREP 15 MINS COOK 1 HR

1 Heat the oil in a large heavy-based pan over a medium heat, add the onion, and cook for 3–4 minutes until soft. Season with salt and pepper, then stir through the garlic and celery and cook for a further 5 minutes or until the celery is soft.

2 Stir in the carrots, tarragon, and rosemary and cook for a minute, then tip in the puréed tomatoes and a little stock, and bring to the boil. Add the remaining stock and return to the boil, then reduce to a simmer, partially cover with the lid, and cook gently for about 45 minutes. If more liquid is needed, top up with a little hot water. Add the potatoes for the last 15 minutes of cooking.

3 When the potatoes are soft, add the beans and cook for a further 10 minutes, or until they are cooked but retain a bite. Taste and season, remove the rosemary, and ladle into warmed large shallow bowls. Sprinkle over the Parmesan, if using, and serve with some crusty French bread.

Lots of complex flavours make up this warming broth. The water chestnuts add an unexpected texture, and the chicken and prawns add plenty of protein, making it a substantial dish.

Asian chicken and prawn broth with ginger and coriander

 SERVES 4–6 **HEALTHY**

1.2 litres (2 pints) hot chicken stock, for
  both methods
salt and freshly ground black pepper
1 tbsp dark soy sauce
3 tbsp fish sauce (nam pla)
3 tbsp mirin
1 tsp tahini
2 garlic cloves, finely chopped
5cm (2in) piece of fresh root ginger, peeled
  and sliced into fine strips

½ tsp dried chilli flakes
225g can bamboo shoots, drained and rinsed
225g can water chestnuts, drained and rinsed
125g (4½oz) button mushrooms, whole or
  larger ones halved
2 skinless chicken breasts, finely sliced
bunch of spring onions, finely chopped
bunch of coriander leaves
250g pack of ready-cooked small prawns
  or shrimps

 in the slow cooker **PREP** 15 MINS **COOK** HIGH 2–2½ HRS

1 Preheat the slow cooker, if required. Put everything into the slow cooker except the spring onions, coriander, and prawns and add 300ml (10fl oz) of hot water.

2 Cover with the lid and cook on high for 2–2½ hours, stirring through the spring onions, coriander, and prawns for the last 20 minutes of cooking. Taste and season as required, and ladle into warmed bowls while piping hot.

 traditional method **PREP** 15 MINS **COOK** 1 HR

1 Put the stock into a large heavy-based pan, season with salt and pepper, and add a further 600ml (1 pint) of hot water. Add the soy sauce, fish sauce, mirin, and tahini and bring to the boil.

2 Reduce to a simmer and add the garlic, ginger, and chilli flakes together with the bamboo shoots, water chestnuts, and mushrooms. Stir, then add the chicken, cover with the lid, and cook gently for 40 minutes. Top up with hot water if necessary.

3 Taste and adjust seasoning as required, then stir through the spring onions and coriander leaves, and simmer on a low heat for a further 10 minutes. Finally, add the prawns and simmer for 5 minutes. Ladle into warmed bowls while piping hot.

The secret of a good French onion soup is to let the onions caramelize slowly so they become wonderfully sweet.
If you like, you could use a dry cider instead of the wine.

French onion soup

⊙ **SERVES** 4 ❄ **FREEZE** UP TO 1 MONTH, WITHOUT THE BREAD OR CHEESE

30g (1oz) butter
1 tbsp sunflower oil
675g (1½lb) onions, thinly sliced
1 tsp caster sugar
salt and freshly ground black pepper
120ml (4fl oz) dry white wine
2 tbsp plain flour

1 litre (1¾ pints) hot beef stock for the slow cooker
  (1.5 litres /2¾ pints for the traditional method)
4 tbsp brandy
1 garlic clove, chopped in half
4 slices of baguette, about 2cm (¾in) thick, toasted
115g (4oz) Gruyère or Emmental cheese, grated

in the slow cooker 🕐 **PREP** 20 MINS **COOK** 45 MINS PRECOOKING; AUTO/LOW 4–6 HRS OR **HIGH** 2–3 HRS

1 Melt the butter with the oil in a large heavy-based pan over a low heat. Stir together the onions and sugar, and season with salt and pepper. Press a piece of wet greaseproof paper over the surface and cook, stirring occasionally, uncovered, for 40 minutes, or until the onions are rich and dark golden brown. Take care that they do not stick and burn at the bottom.

2 Preheat the slow cooker, if required. Remove the paper and stir in the wine. Increase the heat to medium and stir for 5 minutes, or until the onions are glazed. Sprinkle with the flour and stir for 2 minutes. Stir in the stock and bring to the boil. Transfer everything to the slow cooker, cover with the lid, and cook on auto/low for 4–6 hours or on high for 2–3 hours. Taste and adjust the seasoning, if necessary.

3 Preheat the grill on its highest setting. Divide the soup between 4 flameproof bowls and stir 1 tbsp of brandy into each. Rub the garlic clove over the toast and place 1 slice in each bowl. Sprinkle with the cheese and grill for 2–3 minutes, or until the cheese is bubbling and golden. Serve at once.

traditional method 🕐 **PREP** 10 MINS **COOK** 1½ HRS

1 Melt the butter with the oil in a large heavy-based pan over a low heat. Stir together the onions and sugar, and season with salt and pepper. Press a piece of wet greaseproof paper over the surface and cook, stirring occasionally, uncovered, for 40 minutes, or until the onions are rich and dark golden brown. Take care that they do not stick and burn at the bottom.

2 Remove the paper and stir in the wine. Increase the heat to medium and stir for 5 minutes, or until the onions are glazed. Sprinkle with the flour and stir for 2 minutes. Stir in the stock and bring to the boil. Reduce the heat to low, cover with the lid, and leave the soup to simmer for 30 minutes. Taste and adjust the seasoning, if necessary.

3 Meanwhile, preheat the grill on its highest setting. Divide the soup between 4 flameproof bowls and stir 1 tbsp of brandy into each. Rub the garlic clove over the toast and place 1 slice in each bowl. Sprinkle with the cheese and grill for 2–3 minutes, or until the cheese is bubbling and golden. Serve at once.

This is a substantial meal-in-one that is full of complex flavours. It's also one of those dishes that tastes better when reheated, so if you have the time, make it a day ahead and reheat to eat.

Moroccan harira soup

 SERVES 4–6 ❄ **FREEZE** UP TO 1 MONTH

1 tbsp olive oil
1 red onion, finely chopped
salt and freshly ground black pepper
3 garlic cloves, finely chopped
1 celery stick, chopped
675g (1½lb) shoulder or shank of lamb, cut into bite-sized pieces
1 tsp ground turmeric
1 tsp ground cinnamon
5cm (2in) piece of fresh root ginger, peeled and finely chopped

900ml (1½ pints) hot vegetable stock for the slow cooker (1.4 litres/2½ pints for the traditional method)
125g (4½oz) green or brown lentils, rinsed well and picked over for any stones
400g can chickpeas, drained and rinsed
1 tsp harissa paste
few sprigs of coriander, leaves only, to serve

in the slow cooker ● **PREP** 25 MINS **COOK** 25–30 MINS PRECOOKING; **AUTO/LOW** 8 HRS

1 Preheat the slow cooker, if required. Heat the oil in a large flameproof casserole over a medium heat, add the onion, and cook for 3–4 minutes until soft. Season with salt and pepper, then stir through the garlic and celery and cook for a further 6–10 minutes until the celery is soft.

2 Add the lamb, turmeric, cinnamon, and ginger. Increase the heat a little, stir until the lamb is coated, and cook for 6–10 minutes until the lamb is no longer pink. Add a ladleful of stock and bring to the boil. Stir through the lentils and chickpeas, turning them to coat evenly, add the remaining stock, and bring back to the boil.

3 Transfer everything to the slow cooker. Stir through the harissa paste, cover with the lid, and cook on auto/low for 8 hours. Ladle into warmed bowls, top with coriander leaves, and serve with lemon wedges on the side.

 ### traditional method ● **PREP** 25 MINS **COOK** 2 HRS

1 Heat the oil in a large flameproof casserole over a medium heat, add the onion, and cook for 3–4 minutes until soft. Season with salt and pepper, then stir through the garlic and celery and cook for a further 6–10 minutes until the celery is soft.

2 Add the lamb, turmeric, cinnamon, and ginger. Increase the heat a little, stir until the lamb is coated, and cook for 6–10 minutes until the lamb is no longer pink. Add a ladleful of stock and bring to the boil. Stir through the lentils and chickpeas, turning them to coat evenly, add the remaining stock, and bring back to the boil.

3 Reduce to a gentle simmer and cook for 1–1½ hours until the lamb is meltingly tender. Check occasionally that it's not drying out, topping up with a little hot water if needed. Stir through the harissa paste and cook for a few more minutes. Ladle into warmed bowls, top with coriander leaves, and serve with lemon wedges on the side.

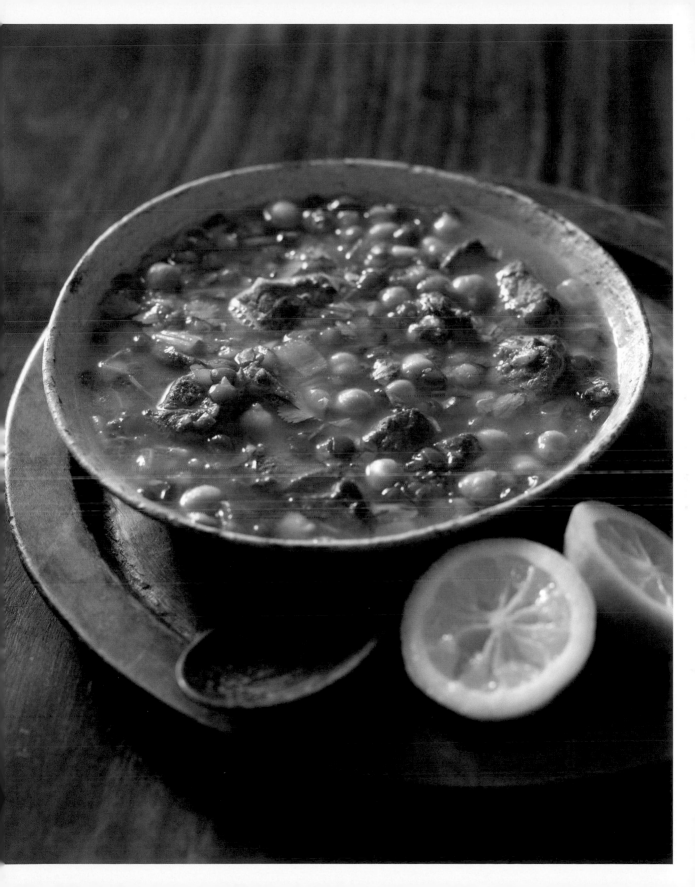

Oxtail has a distinctive flavour and is perfectly suited to slow cooking. You may have to get the meat from your butcher, as not all supermarkets have it. You could use stewing beef if you prefer.

Oxtail soup with nutmeg and star anise

⌾ **SERVES** 4–6 ❄ **FREEZE** UP TO 3 MONTHS

2 tbsp olive oil
600g (1lb 5oz) oxtails
1 red onion, finely chopped
salt and freshly ground black pepper
3 garlic cloves, finely chopped

2 star anise
pinch of grated nutmeg
900ml (1½ pints) hot vegetable stock,
  for both methods
2 x 400g cans whole tomatoes

in the slow cooker ⏱ PREP 15 MINS COOK 15 MINS PRECOOKING; AUTO/LOW 8 HRS

1 Preheat the slow cooker, if required. Heat half the oil in a flameproof casserole over a medium-high heat, add the oxtails, and cook them for about 10 minutes or until beginning to colour on all sides. Remove them and leave to cool, then remove the bones from the oxtails and set aside.

2 Meanwhile, reduce the heat a little, heat the rest of the oil, add the onion, and cook for 3–4 minutes until soft. Season with salt and pepper, stir through the garlic, star anise, and nutmeg, and cook for 1–2 minutes more. Add a little stock and stir to scrape up the bits from the bottom of the pan. Transfer everything to the slow cooker, including the oxtails, tip in the tomatoes and remaining stock, and stir. Cover with the lid and cook on auto/low for 8 hours.

3 Discard the star anise, then remove the oxtails with a slotted spoon. Shred the meat with a fork, and return it to the slow cooker. Use a stick blender to blend the soup until smooth, or transfer in batches to a liquidizer and blend. Transfer the soup to a clean pan to heat through, adding a little hot water if you need to thin it down. Taste and adjust seasoning as needed, and serve piping hot with crusty white bread.

traditional method ⏱ PREP 15 MINS COOK 2¾–3¼ HRS

1 Heat half the oil in a flameproof casserole over a medium-high heat, add the oxtails, and cook them for about 10 minutes or until beginning to colour on all sides. Remove them and set aside. Reduce the heat a little, heat the rest of the oil, add the onion, and cook for 3–4 minutes until soft. Season with salt and pepper, stir through the garlic, star anise, and nutmeg, and cook for 1–2 minutes more. Add a little stock and stir to scrape up the bits from the bottom of the pan.

2 Return the meat to the pan, tip in the tomatoes and the remaining stock, and bring to the boil. Reduce to a simmer, and cook on a gentle heat, partially covered, for 2½–3 hours or until the meat falls off the bone, topping up with a further 300ml (10fl oz) hot water (or more if needed) as required. Discard the star anise, then remove the oxtails with a slotted spoon. Shred the meat with a fork, and return it to the casserole. Use a stick blender to blend the soup until smooth, or transfer in batches to a liquidizer and blend. Transfer the soup to a clean pan to heat through, adding a little hot water if you need to thin it down. Taste and adjust seasoning as needed, and serve piping hot with crusty white bread.

A cure-all soup to which you can add vegetables or some ready-cooked noodles. The key to successful soups is the stock – use the leftover bones in this recipe to make your own.

Chunky chicken soup

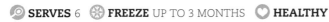 **SERVES** 6 ❀ **FREEZE** UP TO 3 MONTHS ♡ **HEALTHY**

1 whole chicken, weighing about 1.35kg (3lb)
1 tbsp olive oil
1 onion, finely chopped
salt and freshly ground black pepper
3 garlic cloves, finely chopped
2 celery sticks, roughly chopped

4 carrots, peeled and chopped into chunky pieces
340g can sweetcorn, drained
3 potatoes, peeled and roughly chopped
2 leeks, chopped into chunky pieces
few sprigs of curly parsley, finely chopped

 in the slow cooker ● **PREP** 15 MINS **COOK AUTO/LOW** 8 HRS, THEN
AUTO/LOW 6–8 HRS OR **HIGH** 4 HRS

1 Put the chicken, upside down, in the slow cooker. Pour over 900ml (1½ pints) of water, cover, and cook on auto/low for 8 hours. Remove the chicken, cover it, and set aside. Strain and reserve the stock. When cold, store the chicken in the fridge.

2 Preheat the slow cooker, if required. Heat the oil in large heavy-based pan over a medium heat, add the onions, and cook for 3–4 minutes until soft. Season with salt and pepper, add the garlic and celery, and cook for a further 5 minutes until the celery softens. Stir through the carrots, add the sweetcorn, and transfer everything to the slow cooker. Measure the reserved stock and add hot water to make 900ml (1½ pints) and pour this over. Add the potatoes and leeks and stir, then cover with the lid and cook on auto/low for 6–8 hours or on high for 4 hours.

3 Meanwhile, remove the skin from the chicken and pull away the meat. Stir this into the soup for the last 20 minutes of cooking. Taste and season as required. Ladle into wide bowls, sprinkle with a little parsley, and serve with crusty white bread.

 traditional method ● **PREP** 15 MINS **COOK** 1½ HRS

1 Put the chicken in a large heavy-based pan and pour over enough water to just cover it. Season with salt and pepper, then bring to the boil. Reduce to a simmer, cover with the lid, and cook for about 20 minutes until the chicken is cooked and the juices run clear when pierced with a sharp knife. Remove the chicken from the stock, set aside, and cover with foil; strain the stock and also set aside.

2 Heat the oil in another large heavy-based pan over a medium heat, add the onions, and cook for 3–4 minutes until soft. Season with salt and pepper, add the garlic and celery, and cook for a further 5 minutes until the celery softens. Stir through the carrots and add the sweetcorn. Measure the reserved stock and add hot water to make 900ml (1½ pints) and pour this over. Bring the soup to the boil, then reduce to a simmer and cook on a very low heat with the lid partially covering the pan for about 30 minutes, topping up with hot water, if needed. Add the potatoes and leeks and cook for a further 20 minutes, partially covered with the lid.

3 Remove the skin from the chicken and pull away the meat. Stir this into the soup, taste, and season as required. Ladle into wide bowls, sprinkle with a little parsley, and serve with crusty white bread.

A firm favourite with everyone, this soup tastes even better served the next day. Go easy on the salt when adding seasoning as the ham may be salty enough for most people's taste.

Pea, ham, and potato soup

 SERVES 4–6 ❄ **FREEZE** UP TO 3 MONTHS

1.1kg (2½lb) unsmoked ham
1 bay leaf
1 tbsp olive oil
1 onion, finely chopped
salt and freshly ground black pepper
1 tbsp Dijon mustard
3 garlic cloves, finely chopped

2 sprigs of rosemary
handful of thyme, leaves only
900ml (1½ pints) hot beef stock for the slow cooker
  (1.2 litres/2 pints for the traditional method)
450g (1lb) frozen peas
3 potatoes, peeled and chopped into
  bite-sized pieces

 in the slow cooker 🕐 PREP 15 MINS **COOK AUTO/LOW** 8 HRS OR **HIGH** 4 HRS,
                                          THEN **AUTO/LOW** 8 HRS OR **HIGH** 4 HRS

1 Preheat the slow cooker, if required. Sit the ham and bay leaf in the slow cooker and cover with 900ml (1½ pints) of water. Cover and cook on auto/low for 8 hours or on high for 4 hours, then remove the ham and set aside. Discard the stock, or strain and reserve a little to add to the soup.

2 Heat the oil in a large heavy-based pan over a medium heat, add the onion, and cook for 3–4 minutes until soft. Season with salt and pepper, then stir in the mustard, garlic, and herbs (reserve some thyme leaves for garnish). Add a little stock and bring to the boil, then tip in the peas (if you prefer them puréed, pulse them gently in a liquidizer or use a stick blender). Transfer to the slow cooker, add the remaining stock and the potatoes, cover, and cook on auto/low for 8 hours or on high for 4 hours. Remove any fat from the ham, chop into bite-sized pieces, and stir into the soup. Taste and season as needed. Garnish with the reserved thyme leaves and serve with wholemeal bread.

traditional method 🕐 PREP 15 MINS **COOK** 2 HRS

1 Add the ham and bay leaf to a large pan, cover with 1.2 litres (2 pints) of water and bring to the boil. Partially cover, reduce to a simmer, and cook for about 1 hour or until the ham is cooked. Skim away any scum that comes to the surface of the pan as you go. Discard the stock, or strain and reserve a little to add to the soup. Set the ham aside until cool enough to handle.

2 Heat the oil in a large heavy-based pan over a medium heat, add the onion, and cook for 3–4 minutes until soft. Season with salt and pepper, then stir in the mustard, garlic, and herbs (reserve some thyme leaves for garnish). Add a little stock and bring to the boil, then tip in the peas and remaining stock. Bring to the boil, reduce to a simmer, and cook for 45 minutes, topping up with hot water as needed.

3 About 20 minutes before the end of the cooking time, bring a separate pan of water to the boil. Add the potatoes, bring back up to the boil, and then simmer for 12–15 minutes until soft. Drain and set aside. Remove the rosemary from the soup, then use a stick blender to gently purée the peas, or ladle them into a liquidizer and pulse a couple of times. Return them to the pan and stir in the potatoes. Remove any fat from the ham, chop into bite-sized pieces, and stir into the soup. Taste and adjust seasoning as needed. Garnish with the reserved thyme leaves and serve with wholemeal bread.

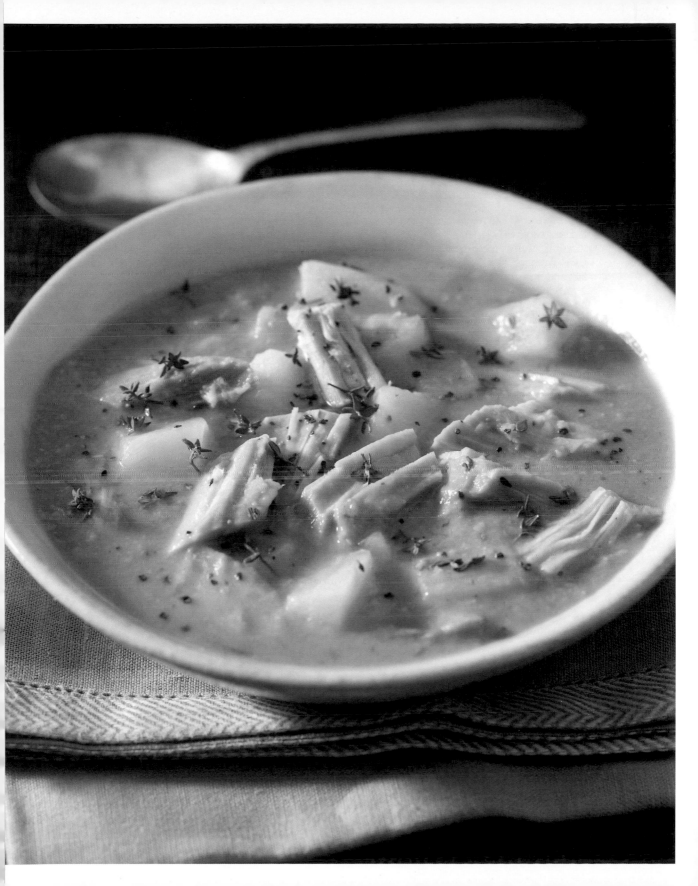

The subtle combinations of meaty monkfish, delicate haddock, aniseed fennel, and the light scent of saffron marry well. You could add some mussels or prawns, if you like.

Rich fish soup

SERVES 4–6 **FREEZE** UP TO 1 MONTH

1 tbsp olive oil
1 onion, finely chopped
salt and freshly ground black pepper
1 sprig of thyme
3 garlic cloves, finely chopped
1 fennel bulb, trimmed and finely chopped
1 red chilli, deseeded and finely chopped

250ml (9fl oz) dry white wine
2 x 400g cans chopped tomatoes
600ml (1 pint) hot light vegetable stock for the slow cooker (900ml/1½ pints for the traditional method)
pinch of saffron threads
200g (7oz) monkfish, cut into bite-sized pieces
200g (7oz) haddock loin, cut into bite-sized pieces

in the slow cooker **PREP** 15 MINS **COOK** 10 MINS PRECOOKING; AUTO/LOW 8 HRS OR HIGH 4 HRS

1 Preheat the slow cooker, if required. Heat the oil in a large heavy-based pan over a medium heat, add the onion, and cook for 3–4 minutes until soft. Season with salt and pepper and throw in the thyme. Add the garlic and fennel, and cook gently for a further 5 minutes until the fennel begins to soften.

2 Stir through the chilli and cook for 1 minute, then increase the heat, add the wine, and let it bubble for a minute. Transfer everything to the hot slow cooker, tip in the tomatoes and stock, and stir through the saffron. Cover with the lid and cook on auto/low for 8 hours or on high for 4 hours.

3 Use a stick blender to blend the soup until smooth, or transfer in batches to a liquidizer and blend until smooth and return to the hot slow cooker. Taste and season as needed, add the fish, put the lid back on, and leave for about 10 minutes or until the fish is opaque and cooked through. Ladle into warmed bowls and serve with white crusty bread. Garnish with chopped fennel fronds, if you like.

traditional method **PREP** 15 MINS **COOK** 1 HR

1 Heat the oil in a large heavy-based pan over a medium heat, add the onion, and cook for 3–4 minutes until soft. Season with salt and pepper and throw in the thyme. Add the garlic and fennel, and cook gently for a further 5 minutes until the fennel begins to soften.

2 Stir through the chilli and cook for 1 minute, then increase the heat, add the wine, let it bubble for a minute, and then tip in the canned tomatoes and stock. Add the saffron, bring to the boil, then reduce to a simmer and cook gently, partially covered with the lid, for about 45 minutes. Take care that the sauce doesn't dry out, topping it up with a little hot water if needed.

3 Use a stick blender to blend the soup until smooth, or transfer in batches to a liquidizer and blend until smooth, and return to a clean pan. Top up with a little hot water – you will probably need about 300ml (10fl oz) in total – and simmer gently. Taste and season as needed, add the fish, put the lid back on, and cook on a low heat for 6–10 minutes or until the fish is opaque and cooked through. Ladle into warmed bowls and serve with white crusty bread. Garnish with chopped fennel fronds, if you like.

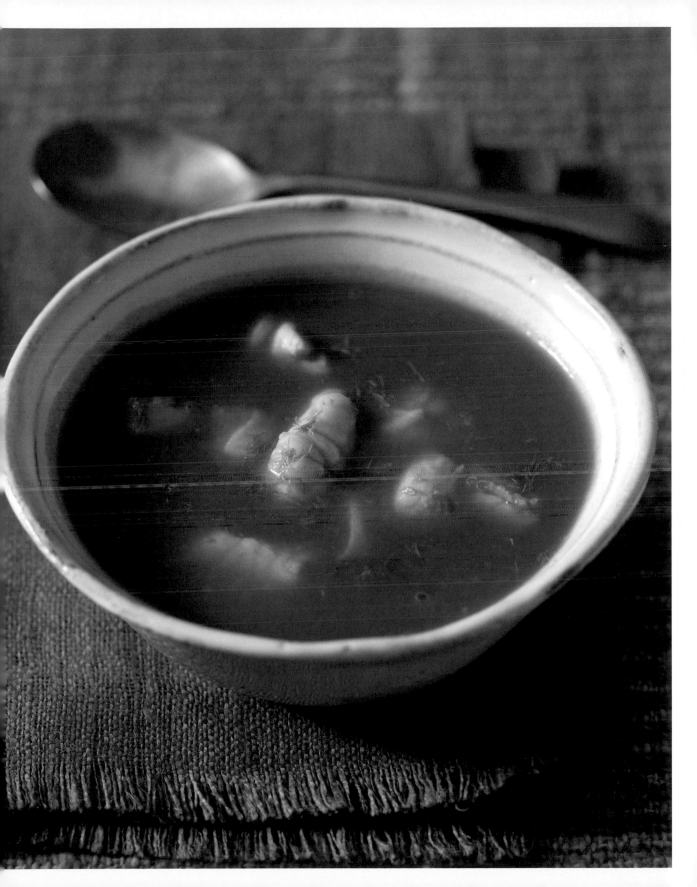

This velvety smooth soup can be made using pumpkin or butternut squash, depending on what is in season. The dried chilli flakes give it just the right kick to cut through the richness.

Pumpkin and ginger soup

⊘ **SERVES** 4–6   ✳ **FREEZE** UP TO 3 MONTHS

1 tbsp olive oil
1 onion, finely chopped
salt and freshly ground black pepper
3 garlic cloves, finely chopped
5cm (2in) piece of fresh root ginger,
  peeled and finely chopped
pinch of dried chilli flakes

1 small cinnamon stick
900g (2lb) pumpkin or butternut squash,
  peeled, deseeded, and diced
600ml (1 pint) hot vegetable stock for the
  slow cooker (900ml/1½ pints for the
  traditional method)

in the slow cooker   ● PREP 15 MINS   COOK 15 MINS PRECOOKING;
AUTO/LOW 8 HRS OR **HIGH** 4 HRS

1 Preheat the slow cooker, if required. Heat the oil in a large heavy-based pan over a medium heat, add the onion, and cook for 3–4 minutes until soft. Season with salt and pepper, add the garlic, ginger, chilli flakes, and cinnamon stick, and cook for a few seconds before adding the pumpkin or squash (and a little more olive oil if needed) and stirring to coat.

2 Pour in a little of the stock, increase the heat, and scrape up the bits from the bottom of the pan. Transfer everything to the slow cooker. Add the remaining stock, cover with the lid, and cook on auto/low for 8 hours or on high for 4 hours.

3 Remove the cinnamon stick and use a stick blender to blend the soup until smooth, or transfer in batches to a liquidizer and blend until smooth. Transfer to a clean pan to heat through, taste, and season as required. Serve with some chunky wholemeal bread or some rye bread.

traditional method   ● PREP 15 MINS   COOK 1 HR

1 Heat the oil in a large heavy-based pan over a medium heat, add the onion, and cook for 3–4 minutes until soft. Season with salt and pepper, add the garlic, ginger, chilli flakes, and cinnamon stick, and cook for a few seconds before adding the pumpkin or squash (and a little more olive oil if needed) and stirring to coat.

2 Pour in a little of the stock, increase the heat, and scrape up the bits from the bottom of the pan. Add the remaining stock, boil for 1 minute, then reduce the heat to barely a simmer, cover with the lid, and cook for about 45 minutes until the pumpkin is soft and the flavours have developed.

3 Remove the cinnamon stick and use a stick blender to blend the soup until smooth, or transfer in batches to a liquidizer and blend until smooth. Add a ladleful of hot water as you go if it is too thick. Transfer to a clean pan to heat through, taste, and season as required. Serve with some chunky wholemeal bread or some rye bread.

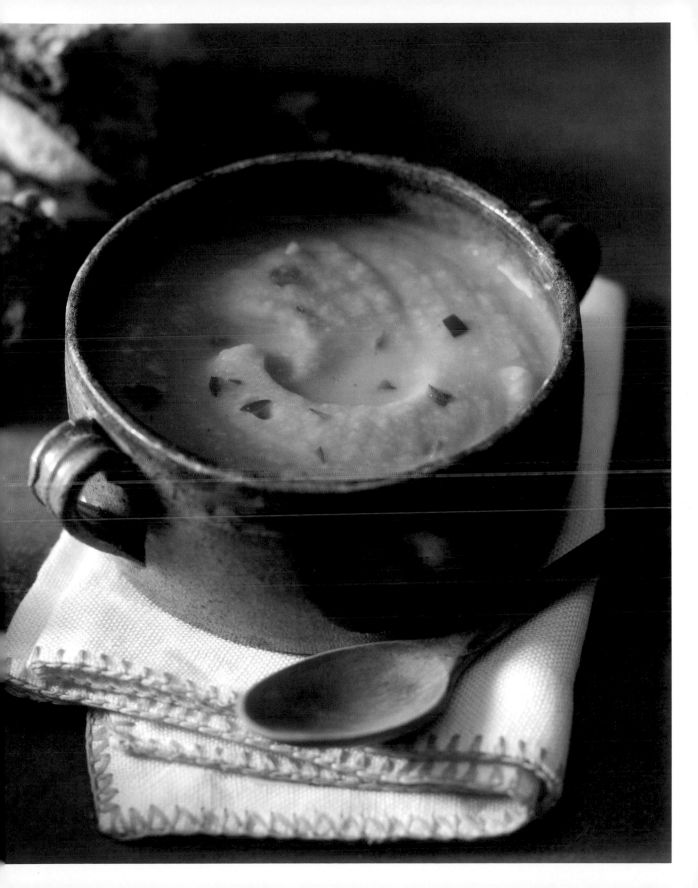

A hearty dish laden with chunks of cod, potatoes, and mussels to add colour and flavour. The traditional accompaniment in New England is oyster crackers, crumbled into the bowls.

New England chowder

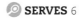 **SERVES** 6

1.2 litres (2 pints) hot fish stock, for both methods
2 bay leaves
120ml (4fl oz) white wine
140g (5oz) smoked streaky bacon rashers, diced
1 onion, finely chopped
2 celery sticks, finely chopped
1 carrot, peeled and finely chopped
2 tsp dried thyme
60g (2oz) plain flour

2 potatoes, total weight about 350g (12oz), peeled and finely diced
200ml (7fl oz) double cream
900g (2lb) skinned sustainable cod fillets, cut into bite-sized pieces
500g (1lb 2oz) mussels, scrubbed and debearded (discard any that do not close when tapped)
salt and freshly ground black pepper
5–7 sprigs of dill, leaves finely chopped, to serve

 in the slow cooker 🕐 **PREP** 15 MINS **COOK** 20 MINS PRECOOKING; **HIGH** 2–3 HRS

1 Preheat the slow cooker, if required. Put the fish stock and bay leaves into a saucepan and pour in the wine. Bring to the boil and simmer for 10 minutes. Put the bacon in a large flameproof casserole over a medium-high heat and cook, stirring occasionally, for 3–5 minutes until crisp and the fat has rendered. Reduce the heat to low, add the onion, celery, carrot, and thyme and cook for 15 minutes, stirring, until soft. Sprinkle the flour over and cook, stirring, for a minute. Add the hot stock mixture and bring to the boil, stirring, until the liquid thickens slightly. Transfer everything to the slow cooker, add the potatoes, cover with the lid, and cook on high for 2–3 hours.

2 For the last 20 minutes of cooking, crush about a third of the potatoes with a fork, and stir in the cream and cod. Cover and cook for 10 minutes. Add the mussels, cover, and cook for 10 minutes or until the mussels have opened (discard any that do not open). Taste and season if needed. Discard the bay leaves. Ladle the chowder into warmed soup bowls and sprinkle each with dill. Serve very hot.

 traditional method 🕐 **PREP** 45–50 MINS **COOK** 55–60 MINS

1 Put the fish stock and bay leaves into a saucepan and pour in the wine. Bring to the boil and simmer for 10 minutes. Put the bacon in a large flameproof casserole over a medium-high heat and cook, stirring occasionally, for 3–5 minutes until crisp and the fat has rendered. Reduce the heat to low, add the onions, celery, carrot, and thyme and cook for 15 minutes, stirring, until soft. Sprinkle the flour over and cook, stirring, for a minute. Add the hot stock mixture and bring to the boil, stirring, until the liquid thickens slightly. Add the potatoes and simmer for about 20 minutes, stirring occasionally, until the potatoes are very tender. Remove the casserole from the heat. With a fork, crush about a third of the potatoes against the side of the casserole, then stir to combine.

2 Return the casserole to the heat, stir in the cod, and simmer for 1–2 minutes. Tip in the mussels and simmer for a further 2–3 minutes until the shells have opened and the fish is opaque and cooked through. Pour in the cream and bring just to the boil. Taste and season if needed. Discard the bay leaves and any mussels that have not opened. Ladle the chowder into warmed soup bowls and sprinkle each with dill. Serve very hot.

This is a delicious tomato-based soup. Mix and match the shellfish to include whatever is available; add ready-cooked lobster and use fresh shellfish stock if you can get hold of it.

Shellfish soup

 SERVES 6

1 tbsp olive oil
2 celery sticks, finely chopped
2 carrots, peeled and finely diced
2 onions, finely diced
175g (6oz) streaky bacon, cut into bite-sized pieces
400g can chopped tomatoes
1 star anise

450ml (15fl oz) hot fish stock for the slow cooker (600ml/1 pint for the traditional method)
about 800g (1¾lb) fresh shellfish, such as clams, mussels, scallops, and shrimps, scrubbed and debearded where necessary (discard any clams and mussels that do not close when tapped)
bunch of flat-leaf parsley, finely chopped

 in the slow cooker   **PREP** 20 MINS   **COOK** 15 MINS PRECOOKING; **AUTO/LOW** 6–8 HRS OR **HIGH** 3–4 HRS

1 Preheat the slow cooker, if required. Heat the oil in a large flameproof casserole, add the celery, carrots, and onions and cook for about 10 minutes until soft. Add the bacon and cook for about 5 minutes, then stir through the tomatoes and add the star anise. Pour in the stock and bring to the boil. Transfer everything to the slow cooker and cook on auto/low for 6–8 hours or on high for 3–4 hours.

2 Add the shellfish for the last 10 minutes of cooking, or until the clams and mussels have opened (discard any that do not open). Sprinkle over the parsley and stir it in. Ladle into warmed bowls and serve with crusty bread and some spicy mayonnaise.

traditional method   **PREP** 20 MINS   **COOK** 1¼ HRS

1 Heat the oil in a large flameproof casserole, add the celery, carrots, and onion and cook for about 10 minutes until soft. Add the bacon and cook for about 5 minutes, then stir through the tomatoes and add the star anise. Pour in the stock and bring to the boil. Reduce the heat and simmer gently for about 45 minutes, topping up with hot water if it starts to reduce too much.

2 Add the shellfish and cook for 5–10 minutes until the clams and mussels have opened (discard any that do not open). Sprinkle over the parsley and stir it in. Ladle into warmed bowls and serve with crusty bread and some spicy mayonnaise.

The poached chicken in this recipe has an incredibly silky texture and is very tender. You can add extras to the soup at the end, such as Asian greens, noodles, shrimps, or crunchy beansprouts.

Malaysian chicken soup

SERVES 4–6   **FREEZE** UP TO 1 MONTH   **HEALTHY**

1.35kg (3lb) free-range chicken
1 onion, quartered
5cm (2in) piece of fresh root ginger, peeled and sliced
6 garlic cloves, crushed
salt and freshly ground black pepper

splash of soy sauce
splash of fish sauce (nam pla)
250ml (9fl oz) hot vegetable stock (optional)
bunch of green spring onions, finely sliced, to serve

in the slow cooker   PREP 15 MINS   COOK AUTO/LOW 6–8 HRS OR HIGH 3–4 HRS

1 Preheat the slow cooker, if required. Put the chicken, upside down, into the slow cooker, add the onion, ginger, and garlic, and season with salt and pepper. Pour over enough water to cover the chicken. Cover with the lid and cook on auto/low for 6–8 hours or on high for 3–4 hours. Remove the chicken from the broth and set aside until it is cool enough to handle.

2 Remove the skin from the chicken and discard, then remove all the meat from the bones. Strain the broth from the slow cooker into a clean heavy-based pan, add the chicken meat, and stir in the soy sauce and fish sauce. Top up with some stock, if necessary, then simmer gently to warm through, taste, and season as required. Ladle into warmed Asian soup bowls and garnish with spring onions.

traditional method   PREP 15 MINS   COOK 40–50 MINS

1 Put the chicken, onion, ginger, and garlic in a large pan and cover with water. Season with salt and pepper and bring to the boil. Reduce to a simmer, cover with the lid, and cook on a low heat for 30–40 minutes or until the chicken is cooked and the juices flow clear when pierced with a sharp knife. Remove the chicken from the broth and set aside until it is cool enough to handle.

2 Remove the skin from the chicken and discard, then remove all the meat from the bones. Strain the broth from the pan into a clean heavy-based pan, add the chicken meat, and stir in the soy sauce and fish sauce. Top up with some stock, if necessary, then simmer gently to warm through, taste, and season as required. Ladle into warmed Asian soup bowls and garnish with spring onions.

This is a rich and lightly curried soup with a hint of apple added for sweetness. The lentils give it real substance, making it a perfect main meal soup.

Beef mulligatawny soup

 SERVES 4–6 ✳ **FREEZE** UP TO 3 MONTHS

1 tbsp olive oil
1 onion, finely chopped
salt and freshly ground black pepper
1 tbsp coriander seeds
1 red chilli, deseeded and finely chopped
1–2 tsp garam masala (depending on how much spice you like)
550g (1¼lb) skirt beef or braising steak, cut into bite-sized pieces

3 garlic cloves, finely chopped
3 carrots, peeled and diced
1 eating apple, peeled, cored, and diced
125g (4½oz) red lentils, rinsed well and picked over for any stones
900ml (1½ pints) hot beef stock for the slow cooker (1.2 litres/2 pints for the traditional method)
coriander leaves, chopped, to serve

 ### in the slow cooker 🕐 PREP 35 MINS   COOK 25 MINS PRECOOKING; AUTO/LOW 8 HRS OR HIGH 4 HRS

1 Preheat the slow cooker, if required. Heat the oil in a large heavy-based pan over a medium heat, add the onion, and cook for 3–4 minutes until soft. Season with salt and pepper, then stir in the coriander seeds, chilli, and garam masala. Cook for a few minutes, increase the heat a little, add the beef (adding a little more oil if necessary), and cook for about 6 minutes until the beef is no longer pink.

2 Reduce the heat, add the garlic, carrots, and apple, and cook for about 5 minutes until the carrots begin to soften. Tip in the lentils and stir to coat. Transfer everything to the slow cooker and stir in the beef stock. Cover with the lid and cook on auto/low for 8 hours or on high for 4 hours. Taste and adjust the seasoning, then blend with a stick blender, or transfer to a liquidizer and pulse very briefly. Don't purée the soup too much as it still needs plenty of texture. Add a little hot water as you go, if needed. Return to a clean pan, taste and adjust seasoning as needed, and heat through. Ladle into warmed bowls and garnish with the coriander.

traditional method 🕐 PREP 35 MINS   COOK 1½ HRS

1 Heat the oil in a large heavy-based pan over a medium heat, add the onion, and cook for 3–4 minutes until soft. Season with salt and pepper, then stir in the coriander seeds, chilli, and garam masala. Cook for a few minutes, increase the heat a little, add the beef (adding a little more oil if necessary), and cook for about 6 minutes until the beef is no longer pink.

2 Reduce the heat, add the garlic, carrots, and apple, and cook for about 5 minutes until the carrots begin to soften. Tip in the lentils and stir to coat, then pour over the stock. Bring to the boil, reduce to a simmer, and cook gently, covered, for about 1 hour. Check occasionally that it's not drying out, topping up with hot water if needed. You will probably need to add at least 300ml (10fl oz). Don't worry if it is a little thick, you can dilute it when you liquidize it. Taste and adjust the seasoning, then blend with a sticker blender, or transfer to a liquidizer and pulse very briefly. Don't purée it too much as it still needs plenty of texture. Add a little hot water as you go, if needed. Return to a clean pan, taste and adjust seasoning as needed, and heat through. Ladle into warmed bowls and garnish with the coriander.

This main meal soup has a great balance of flavours with the aromatic orange zest and juice giving it an extra tang that really lifts the poached chicken and earthy celeriac.

Chicken broth with celeriac and orange

SERVES 4–6 ❄ **FREEZE** UP TO 3 MONTHS

1 tbsp olive oil
1 onion, finely chopped
1 bay leaf
salt and freshly ground black pepper
2 garlic cloves, finely chopped
zest of 1 orange and juice of ½ orange

few sprigs of oregano, leaves only
1 celeriac, peeled and chopped into small chunks
1 litre (1¾ pints) hot chicken stock, for both methods
4 skinless chicken breasts
4 sprigs of flat-leaf parsley, finely chopped, to serve

in the slow cooker ⏱ **PREP** 15 MINS **COOK** 10 MINS PRECOOKING, AUTO/LOW 8 HRS OR **HIGH** 4 HRS

1 Preheat the slow cooker, if required. Heat the oil in a large heavy-based pan over a medium heat, add the onion and bay leaf, and cook for 3–4 minutes until the onion is just beginning to soften. Season with salt and pepper, then add the garlic, orange zest, and oregano and cook for a few seconds.

2 Stir in the celeriac and orange juice, scraping up the bits from the bottom of the pan. Transfer everything to the slow cooker, pour over the stock, and stir in the chicken breasts. Cover with the lid and cook on auto/low for 8 hours or on high for 4 hours.

3 Remove the chicken breasts with a slotted spoon and set aside until cool enough to handle, then shred into chunky pieces using your hands or two forks, and return the meat to the slow cooker. Taste and adjust the seasoning, if needed, and remove the bay leaf. Serve in warmed bowls, garnished with parsley.

traditional method ⏱ **PREP** 15 MINS **COOK** 1 HR

1 Heat the oil in a large heavy-based pan over a medium heat, add the onion and bay leaf, and cook for 3–4 minutes until the onion is just beginning to soften. Season with salt and pepper, then add the garlic, orange zest, and oregano and cook for a few seconds.

2 Stir in the celeriac and orange juice, scraping up the bits from the bottom of the pan. Then pour in the stock, add the chicken breasts, and bring to the boil. Reduce to a simmer and cook gently for 20–30 minutes or until the chicken breasts are cooked. Remove the chicken breasts with a slotted spoon and set aside until cool enough to handle, then shred into chunky pieces using your hands or two forks.

3 Continue simmering the stock for a further 15 minutes or so, topping up with a little hot water if needed. Taste and adjust the seasoning, if needed, and remove the bay leaf. Return the shredded chicken to the pan and stir. Serve in warmed bowls, garnished with parsley.

It's the slow-cooked beef stock, flavoured with gentle spices, that really makes this dish. Use glass noodles, if you can find them, for a traditional Vietnamese touch.

Vietnamese beef soup

⊘ **SERVES** 4–6   ❄ **FREEZE** STOCK UP TO 1 MONTH

about 675g (1½lb) beef bones, rinsed and dried
1 tbsp dark soy sauce
1 tbsp olive oil
1 star anise
1 tsp black peppercorns
1 cinnamon stick
½ tbsp fish sauce (nam pla)
1 onion, finely chopped
3 garlic cloves, finely chopped
1 chilli, deseeded and finely chopped

1 lemongrass stalk, trimmed, woody outer leaves
    removed and very finely chopped
2.5cm (1in) piece of fresh root ginger, peeled and
    finely sliced
salt and freshly ground black pepper
350g (12oz) fillet steak, very finely sliced across
    the grain
60g (2oz) vermicelli noodles, soaked in hot water for
    5 minutes (or as per pack instructions) and drained
bunch of green spring onions, finely sliced

in the slow cooker   ⊙ PREP 15 MINS   COOK 20 MINS PRECOOKING;
AUTO/LOW 8 HRS OR HIGH 4 HRS

1 First make the beef stock. Preheat the slow cooker, if required. In a bowl, toss the beef bones with the soy sauce. Heat a little of the oil in a large heavy-based pan over a medium-high heat, add the bones and cook, stirring, for about 15 minutes until the meat is no longer pink. Transfer them to the slow cooker together with the star anise, peppercorns, cinnamon stick, and fish sauce. Pour over 900ml (1½ pints) of water, cover with the lid, and cook on auto/low for 8 hours or on high for 4 hours.

2 Halfway through the cooking time, heat the remaining oil in a large heavy-based pan over a medium heat, add the onion, and cook for 3–4 minutes until soft. Stir in the garlic, chilli, and lemongrass and cook for a minute. Strain the stock from the slow cooker through a sieve and return to the slow cooker with the onion mixture. Add the ginger and taste, adding seasoning if needed.

3 Just before serving, add the beef to the stock and put the lid on. The beef will cook in the hot stock in minutes. Stir through the noodles and spring onions and ladle into warmed bowls.

traditional method   ⊙ PREP 15 MINS   COOK 1¼ HRS

1 First make the beef stock. In a bowl, toss the beef bones with the soy sauce. Heat a little of the oil in a large heavy-based pan over a medium-high heat, add the bones and cook, stirring, for about 15 minutes until the meat is no longer pink. Transfer them to a large stock pan, pour over 1.4 litres (2½ pints) of water and add the star anise, peppercorns, cinnamon stick, and fish sauce. Bring to the boil, then partially cover with the lid, reduce to a simmer and cook for 1 hour. Strain the stock through a sieve into a clean pan, topping up with water to 900ml (1½ pints), if necessary, and reserve.

2 Heat the remaining oil in a large heavy-based pan, add the onion, and cook for 3–4 minutes until soft. Do not brown. Stir in the garlic, chilli, and lemongrass and cook for a minute. Then pour in the beef stock, add the ginger, and taste, adding seasoning if needed. Gently simmer for a few minutes, then add the sliced steak to the stock and cook for 2–3 minutes. Stir through the noodles and spring onions and ladle into warmed bowls.

To ring the changes in this vegetarian soup, you could swap the cannellini beans for butter beans if you wish. Butter beans can be used, like potatoes, as a thickener.

Cannellini bean, garlic, and mushroom soup

◎ **SERVES** 4–6 ✳ **FREEZE** UP TO 3 MONTHS

1 tbsp olive oil
1 onion, finely chopped
salt and freshly ground pepper
3 garlic cloves, finely chopped
few sprigs of oregano, leaves only
200g (7oz) mushrooms, finely chopped

20g (¾oz) porcini mushrooms
900ml (1½ pints) hot vegetable stock, for both methods
2 x 400g cans cannellini beans
handful of basil leaves
drizzle of basil oil, to serve (optional)

in the slow cooker 🕐 PREP 15 MINS COOK 15 MINS PRECOOKING; HIGH 4 HRS

1 Preheat the slow cooker, if required. Heat the oil in a large heavy-based pan over a medium heat, add the onion, and cook for 3–4 minutes until soft. Then season with salt and pepper, add the garlic and oregano, and cook for a few seconds.

2 Add all the mushrooms and cook for about 5 minutes until they begin to release their juices, then increase the heat, add a little stock, and let it simmer. Transfer everything to the slow cooker, add the remaining stock and the beans, cover with the lid, and cook on high for 4 hours.

3 Add the basil leaves to the soup and use a stick blender to blend until smooth, or transfer in batches to a liquidizer and blend. Add a ladleful of hot water if it is too thick. Pour the soup into a clean pan, taste and season as needed, and heat through. Garnish with a drizzle of basil oil and serve with some crusty bread.

traditional method 🕐 PREP 15 MINS COOK 50 MINS

1 Heat the oil in a large heavy-based pan over a medium heat, add the onion, and cook for 3–4 minutes until soft. Then season with salt and pepper, add the garlic and oregano, and cook for a few seconds.

2 Add all the mushrooms and cook for about 5 minutes until they begin to release their juices, then increase the heat, add a little stock, and let it simmer. Add the remaining stock and bring to the boil, then reduce to a simmer, add the beans and cook gently, partially covered with a lid, for about 40 minutes, topping up with more hot water if needed.

3 Add the basil leaves to the soup and use a stick blender to blend until smooth, or transfer in batches to a liquidizer and blend. Add a ladleful of hot water if it is too thick. Pour the soup into a clean pan, taste and season as needed, and heat through. Garnish with a drizzle of basil oil and serve with some crusty bread.

Just a touch of chilli and paprika enlivens this soup and the slow cooking of the peppers enhances their sweet flavour. You could add canned chickpeas for a more substantial soup.

Spanish pepper and tomato soup

⊙ **SERVES** 4–6   ❄ **FREEZE** UP TO 3 MONTHS

1 tbsp olive oil
1 onion, finely chopped
salt and freshly ground black pepper
2 celery sticks, roughly chopped
3 garlic cloves, finely chopped
1 large carrot, peeled and chopped
pinch of dried chilli flakes

pinch of paprika
6 red peppers, deseeded and roughly chopped
3 tomatoes, roughly chopped
900ml (1½ pints) hot vegetable stock for the
    slow cooker (1.4 litres/2½ pints for the
    traditional method)
85g (3oz) feta cheese, crumbled, to serve (optional)

in the slow cooker   🕐 **PREP** 20 MINS   **COOK** 35 MINS PRECOOKING;
AUTO/LOW 8 HRS OR **HIGH** 3 HRS

1 Preheat the slow cooker, if required. Heat the oil in a large heavy-based pan over a medium heat, add the onion, and cook for 3–4 minutes until soft. Season with salt and pepper, add the celery, garlic, and carrot, and cook for 5–10 minutes until soft, stirring occasionally.

2 Stir through the chilli flakes and paprika and cook for a minute, then add the peppers and tomatoes. Cook on a very low heat for about 20 minutes, stirring so they don't stick. Transfer everything to the slow cooker. Pour over the stock, stir, then cover with the lid and cook on auto/low for 8 hours or on high for 3 hours.

3 Use a stick blender to blend the soup until smooth, or transfer in batches to a liquidizer and blend. Add a ladleful of hot water if it is too thick. Pour the soup into a clean pan, taste and season as needed, and heat through. Serve with a little feta cheese on top, if using, together with some crusty bread on the side.

traditional method   🕐 **PREP** 20 MINS   **COOK** 1¼–1½ HRS

1 Heat the oil in a large heavy-based pan over a medium heat, add the onion, and cook for 3–4 minutes until soft. Season with salt and pepper, add the celery, garlic, and carrot, and cook for 5–10 minutes until soft, stirring occasionally.

2 Stir through the chilli flakes and paprika and cook for a minute, then add the peppers and tomatoes. Cook on a very low heat for about 20 minutes, stirring so they don't stick. Pour in half of the stock and bring to the boil, then reduce to a simmer, partially cover with the lid, and cook on a low heat for 45–60 minutes, topping up with the reserved stock as the cooking liquid reduces.

3 Use a stick blender to blend the soup until smooth, or transfer in batches to a liquidizer and blend. Add a ladleful of hot water if it is too thick. Pour the soup into a clean pan, taste and season as needed, and heat through. Serve with a little feta cheese on top, if using, together with some crusty bread on the side.

The two main ingredients of a laksa are noodles and coconut milk, and it is often served with the addition of shellfish, in this case king prawns. You could replace the noodles with rice vermicelli.

Prawn laksa

SERVES 4–6

550g (1¼lb) raw king prawns with shells on, peeled (but keep the tails on) and shells reserved
2 tbsp sunflower oil
2–3 tbsp fish sauce (nam pla)
6 shallots, peeled
5cm (2in) piece of fresh root ginger, peeled and finely chopped
3 garlic cloves, peeled

2 red chillies, deseeded
salt and freshly ground black pepper
400ml can coconut milk
175g (6oz) medium rice noodles, soaked in hot water for 10 minutes
pinch of sugar (optional)
handful of mint leaves, finely chopped
handful of coriander leaves, finely chopped

in the slow cooker ⏱ PREP 15 MINS COOK 10 MINS PRECOOKING; **HIGH** 3–4 HRS, THEN 3–4 HRS

1 Preheat the slow cooker, if required. To make the soup base, put the prawn shells into a heavy-based pan with a sprinkling of oil and cook for a few minutes, stirring, until they turn pink. Transfer to the slow cooker, then pour over 1.2 litres (2 pints) of water and add the fish sauce, to taste. Cover with the lid, and cook on high for 3–4 hours. Strain the stock and reserve.

2 Keep the slow cooker heated, if required. Put the shallots, ginger, garlic, chillies, and 1 tbsp of the oil in a food processor and blend to a paste. Season with salt and pepper. Heat the remaining oil in a small heavy-based pan over a medium heat, stir in the paste, and cook for a couple of minutes. Ladle in a little of the stock, stir, and transfer everything to the slow cooker. Pour in the coconut milk and the remaining stock, cover with the lid, and cook on high for another 3–4 hours.

3 Taste and adjust seasoning as required, adding a little more fish sauce, if you like, or you may wish to sweeten it with a little sugar. Stir through the noodles and the prawns to cook for 10 minutes more. To serve, stir through the mint and coriander and ladle into warmed shallow bowls.

traditional method ⏱ PREP 15 MINS COOK 1½ HRS

1 To make the soup base, put the prawn shells into a large heavy-based pan with a sprinkling of oil and cook for a few minutes, stirring, until they turn pink. Pour over 1.2 litres (2 pints) of water and add the fish sauce, to taste. Bring to the boil, then reduce to a simmer, partially cover with the lid, and cook gently for 30–45 minutes. Strain the stock and reserve.

2 Put the shallots, ginger, garlic, chillies, and 1 tbsp of the oil in a food processor and blend to a paste. Season with salt and pepper. Heat the remaining oil in a large heavy-based pan over a medium heat, stir in the paste, and cook for a couple of minutes. Ladle in a little of the stock and bring to the boil, then pour in the coconut milk and the remaining stock, and let it bubble for a few minutes. Reduce to a gentle simmer, partially cover, and cook for 30–40 minutes topping up with a little hot water if needed.

3 Taste and adjust seasoning as required, adding a little more fish sauce, if you like, or you may wish to sweeten it with a little sugar. Stir through the noodles and the prawns, and simmer for a couple of minutes. To serve, stir through the mint and coriander and ladle into warmed shallow bowls.

Stews

A colourful and gutsy dish, you could always add some spicy sausage or chorizo if you prefer a meaty meal. Black beans are also called turtle beans and need soaking overnight.

Brazilian black bean and pumpkin stew

 SERVES 4–6 ✸ **FREEZE** UP TO 3 MONTHS ♡ **HEALTHY**

325g (11oz) dried black beans, soaked
  overnight and drained
1 tbsp olive oil
1 onion, finely chopped
salt and freshly ground black pepper
3 garlic cloves, finely chopped
1 small pumpkin or butternut squash, peeled,
  deseeded, and diced

2 red peppers, deseeded and diced
2 x 400g cans chopped tomatoes
1 small green chilli, deseeded and diced
600ml (1 pint) hot vegetable stock for the slow
  cooker (900ml/1½ pints for the traditional method)
1 mango, peeled, stone removed, and diced
bunch of coriander, chopped

 in the slow cooker 🕐 **PREP** 25 MINS, PLUS SOAKING **COOK** 10 MINS PRECOOKING; AUTO/LOW 6–8 HRS

1 Preheat the slow cooker, if required. Put the beans in a large heavy-based pan and cover with water. Bring to the boil, and then drain the beans and set aside.

2 Dry the pan and heat the oil in it over a medium heat, add the onion, and cook for 3–4 minutes until soft. Season with salt and pepper, stir in the garlic, and cook for 1–2 minutes until soft. Stir in the pumpkin or butternut squash and also cook for about a minute.

3 Transfer everything to the slow cooker and add the beans, red peppers, tomatoes, and chilli together with the stock. Season well, cover with the lid, and cook on auto/low for 6–8 hours. Taste and season, if necessary, then stir through the mango and coriander. Serve with some soured cream and rice on the side.

 traditional method 🕐 **PREP** 25 MINS, PLUS SOAKING **COOK** 2½–3 HRS

1 Preheat the oven to 160°C (325°F/Gas 3). Put the beans in a large heavy-based pan and cover with water. Bring to the boil, then reduce to a simmer, partially cover with the lid, and cook on a low heat for 1 hour. Drain and set aside.

2 Heat the oil in a large heavy-based pan over a medium heat, add the onion, and cook for 3–4 minutes until soft. Season with salt and pepper, stir in the garlic, and cook for 1–2 minutes until soft. Stir in the pumpkin or butternut squash, red peppers, tomatoes, and chilli.

3 Add the beans, pour over the stock, and bring to the boil. Then reduce to a simmer, cover with the lid and put in the oven for 1½–2 hours. Taste and season, if necessary, then stir through the mango and coriander. Serve with some soured cream and rice on the side.

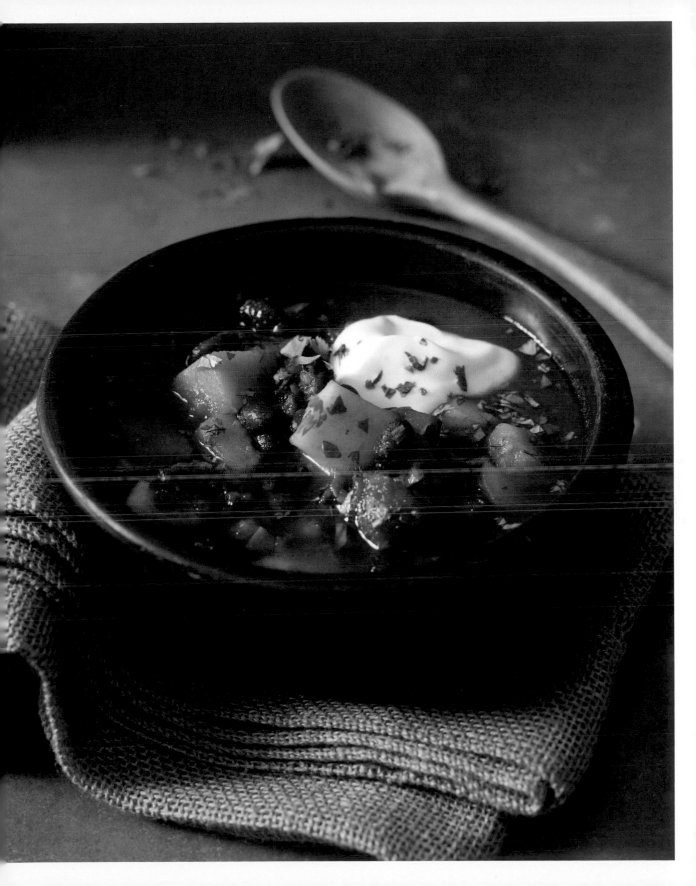

This combination of rich pork and salty clams – and, indeed, any pork with shellfish – has been enjoyed for centuries in Portugal. A squeeze of lemon at the end brings out the flavours.

Pork and clam cataplana

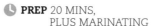 **SERVES** 4 ❄ **FREEZE** UP TO 1 MONTH, WITHOUT THE CLAMS ♥ **HEALTHY**

900g (2lb) pork tenderloin, cut into 2.5cm (1in) cubes
2 tbsp olive oil
1 large onion, thinly sliced
2 garlic cloves, finely chopped
400g can whole tomatoes
1 tbsp tomato purée
dash of Tabasco sauce (or more to taste)
1kg (2¼lb) clams, such as amandes, scrubbed
    (discard any that do not close when tapped)
bunch of parsley, leaves chopped

FOR THE MARINADE
2 garlic cloves, finely chopped
1 bay leaf
1½ tbsp paprika
1 tbsp olive oil
375ml (13fl oz) dry white wine
pinch of freshly ground black pepper

 in the slow cooker 🕐 PREP 20 MINS, PLUS MARINATING COOK 30 MINS PRECOOKING; AUTO/LOW 6–8 HRS OR HIGH 3–4 HRS

1 To make the marinade, put all the ingredients into a bowl and whisk to combine. Add the pork and mix well. Cover and refrigerate for 2 hours, or 12 hours if time permits, stirring occasionally. Preheat the slow cooker, if required. Lift the meat from the marinade with a slotted spoon and pat dry with kitchen paper. Reserve the marinade. Heat the oil in a large flameproof casserole over a medium-high heat. Add the pork, in batches, and brown well on all sides. Transfer to a bowl and set aside.

2 Reduce the heat and add the onion and garlic to the casserole. Cover and cook very gently for about 15 minutes, until the onion is very soft and brown. Add the tomatoes, tomato purée, Tabasco, and pork. Pour in the marinade and stir. Transfer everything to the slow cooker, cover with the lid, and cook on auto/low for 6–8 hours or on high for 3–4 hours. Add the clams for the last 20 minutes of cooking, or until all the clams are open (discard any that do not open). Transfer to a warmed serving bowl, remove the bay leaf, sprinkle with the parsley, and serve with lemon wedges on the side.

 traditional method 🕐 PREP 20 MINS, PLUS MARINATING COOK 2¼–2½ HRS

1 To make the marinade, put all the ingredients into a bowl and whisk to combine. Add the pork and mix well. Cover and refrigerate for 2 hours, or 12 hours if time permits, stirring occasionally. Preheat the oven to 180°C (350°F/Gas 4). Lift the meat from the marinade with a slotted spoon and pat dry with kitchen paper. Reserve the marinade. Heat the oil in a large flameproof casserole over a medium-high heat. Add the pork, in batches, and brown well on all sides. Transfer to a bowl and set aside.

2 Reduce the heat and add the onion and garlic to the casserole. Cover and cook very gently for about 15 minutes, until the onion is very soft and brown. Add the tomatoes, tomato purée, Tabasco, and pork. Pour in the marinade and stir. Cover with the lid and cook in the oven for 1½–1¾ hours, until tender when pierced. Check occasionally that it's not drying out, topping up with a little hot water if needed. Arrange the clams on top of the pork, cover with the lid, and cook in the oven for 15–20 minutes longer until the clams open (discard any that do not open). Transfer to a warmed serving bowl, remove the bay leaf, sprinkle with the parsley, and serve with lemon wedges on the side.

This is a filling one-pot meal, known as *Cocido* in Spain. Vary the vegetables, if you wish – turnip, green beans, or even pumpkin are all delicious. Chickpeas are a must for this dish.

Spanish stew

SERVES 6

3 tbsp olive oil

2 small onions, quartered

2 garlic cloves, sliced

2 slices pork belly, about 550g (1¼lb),
  cut into large chunks

4 chicken thighs, about 600g (1lb 5oz) total weight

115g (4oz) beef braising steak, cut into
  bite-sized pieces

115g (4oz) tocino or smoked streaky bacon, cut
  into bite-sized pieces

4 small pork spare ribs, 150g (5½oz) total weight

100ml (3½fl oz) white wine

115g (4oz) chorizo, chopped into 4 pieces

115g (4oz) morcilla (Spanish black pudding) (optional)

1 bay leaf

salt and freshly ground black pepper

6 small waxy potatoes, chopped into large chunks

3 carrots, peeled and chopped into large chunks

400g can chickpeas, drained

½ Savoy cabbage or green cabbage heart, cored
  and quartered

3 tbsp chopped parsley, to serve

in the slow cooker   ⏱ PREP 35 MINS   COOK 30 MINS PRECOOKING; AUTO/LOW 6–8 HRS

1 Preheat the slow cooker, if required. Heat 1 tbsp of the oil in a large flameproof casserole over a medium heat, add the onions and garlic, and cook for 10 minutes, stirring occasionally. Transfer to the slow cooker. Heat the remaining oil in the casserole and cook the pork, chicken, beef, tocino or bacon, and spare ribs, in batches, until lightly browned on all sides. Also transfer to the slow cooker.

2 Pour the wine into the casserole and reduce by half over a high heat. Add to the slow cooker along with the chorizo, morcilla, if using, and bay leaf, season with salt and pepper, then pour in enough hot water to cover. Cover with the lid and cook on auto/low for 6–8 hours, adding the potatoes, carrots, chickpeas, and cabbage for the last hour of cooking. Remove the bay leaf, bones, and chicken skin from the stew. Divide the meat and vegetables between warmed serving plates. Add a few spoonfuls of the hot broth and sprinkle with parsley. Serve with crusty bread.

traditional method   ⏱ PREP 35 MINS   COOK 2¾ HRS

1 Heat 1 tbsp of the oil in a large flameproof casserole over a medium heat, add the onions and garlic, and cook for 10 minutes, stirring occasionally. Remove and set aside in a bowl. Heat the remaining oil in the casserole and cook the pork, chicken, beef, tocino, and spare ribs, in batches, until lightly browned on all sides. Transfer to the bowl with the onions.

2 Pour the wine into the casserole and reduce by half over a high heat. Add the chorizo, morcilla, if using, and bay leaf together with the onions and browned meat. Season with salt and pepper, then pour in enough cold water to cover. Bring to the boil, then reduce the heat and simmer, covered, for 1½ hours. Add the potatoes and carrots to the casserole, continue to cook for 15 minutes, then add the chickpeas and cabbage and cook for a further 15 minutes. Remove the bay leaf, bones, and chicken skin from the stew. Divide the meat and vegetables between warmed serving plates. Add a few spoonfuls of the hot broth and sprinkle with parsley. Serve with crusty bread.

Slow-cooked sweet cabbage is the perfect complement to ham, and with the addition of spices and dried fruit, the humble piece of meat is transformed. Ham hocks are also known as knuckles.

Ham hock with red cabbage

 SERVES 4–6 **HEALTHY**

2 ham hocks, about 1.35kg (3lb) each
1 red cabbage, cored and finely shredded
2 onions, sliced
4 garlic cloves, finely chopped
few sprigs of thyme
60g (2oz) raisins

pinch of freshly grated nutmeg
pinch of ground cinnamon
150ml (5fl oz) white wine vinegar for the slow cooker
  (300ml/10fl oz for the traditional method)
600ml (1 pint) hot vegetable stock, for both methods
salt and freshly ground black pepper

 in the slow cooker ⏱ **PREP** 20 MINS **COOK** AUTO/LOW 6–8 HRS, THEN **AUTO/LOW** 6–8 HRS

1 Preheat the slow cooker, if required. Put the ham hocks in the pot and cover with water so that the cooker is three-quarters full. Cover with the lid and cook on auto/low for 6–8 hours.

2 Remove the hams and reserve the cooking liquid, if you wish to use it instead of the vegetable stock (it can be salty). When the hams are cool enough to handle, remove the skin and discard, then sit the hams back in the slow cooker. Add all the other ingredients, using either the stock or the cooking liquid, and season with salt and pepper. Cover with the lid and cook on auto/low for 6–8 hours. Remove the hams, shred the meat, and stir it into the slow cooker. Serve with baked or roast potatoes.

 traditional method ⏱ **PREP** 20 MINS **COOK** 3 HRS

1 Preheat the oven to 160°C (325°F/Gas 3). Sit the ham hocks in a large heavy-based pan and cover with water. Bring to the boil, then reduce to a simmer, partially cover, and cook gently for 1 hour. Remove the hams and reserve the stock, if you wish to use it instead of the vegetable stock (it can be salty). When the hams are cool enough to handle, remove the skin and discard, then sit the hams in a large flameproof casserole.

2 Add all the other ingredients to the casserole, using either the stock or the cooking liquid, and tuck the hams in neatly. Season with salt and pepper, cover, and put in the oven for 2 hours. Check occasionally that it's not drying out, topping up with a little hot water if necessary. Remove the hams, shred the meat, and stir it into the casserole. Serve with baked or roast potatoes.

Barley is a grain that used to be overlooked, but it has made a well-deserved comeback due to its ability to add body and earthy flavour to all sorts of dishes. For a treat, use wild mushrooms, too.

Beef with barley and mushrooms

SERVES 4–6   **FREEZE** UP TO 3 MONTHS

3 tbsp vegetable oil
1kg (2¼lb) braising steak, cut into 5cm (2in) pieces
450g (1lb) onions, thinly sliced
salt and freshly ground black pepper
1 bouquet garni, made with 5–6 parsley sprigs,
  2–3 thyme sprigs, and 1 bay leaf
700ml (1 pint 3½fl oz) hot beef stock for the slow
  cooker (1 litre/1¾ pints for the traditional method)

225g (8oz) carrots, sliced
2 celery sticks, sliced
150g (5½oz) pearl barley
500g (1lb 2oz) mushrooms, trimmed and sliced
2–3 sprigs of parsley, leaves finely chopped, to serve

in the slow cooker   **PREP** 30 MINS   **COOK** 20 MINS PRECOOKING;
AUTO/LOW 6–8 HRS OR **HIGH** 3–4 HRS

1 Preheat the slow cooker, if required. Heat the oil in a large flameproof casserole over a medium-high heat, add the beef (in batches, if necessary) and cook for about 5 minutes until well browned. Remove and set aside.

2 Reduce the heat to medium, add the onions and a little salt and pepper, and cook for 5–7 minutes until lightly browned. Return the beef and add the bouquet garni and more seasoning. Pour in the stock, stir, and then add the carrots, celery, and barley. Transfer everything to the slow cooker, cover, and cook on auto/low for 6–8 hours or on high for 3–4 hours. Add the mushrooms for the last 20 minutes of cooking.

3 Discard the bouquet garni and taste the stew for seasoning, adding more if needed. Serve in warmed bowls, sprinkled with the parsley and with crusty bread on the side.

traditional method   **PREP** 30 MINS   **COOK** 2¼–2½ HRS

1 Preheat the oven to 180°C (350°F/Gas 4). Heat the oil in a large flameproof casserole over a medium-high heat, add the beef (in batches, if necessary) and cook for about 5 minutes until well browned. Remove and set aside.

2 Reduce the heat to medium, add the onions and a little salt and pepper, and cook for 5–7 minutes until lightly browned. Return the beef and add the bouquet garni and more seasoning. Pour in the stock and stir. Cover with the lid and put in the oven for 1½ hours, stirring occasionally. Then add the carrots, celery, and barley, together with more hot water, if necessary, to keep the casserole moist. Cover, and continue to cook for a further 40–45 minutes until the meat and vegetables are tender when pierced. The barley should be tender but still slightly chewy. About 20 minutes before the end of cooking, stir in the mushrooms.

3 Discard the bouquet garni and taste the stew for seasoning, adding more if needed. Serve in warmed bowls, sprinkled with the parsley and with crusty bread on the side.

In this dish, salt cod is tender and fragrant with the classic Spanish aromas of garlic, bay leaves, and saffron. If you can't get salt cod, use a white fish and add it in for the last 15 minutes of cooking.

Salt cod braised with vegetables

SERVES 4 **HEALTHY**

800g (1¾lb) thick-cut salt cod, or fresh white fish
  such as sustainable cod, haddock, or halibut
3 tbsp olive oil
1 onion, finely diced
2 leeks, trimmed and white parts finely sliced
3 garlic cloves, finely chopped
3 tomatoes, skinned and chopped

500g (1lb 2oz) potatoes, diced
salt and freshly ground black pepper
2 bay leaves
large pinch of saffron threads
120ml (4fl oz) dry white wine
2 tbsp chopped parsley, to serve

in the slow cooker ⏱ **PREP** 20 MINS, PLUS SOAKING **COOK** 10 MINS PRECOOKING;
AUTO/LOW 6–8 HRS OR **HIGH** 3–4 HRS

1 If using the salt cod, soak the pieces of cod in enough cold water to cover them for at least 24 hours, changing the water 2–3 times to remove the saltiness of the brine. Drain and cut the fish into 4 pieces, then pat dry with kitchen paper. If using the fresh fish, simply cut the fish into 4 pieces.

2 Preheat the slow cooker, if required. Heat the oil in a large heavy-based pan over a medium heat, add the onion and leeks, and cook for about 5 minutes until soft. Add the garlic and tomatoes and cook for a further 2 minutes, stirring. Add the potatoes, seasoning, bay leaves, and saffron.

3 Transfer everything to the slow cooker, then pour in the wine and 100ml (3½fl oz) of water. Cover with the lid and cook on auto/low for 6–8 hours or on high for 3–4 hours. Sit the salt cod, skin-side up, on top of the vegetables for the last hour of cooking. Ladle into warmed bowls, sprinkle with the parsley, and serve with a crisp mixed salad and some crusty bread.

traditional method ⏱ **PREP** 20 MINS, PLUS SOAKING **COOK** 40 MINS

1 If using the salt cod, soak the pieces of cod in enough cold water to cover them for at least 24 hours, changing the water 2–3 times to remove the saltiness of the brine. Drain and cut the fish into 4 pieces, then pat dry with kitchen paper. If using the fresh fish, simply cut the fish into 4 pieces.

2 Heat the oil in a large heavy-based pan over a medium heat, add the onion and leeks, and cook for about 5 minutes until soft. Add the garlic and tomatoes and cook for a further 2 minutes, stirring. Add the potatoes, seasoning, bay leaves, and saffron.

3 Pour in the wine and 250ml (9fl oz) water and sit the cod, skin-side up, on top of the vegetables. Bring gently to a simmer and cook for 25–30 minutes until the fish is opaque and cooked through. Shake the pan once or twice every 5 minutes to help release gelatine from the fish, to thicken the sauce. Ladle into warmed bowls, sprinkle with the parsley, and serve with a crisp mixed salad and some crusty bread.

Asian flavours perk up the pork in this stew. Five-spice powder is a favourite ingredient in Asian dishes, and is made from Szechuan pepper, star anise, fennel seeds, cloves, and cinnamon.

Braised pork in soy and cinnamon

 SERVES 4–6 **FREEZE** UP TO 3 MONTHS **HEALTHY**

1.1kg (2½lb) pork shoulder or leg, cut into bite-sized pieces
2 tsp five-spice powder
2–3 tbsp olive oil
2 bunches of spring onions, white and green parts separated and finely chopped
3 garlic cloves, sliced
5cm (2in) piece of fresh root ginger, peeled and sliced

100ml (3½fl oz) dark soy sauce
2 cinnamon sticks, broken in half
250g (9oz) small button mushrooms, any large ones halved
about 200ml (7fl oz) hot chicken stock for the slow cooker (900ml/1½ pints for the traditional method)
freshly ground black pepper

 in the slow cooker **PREP** 15 MINS **COOK** 15 MINS PRECOOKING; AUTO/LOW 6–8 HRS OR HIGH 4 HRS

1 Preheat the slow cooker, if required, and toss the pork in the five-spice powder. Heat half the oil in a large flameproof casserole over a medium-high heat, and cook the pork in batches for 5–6 minutes until it turns golden. Remove and set aside.

2 Heat the remaining oil in the casserole over a medium heat. Add the spring onion whites and cook for a minute, then stir in the garlic and ginger until coated. Add the soy sauce and bring to the boil, then reduce to a simmer, and transfer everything to the slow cooker, including the pork.

3 Stir in the cinnamon and mushrooms, and then pour over the stock just to cover. Season with pepper, cover with the lid, and cook on auto/low for 6–8 hours or on high for 4 hours. Taste and season some more with soy sauce, if needed, remove the cinnamon sticks, and top with the spring onion greens. Ladle into warmed bowls and serve with noodles or rice.

 traditional method **PREP** 15 MINS **COOK** 2¼–2½ HRS

1 Preheat the oven to 160°C (325°F/Gas 3) and toss the pork in the five-spice powder. Heat half the oil in a large flameproof casserole over a medium-high heat, and cook the pork in batches for 5–6 minutes until it turns golden. Remove and set aside.

2 Heat the remaining oil in the casserole over a medium heat. Add the spring onion whites and cook for a minute, then stir in the garlic and ginger until coated. Stir in the soy sauce, add the cinnamon and mushrooms, and return the pork to the casserole. Finally, add the stock, bring to the boil, then reduce to a simmer and season with pepper. Cover with the lid and put in the oven for 2 hours.

3 If the sauce is too thin, remove the meat with a slotted spoon and set aside, then sit the casserole on the hob and let it simmer for about 10 minutes, to reduce a little and intensify the flavours. Return the meat, remove the cinnamon sticks, and top with the spring onion greens. Ladle into warmed bowls and serve with noodles or rice.

Bok choy is a versatile vegetable used frequently in Chinese stir-fries, appetizers, and main dishes. Also known as pak choi, it cooks quickly, so it is added towards the end of the cooking time.

Asian beef and bok choy

🔵 **SERVES** 4–6 ❄ **FREEZE** UP TO 3 MONTHS

2 tbsp olive oil
1 onion, roughly chopped
freshly ground black pepper
4 garlic cloves, peeled and left whole
5cm (2in) piece of fresh root ginger,
  peeled and sliced
2 dried chillies, left whole
2 star anise

175ml (6fl oz) Chinese rice wine or dry pale sherry
2 tbsp demerara sugar
2 tbsp oyster sauce
1 tbsp dark soy sauce
1 tsp toasted sesame oil
1.1kg (2½lb) shin beef, cut into bite-sized pieces
250g (9oz) bok choy, sliced lengthways

in the slow cooker 🕐 **PREP** 15 MINS **COOK** 15 MINS PRECOOKING; **AUTO/LOW** 6–8 HRS

1 Preheat the slow cooker, if required. Heat the oil in a large flameproof casserole over a medium heat, add the onion, and cook for 3–4 minutes until soft. Season with pepper, then stir in the garlic, ginger, chillies, and star anise.

2 Increase the heat, pour in the Chinese wine or sherry, and let it simmer for a few minutes. Stir through the sugar, oyster sauce, soy sauce, and sesame oil. Boil for a minute, then reduce to a simmer, add the beef, and stir to coat.

3 Transfer everything to the slow cooker and pour over just enough water to cover. Cover with the lid and cook on auto/low for 6–8 hours. Add the bok choy for the last hour of cooking, pushing it under the liquid slightly so it doesn't go dry at the edges. Remove the whole dried chillies and serve with white rice.

traditional method 🕐 **PREP** 15 MINS **COOK** 2¼–2¾ HRS

1 Preheat the oven to 160°C (325°F/Gas 3). Heat the oil in a large flameproof casserole over a medium heat, add the onion, and cook for 3–4 minutes until soft. Season with pepper, then stir in the garlic, ginger, chillies, and star anise.

2 Increase the heat, pour in the Chinese wine or sherry, and let it simmer for a few minutes. Stir through the sugar, oyster sauce, soy sauce, and sesame oil. Boil for a minute, then reduce to a simmer, add the beef, and stir to coat.

3 Pour over just enough water to cover, cover with the lid, and put in the oven for 2–2½ hours, until the meat is tender. Check occasionally that it's not drying out, topping up with a little hot water if needed. Add the bok choy for the last 15 minutes of cooking, pushing it under the liquid slightly so it doesn't go dry at the edges. Remove the whole dried chillies and serve with white rice.

In Italy, this dish is called *alla cacciatora*, meaning "hunter's style". Chicory, with its slight bitterness, makes a flavoursome addition and must be added towards the end of cooking.

Hunter's chicken stew

SERVES 4 ❊ **FREEZE** UP TO 3 MONTHS, WITHOUT THE CHICORY

1.5kg (3lb 3oz) chicken, jointed into 8 pieces
salt and freshly ground black pepper
4 tbsp olive oil
1 onion, chopped
4 garlic cloves, finely chopped
1 sprig of rosemary

1 bay leaf
4 tbsp dry white wine
120ml (4fl oz) hot chicken stock, for both methods
2 heads of chicory (also known as Belgian endive),
    trimmed, leaves separated, and roughly chopped

in the slow cooker   🕐 **PREP** 15 MINS   **COOK** 30 MINS PRECOOKING;
                                                AUTO/LOW 5–6 HRS OR HIGH 3–4 HRS

1 Preheat the slow cooker, if required. Season the chicken all over with salt and pepper. Heat half the oil in a large flameproof casserole over a medium heat, add the thighs and drumsticks, skin-side down, and cook for about 5 minutes until they begin to brown. Add the breast pieces and cook gently for 10–15 minutes until very brown. Turn and brown the other side. Lower the heat.

2 Add the onion and garlic, stir, and continue cooking gently for 3–4 minutes until they are soft. Season with salt and pepper, then stir in the rosemary, bay leaf, wine, and stock, and bring to the boil. Transfer everything to the slow cooker, cover with the lid, and cook on auto/low for 5–6 hours or on high for 3–4 hours.

3 Add the chicory for the last 15 minutes of cooking. Discard the bay leaf and rosemary from the sauce, taste, and add seasoning if needed. Spoon out into warmed bowls and serve with crusty bread.

traditional method   🕐 **PREP** 20–25 MINS   **COOK** 45–60 MINS

1 Season the chicken all over with salt and pepper. Heat half the oil in a large flameproof casserole over a medium heat, add the thighs and drumsticks, skin-side down, and cook for about 5 minutes until they begin to brown. Add the breast pieces and cook gently for 10–15 minutes until very brown. Turn and brown the other side. Lower the heat.

2 Add the onion and garlic, stir, and continue cooking gently for 3–4 minutes until they are soft. Season with salt and pepper, then stir in the rosemary, bay leaf, wine, and stock. Cover and simmer for 15–20 minutes until tender.

3 Add the chicory for the last 5 minutes of cooking, return the lid, and cook gently until it has just softened. Discard the bay leaf and rosemary from the sauce, taste, and add seasoning if needed. Spoon out into warmed bowls and serve with crusty bread.

The darker the beer, the richer this dish will be. Cognac is also added, to add depth of flavour. Mashed potatoes would be good with it and, naturally, you can guess what is the best drink to serve.

Chicken and beer stew

SERVES 4–6   **FREEZE** UP TO 3 MONTHS

4 chicken breasts on the bone
salt and freshly ground black pepper
30g (1oz) butter
2 tbsp vegetable oil
750g (1lb 10oz) onions, thinly sliced
30g (1oz) plain flour
3–4 tbsp Cognac
500g (1lb 2oz) mushrooms, quartered

1 bouquet garni, made with 5–6 parsley sprigs,
  2–3 thyme sprigs, and 1 bay leaf
2 tsp juniper berries, gently crushed
500ml (16fl oz) beer
250ml (9fl oz) hot chicken stock, for both methods
4 tbsp double cream
small bunch of flat-leaf parsley, leaves
  finely chopped

in the slow cooker   **PREP** 15 MINS   **COOK** 20 MINS PRECOOKING; AUTO/LOW 6–8 HRS OR **HIGH** 3–4 HRS

1 Preheat the slow cooker, if required. Season the chicken pieces. Heat the butter and oil in a large flameproof casserole over a medium-high heat until foaming. Add the chicken, skin-side down (in batches, if necessary) and cook for about 5 minutes on each side until browned. Remove and set aside.

2 Reduce the heat to medium, add the onions, and cook for about 10 minutes until soft and well browned. Sprinkle with the flour and cook, stirring, for 1–2 minutes until the flour is just lightly browned. Return the chicken to the casserole in a single layer. Add the Cognac and bring to the boil for a few minutes, basting the chicken with the Cognac. Add the mushrooms, bouquet garni, and crushed juniper berries. Pour in the beer and stock, bring to the boil, and transfer everything to the slow cooker. Cover with the lid and cook on auto/low for 6–8 hours or on high for 3–4 hours.

3 Discard the bouquet garni and skim off excess fat from the surface. Stir in the cream for the last 15 minutes of cooking. Taste, and add seasoning if needed. Sprinkle with the parsley and serve.

traditional method   **PREP** 15 MINS   **COOK** 1 HR

1 Season the chicken pieces. Heat the butter and oil in a large flameproof casserole over a medium-high heat until foaming. Add the chicken, skin-side down (in batches, if necessary) and cook for about 5 minutes on each side until browned. Remove and set aside.

2 Reduce the heat to medium, add the onions, and cook for about 10 minutes until soft and well browned. Sprinkle with the flour and cook, stirring, for 1–2 minutes until the flour is just lightly browned. Return the chicken to the casserole in a single layer. Add the Cognac and bring to the boil for a few minutes, basting the chicken with the Cognac. Add the mushrooms, bouquet garni, and crushed juniper berries. Pour in the beer and stock, bring to the boil, cover with the lid, and simmer for 40–50 minutes until the chicken is tender when pierced and the juices run clear.

3 Discard the bouquet garni and skim off excess fat from the surface. Stir in the cream for the last 15 minutes of cooking. Taste, and add seasoning if needed. Sprinkle with the parsley and serve.

This stew is a favourite dish in northern Italy. Barbera is the preferred wine, but substitute any good-quality dry red; you will taste a bad wine if you use it in a dish.

Italian beef braised in red wine

SERVES 6

2 tbsp olive oil
1kg (2¼lb) stewing beef, cut into bite-sized pieces
1 small onion, finely chopped
1 small carrot, peeled and finely chopped
1 celery stick, finely chopped
500ml (16fl oz) dry red wine

2 tbsp tomato purée
about 300ml (10fl oz) hot beef stock for the slow cooker (about 500ml/16fl oz for the traditional method)
2–3 thyme sprigs
salt and freshly ground black pepper

in the slow cooker   PREP 15 MINS   COOK 15 MINS PRECOOKING; AUTO/LOW 6–8 HRS

1 Preheat the slow cooker, if required. Heat the oil in a large flameproof casserole over a medium-high heat, add the beef (in batches, if necessary) and cook for about 5 minutes until browned on all sides. Remove from the casserole and set aside. Add the onion, carrot, and celery, and cook, stirring, for 3–5 minutes until the vegetables are soft.

2 Add the red wine, stir to dissolve the casserole juices, and bring to the boil. Stir in the tomato purée, then transfer everything to the slow cooker, including the meat. Add enough stock to cover the meat and add the thyme and seasoning. Cover with the lid and cook on auto/low for 6–8 hours. Discard the thyme, taste, and add seasoning if needed. Ladle into shallow bowls and serve with some crusty bread.

traditional method   PREP 15 MINS   COOK 2¼–3¼ HRS

1 Preheat the oven to 150°C (300°F/Gas 2). Heat the oil in a large flameproof casserole over a medium-high heat, add the beef (in batches, if necessary) and cook for about 10 minutes until browned on all sides. Remove from the casserole and set aside. Add the onion, carrot, and celery, and cook, stirring, for 3–5 minutes until the vegetables are soft.

2 Add the red wine, stir to dissolve the casserole juices, and bring to the boil. Stir in the tomato purée and return the beef. Add enough stock to cover the meat, add the thyme and seasoning, and bring to the boil. Cover with the lid and put in the oven to cook for 2–3 hours or until the meat is very tender when pierced with a fork. Check occasionally that it's not drying out, topping up with a little hot water if needed. Discard the thyme, taste, and add seasoning if needed. Ladle into shallow bowls and serve with some crusty bread.

Chianti is the wine of Tuscany, but you can use any good-quality, full-bodied red wine. This dish benefits from being made ahead and kept in the refrigerator; its flavours will mellow.

Peppery Tuscan beef

SERVES 4–6 ❄ **FREEZE** UP TO 3 MONTHS

2 tbsp freshly ground black pepper
200ml (7fl oz) olive oil, plus 3 tbsp for cooking
1.1kg (2½lb) braising steak, cut into 5cm (2in) cubes
125g (4½oz) pancetta lardons
1 large onion, chopped
5 garlic cloves, finely chopped

400g can chopped tomatoes
2 bay leaves
3–4 sprigs of sage, leaves chopped
250ml (9fl oz) hot beef stock, for both methods
300ml (10fl oz) red wine for the slow cooker
    (500ml/16fl oz for the traditional method)

in the slow cooker
PREP 20 MINS, PLUS MARINATING **COOK** 20 MINS PRECOOKING; AUTO/LOW 8 HRS

1 In a large bowl, combine 1 tbsp of the black pepper with the oil. Add the beef and stir until well coated. Cover with cling film and refrigerate, stirring occasionally, for 8–12 hours.

2 Preheat the slow cooker, if required. Remove the beef from the marinade and pat dry with kitchen paper. Heat the cooking oil in a large flameproof casserole over a high heat, add the meat (in batches, if necessary), and cook for 3–5 minutes until browned on all sides. Remove and set aside. Reduce the heat to medium, add the lardons, and cook, stirring occasionally, for 2–3 minutes, until the fat has rendered. Add the onion and cook for 3–4 minutes until soft. Return the beef and add the garlic, tomatoes, bay leaves, sage, stock, and wine, together with the remaining pepper. Bring to the boil, then transfer everything to the slow cooker, cover with the lid, and cook on auto/low for 8 hours.

3 Discard the bay leaves, taste, and add seasoning if needed. Serve with some greens, such as Savoy cabbage or broccoli, and Italian-style cubed roast potatoes and rosemary.

traditional method
PREP 20 MINS, PLUS MARINATING **COOK** 2–2½ HRS

1 In a large bowl, combine 1 tbsp of the black pepper with the oil. Add the beef and stir until well coated. Cover with cling film and refrigerate, stirring occasionally, for 8–12 hours.

2 Remove the beef from the marinade and pat dry with kitchen paper. Heat the cooking oil in a large flameproof casserole over a high heat, add the meat (in batches, if necessary), and cook for 3–5 minutes until browned on all sides. Remove and set aside. Reduce the heat to medium, add the lardons, and cook, stirring occasionally, for 2–3 minutes, until the fat has rendered. Add the onion and cook for 3–4 minutes until soft. Return the beef and add the garlic, tomatoes, bay leaves, sage, stock, and wine, together with the remaining pepper. Bring to the boil, cover, reduce the heat, and leave to simmer for 1¾–2 hours until very tender, stirring occasionally. During cooking, add more hot water if the stew seems dry. The beef is ready when it is tender enough to crush in your fingers.

3 Discard the bay leaves, taste, and add seasoning if needed. Serve with some greens, such as Savoy cabbage or broccoli, and Italian-style cubed roast potatoes and rosemary.

In Mexico, chorizo is made with fresh pork, but in Spain, the pork is smoked first for even more flavour. Chorizo works its magic as it cooks and gives the sauce a rich, deep flavour.

Chicken with chorizo

SERVES 4 ❄ **FREEZE** UP TO 1 MONTH

2 tbsp olive oil
4 skinless chicken legs
250g (9oz) chorizo, chopped into bite-sized pieces
1 red onion, thinly sliced
1 tsp ground coriander
1 tsp chopped thyme leaves
1 red pepper, deseeded and chopped
1 yellow pepper, deseeded and chopped

1 courgette, trimmed and sliced
2 garlic cloves, crushed
400g can chopped tomatoes
100ml (3½fl oz) hot chicken stock for the slow cooker (200ml/7fl oz for the traditional method)
60ml (2fl oz) dry sherry
freshly ground black pepper

in the slow cooker 🕐 PREP 10 MINS COOK 20 MINS PRECOOKING; AUTO/LOW 6–8 HRS OR HIGH 3–4 HRS

1 Preheat the slow cooker, if required. Heat the oil in a large flameproof casserole over a medium-high heat, add the chicken, and fry for 5–8 minutes, turning frequently, until evenly browned. Remove and set aside. Then add the chorizo to the casserole and cook for 2–3 minutes until lightly browned, stirring frequently. Also remove and set aside.

2 Reduce the heat to medium, add the onion to the casserole, and cook for 3–4 minutes until soft. Add the coriander, cook for 1 minute, and then add the thyme, peppers, courgette, and garlic and cook for 5 minutes. Add the tomatoes, stock, and sherry. Season with black pepper, if needed, and bring to the boil. Transfer everything to the slow cooker, including the chicken and chorizo. Cover with the lid and cook on auto/low for 6–8 hours or on high for 3–4 hours. Serve with mashed sweet potatoes and peas.

traditional method 🕐 PREP 10 MINS COOK 1 HR

1 Preheat the oven to 180°C (350°F/Gas 4). Heat the oil in a large flameproof casserole over a medium-high heat, add the chicken, and fry for 5–8 minutes, turning frequently, until evenly browned. Remove and set aside. Then add the chorizo to the casserole and cook for 2–3 minutes until lightly browned, stirring frequently. Also remove and set aside.

2 Reduce the heat to medium, add the onion to the casserole, and cook for 3–4 minutes until soft. Add the coriander, cook for 1 minute, and then add the thyme, peppers, courgette, and garlic and cook for 5 minutes. Add the tomatoes, stock, and sherry. Season with black pepper, if needed, and bring to the boil. Return the chicken and chorizo, and cook in the oven for about 40 minutes until the chicken is tender when pierced with a fork. Serve with mashed sweet potatoes and peas.

Olives, feta cheese, and thyme are all synonymous with Greek cuisine, and here they are combined with a succulent leg of lamb. The feta adds a fabulous saltiness to the finished dish.

Stuffed lamb, Greek style

SERVES 4–6

1 leg of lamb, boned and butterflied
  (about 1.8kg/4lb after boning – ask your butcher
  to do this), or use a boneless shoulder
salt and freshly ground black pepper
2 tbsp olive oil
1 tbsp dried oregano
2 red peppers, deseeded and finely chopped

60g (2oz) stoned black olives, finely chopped
175g (6oz) feta cheese, finely chopped
3 red onions, roughly chopped
4–6 tomatoes, roughly chopped
450ml (15fl oz) red wine
few sprigs of thyme

in the slow cooker   **PREP** 30 MINS   **COOK** 10 MINS PRECOOKING; **AUTO/LOW** 8 HRS

1 Preheat the slow cooker, if required. Lay the lamb out flat and season well. Rub both sides all over with the oil and oregano. Cover one side of the lamb with the red peppers, then the olives, and then the feta. Starting from one end, roll up the lamb, tucking in any loose pieces to neaten it. Tie it up with butcher's string so it is secure.

2 Heat a large flameproof casserole over a medium heat, add the lamb, and cook for 4–6 minutes on each side until it begins to colour. Transfer the lamb to the slow cooker and add the onions, tomatoes, and wine. Season and add the thyme, cover with the lid, and cook on auto/low for 8 hours.

3 Remove the meat from the slow cooker, cover loosely with foil, and leave to rest for 15 minutes. Remove the string and carve into slices. Serve with some of the sauce, together with baby roast potatoes with rosemary, and some wilted spinach.

traditional method   **PREP** 30 MINS   **COOK** 2¼–2¾ HRS

1 Preheat the oven to 160°C (325°F/Gas 3). Lay the lamb out flat and season well. Rub both sides all over with the oil and oregano. Cover one side of the lamb with the red peppers, then the olives, and then the feta. Starting from one end, roll up the lamb, tucking in any loose pieces to neaten it. Tie it up with butcher's string so it is secure.

2 Heat a large flameproof casserole over a medium heat, add the lamb, and cook for 4–6 minutes on each side until it begins to colour. Throw in the red onions and tomatoes and cook for a minute more, then pour in the wine. Bring to the boil, then reduce to a simmer and add some seasoning and the thyme. Cover with the lid and put in the oven for 2–2½ hours or until cooked to your liking. Check occasionally that it's not drying out, topping up with a little hot water if needed.

3 Remove from the oven, cover the meat loosely with foil, and leave to rest for 15 minutes. Remove the string and carve into slices. Serve with some of the sauce, together with baby roast potatoes with rosemary, and some wilted spinach.

Stifado is a rich mix of beef and onions, but the onions are added later in the recipe as this helps them to keep their shape. This is a good "make-ahead" stew, as it tastes great reheated the next day.

Greek stifado

 SERVES 4–6 **FREEZE** UP TO 3 MONTHS

3 tbsp olive oil
1.1kg (2½lb) chuck steak, cut into bite-sized pieces
salt and freshly ground black pepper
175ml (6fl oz) red wine
2 tbsp red wine vinegar
1 cinnamon stick
1 tsp ground cloves
½ tsp grated nutmeg

3 garlic cloves, finely chopped
4 tomatoes, roughly chopped
1 tbsp tomato purée
450ml (15fl oz) hot vegetable stock for the slow cooker (600ml/1 pint for the traditional method)
few sprigs of thyme
knob of butter
500g (1lb 2oz) shallots, peeled and left whole

 in the slow cooker **PREP** 30 MINS **COOK** 20 MINS PRECOOKING; **AUTO/LOW** 8 HRS

1 Preheat the slow cooker, if required. Heat 2 tbsp of the oil in a large flameproof casserole over a medium-high heat. Add the meat, season with salt and pepper, and cook for about 6 minutes until lightly browned. Increase the heat and add the wine and vinegar. Cook for a couple of minutes, then stir in the cinnamon stick, cloves, nutmeg, and garlic and cook for a further minute.

2 Add the tomatoes and tomato purée and cook for a few minutes. Transfer everything to the slow cooker, pour in the stock, and add the thyme. Cover with the lid and cook on auto/low for 8 hours.

3 About halfway through the cooking time, heat the remaining oil together with the butter in a heavy-based pan over a medium heat. Add the shallots and cook for 6–8 minutes until golden, then add them to the slow cooker. Taste and season, remove the cinnamon stick and thyme, and serve with creamy mashed potatoes or baby roast potatoes with rosemary.

traditional method **PREP** 30 MINS **COOK** 2¼ HRS

1 Preheat the oven to 180°C (350°F/Gas 4). Heat 2 tbsp of the oil in a large flameproof casserole over a medium-high heat. Add the meat, season with salt and pepper, and cook for about 6 minutes until lightly browned. Increase the heat and add the wine and vinegar. Cook for a couple of minutes, then stir in the cinnamon stick, cloves, nutmeg, and garlic and cook for a further minute.

2 Add the tomatoes and tomato purée and then add the stock. Bring the sauce to the boil, then throw in the thyme, cover with the lid, and put in the oven for about 1 hour. Check occasionally that it's not drying out, topping up with a little hot water if needed.

3 Heat the remaining oil together with the butter in a heavy-based pan over a medium heat, add the shallots and cook for 6–8 minutes until golden, then spoon these into the stew and stir carefully. Cover and return to the oven. Reduce the temperature to 160°C (325°F/Gas 3) and cook for a further hour. Check occasionally that it's not drying out, topping up with a little hot water if needed. Taste and season, remove the cinnamon stick and thyme, and serve with creamy mashed potatoes or baby roast potatoes with rosemary.

Lamb works very well with fruit, and the prunes and apple in this recipe are no exception. If you're not a fan of prunes, use dried apricots or dates instead. They add a piquant flavour.

Fruity lamb shanks

⊘ **SERVES** 4 ❄ **FREEZE** UP TO 3 MONTHS

4 tbsp olive oil
4 lamb shanks
1 tbsp plain flour
250ml (9fl oz) white wine
1 large onion, sliced
salt and freshly ground black pepper
3 garlic cloves, finely chopped
1 tsp fennel seeds

few sprigs of thyme
2 bay leaves
1 celeriac, peeled and chopped into bite-sized pieces
1 cooking apple, peeled, cored, and diced
200g (7oz) soft prunes, stoned and left whole
175ml (6fl oz) fresh orange juice
150ml (5fl oz) hot vegetable stock for the slow cooker (900ml/1½ pints for the traditional method)

in the slow cooker ⏱ PREP 15 MINS COOK 20 MINS PRECOOKING; AUTO/LOW 8 HRS

1 Preheat the slow cooker, if required. Heat half the oil in a large flameproof casserole over a medium-high heat, and toss the lamb shanks in the flour. Add the shanks to the casserole, one or two at a time, and cook for about 10 minutes until golden on all sides. Remove and set aside in a bowl. Pour the wine into the casserole, increase the heat, and let it simmer while stirring to remove the bits from the bottom of the casserole. Pour this over the lamb and wipe the casserole with kitchen paper.

2 Heat a little more oil over a medium heat, add the onion, and cook for 3–4 minutes until soft. Season with salt and pepper, then stir through the garlic, fennel seeds, thyme, bay leaves, and celeriac, and cook for about 5 minutes, adding more oil if necessary, until just beginning to turn golden.

3 Add the apple and prunes, season, and cook for 1–2 minutes. Return the lamb and sauce to the casserole, add the orange juice and stock, and bring to the boil. Transfer everything to the slow cooker, cover with the lid, and cook on auto/low for 8 hours. Serve with creamy mashed potatoes.

traditional method ⏱ PREP 15 MINS COOK 3¼–3¾ HRS

1 Preheat the oven to 150°C (300°F/Gas 2). Heat half the oil in a large flameproof casserole over a medium-high heat, and toss the lamb shanks in the flour. Add the shanks to the casserole, one or two at a time, and cook for about 10 minutes until golden on all sides. Remove and set aside in a bowl. Pour the wine into the casserole, increase the heat, and let it simmer while stirring to remove the bits from the bottom of the casserole. Pour this over the lamb and wipe the casserole with kitchen paper.

2 Heat a little more oil over a medium heat, add the onion, and cook for 3–4 minutes until soft. Season with salt and pepper, then stir through the garlic, fennel seeds, thyme, bay leaves, and celeriac, and cook for about 5 minutes, adding more oil if necessary, until just beginning to turn golden.

3 Add the apple and prunes, season, and cook for 1–2 minutes. Return the lamb and sauce to the casserole, add the orange juice and stock, and bring to the boil. Reduce to a simmer, cover with the lid, and put in the oven for 3–3½ hours until the lamb is falling off the bone. Check occasionally that it's not drying out, topping up with a little hot water if needed. Serve with creamy mashed potatoes.

Pear makes the perfect partner to venison and is tasty served with steamed Savoy cabbage with butter and black pepper. You could use beef instead of venison, cooking it for the same length of time.

Venison stew with pears

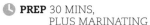 **SERVES** 6 ❄ **FREEZE** UP TO 3 MONTHS ♥ **HEALTHY**

2 tsp black peppercorns, crushed
2 tsp juniper berries, crushed
4 shallots, roughly chopped
2 garlic cloves, peeled and left whole
2 onions, quartered
2 carrots, peeled and roughly sliced
1 bouquet garni
2 tbsp red wine vinegar
450ml (15fl oz) dry red wine for the slow cooker
  (750ml/1¼ pints for the traditional method)

1kg (2¼lb) stewing venison (leg or shoulder), fat trimmed and cut into 4cm (1½in) cubes
3 tbsp vegetable oil
30g (1oz) plain flour
450ml (15fl oz) hot beef stock for the slow cooker
  (750ml/1¼ pints for the traditional method)
salt and freshly ground black pepper
4 ripe pears, peeled, cored, and chopped
3 tbsp redcurrant jelly

 in the slow cooker 🕐 **PREP** 30 MINS, PLUS MARINATING   **COOK** 20 MINS PRECOOKING; **AUTO/LOW** 6–8 HRS OR **HIGH** 3–4 HRS

1 To make the marinade, put the spices, vegetables, bouquet garni, vinegar, and wine in a pan and bring to the boil, then simmer for about 2 minutes. Transfer to a shallow dish and leave to cool. Add the venison, stir to coat evenly, cover, and refrigerate for 6–8 hours, turning occasionally.

2 Preheat the slow cooker, if required. Remove the venison and pat dry. Strain the marinade, reserving the bouquet garni, vegetables, and marinade separately. Heat half the oil in a large flameproof casserole over a high heat, add the venison (in batches and with extra oil, if necessary) and cook for 3–5 minutes until brown all over. Transfer to a bowl. Heat the remaining oil over a medium heat, add the reserved vegetables, and cook, stirring, for 5–7 minutes until they start to brown. Add the flour and cook, stirring, for 3–5 minutes until it has been absorbed. Stir in the marinade, venison, bouquet garni, stock, and seasoning. Transfer to the slow cooker, cover, and cook on auto/low for 6–8 hours or on high for 3–4 hours. Stir in the pears and redcurrant jelly for the last 20 minutes of cooking.

 traditional method 🕐 **PREP** 30 MINS, PLUS MARINATING   **COOK** 1½–1¾ HRS

1 To make the marinade, put the spices, vegetables, bouquet garni, vinegar, and wine in a pan and bring to the boil, then simmer for about 2 minutes. Transfer to a shallow dish and leave to cool. Add the venison, stir to coat evenly, cover, and refrigerate for 6–8 hours, turning occasionally.

2 Preheat the oven to 180°C (350°F/Gas 4). Remove the venison and pat dry. Strain the marinade, reserving the bouquet garni, vegetables, and marinade separately. Heat half the oil in a large flameproof casserole over a high heat, add the venison (in batches and with extra oil, if necessary) and cook for 3–5 minutes until brown all over. Transfer to a bowl. Heat the remaining oil over a medium heat, add the reserved vegetables, and cook, stirring, for 5–7 minutes until they start to brown. Add the flour and cook, stirring, for 3–5 minutes until it has been absorbed. Stir in the marinade, venison, bouquet garni, stock, and seasoning. Cover and cook in the oven for 1¼–1½ hours until tender. Stir in the pears and redcurrant jelly and cook for 6–8 minutes until the pears are tender.

This colonial American dish uses lots of Southern ingredients, such as smoked ham, beans, sweetcorn, and chilli – although it was originally made with squirrel!

American Brunswick stew

SERVES 4–6 **FREEZE** UP TO 3 MONTHS

4 chicken thighs on the bone
1kg (2¼lb) ham hock
1 tbsp dark soft brown sugar
1 bouquet garni
1 onion, chopped
3 celery sticks, trimmed and thinly sliced
400g can chopped tomatoes

200g (7oz) thawed frozen or canned sweetcorn
salt and freshly ground black pepper
250g (9oz) fresh or thawed frozen broad beans
375g (13oz) potatoes, peeled and chopped
  into chunks
1 tsp dried chilli flakes

in the slow cooker **PREP** 25 MINS **COOK** AUTO/LOW 6–8 HRS

1 Preheat the slow cooker, if required. Put the chicken and ham hock in the slow cooker and add the sugar, bouquet garni, onion, celery, tomatoes, sweetcorn, and seasoning. Pour in water to cover. Cover with the lid and cook on auto/low for 6–8 hours. Add the broad beans for the last hour of cooking.

2 Meanwhile, put the potatoes in a saucepan of salted water. Bring to the boil, cover, and simmer for 15–20 minutes until tender. Drain, mash until very smooth, and set aside.

3 Stir in the chilli flakes into the slow cooker for the last 10 minutes of cooking. Lift out the ham and chicken and pull the meat from the bones of both, in large pieces, using a knife and fork. Discard the skin and fat, shred the meat into chunky bits, and stir it back into the stew. Stir the mashed potatoes into the stew. Discard the bouquet garni and taste, adding seasoning if needed.

traditional method **PREP** 10 MINS **COOK** 2–2½ HRS

1 Put the chicken in a large flameproof casserole with the ham hock and pour in enough water to cover. Add the sugar and bouquet garni. Bring to the boil and skim well with a slotted spoon. Cover and simmer gently until the chicken joints are almost tender when pierced; it will take about 1 hour. Lift out the chicken with a slotted spoon and reserve. Remove the casserole from the heat and set aside. Bring the cooking liquid in the casserole back to the boil. Add the onion, celery, and tomatoes and simmer, stirring often, for 20–30 minutes. Make sure the heat is gentle; the liquid should be barely bubbling. Add the sweetcorn and simmer for 10 minutes longer.

2 Put the potatoes in a saucepan of salted water. Bring to the boil, cover, and simmer for 15–20 minutes, until tender. Drain and mash until smooth (an old-fashioned potato ricer can make potatoes really smooth). Stir the potatoes, chilli flakes, and beans into the stew and season to taste. The heat of the chillies will mellow, if you are cooking this dish in advance. Return the chicken to the stew and simmer, stirring often, for about 15 minutes more, or until the meats and vegetables are tender.

3 Lift out the ham. Using a fork and knife, pull the meat from the bones in large pieces, discarding the skin and fat. Shred the meat into chunky bits and stir it back into the stew. The sauce should be thick, but if it is too sticky (which it may be, depending on the potatoes you used), add a little more water to thin it out. Discard the bouquet garni and taste, adding seasoning if needed.

There is plenty of vibrant colour and a lot of heat in this vegetable dish. This is good on its own or with plain boiled rice and, to ring the changes, you may wish to add some chorizo or chicken.

Jamaican corn stew

SERVES 4–6

2 tbsp olive oil
2 onions, finely chopped
salt and freshly ground black pepper
3 garlic cloves, finely chopped
1 tsp cayenne pepper
3 sweetcorn cobs, cut into slices about
   1cm (½in) thick
2 red peppers, deseeded and roughly chopped

3 sweet potatoes, peeled and diced
175g (6oz) yellow split peas
150ml (5fl oz) hot vegetable stock for the slow
   cooker (300ml/10fl oz for the traditional method)
400ml can coconut milk
small handful of thyme
1 Scotch bonnet chilli, left whole

in the slow cooker   **PREP** 20 MINS   **COOK** 10 MINS PRECOOKING; AUTO/LOW 6–8 HRS OR **HIGH** 3–4 HRS

1 Preheat the slow cooker, if required. Heat the oil in a large heavy-based pan over a medium heat, add the onions, and cook for 3–4 minutes until soft. Season with salt and pepper, then stir through the garlic and cayenne pepper, and cook for 1 minute. Add the sweetcorn, peppers, and sweet potatoes and turn so it is all coated evenly. Then stir through the split peas and a little of the stock.

2 Transfer the mixture to the slow cooker. Pour in the coconut milk and the remaining stock. Add seasoning, the thyme, and the Scotch bonnet, then stir, cover with the lid, and cook on auto/low for 6–8 hours or on high for 3–4 hours.

3 Remove the Scotch bonnet, taste, and season as required. Ladle into warmed bowls and serve with rice and some lime wedges on the side.

traditional method   **PREP** 20 MINS   **COOK** 1½–2 HRS

1 Preheat the oven to 160°C (325°F/Gas 3). Heat the oil in a large flameproof casserole over a medium heat, add the onions, and cook for 3–4 minutes until soft. Season with salt and pepper, then stir through the garlic and cayenne pepper, and cook for 1 minute. Add the sweetcorn, peppers, and sweet potatoes and turn so it is all coated evenly. Then stir through the split peas and a little of the stock.

2 Bring to the boil, then add the remaining stock and coconut milk. Bring back to the boil, reduce to a simmer, season, and add the thyme and the Scotch bonnet. Cover and put in the oven to cook for 1½–2 hours. Check occasionally that it's not drying out, topping up with a little hot water if needed.

3 Remove the Scotch bonnet, taste, and season as required. Ladle into warmed bowls and serve with rice and some lime wedges on the side.

A medley of earthy mushrooms and potatoes makes this vegetarian dish a really hearty supper. Portabella mushrooms are especially meaty in texture so cut them into substantial chunks.

Mixed mushroom stew

⊘ **SERVES** 4–6   ❄ **FREEZE** UP TO 3 MONTHS   ♡ **HEALTHY**

1 tbsp olive oil
1 onion, finely chopped
salt and freshly ground black pepper
175g (6oz) chestnut mushrooms, grated
450g (1lb) white mushrooms, thickly sliced
1 sprig of rosemary
3 garlic cloves, finely chopped
4 portabella mushrooms, roughly chopped
1 tbsp sherry vinegar

6 tomatoes, roughly chopped
1 tbsp tomato purée
300ml (10fl oz) hot vegetable stock for the slow cooker (450ml/15fl oz for the traditional method)
3 potatoes, peeled and chopped into bite-sized pieces
pinch of dried chilli flakes
small bunch of curly parsley, finely chopped
25g (scant 1oz) Parmesan cheese, grated (optional)

in the slow cooker   🕑 PREP 30 MINS   COOK 20 MINS PRECOOKING; HIGH 3–4 HRS

1 Preheat the slow cooker, if required. Heat the oil in a large heavy-based pan over a medium heat, add the onion, and cook for 3–4 minutes until soft. Season with salt and pepper, then add the grated chestnut mushrooms and cook for 5 minutes until they start to release their juices.

2 Throw in the white mushrooms, rosemary, garlic, and portabella mushrooms, and stir. Add the sherry vinegar and allow the sauce to bubble for 1 minute, then add the tomatoes and tomato purée. Cook on a gentle heat for 5 minutes, stirring occasionally, then transfer everything to the slow cooker. Add the stock and potatoes, season and cover with the lid, and then cook on high for 3–4 hours.

3 Taste and season as needed, remove the rosemary, then stir through the chilli flakes and parsley. Ladle into warmed bowls and serve with the grated Parmesan cheese, if using, and some chunky wholemeal bread.

traditional method   🕑 PREP 30 MINS   COOK 1 HR

1 Heat the oil in a large heavy-based pan over a medium heat, add the onion, and cook for 3–4 minutes until soft. Season with salt and pepper, then add the grated chestnut mushrooms and cook for 5 minutes until they start to release their juices.

2 Throw in the white mushrooms, rosemary, garlic, and portabella mushrooms, and stir. Add the sherry vinegar and allow the sauce to bubble for 1 minute, then add the tomatoes and tomato purée. Cook on a gentle heat for 5 minutes, stirring occasionally, then add the stock and bring to the boil. Reduce the heat to a simmer and cook, uncovered, on a low heat for 40–45 minutes.

3 Stir through the potatoes for the last 20 minutes of cooking, and cook until tender. Taste and season as needed, remove the rosemary, then stir through the chilli flakes and parsley. Ladle into warmed bowls and serve with the grated Parmesan cheese, if using, and some chunky wholemeal bread.

Puy lentils add texture to this dish as they hold their shape well when cooked. Add a little chilli heat, if you wish, and use butternut squash if pumpkin isn't available or out of season.

Sweet and sour pumpkin stew

◎ **SERVES** 4 ✳ **FREEZE** UP TO 3 MONTHS ♥ **HEALTHY**

2 tbsp olive oil
1 onion, finely chopped
salt and freshly ground black pepper
3 garlic cloves, finely chopped
1 carrot, peeled and finely diced
2 celery sticks, finely diced
2 bay leaves
4 tbsp red wine vinegar
pinch of demerara sugar

1 pumpkin or large butternut squash, peeled and chopped into chunky pieces (about 500g/1lb 2oz prepared weight)
450ml (15fl oz) hot vegetable stock for the slow cooker (900ml/1½ pints for the traditional method)
150g (5½oz) Puy lentils, rinsed and picked over for any stones
bunch of mint leaves, roughly chopped
pumpkin seeds, to serve

in the slow cooker 🕐 **PREP** 15 MINS **COOK** 15 MINS PRECOOKING; **AUTO/LOW** 8 HRS OR **HIGH** 4 HRS

1 Preheat the slow cooker, if required. Heat the oil in a large flameproof casserole over a medium heat, add the onion, and cook for 3–4 minutes until soft. Season well with salt and pepper, then stir in the garlic, carrot, celery, and bay leaves, and cook for a further 5 minutes until soft.

2 Increase the heat, add the vinegar, and let it bubble for a minute, then stir in the sugar and pumpkin. Turn to coat well and add a little stock before cooking on high for a minute. Then stir through the lentils.

3 Transfer everything to the slow cooker, stir in the stock, cover with the lid, and cook on auto/low for 8 hours or on high for 4 hours. Taste and season, if needed, and remove the bay leaf. Stir through the mint, then serve on a bed of rice with some pumpkin seeds scattered over.

traditional method 🕐 **PREP** 15 MINS **COOK** 1 HR

1 Heat the oil in a large flameproof casserole over a medium heat, add the onion, and cook for 3–4 minutes until soft. Season well with salt and pepper, then stir in the garlic, carrot, celery, and bay leaves, and cook for a further 5 minutes until soft.

2 Increase the heat, add the vinegar, and let it bubble for a minute, then stir in the sugar and pumpkin. Turn to coat well and add a little stock before cooking on high for a minute. Stir through the lentils, add the remaining stock, and bring to the boil.

3 Partially cover with the lid, reduce the heat, and simmer gently for about 45 minutes or until the lentils are soft. Top up with hot water if the stew is becoming to dry. Taste and season, if needed, and remove the bay leaf. Stir through the mint, then serve on a bed of rice with some pumpkin seeds scattered over.

Except for squid, seafood doesn't take kindly to slow cooking, so make the stew base first and add the fish at the last minute. For ease of preparation, you could always make this the day before.

Seafood stew

🔍 **SERVES** 4–6 🤍 **HEALTHY**

2 tbsp olive oil, plus extra for drizzling
1 onion, finely chopped
2 celery sticks, finely chopped
salt and freshly ground black pepper
1 tbsp dried oregano
1 fennel bulb, trimmed and roughly chopped
450g (1lb) cleaned squid, sliced into 1cm (½in) rings
350ml (12fl oz) dry white wine
2 lemons, zest peeled into strips using a
  vegetable peeler

1 tbsp tomato purée
400g can chopped tomatoes
600ml (1 pint) hot fish stock for the slow cooker
  (900ml/1½ pints for the traditional method)
1kg (2¼lb) mussels, scrubbed and debearded
  (discard any that do not close when tapped)
250g (9oz) raw shelled king prawns
350g (12oz) sea bass fillet (or other white fish such
  as haddock), skinned and cut into chunky pieces
few sprigs of flat-leaf parsley, finely chopped

 in the slow cooker 🕐 **PREP** 20–30 MINS **COOK** 15 MINS PRECOOKING; **HIGH** 3–4 HRS

1 Preheat the slow cooker, if required. Heat the oil in a large heavy-based pan over a medium heat, add the onion and celery, and cook for about 5 minutes until soft. Season with salt and pepper, then stir in the oregano and fennel and cook for a further 5 minutes.

2 Add the squid and cook over a low heat for a few minutes, stirring occasionally, then stir in the wine, and bring to the boil for 5 minutes. Stir in the strips of lemon zest and tomato purée, season well, and then add the canned tomatoes and stock. Transfer everything to the slow cooker, cover with the lid, and cook on high for 3–4 hours.

3 For the last 10 minutes of cooking, add the mussels, prawns, and sea bass, cover, and cook until the mussels have opened (discard any that do not open) and the fish is opaque and cooked through. Taste and season as needed. Ladle into deep, warmed bowls and serve with rice, couscous, or quinoa, a drizzle of olive oil, and a sprinkling of parsley.

 traditional method 🕐 **PREP** 20–30 MINS **COOK** 1½ HRS

1 Preheat the oven to 160°C (325°F/Gas 3). Heat the oil in a large flameproof casserole over a medium heat, add the onion and celery, and cook for about 5 minutes until soft. Season with salt and pepper, then stir in the oregano and fennel and cook for a further 5 minutes.

2 Add the squid and cook over a low heat for a few minutes, stirring occasionally, then stir in the wine, and bring to the boil for 5 minutes. Stir in the strips of lemon zest and tomato purée, season well, and then add the canned tomatoes and stock. Bring back to the boil, reduce to a simmer, cover, and put in the oven for 1 hour, topping up with hot stock if needed.

3 Add the mussels, prawns, and sea bass to the casserole, cover with the lid once more, and put back in the oven for 5 minutes or until the mussels have opened (discard any that do not open) and the fish is opaque and cooked through. Taste and season as needed. Ladle into deep, warmed bowls and serve with rice, couscous, or quinoa, a drizzle of olive oil, and a sprinkling of parsley.

Originally nothing more than a humble fisherman's stew using the remains of the day's catch, bouillabaisse has evolved into one of the great Provençal dishes. The rouille has a fine garlic kick to it.

Bouillabaisse

SERVES 4

4 tbsp olive oil
1 onion, thinly sliced
2 leeks, trimmed and thinly sliced
1 small fennel bulb, thinly sliced
2–3 garlic cloves, finely chopped
4 tomatoes, skinned, deseeded, and chopped
1 tbsp tomato purée
250ml (9fl oz) dry white wine
450ml (15fl oz) hot fish stock for the slow cooker
   (1.5 litres/2¾ pints for the traditional method)
pinch of saffron threads
strip of orange zest
1 bouquet garni

salt and freshly ground black pepper
1.1kg (2½lb) mixed white and oily fish and
   shellfish, heads and bones removed, and cut,
   if needed, into bite-sized pieces
2 tbsp Pernod
8 thin slices day-old French bread, toasted, to serve

FOR THE ROUILLE
125g (4½oz) mayonnaise
1 bird's-eye chilli, deseeded and roughly chopped
4 garlic cloves, roughly chopped
1 tbsp tomato purée
pinch of salt

in the slow cooker   🕐 PREP 30 MINS   COOK 20 MINS PRECOOKING; HIGH 2–3 HRS

1 To make the rouille, put all the ingredients in a liquidizer or food processor and blend until smooth. Transfer to a bowl, cover with cling film, and chill until required.

2 Preheat the slow cooker, if required. Heat the oil in a large heavy-based pan over a medium heat. Add the onion, leeks, fennel, and garlic and cook, stirring, for 5–8 minutes until the vegetables are softened. Stir in the tomatoes, tomato purée, and wine and bring to the boil. Transfer everything to the slow cooker, add the stock, saffron, orange zest, and bouquet garni and season with salt and pepper. Cover with the lid and cook on high for 2–3 hours. Add the fish for the last 10 minutes of cooking. Remove the orange zest and bouquet garni. Stir in the Pernod and season, if needed. To serve, spread each piece of toast with rouille and put 2 slices in the bottom of each bowl. Ladle the stew on top and serve.

traditional method   🕐 PREP 30 MINS   COOK 45 MINS

1 To make the rouille, put all the ingredients in a liquidizer or food processor and blend until smooth. Transfer to a bowl, cover with cling film, and chill until required.

2 Heat the oil in a large heavy-based pan over a medium heat. Add the onion, leeks, fennel, and garlic, and cook, stirring, for 5–8 minutes until the vegetables are softened. Stir in the tomatoes, tomato purée, and wine. Add the stock, saffron, orange zest, and bouquet garni, season with salt and pepper, and bring to the boil. Reduce the heat, partially cover the pan, and simmer for 30 minutes, or until the stew is reduced slightly, stirring occasionally. Remove the orange zest and bouquet garni from the soup and add the firm fish. Reduce the heat to low and let the soup simmer for 5 minutes, then add the delicate fish and simmer for a further 2–3 minutes, or until all the fish is opaque, cooked through, and flakes easily. Stir in the Pernod, and season if needed. To serve, spread each piece of toast with rouille and put 2 slices in the bottom of each bowl. Ladle the soup on top and serve.

Often made with beef and the addition of peppers, goulash should have a fairly thick consistency. Caraway seeds give goulash its distinctive taste, but be restrained as they can be overpowering.

Pork goulash

 SERVES 6 ✲ **FREEZE** UP TO 3 MONTHS

900g (2lb) stewing pork, cut into bite-sized pieces
1 tbsp plain flour
2 tsp paprika
2 tsp caraway seeds, crushed
salt and freshly ground black pepper
2 tbsp olive oil
1 tbsp cider vinegar

2 tbsp tomato purée
450ml (15fl oz) hot vegetable stock for
  the slow cooker (1.2 litres/2 pints for the
  traditional method)
4 tomatoes, skinned and roughly chopped
1 onion, sliced into rings
handful of curly parsley, finely chopped

 in the slow cooker 🕐 PREP 25 MINS   **COOK** 15 MINS PRECOOKING;
                                                          AUTO/LOW 6–8 HRS OR **HIGH** 3–4 HRS

1 Preheat the slow cooker, if required. Toss the meat with the flour, paprika, and caraway seeds, and season well with salt and pepper. Heat the oil in a large flameproof casserole over a high heat, add the meat and cook, stirring occasionally, for 8–10 minutes or until it begins to brown. Add the vinegar and stir well for a couple of minutes, scraping up all the sticky bits from the bottom of the casserole.

2 Add the tomato purée, followed by the stock, and bring to the boil. Transfer everything to the slow cooker, cover with the lid, and cook on auto/low for 6–8 hours or on high for 3–4 hours.

3 Stir through the tomatoes, taste, and season again if needed. Top with the onion rings and parsley, and serve with rice.

 traditional method 🕐 PREP 25 MINS   **COOK** 1 HR

1 Toss the meat with the flour, paprika, and caraway seeds, and season well with salt and pepper. Heat the oil in a large flameproof casserole over a high heat, add the meat and cook, stirring occasionally, for 8–10 minutes or until it begins to brown. Add the vinegar and stir well for a couple of minutes, scraping up all the sticky bits from the bottom of the casserole.

2 Add the tomato purée, followed by the stock, and bring to the boil. Reduce to a simmer, cover with the lid, and cook gently for 1 hour. Check occasionally that it's not drying out, topping up with a little hot water if needed – the goulash should be fairly thick though.

3 Stir through the tomatoes, taste, and season again if needed. Top with the onion rings and parsley, and serve with rice.

Duck legs are very succulent with lots of tasty meat on them. They can, however, be fatty so the addition of redcurrant jelly and raisins helps to balance this. Pine nuts give an added twist.

Duck legs with cabbage, pine nuts, and raisins

 SERVES 4–6

6 duck legs
2 red onions, roughly chopped
2 garlic cloves, finely chopped
few sprigs of thyme
1 bay leaf
1 tbsp redcurrant jelly

350ml (12fl oz) hot chicken stock for the slow cooker (600ml/1 pint for the traditional method)
salt and freshly ground black pepper
30g (1oz) raisins
30g (1oz) pine nuts, toasted
1 Savoy cabbage, cored and chopped into eighths

 in the slow cooker   **PREP** 15 MINS   **COOK** 30 MINS PRECOOKING; **AUTO/LOW** 6 HRS OR **HIGH** 3–4 HRS

1 Preheat the slow cooker, if required. Heat a large flameproof casserole over a medium heat, then add the duck legs and cook for 15–20 minutes, turning them as you go, until they begin to turn golden. Remove them from the casserole, set aside, and pour off any fat.

2 Add the onions, garlic, thyme, and bay leaf and cook for 5 minutes, then add the redcurrant jelly and cook for a few minutes more. Transfer everything to the slow cooker and add the duck legs, nestling them into the onion mixture, skin-side up. Pour over the stock, season with salt and pepper, cover with the lid, and cook on auto/low for 6 hours or on high for 3–4 hours.

3 Add the raisins, pine nuts, and cabbage to the casserole for the last 1 hour of cooking. Discard the bay leaf, taste, and adjust the seasoning. Serve with creamy mashed potatoes and some chilli jelly on the side.

traditional method   **PREP** 15 MINS   **COOK** 2½ HRS

1 Preheat the oven to 180°C (350°F/Gas 4). Heat a large flameproof casserole over a medium heat, then add the duck legs and cook for 15–20 minutes, turning them as you go, until they begin to turn golden. Remove them from the casserole, set aside, and pour off any fat.

2 Add the onions, garlic, thyme, and bay leaf and cook for 5 minutes, then add the redcurrant jelly and cook for a few minutes more. Return the duck legs to the casserole and nestle them into the onion mixture, skin-side up. Pour over the stock, bring to the boil, and then reduce to a simmer. Season with salt and pepper, cover with the lid, and put in the oven for 2 hours. Check occasionally that it's not drying out, topping up with a little hot water if needed.

3 Add the raisins, pine nuts, and cabbage to the casserole for the last 30 minutes of cooking. Discard the bay leaf, taste, and adjust the seasoning. Serve with creamy mashed potatoes and some chilli jelly on the side.

Red cabbage is transformed when slow cooked, becoming sweet and tender. Add a handful of sultanas, if you wish, for extra flavour, and serve with couscous or sausages for a simple supper.

Red cabbage with cider

SERVES 4   **HEALTHY**

½ red onion, sliced
1 large red cabbage (weighing about 1kg/2¼lb),
  cored and shredded
1 apple, cored (but not peeled) and finely chopped

1 tsp five-spice powder
salt and freshly ground black pepper
150ml (5fl oz) dry cider for the slow cooker
  (300ml/10fl oz for the traditional method)

in the slow cooker   **PREP** 15 MINS   **COOK** AUTO/LOW 8 HRS OR **HIGH** 4 HRS

1 Preheat the slow cooker, if required. Put the onion, cabbage, apple, and five-spice powder into the slow cooker and season well with salt and pepper. Turn to mix everything together.

2 Pour in the cider and stir, then cover with the lid and cook on auto/low for 8 hours or on high for 4 hours. Taste and season as needed.

traditional method   **PREP** 15 MINS   **COOK** 1–1½ HRS

1 Put the onion, cabbage, apple, and five-spice powder into a large heavy-based pan, and season well with salt and pepper. Turn to mix everything together.

2 Pour in the cider and stir, then cover with the lid and cook on a low heat for 1–1½ hours, stirring occasionally. Taste and season as needed.

The venison is marinated in red wine to tenderize the meat – the longer you can leave it to marinate, the better. You could switch the venison to beef if you prefer.

Venison stew

🕐 **SERVES** 4–6 ❄️ **FREEZE** UP TO 3 MONTHS

500ml (16fl oz) red wine
3 tbsp olive oil
1 tbsp crushed juniper berries
2 sprigs of rosemary
1.1kg (2½lb) venison, cut into bite-sized pieces
2 tbsp plain flour, seasoned with salt and pepper
1 onion, roughly chopped
200g (7oz) pancetta cubes

30g (1oz) dried porcini mushrooms, soaked in
    warm water for 30 minutes
coarsely chopped zest of 1 orange
450ml (15fl oz) hot vegetable stock for the slow
    cooker (900ml/1½ pints for the traditional method)
knob of butter
250g (9oz) chestnut mushrooms, halved
salt and freshly ground black pepper

in the slow cooker 🕐 PREP 15 MINS, PLUS MARINATING **COOK** 15 MINS PRECOOKING; AUTO/LOW 8 HRS

1 Preheat the slow cooker, if required. Put the wine, 2 tbsp of the oil, the juniper berries, 1 sprig of rosemary, and the venison in a large bowl. Ensure the meat is immersed in the wine, cover, and leave to marinate for 1 hour or overnight, if possible. Drain the meat, reserving the liquid and rosemary.

2 Heat the remaining oil in a large flameproof casserole over a medium-high heat, and toss the venison in the flour. Cook in batches for about 5 minutes until golden on all sides. Remove and set aside. Reduce the heat to medium, add the onion and pancetta, and cook for about 5 minutes until the pancetta begins to colour. Drain the porcini and strain the juice. Add the mushrooms and a little of the juice to the casserole with the orange zest, wine marinade, and rosemary. Bring to the boil.

3 Transfer everything, including the venison, to the slow cooker and pour over the stock. Heat the butter in a frying pan, add the chestnut mushrooms, and cook for a few minutes until golden, then stir into the slow cooker. Cover with the lid, and cook on auto/low for 8 hours. Taste and season as needed. Ladle into shallow bowls and serve with polenta.

traditional method 🕐 PREP 15 MINS, PLUS MARINATING **COOK** 1¾–2¼ HRS

1 Put the wine, 2 tbsp of the oil, the juniper berries, 1 sprig of rosemary, and the venison in a large bowl. Ensure the meat is immersed in the wine, cover, and leave to marinate for 1 hour or overnight, if possible. Drain the meat, reserving the liquid and rosemary.

2 Heat the remaining olive oil in a large flameproof casserole over a medium-high heat, and toss the venison in the flour. Cook in batches for about 5 minutes until golden on all sides. Remove and set aside. Reduce the heat to medium, add the onion and pancetta, and cook for about 5 minutes until the pancetta begins to colour. Drain the porcini and strain the juice. Add the mushrooms and a little of the juice to the casserole with the orange zest, wine marinade, and rosemary. Add the stock and boil. Add the meat, reduce to a simmer, cover, and cook on a low heat for 1½–2 hours until tender. Top up with the reserved porcini juice or hot water to keep the meat covered. For the last 30 minutes, heat the butter in a frying pan and cook the chestnut mushrooms for a few minutes until golden, then stir into the stew. Taste and season as needed. Ladle into shallow bowls and serve with polenta.

The delicate flavour of the monkfish is highlighted by white wine, and the sauce is given a velvety consistency by adding a kneaded butter and flour paste, known as beurre manié.

Monkfish and white wine stew

SERVES 4–6 **FREEZE** UP TO 1 MONTH

75g (2½oz) butter, softened
2 shallots, diced
2 garlic cloves, finely chopped
2 leeks, trimmed, cut lengthways, and chopped into bite-sized diagonal pieces
500g (1lb 2oz) small courgettes, trimmed and chopped into bite-sized pieces
salt and freshly ground black pepper
250g (9oz) mushrooms, trimmed and quartered
3–5 thyme sprigs, leaves only

1 bay leaf
250ml (9fl oz) dry white wine
300ml (10fl oz) hot fish stock for the slow cooker (500ml/16fl oz for the traditional method)
750g (1lb 10oz) skinned monkfish fillets, membrane removed and cut into bite-sized diagonal pieces
3 tbsp flour
small bunch of parsley, leaves chopped

in the slow cooker ● PREP 30 MINS COOK 5 MINS PRECOOKING; **AUTO/LOW** 2–3 HRS

1 Preheat the slow cooker, if required. Melt 30g (1oz) of the butter in a large heavy-based pan over a medium heat, add the shallots, garlic, leeks, and courgettes, and cook for 3–5 minutes until soft. Season with salt and pepper, then add the mushrooms, thyme, bay, wine, and stock and bring to the boil. Transfer everything to the slow cooker, cover with the lid, and cook on auto/low for 2–3 hours.

2 Add the monkfish for the last 15 minutes of cooking and stir very gently to combine. Do not stir too vigorously or the fish may fall apart.

3 Fork together the remaining butter with the flour to form a smooth paste. Add to the slow cooker for the last 5 minutes of cooking and stir to combine. Discard the bay leaf, stir in half the parsley, and add seasoning, if needed. Serve sprinkled with the remaining parsley.

traditional method ● PREP 30 MINS COOK 40–45 MINS

1 Melt 30g (1oz) of the butter in a large heavy-based pan over a medium heat, add the shallots, garlic, leeks, and courgettes, and cook for 3–5 minutes until soft. Season with salt and pepper, then add the mushrooms, thyme, bay, wine, and stock, cover with the lid, and simmer gently for 25–30 minutes.

2 Add the monkfish and stir very gently to combine. Do not stir too vigorously or the fish may fall apart. Cover the pan, bring back to the boil, and simmer for 3–5 minutes until the fish is opaque and cooked through.

3 Fork together the remaining butter with the flour to form a smooth paste. Add to the pan, stir to combine, and simmer for 2 minutes. Discard the bay leaf, stir in half the parsley, and add seasoning, if needed. Serve sprinkled with the remaining parsley.

The lamb is tossed in cumin and chilli, which lends a gentle touch of spice to the mixture and the wine adds depth to the sauce. The trick with this dish is to cook the vegetables separately.

Lamb ratatouille

⊚ **SERVES** 6   ❄ **FREEZE** UP TO 3 MONTHS

2 tbsp vegetable oil
750g (1lb 10oz) boneless lamb shoulder, cut
  into 2.5–4cm (1–1½in) cubes
2 tbsp plain flour
salt and freshly ground black pepper
1 tsp ground cumin
1 tsp dried chilli flakes
250ml (9fl oz) red wine
400g can chopped tomatoes

300ml (10fl oz) hot chicken or lamb stock for
  the slow cooker (500ml/16fl oz for the
  traditional method)
3 tbsp olive oil
1 large onion, sliced
3 garlic cloves, finely chopped
1 red pepper, deseeded and sliced
1 green pepper, deseeded and sliced
1 aubergine, chopped into 2.5cm (1in) chunks

in the slow cooker   ⏱ **PREP** 20 MINS   **COOK** 15 MINS PRECOOKING;
AUTO/**LOW** 6–8 HRS OR **HIGH** 3–4 HRS

1 Preheat the slow cooker, if required. Heat the vegetable oil in a large flameproof casserole over a high heat. In a bowl, toss the lamb with the flour, seasoning, cumin, and chilli flakes. Add the meat to the casserole (in batches, if necessary) and cook for 3–5 minutes, stirring occasionally, until evenly browned.

2 Pour in the wine, increase the heat, and let it bubble for a minute, then add the tomatoes and the stock and bring to the boil. Transfer everything to the slow cooker, cover with the lid, and cook on auto/low for 6–8 hours or on high for 3–4 hours.

3 Meanwhile, heat the olive oil in a large heavy-based pan over a medium heat, add the onion and garlic, and cook for 3–5 minutes until soft. Stir in the peppers and cook for 2–3 minutes, then add the aubergine and cook for about 10 minutes, stirring, until just tender. Stir these into the slow cooker for the last hour of cooking. Serve with rice.

traditional method   ⏱ **PREP** 20 MINS   **COOK** 2–2¼ HRS

1 Heat the vegetable oil in a large flameproof casserole over a high heat. In a bowl, toss the lamb with the flour, seasoning, cumin, and chilli flakes. Add the meat to the casserole (in batches, if necessary) and cook for 3–5 minutes, stirring occasionally, until evenly browned.

2 Pour in the wine, increase the heat, and let it bubble for a minute, then add the tomatoes and the stock and bring to the boil. Reduce the heat and simmer, partially covered, for 1¼ hours.

3 Meanwhile, heat the olive oil in a large heavy-based pan over a medium heat, add the onion and garlic, and cook for 3–5 minutes until soft. Stir in the peppers and cook for 2–3 minutes, then add the aubergine and cook for about 10 minutes, stirring, until just tender. Stir these into the casserole, top up with a little hot water if too dry, and cook, uncovered, for a further 15 minutes. Serve with rice.

Tender beef with robust kale is a great combination. The chilli hint is subtle, but just enough to add interest to the dish, while the anchovies are added to enrich the sauce.

Beef and greens

 SERVES 4–6 **FREEZE** UP TO 3 MONTHS

3–4 tbsp olive oil
1.25kg (2¾lb) chuck beef, cut into bite-sized pieces
salt and freshly ground black pepper
1 tsp paprika
1 tbsp plain flour
2 onions, roughly chopped
3 garlic cloves, finely chopped
1 green chilli, deseeded and finely chopped
8 salted anchovies

4 large carrots, peeled and roughly chopped
250ml (9fl oz) red wine
600ml (1 pint) hot beef or vegetable stock for the slow cooker (900ml/1½ pints for the traditional method)
4 large potatoes, peeled and roughly chopped
200g pack curly kale, stems trimmed and leaves roughly chopped

 in the slow cooker ⏱ PREP 15 MINS COOK 20 MINS PRECOOKING; **AUTO/LOW** 6–8 HRS

1 Preheat the slow cooker, if required. Heat 1 tbsp of the oil in a large flameproof casserole over a medium heat. Season the meat with salt, pepper, and paprika, then toss in the flour. Add the beef to the casserole (in batches and with extra oil, if necessary), and cook for 5–8 minutes until browned all over. Remove with a slotted spoon and set aside.

2 Add the remaining oil to the casserole, add the onions, and cook for 3–4 minutes until soft. Then stir in the garlic, chilli, and anchovies and cook for a minute. Add the carrots and cook for a further 2–3 minutes. Pour in the wine and bring to the boil, stirring and scraping up the bits from the bottom of the casserole.

3 Transfer everything to the slow cooker, add the stock, and then the meat and potatoes. Cover with the lid and cook on auto/low for 6–8 hours. Add the kale for the last 1 hour of cooking. Serve while piping hot with some crusty bread.

 traditional method ⏱ PREP 15 MINS COOK 1¾ HRS

1 Preheat the oven to 160°C (325°F/Gas 3). Heat 1 tbsp of the oil in a large flameproof casserole over a medium heat. Season the meat with salt, pepper, and paprika, then toss in the flour. Add the beef to the casserole (in batches and with extra oil, if necessary), and cook for 5–8 minutes until browned all over. Remove with a slotted spoon and set aside.

2 Add the remaining oil to the casserole, add the onions, and cook for 3–4 minutes until soft. Then stir in the garlic, chilli, and anchovies and cook for a minute. Add the carrots and cook for a further 2–3 minutes.

3 Pour in the wine and bring to the boil, stirring and scraping up the bits from the bottom of the casserole. Pour in the stock and bring back to the boil, add the meat and potatoes, cover, and put in the oven for 1½ hours. Check occasionally that it's not drying out, topping up with a little hot water if needed. Add the kale and cook for a further hour, again checking that it doesn't dry out too much. Serve while piping hot with some crusty bread.

Aubergine and lamb and are a classic combination from the Middle East, and the paprika adds a fine smoky flavour. The aubergine can sop up the oil, so keep topping it up.

Smoky aubergine and lamb stew

⊚ **SERVES** 6–8 ❄ **FREEZE** UP TO 3 MONTHS

3–4 tbsp olive oil
2 aubergines, cubed
1–2 tsp smoked paprika
750g (1lb 10oz) middle neck of lamb,
  chopped into large chunks
1 onion, roughly chopped
200g (7oz) chorizo, diced
1 tbsp sherry vinegar

3 garlic cloves, finely chopped
1 tsp ground cumin
400g can chickpeas, drained and rinsed
450ml (15fl oz) hot vegetable stock
  for the slow cooker (900ml/1½ pints
  for the traditional method)
few sprigs of thyme, leaves only
bunch of mint, leaves roughly chopped

in the slow cooker ⏱ **PREP** 15 MINS **COOK** 20 MINS PRECOOKING; **AUTO/LOW** 6–8 HRS

1 Preheat the slow cooker, if required. Heat 2 tbsp of the oil in a large flameproof casserole over a medium-high heat, add the aubergine and smoked paprika, and toss to coat. Cook, stirring, and adding more oil as needed, for 6–8 minutes until the aubergine begins to colour. Remove with a slotted spoon and set aside.

2 Add a drizzle of oil and cook the lamb (in batches, if necessary) for 4–6 minutes until it browns on all sides. Remove and set aside. Add the onion and chorizo (again, with a little oil, if needed), and cook for 2 minutes, then add the vinegar. Increase the heat and cook for 2 minutes until the vinegar has evaporated. Stir to scrape up the bits from the bottom of the casserole, then add the garlic and cumin.

3 Return the lamb to the casserole, add the chickpeas, and transfer everything to the slow cooker. Pour in the stock and throw in the thyme, cover with the lid, and cook on auto/low for 6–8 hours. Taste and season as needed, then remove the thyme, and stir through the mint. Serve with couscous and crusty bread.

traditional method ⏱ **PREP** 15 MINS **COOK** 1¾ HRS

1 Heat 2 tbsp of the oil in a large flameproof casserole over a medium-high heat, add the aubergine and smoked paprika, and toss to coat. Cook, stirring, and adding more oil as needed, for 6–8 minutes until the aubergine begins to colour. Remove with a slotted spoon and set aside.

2 Add a drizzle of oil and cook the lamb (in batches, if necessary) for 4–6 minutes until it browns on all sides. Remove and set aside. Add the onion and chorizo (again, with a little oil, if needed), and cook for 2 minutes, then add the vinegar. Increase the heat and cook for 2 minutes until the vinegar has evaporated. Stir to scrape up the bits from the bottom of the casserole, then add the garlic and cumin.

3 Return the lamb to the casserole, add the chickpeas, and pour in the stock. Throw in the thyme and bring to the boil, then partially cover and cook for 1 hour, checking the liquid level and topping up with hot water if needed. Stir through the aubergine and cook for a further 30 minutes, then remove the thyme, and stir through the mint. Serve with couscous and crusty bread.

This is a deep-flavoured stew to be served up on cold days. The anchovies melt into it and the redcurrant jelly adds a distinctive sweetness. It is delicious spooned over mashed or baked potatoes.

Beef and anchovy stew

⊚ **SERVES** 4–6 ❄ **FREEZE** UP TO 3 MONTHS

4 tbsp olive oil, plus extra if necessary
knob of butter
12 baby onions, peeled
few sprigs of thyme
salt and freshly ground black pepper
1.1kg (2½lb) chuck beef, cut into chunky cubes
1 tbsp plain flour, seasoned with salt and pepper
2 leeks, trimmed and sliced

pinch of ground allspice
250ml (9fl oz) red wine
6 anchovy fillets in oil, drained and chopped
1 tbsp small capers
300ml (10fl oz) hot beef stock for the slow cooker
  (800ml/1 pint 7fl oz for the traditional method)
1–2 tbsp redcurrant jelly

in the slow cooker ⏱ **PREP** 20 MINS **COOK** 20 MINS PRECOOKING; **AUTO/LOW** 6–8 HRS

1 Preheat the slow cooker, if required. Heat half the oil and the butter in a large flameproof casserole over a medium heat, then add the onions, thyme, and salt and pepper. Cook for about 10 minutes until the onions start to take on some colour. Remove with a slotted spoon and set aside. Toss the beef in the flour. Add the remaining oil to the casserole, increase the heat to medium-high, and cook the beef in batches for a few minutes on each side until browned all over. Remove and set aside. Add a little more oil, stir in the leeks and allspice, and cook for about 5 minutes. Also remove and set aside.

2 Add the wine and bring to the boil, scraping up the bits from the bottom of the casserole. Let it bubble for a few minutes, then stir through the anchovies, capers, stock, and redcurrant jelly. Bring to the boil, then reduce to a simmer and transfer everything to the slow cooker along with the meat, leeks, and onions. Taste and season if needed, then pour over just enough of the hot stock to cover. Put the lid on and cook on auto/low for 6–8 hours. Serve while piping hot.

traditional method ⏱ **PREP** 20 MINS **COOK** 2¼–2¾ HRS

1 Preheat the oven to 160°C (325°F/Gas 3). Heat half the oil and the butter in a large flameproof casserole over a medium heat, then add the onions, thyme, and salt and pepper. Cook for about 10 minutes until the onions start to take on some colour. Remove with a slotted spoon and set aside.

2 Toss the beef in the flour. Add the remaining oil to the casserole, increase the heat to medium-high, and cook the beef in batches for a few minutes on each side until browned all over. Remove and set aside. Add a little more oil, stir in the leeks and allspice, and cook for about 5 minutes. Also remove and set aside.

3 Add the wine and bring to the boil, scraping up the bits from the bottom of the casserole. Let it bubble for a few minutes, then stir through the anchovies, capers, stock, and redcurrant jelly. Bring to the boil, then reduce to a simmer, return the meat, leeks, and onions to the casserole, and season again if you wish. Cover with the lid and cook in the oven for 2–2½ hours until the beef is tender. Check occasionally that it's not drying out, topping up with a little hot water, if needed. Serve while piping hot.

Rich and robust, oxtail makes a change to beef and braising it very slowly tenderizes it to the full. Prunes are always a tasty addition to a stew as their sweetness and texture complement the meat.

Braised oxtail with star anise

 SERVES 4–6 ❄ **FREEZE** UP TO 3 MONTHS

2 oxtails, about 1.35kg (3lb) each, cut
  into bite-sized pieces
salt and freshly ground black pepper
2 tbsp olive oil
2 red onions, sliced
3 garlic clove, finely chopped
pinch of dried chilli flakes
350ml (12fl oz) red wine
4 star anise

handful of black peppercorns
1 bay leaf
8 soft prunes, stoned and chopped
600ml (1 pint) hot beef stock for the slow cooker
  (900ml/1½ pints for the traditional method)
4 clementines or 2 oranges, peeled and sliced
  into rings
small bunch of curly parsley leaves, finely chopped

 in the slow cooker 🕐 **PREP** 20 MINS **COOK** 15 MINS PRECOOKING; **AUTO/LOW** 8 HRS

1 Preheat the slow cooker, if required. Season the oxtail with salt and pepper. Heat half the oil in a large flameproof casserole over a medium heat, then add the meat in batches, and fry for 8–10 minutes until browned on all sides. Remove from the casserole and set aside.

2 Heat the remaining oil in the casserole over a medium heat, add the onions, and cook for 3–4 minutes to soften. Stir through the garlic and chilli flakes, then pour in the wine and let it simmer before adding it to the slow cooker together with the meat, star anise, peppercorns, bay leaf, prunes, and stock. Cover with the lid and cook on auto/low for 8 hours. Add the clementines for the last 30 minutes of cooking.

3 Shred the meat from the bone into the slow cooker, and discard the bone, bay leaf, and star anise. Serve on a bed of pasta, sprinkled with the parsley.

traditional method 🕐 **PREP** 20 MINS **COOK** 3¼ HRS

1 Preheat the oven to 150°C (300°F/Gas 2). Season the oxtail with salt and pepper. Heat half the oil in a large flameproof casserole over a medium heat, then add the meat in batches, and fry for 8–10 minutes until browned on all sides. Remove with a slotted spoon and set aside.

2 Heat the remaining oil in the casserole over a medium heat, add the onions, and cook for 3–4 minutes to soften. Stir through the garlic and chilli flakes, then pour in the wine and let it simmer for about 5 minutes until slightly reduced. Return the meat to the casserole and add the star anise, peppercorns, bay leaf, and prunes, and pour over just enough stock to cover the meat.

3 Bring to the boil, then reduce to a simmer, add the remaining stock, cover, and put in the oven for about 3 hours. Check occasionally that it's not drying out, topping up with a little hot water if needed. Add the clementines or oranges for the last 30 minutes of cooking and leave the casserole uncovered to allow the liquid to thicken slightly. Stir it occasionally to keep the oxtail moist and coated with the gravy. When ready, the meat will fall away from the bone. Remove the bone and discard it together with the bay leaf and star anise. Serve on a bed of pasta, sprinkled with the parsley.

Casseroles, cassoulets, & meatballs

A robust dish that will hit the spot on cold days and fill you up. The lentils become soft and tender and, because they are cooked for so long, they are flavoured by the sausages.

Lentil and Toulouse sausage casserole

🔍 **SERVES** 4–6　❄️ **FREEZE** UP TO 1 MONTH

2 tbsp olive oil
8 Toulouse sausages, roughly chopped
1 onion, finely chopped
2 carrots, peeled and finely diced
freshly ground black pepper
3 garlic cloves, finely chopped
140g (5oz) chorizo, diced
3 sprigs of rosemary

few sprigs of thyme
200g (7oz) Puy lentils or brown lentils, rinsed and picked over for any stones
175ml (6fl oz) red wine
600ml (1 pint) hot chicken stock for the slow cooker (900ml/1½ pints for the traditional method)
1 red chilli, left whole
splash of extra virgin olive oil, to serve

in the slow cooker　⏱ **PREP** 15 MINS　**COOK** 15 MINS PRECOOKING; **AUTO/LOW** 6–8 HRS

1 Preheat the slow cooker, if required. Heat half the oil in a large flameproof casserole over a high heat, add the Toulouse sausages, and cook for a few minutes until they begin to turn golden. Remove from the casserole and set aside.

2 Add the remaining oil, stir in the onion and carrot, and turn to coat. Season with pepper and leave to cook for a few minutes, stirring occasionally. Add the garlic, chorizo, and herbs, give it all a stir, then return the Toulouse sausages to the casserole and stir in the lentils. Add the wine, bring to the boil, and cook for a minute. Transfer everything to the slow cooker, add the chicken stock and chilli, cover with the lid, and cook on auto/low for 6–8 hours.

3 Taste and season, if necessary, remove the whole chilli, then ladle into warmed bowls and serve with a splash of extra virgin olive oil and some crusty bread.

traditional method　⏱ **PREP** 15 MINS　**COOK** 1¾ HRS

1 Preheat the oven to 160°C (325°F/Gas 3). Heat half the oil in a large flameproof casserole over a high heat, add the Toulouse sausages, and cook for a few minutes until they begin to turn golden. Remove from the casserole and set aside.

2 Add the remaining oil, stir in the onion and carrot, and turn to coat. Season with pepper and leave to cook for a few minutes, stirring occasionally. Add the garlic, chorizo, and herbs, give it all a stir, then return the Toulouse sausages to the casserole and stir in the lentils. Add the wine, bring to the boil, and cook for a minute.

3 Pour in the stock, bring to the boil, then reduce to a simmer. Add the chilli, cover with the lid, and put in the oven for 1½ hours. Check occasionally that it's not drying out, topping up with a little hot water if needed. Taste and season, if necessary, remove the whole chilli, then ladle into warmed bowls and serve with a splash of extra virgin olive oil and some crusty bread.

Look for ready-diced packs of game meat, which cut down on preparation time. Cider, carrot, and parsnip lend a sweetness to this dish and the fennel seeds add a welcome touch of aniseed.

Autumn game casserole

⊘ SERVES 4   **❄ FREEZE** UP TO 3 MONTHS

2 tbsp olive oil
500g (1lb 2oz) mixed casserole game, such as
   pheasant, partridge, venison, rabbit, and
   pigeon, cut into bite-sized cubes
1 onion, chopped
1 carrot, peeled and chopped
1 parsnip, peeled and chopped
1 fennel bulb, diced, fronds reserved

2 tbsp plain flour
200ml (7fl oz) dry cider or apple juice
200ml (7fl oz) hot chicken stock, for both methods
250g (9oz) chestnut mushrooms, thickly sliced
½ tsp fennel seeds
salt and freshly ground black pepper
small handful of flat-leaf parsley, chopped (optional)

in the slow cooker   **⏱ PREP** 20 MINS   **COOK** 15 MINS PRECOOKING; **AUTO/LOW** 6–8 HRS OR **HIGH** 2–3 HRS

1 Preheat the slow cooker, if required. Heat the oil in a large flameproof casserole over a medium-high heat and cook the game meat, stirring occasionally, for 3–4 minutes until lightly browned. Remove and set aside.

2 Lower the heat to medium, add the onion, carrot, parsnip, and fennel to the casserole and cook, stirring occasionally, for 4–5 minutes until lightly coloured. Sprinkle in the flour and gradually stir in the cider and stock. Add the mushrooms and fennel seeds, then bring to the boil. Transfer everything to the slow cooker, including the game meat, season well, and cover with the lid. Cook on auto/low for 6–8 hours or on high for 2–3 hours. Sprinkle the finished dish with the reserved fennel fronds or chopped parsley and serve hot with some creamy mashed potatoes.

traditional method   **⏱ PREP** 20 MINS   **COOK** 1½ HRS

1 Preheat the oven to 160°C (325°F/Gas 3). Heat the oil in a large flameproof casserole over a medium-high heat and cook the game meat, stirring occasionally, for 3–4 minutes until lightly browned. Remove and set aside.

2 Lower the heat to medium, add the onion, carrot, parsnip, and fennel to the casserole and cook, stirring occasionally, for 4–5 minutes until lightly coloured. Sprinkle in the flour and gradually stir in the cider and stock. Add the mushrooms and fennel seeds, then return the meat, season well, and bring to the boil. Cover tightly with the lid and put in the oven for about 1¼ hours, or until the meat and vegetables are tender. Sprinkle the finished dish with the reserved fennel fronds or chopped parsley and serve hot with some creamy mashed potatoes.

Try using a Normandy cider for this dish, for an authentic flavour. Crème fraîche can be used in place of the cream. Stir through a handful of walnuts at the end to add flavour.

Pork Normandy

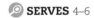 **SERVES** 4–6

2 tbsp olive oil
knob of butter
900g (2lb) lean pork, cut into bite-sized pieces
2 onions, finely chopped
2 tbsp Dijon mustard
4 garlic cloves, finely chopped
4 celery sticks, finely chopped
3 carrots, peeled and finely chopped

1 tbsp chopped rosemary leaves
2 Bramley apples, peeled, cored, and
 roughly chopped
200ml (7fl oz) dry cider
200ml (7fl oz) hot light chicken stock,
 for both methods
200ml (7fl oz) double cream
1 tsp black peppercorns

 in the slow cooker 🕑 **PREP** 30 MINS **COOK** 25 MINS PRECOOKING;
AUTO/LOW 6 8 HRS OR **HIGH** 3–4 HRS

1 Preheat the slow cooker, if required. Heat the oil and butter in a large flameproof casserole over a medium heat, add the pork (in batches, if necessary), and cook for about 10 minutes, stirring occasionally, until golden brown on all sides. Remove and set aside.

2 Reduce the heat to low, add the onions, and cook for about 5 minutes until soft. Stir in the mustard, garlic, celery, carrots, and rosemary, and cook, stirring often, for about 10 minutes until tender. Add the apples and cook for a further 5 minutes.

3 Pour in the cider, increase the heat, and boil for a couple of minutes while the alcohol evaporates. Transfer everything to the slow cooker, including the pork, and pour over the stock. Cover with the lid and cook on auto/low for 6–8 hours or on high for 3–4 hours. Add the cream and peppercorns for the last 20 minutes of cooking. Serve with fluffy rice or creamy mashed potatoes.

 traditional method 🕑 **PREP** 30 MINS **COOK** 1½ HRS

1 Preheat the oven to 180°C (350°F/Gas 4). Heat the oil and butter in a large flameproof casserole over a medium heat, add the pork (in batches, if necessary), and cook for about 10 minutes, stirring occasionally, until golden brown on all sides. Remove and set aside.

2 Reduce the heat to low, add the onions, and cook for about 5 minutes until soft. Stir in the mustard, garlic, celery, carrots, and rosemary, and cook, stirring often, for about 10 minutes until tender. Add the apples and cook for a further 5 minutes.

3 Pour in the cider, increase the heat, and boil for a couple of minutes while the alcohol evaporates. Return the pork to the casserole and pour in the stock and cream. Stir in the peppercorns, bring to the boil, cover with the lid, and put in the oven for 1 hour, or until the sauce has reduced and the pork is tender. Serve with fluffy rice or creamy mashed potatoes.

In this classic French casserole, long, slow braising ensures the meat becomes tender, cooked as it is in red wine. Traditionally, the French use red Burgundy wine, but it's not obligatory.

Boeuf bourguignon

SERVES 4 ❄ **FREEZE** UP TO 3 MONTHS

175g (6oz) streaky bacon rashers, chopped
1–2 tbsp olive oil
900g (2lb) braising steak, cut into 4cm (1½in) cubes
12 small shallots, peeled and left whole
1 tbsp plain flour
300ml (10fl oz) red wine
200ml (7fl oz) hot beef stock for the slow cooker
  (300ml/10fl oz for the traditional method)

115g (4oz) button mushrooms
1 bay leaf
1 tsp dried herbes de Provence
salt and freshly ground black pepper
4 tbsp chopped flat-leaf parsley

in the slow cooker ⏱ PREP 20 MINS COOK 20 MINS PRECOOKING; **AUTO/LOW** 6–8 HRS

1 Preheat the slow cooker, if required. Fry the bacon in a large flameproof casserole over a medium heat until lightly browned. Drain on kitchen paper, then set aside and keep warm. Depending on how much fat is left from the bacon, add a little oil to the casserole, if necessary, so you have 2–3 tbsp, and increase the heat to high. Fry the beef (in batches, if necessary) for 8–10 minutes until browned all over. Remove, set aside, and keep warm. Reduce the heat to medium and fry the shallots for 6–8 minutes and then remove these too, and set aside with the meat.

2 Stir the flour into the remaining fat in the casserole. If the casserole is quite dry, mix the flour with a little of the wine or stock. Pour the remaining wine and stock into the casserole and bring to the boil, stirring, until smooth. Add the mushrooms, bay leaf, and dried herbs. Add seasoning and then transfer everything to the slow cooker, including the bacon, beef, and shallots. Cover with the lid and cook on auto/low for 6–8 hours. Sprinkle with the chopped parsley, remove the bay leaf, and serve with mashed potatoes, baby carrots, and a green vegetable such as broccoli or French beans.

traditional method ⏱ PREP 25 MINS COOK 2½ HRS

1 Preheat the oven to 160°C (325°F/Gas 3). Fry the bacon in a large flameproof casserole over a medium heat until lightly browned. Drain on kitchen paper, then set aside and keep warm. Depending on how much fat is left from the bacon, add a little oil to the casserole, if necessary, so you have 2–3 tbsp, and increase the heat to high. Fry the beef (in batches, if necessary) for 8–10 minutes until browned all over. Remove, set aside, and keep warm. Reduce the heat to medium and fry the shallots for 6–8 minutes and then remove these too, and set aside with the meat.

2 Stir the flour into the remaining fat in the casserole. If the casserole is quite dry, mix the flour with a little of the wine or stock. Pour the remaining wine and stock into the casserole and bring to the boil, stirring, until smooth. Add the mushrooms, bay leaf, and dried herbs. Add seasoning and return the meat and shallots to the casserole. Cover and cook in the oven for 2 hours, or until the meat is very tender. Check occasionally that it's not drying out, topping up with a little hot water if needed.

3 Sprinkle with the chopped parsley, remove the bay leaf, and serve with mashed potatoes, baby carrots, and a green vegetable such as broccoli or French beans.

The flavour varies with the wine used: a Rhône wine gives a rich sauce; a Loire wine, a fruitier dish. Start the recipe a day ahead to allow time for marinating. Serve with new potatoes.

Coq au vin

SERVES 4–6

1 onion, thinly sliced
1 celery stick, thinly sliced
1 carrot, peeled and thinly sliced
2 garlic cloves, 1 peeled and left whole,
   1 finely chopped
6 black peppercorns
375ml (13fl oz) red wine
2kg (4½lb) chicken, jointed into 8 pieces
2 tbsp olive oil
1 tbsp vegetable oil

15g (½oz) butter
125g (4½oz) piece of bacon, diced
18–20 baby onions, peeled
3 tbsp flour
500ml (16fl oz) hot chicken stock, for
   both methods
2 shallots, finely chopped
1 bouquet garni
salt and freshly ground black pepper
250g (9oz) mushrooms, quartered

in the slow cooker   **PREP** 30 MINS,   **COOK** 20 MINS PRECOOKING;
                        PLUS MARINATING   **AUTO/LOW** 6–8 HRS OR **HIGH** 3–4 HRS

1 For the marinade, put the onion, celery, carrot, whole garlic clove, and peppercorns in a pan. Pour in the wine and bring to the boil. Simmer for about 5 minutes, then cool and pour into a large bowl. Add the chicken and olive oil, cover, and refrigerate for 12–18 hours, turning the chicken occasionally.

2 Preheat the slow cooker, if required. Remove the chicken from the marinade and dry on kitchen paper. Strain the marinade and reserve the liquid and vegetables. Heat the vegetable oil and butter in a flameproof casserole until foaming. Add the bacon, brown it, remove, and set aside. Add the chicken and cook for 10–15 minutes until brown. Remove and set aside. Discard all but 2 tbsp of the fat. Reduce the heat to medium and cook the baby onions for 3–4 minutes until soft. Add the reserved vegetables and cook over a very low heat for 5 minutes until soft. Add the flour and cook for 2 minutes until lightly browned. Stir in the reserved marinade, stock, chopped garlic, shallots, bouquet garni, and seasoning. Bring to the boil, then transfer to the slow cooker, adding the bacon and chicken. Cover with the lid and cook on auto/low for 6–8 hours or on high for 3–4 hours. Add the mushrooms with 15 minutes remaining.

traditional method   **PREP** 30 MINS, PLUS MARINATING   **COOK** 1½–1¾ HRS

1 For the marinade, put the onion, celery, carrot, whole garlic clove, and peppercorns in a pan. Pour in the wine and bring to the boil. Simmer for about 5 minutes, then cool and pour into a large bowl. Add the chicken and olive oil, cover, and refrigerate for 12–18 hours, turning the chicken occasionally.

2 Remove the chicken from the marinade and dry on kitchen paper. Strain the marinade and reserve the liquid and vegetables. Heat the vegetable oil and butter in a flameproof casserole until foaming. Add the bacon, brown it, remove, and set aside. Add the chicken and cook for 10–15 minutes until brown. Remove and set aside. Discard all but 2 tbsp of the fat. Reduce the heat to medium and cook the baby onions for 3–4 minutes until soft. Add the reserved vegetables and cook over a low heat for 5 minutes until soft. Add the flour and cook for 2 minutes until lightly browned. Stir in the reserved marinade, stock, chopped garlic, shallots, bouquet garni, and seasoning. Bring to the boil. Return the chicken, cover, and simmer over a low heat for 45–60 minutes until tender. Add the mushrooms with 15 minutes remaining.

This Italian classic is served with a zesty gremolata, and it would be delicious with a saffron and Parmesan risotto. Ask your butcher for a hindleg of veal as they are meatier than the front legs.

Osso bucco

SERVES 4–6

30g (1oz) plain flour
salt and freshly ground black pepper
4–6 pieces of veal shin on the bone (about 1.8kg/4lb)
2 tbsp vegetable oil
30g (1oz) butter
1 carrot, peeled and thinly sliced
2 onions, finely chopped
250ml (9fl oz) white wine
400g can Italian plum tomatoes, drained and
  coarsely chopped

1 garlic clove, finely chopped
finely grated zest of 1 orange
120ml (4fl oz) hot chicken or veal stock for
  both methods

FOR THE GREMOLATA
small bunch of flat-leaf parsley, leaves
  finely chopped
finely grated zest of 1 lemon
1 garlic clove, finely chopped

 in the slow cooker **PREP** 15 MINS **COOK** 15 MINS PRECOOKING;
AUTO/LOW 6–8 HRS OR **HIGH** 4 HRS

1 Preheat the slow cooker, if required. Put the flour on a large plate, season with salt and pepper, and stir to combine. Lightly coat the veal pieces with the seasoned flour. Heat the oil and butter in a large flameproof casserole over a medium heat, add the veal pieces (in batches and with extra oil, if necessary), and brown thoroughly on all sides. Transfer to a plate with a slotted spoon and set aside.

2 Add the carrot and onions and cook, stirring occasionally, until soft. Add the wine and boil until reduced by half. Stir in the tomatoes, garlic, and orange zest, and add seasoning. Transfer everything to the slow cooker, then lay the veal on top, and pour over the stock. Cover with the lid and cook for 6–8 hours on auto/low or on high for 4 hours.

3 For the gremolata, mix the parsley, lemon, and garlic in a small bowl. Put the veal on warmed plates, spoon the sauce on top and sprinkle with the gremolata.

 traditional method **PREP** 30–35 MINS **COOK** 1¾–2¼ HRS

1 Preheat the oven to 180°C (350°F/Gas 4). Put the flour on a large plate, season with salt and pepper, and stir to combine. Lightly coat the veal pieces with the seasoned flour. Heat the oil and butter in a large flameproof casserole over a medium heat, add the veal pieces (in batches and with extra oil, if necessary), and brown thoroughly on all sides. Transfer to a plate with a slotted spoon and set aside.

2 Add the carrot and onions and cook, stirring occasionally, until soft. Add the wine and boil until reduced by half. Stir in the tomatoes, garlic, and orange zest, and add seasoning. Transfer everything to the slow cooker, then lay the veal on top, and pour over the stock. Cover with the lid and put in the oven for 1½–2 hours until very tender. Check occasionally that it's not drying out, topping up with a little hot water if needed.

3 For the gremolata, mix the parsley, lemon, and garlic in a small bowl. Put the veal on warmed plates, spoon the sauce on top and sprinkle with the gremolata.

The vivid flavours of young lamb and baby vegetables marry perfectly in this springtime stew. Cook the lamb until it is soft enough to fall from a fork, while only lightly cooking the vegetables.

Navarin of lamb

SERVES 6 ❄ **FREEZE** UP TO 3 MONTHS

2 tbsp vegetable oil
500g (1lb 2oz) baby onions, peeled and left whole
750g (1lb 10oz) boneless lamb shoulder, cut into bite-sized pieces
2 tbsp plain flour, seasoned with salt and pepper
1 tbsp tomato purée
2 garlic cloves, finely chopped
1 bouquet garni made with 5–6 parsley sprigs, 2–3 thyme sprigs, and 1 bay leaf
about 600ml (1 pint) hot chicken or lamb stock for the slow cooker (750ml/1¼ pints for the traditional method)

750g (1lb 10oz) small new potatoes, peeled or scrubbed
250g (9oz) turnips, peeled and quartered
375g (13oz) tomatoes, skinned, deseeded, and coarsely chopped
250g (9oz) baby carrots, topped and small ones left whole or halved
150g (5½oz) fresh or frozen peas (optional)
250g (9oz) French beans, topped and chopped into 2.5cm (1in) pieces
salt and freshly ground black pepper
few sprigs of flat-leaf parsley, leaves chopped

 in the slow cooker 🕐 **PREP** 20 MINS **COOK** 20 MINS PRECOOKING; AUTO/LOW 6–8 HRS OR **HIGH** 3–4 HRS

1 Preheat the slow cooker, if required. Heat the oil in a large flameproof casserole over a medium heat, add the baby onions, and cook for 5–7 minutes until golden. Remove and set aside. Toss the lamb in the flour and cook (in batches, if necessary) for 5–8 minutes over a high heat until browned. Stir in the tomato purée, garlic, and bouquet garni, pour in enough stock to just cover, and bring to the boil.

2 Transfer to the slow cooker, cover with the lid, and cook on auto/low for 6–8 hours or on high for 3–4 hours. Add the baby onions, potatoes, turnips, tomatoes, and carrots for the last 2 hours of cooking and top up with a small amount of hot water to cover, if needed. Add the peas, if using, and beans for the last 15 minutes of cooking until they are just tender. Taste and season, if needed. To serve, ladle onto warmed plates and sprinkle over the parsley.

 traditional method 🕐 **PREP** 20 MINS **COOK** 2 HRS

1 Heat the oil in a large flameproof casserole over a medium heat, add the baby onions, and cook for 5–7 minutes until golden. Remove and set aside. Toss the lamb in the flour and cook (in batches, if necessary) for 5–8 minutes over a high heat until browned. Stir in the tomato purée, garlic, and bouquet garni, pour in enough stock to just cover, and bring to the boil. Cover with the lid and simmer for 1 hour.

2 Add the baby onions, potatoes, turnips, tomatoes, and carrots. Pour in more stock to almost cover the meat and vegetables. Cover and simmer for 20–25 minutes until the potatoes are tender to the point of a knife. Add the peas, if using, and beans and simmer until they are just tender. Be sure not to cook the navarin for any longer than necessary to cook the vegetables through; they should retain their fresh crunch and bright colours. Taste and adjust the seasoning, if needed. To serve, ladle onto warmed plates and sprinkle over the parsley.

This is a classic one-pot French dish in which chicken is simmered until the meat falls off the bone. If you can use a fresh chicken stock for this, all the better.

Chicken fricassée

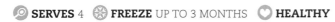 **SERVES** 4　**FREEZE** UP TO 3 MONTHS　**HEALTHY**

2 tbsp olive oil
4 chicken legs, divided into drumstick and thigh
  joints, skin removed
2 tbsp plain flour, seasoned with salt and pepper
4 shallots, sliced
2 garlic cloves, crushed
115g (4oz) button mushrooms, sliced

4 waxy potatoes, peeled and chopped into
  small pieces
2 tsp finely chopped rosemary leaves
150ml (5fl oz) dry white wine
300ml (10fl oz) hot chicken stock, for both methods
1 bay leaf
salt and freshly ground black pepper

 in the slow cooker　🕐 **PREP** 15 MINS　**COOK** 15 MINS PRECOOKING;
AUTO/LOW 5–6 HRS OR HIGH 3–4 HRS

1 Preheat the slow cooker, if required. Heat the oil in a large flameproof casserole over a medium heat. Toss the chicken pieces in the flour and then cook for 8–10 minutes, turning often, until golden brown. Remove and set aside.

2 Add the shallots to the casserole and cook for 2–3 minutes, stirring often. Stir in the garlic, mushrooms, potatoes, and rosemary and also cook for 2 minutes.

3 Pour in the wine and bring to the boil, then allow it to simmer and reduce for 1 minute. Transfer everything to the slow cooker and pour in the stock. Add the chicken and the bay leaf, cover with the lid, and cook on auto/low for 5–6 hours or on high for 3–4 hours. Discard the bay leaf and adjust the seasoning, if needed. Serve hot with courgettes or sautéed cabbage.

 traditional method　🕐 **PREP** 15 MINS　**COOK** 1 HR

1 Heat the oil in a large flameproof casserole over a medium heat. Toss the chicken pieces in the flour and then cook for 8–10 minutes, turning often, until golden brown. Remove and set aside.

2 Add the shallots to the casserole and cook for 2–3 minutes, stirring often. Stir in the garlic, mushrooms, potatoes, and rosemary and also cook for 2 minutes.

3 Pour in the wine and bring to the boil, then allow it to simmer and reduce for 1 minute. Pour in the stock, and bring to the boil. Return the chicken to the casserole, add the bay leaf, and cover tightly. Reduce the heat and cook gently for 45 minutes or until the chicken is very tender. Discard the bay leaf and adjust the seasoning, if needed. Serve hot with courgettes or sautéed cabbage.

This popular Mediterranean dish makes an easy vegetarian supper. Make ahead so the flavours become well acquainted, then reheat to serve. Any leftovers are just as good served cold.

Ratatouille

 SERVES 4 ❄ **FREEZE** UP TO 3 MONTHS

4 tbsp olive oil
1 small aubergine, about 225g (8oz), chopped
  into 2.5cm (1in) cubes
1 courgette, trimmed and sliced
1 onion, chopped
1 garlic clove, chopped

1 red pepper, deseeded and chopped into 2.5cm
  (1in) pieces
150ml (5fl oz) hot vegetable stock, for both methods
400g can chopped tomatoes
2 tsp chopped oregano, plus 2–3 sprigs to serve
salt and freshly ground black pepper

 in the slow cooker 🕐 **PREP** 15 MINS **COOK** 30 MINS PRECOOKING;
                                                    AUTO/LOW 4–5 HRS OR **HIGH** 2–3 HRS

1 Preheat the slow cooker, if required. Heat half the oil in a large heavy-based pan over a medium heat, add the aubergine, and cook for about 10 minutes until beginning to colour. Remove and set aside. Add the courgette, with more oil if necessary, and cook for 5–8 minutes until golden. Remove and set aside. Now add the onion together with any remaining oil, and cook for 4–5 minutes until soft. Stir in the garlic and peppers and cook for about 5 minutes to soften.

2 Pour in the stock and tomatoes with their juice, stir in the chopped oregano, and bring to the boil. Transfer to the slow cooker, cover with the lid, and cook on auto/low for 4–5 hours or on high for 2–3 hours. Stir through the aubergine and courgette for the last 30 minutes of cooking.

3 Taste and add seasoning, if needed. Spoon the ratatouille into a warmed serving bowl and top with the oregano sprigs. Serve with rice, bulgur wheat, or couscous, and sprinkle some grated cheese over the ratatouille, if you wish.

 traditional method 🕐 **PREP** 15 MINS **COOK** 1¼ HRS

1 Heat half the oil in a large heavy-based pan over a medium heat, add the aubergine, and cook for about 10 minutes until beginning to colour. Remove and set aside. Add the courgette, with more oil if necessary, and cook for 5–8 minutes until golden. Also remove and set aside. Now add the onion together with any remaining oil, and cook for 4–5 minutes until soft. Stir in the garlic and peppers and cook for about 5 minutes to soften.

2 Pour in the stock and tomatoes with their juice, stir in the chopped oregano, and bring to the boil. Reduce the heat to low and partially cover with the lid. Cook, stirring occasionally, for about 40 minutes, topping up with a little hot water if needed. Stir through the aubergine and courgette, and simmer for 10 minutes more.

3 Taste and add seasoning, if needed. Spoon the ratatouille into a warmed serving bowl and top with the oregano sprigs. Serve with rice, bulgur wheat, or couscous, and sprinkle some grated cheese over the ratatouille, if you wish.

This is a hearty bean and meat dish from southwest France. Use dried beans if you prefer, but they will need overnight soaking and boiling for 10 minutes before adding to the casserole.

Cassoulet de Toulouse

⊘ **SERVES** 4 ❄ **FREEZE** UP TO 3 MONTHS

1 tbsp olive oil
2 duck legs
4 Toulouse sausages
150g (5½oz) piece of pancetta or a whole chorizo sausage, chopped into small pieces
1 onion, peeled and finely chopped
1 carrot, peeled and chopped
4 garlic cloves, crushed
2 x 400g cans haricot beans, drained and rinsed

1 sprig of thyme, plus ½ tbsp chopped leaves
1 bay leaf
salt and freshly ground black pepper
2 tbsp tomato purée
400g can chopped tomatoes
150ml (5fl oz) white wine
½ day-old baguette, crusts removed and torn into pieces
1 tbsp chopped parsley

in the slow cooker 🕑 **PREP** 30 MINS **COOK** 50 MINS PRECOOKING; **AUTO/LOW** 6–8 HRS

1 Preheat the slow cooker, if required. Heat the oil in a large flameproof casserole over a medium-high heat and add the duck legs, skin-side down. Cook each side for 3–6 minutes until golden. Remove and reserve the duck fat. Add the sausages, cook for 7–8 minutes until browned, then remove and set aside. Cook the pancetta for 5 minutes and also remove and set aside. Add the onions and carrot, cook over a medium heat for 10 minutes until soft, then cook most of the garlic for 1 minute. Layer the ingredients in the slow cooker, beginning with half the beans, then the onion, carrot, sausages, pancetta, and duck legs, followed by the remaining beans, and adding the bay leaf and thyme as you go. Season with salt and pepper. Mix 400ml (14fl oz) of hot water with the tomato purée, tomatoes, and wine, then add to the slow cooker. Cover with the lid and cook on auto/low for 6–8 hours.

2 Put the baguette in a food processor with the remaining garlic. Process into coarse crumbs. Heat 2 tbsp of the duck fat in a heavy-based pan over a medium heat and fry the crumbs for 7–8 minutes until golden. Drain on kitchen paper and stir in the parsley. Sprinkle over the cassoulet and serve.

traditional method 🕑 **PREP** 30 MINS **COOK** 3¾ HRS

1 Preheat the oven to 140°C (275°F/Gas 1). Heat the oil in a large flameproof casserole over a medium-high heat and add the duck legs, skin-side down. Cook each side for 3–6 minutes until golden. Remove and reserve the duck fat. Add the sausages, cook for 7–8 minutes until browned, then remove and set aside. Cook the pancetta for 5 minutes and also remove and set aside. Add the onions and carrot, cook over a medium heat for 10 minutes until soft, then cook most of the garlic for 1 minute. Layer the ingredients in the casserole, beginning with half the beans, then onions, carrot, sausages, pancetta, and duck legs, followed by the remaining beans, and adding the bay leaf and thyme as you go. Season with salt and pepper. Mix 900ml (1½ pints) hot water with the tomato purée, tomatoes, and wine, then add to the casserole. Cover and cook in the oven for 3 hours, adding extra water if required.

2 Put the baguette in a food processor with the remaining garlic. Process into coarse crumbs. Heat 2 tbsp of the duck fat in a heavy-based pan over a medium heat and fry the crumbs for 7–8 minutes until golden. Drain on kitchen paper and stir in the parsley. Sprinkle over the cassoulet and serve.

Dumplings are the perfect addition to a casserole or stew as they make the dish a complete meal. For variety, add other herbs, such as thyme or tarragon, to the parsley in the mixture.

Vegetable casserole with dumplings

 SERVES 4–6 ❄ **FREEZE** UP TO 1 MONTH

1 tbsp olive oil
1 onion, roughly chopped
salt and freshly ground black pepper
3 garlic cloves, finely chopped
pinch of dried chilli flakes
2 leeks, trimmed and thickly sliced
3 carrots, peeled and roughly chopped
2 celery sticks, roughly chopped

1 tbsp plain flour
600ml (1 pint) hot vegetable stock for the slow cooker (900ml/1½ pints for the traditional method)
400g can haricot beans, drained and rinsed
few sprigs of rosemary
225g (8oz) self-raising flour
115g (4oz) vegetable suet
2 tbsp finely chopped flat-leaf parsley

 ### in the slow cooker 🕐 PREP 25 MINS COOK 20 MINS PRECOOKING; AUTO/LOW 6–8 HRS OR **HIGH** 4 HRS

1 Preheat the slow cooker, if required. Heat the oil in a large heavy-based pan over a medium heat, add the onion, and cook for 3–4 minutes until soft. Season with salt and pepper, then stir through the garlic and chilli flakes. Add the leeks, carrots, and celery and continue cooking for a further 10 minutes, stirring occasionally, until softened. Stir in the plain flour, then gradually stir in the stock. Add the haricot beans and rosemary, and transfer everything to the slow cooker. Cover with the lid and cook on auto/low for 6–8 hours or on high for 4 hours.

2 About 45 minutes before the end of the cooking time, prepare the dumplings. Mix together the self-raising flour, suet, and parsley and season well. Add about 120ml (4fl oz) cold water to form a soft, slightly sticky dough, trickling in more water if it seems too dry. Form into 12 balls and drop them into the stew for the last 30 minutes of cooking. Push them down a little so they are just immersed and cover with the lid. Remove the rosemary, ladle the casserole into warmed bowls, and serve with crusty bread.

traditional method 🕐 PREP 25 MINS COOK 1¼ HRS

1 Preheat the oven to 160°C (325°F/Gas 3). Heat the oil in a large flameproof casserole over a medium heat, add the onion, and cook for 3–4 minutes until soft. Season with salt and pepper, then stir through the garlic and chilli flakes. Add the leek, carrots, and celery and continue cooking for a further 10 minutes, stirring occasionally, until softened. Stir in the plain flour, then gradually stir in the stock. Add the haricot beans and rosemary. Bring to the boil, then reduce to a simmer, cover, and put in the oven for 1 hour, checking on the liquid level as it cooks and topping up with hot stock if needed.

2 While this is cooking, prepare the dumplings. Mix together the self-raising flour, suet, and parsley and season well. Add about 120ml (4fl oz) cold water to form a soft, slightly sticky dough, trickling in more water if it seems too dry. Form into 12 balls and drop them into the stew for the last 30 minutes of cooking. Push them down a little so they are just immersed and cover with the lid. Remove the lid for the final 10 minutes or until the dumplings are browned. Remove the rosemary, ladle the casserole into warmed bowls, and serve with crusty bread.

The all-important ingredient in a carbonnade – a classic Belgian casserole – is the beer. Here it is topped with slices of French bread and mustard, which soak into the pot and enhance the gravy.

Beef carbonnade

⊚ **SERVES** 4–6 ❊ **FREEZE** UP TO 3 MONTHS

knob of butter
2 tbsp olive oil
1.1kg (2½lb) skirt beef, cut into chunks
1–2 tbsp plain flour, seasoned with salt and pepper
12 baby shallots, peeled and left whole
salt and freshly ground black pepper
3 garlic cloves, finely chopped
1 tbsp demerara sugar

300ml (10fl oz) Belgian beer or dark brown ale
pinch of grated nutmeg
1 bouquet garni
450ml (15fl oz) hot beef stock for the slow cooker
  (900ml/1½ pints for the traditional method)
1 tbsp Dijon mustard
1 small French stick, cut into slices
handful of flat-leaf parsley, finely chopped

in the slow cooker 🕐 **PREP** 10 MINS **COOK** 25 MINS PRECOOKING; AUTO/LOW 8 HRS OR **HIGH** 4 HRS

1 Preheat the slow cooker, if required. Heat the butter and 1 tbsp of the oil in a large flameproof casserole over a medium-high heat. Toss the meat in the flour, and cook in batches for about 10 minutes until golden. Remove and set aside. Reduce the temperature, add the remaining oil, and cook the shallots for 8–10 minutes, stirring so they don't burn. Add seasoning, garlic, and sugar, and cook for a few minutes, adding more oil if needed. Remove and set aside.

2 Increase the heat, add the beer, and let it boil for a few minutes. Transfer the beer to the slow cooker, adding the meat, shallot mixture, nutmeg, and bouquet garni. Pour over the stock so it just covers the meat, cover with the lid, and cook on auto/low for 8 hours or on high for 4 hours.

3 Spread the mustard over the slices of French bread and place on top of the stew halfway through the cooking time. Remove the bouquet garni and sprinkle with parsley. Ladle into warmed large shallow bowls to serve.

traditional method 🕐 **PREP** 10 MINS **COOK** 3¼ HRS

1 Preheat the oven to 160°C (325°F/Gas 3). Heat the butter and 1 tbsp of the oil in a large flameproof casserole over a medium-high heat. Toss the meat in the flour, and cook in batches for about 10 minutes until golden. Remove and set aside. Reduce the temperature, add the remaining oil, and cook the shallots for 8–10 minutes, stirring so they don't burn. Add seasoning, garlic, and sugar, and cook for a few minutes, adding more oil if needed. Remove and set aside.

2 Increase the heat, add the beer, and let it boil for a few minutes. Then reduce the heat, return the meat and shallot mixture to the casserole, and add the nutmeg and bouquet garni. Pour over the stock, cover with the lid, and put the casserole in the oven for 2 hours or until the beef is meltingly tender. Check occasionally that it's not drying out, topping up with a little hot water if needed.

3 Spread the mustard over the slices of French bread and place on top of the stew. Cover with the lid and return to the oven for 30 minutes. Uncover and give the topping about 10 minutes to brown. Remove the bouquet garni and sprinkle with parsley. Ladle into warmed large shallow bowls to serve.

Cooking lamb on the bone in the pot adds lots more flavour to the dish. If you can't get hold of lamb shanks, neck of lamb would be a good alternative, and will take the same length of time to cook.

Lamb shanks with harissa and shallots

 SERVES 4 ❄ **FREEZE** UP TO 3 MONTHS

3–4 tbsp olive oil
2 large lamb shanks
1 tbsp plain flour, seasoned with salt and pepper
12 shallots, peeled and left whole
salt and freshly ground black pepper
2 garlic cloves, crushed
125g (4½oz) red lentils, rinsed and picked over for stones

400g can chopped tomatoes
450ml (15fl oz) hot chicken or vegetable stock for the slow cooker (600ml/1pint for the traditional method)
1 tbsp harissa paste
½ bunch of flat-leaf parsley, finely chopped
handful of mint, roughly chopped

 in the slow cooker 🕐 **PREP** 20 MINS   **COOK** 20 MINS PRECOOKING; **AUTO/LOW** 6–8 HRS OR **HIGH** 4–5 HRS

1 Preheat the slow cooker, if required. Heat 1 tbsp of the oil in a large flameproof casserole over a medium-high heat, and toss the lamb shanks in the flour. Cook the shanks in the oil for 5–6 minutes, turning so they become golden on all sides. Top up with oil as needed. Remove and set aside.

2 Add the remaining oil and reduce the heat to medium. Season the shallots with salt and pepper and cook, stirring, for 8–10 minutes until they begin to colour a little. Stir in the garlic and lentils, and transfer everything to the slow cooker, including the lamb.

3 Stir in the tomatoes and stock and add the harissa paste. Season, cover with the lid, and cook on auto/low for 6–8 hours or on high for 4–5 hours until the meat falls off the bone. Shred the meat off the bone and return to the slow cooker. Add the parsley and mint, and serve with boiled potatoes.

traditional method 🕐 **PREP** 20 MINS   **COOK** 2¼–2¾ HRS

1 Preheat the oven to 150°C (300°F/Gas 2). Heat 1 tbsp of the oil in a large flameproof casserole over a medium-high heat, and toss the lamb shanks in the flour. Cook the shanks in the oil for 5–6 minutes, turning so they become golden on all sides. Top up with oil as needed. Remove and set aside.

2 Add the remaining oil and reduce the heat to medium. Season the shallots with salt and pepper and cook, stirring, for 8–10 minutes until they begin to colour a little. Stir in the garlic and lentils, then tip in the tomatoes and stock, and bring to the boil. Reduce the heat and stir in the harissa paste, then return the lamb shanks to the casserole.

3 Cover the casserole with the lid and put in the oven for 2–2½ hours until the lamb is tender and falling off the bone. Check occasionally that it's not drying out, topping up with a little hot water if needed. Shred the meat off the bone and return to the casserole. Add the parsley and mint, and serve with boiled potatoes.

This is a lighter, vegetarian version of the traditional meaty cassoulet, featuring creamy haricot beans and a crispy, herby breadcrumb and Parmesan cheese topping.

Pumpkin and parsnip cassoulet

⊘ **SERVES** 4–6 ❄ **FREEZE** UP TO 3 MONTHS ♡ **HEALTHY**

2 tbsp olive oil
1 onion, finely chopped
salt and freshly ground black pepper
3 garlic cloves, finely chopped
1 tsp ground cloves
2 carrots, peeled and finely chopped
2 celery sticks, finely chopped
1 bay leaf
450g (1lb) pumpkin (prepared weight), chopped into bite-sized pieces
450g (1lb) small parsnips, sliced into rounds

250ml (9fl oz) white wine
few sprigs of thyme
4 tomatoes, chopped, or use a 400g can tomatoes
400g can haricot beans, rinsed and drained
300ml (10fl oz) hot vegetable stock for the slow cooker (900ml/1½ pints for the traditional method)

FOR THE TOPPING
125g (4½oz) breadcrumbs, lightly toasted
30g (1oz) Parmesan cheese, grated
1 tbsp chopped flat-leaf parsley

in the slow cooker ⏱ PREP 15 MINS COOK 20 MINS PRECOOKING; AUTO/LOW 8 HRS OR HIGH 4 HRS

1 Preheat the slow cooker, if required. Heat the oil in a large heavy-based pan over a medium heat, add the onion, and cook for 3–4 minutes until soft. Season with salt and pepper, add the garlic, cloves, carrots, celery, and bay leaf, and cook, stirring occasionally, on a very low heat for 8–10 minutes until it is all soft. Stir through the pumpkin and parsnip and cook for a few minutes more, then pour in the wine. Increase the heat, stir, and let it bubble for a minute or two. Then add the thyme, tomatoes, and beans.

2 Transfer everything to the slow cooker, pour over the stock, season, and stir. Cover with the lid and cook on auto/low for 8 hours or on high for 4 hours. An hour before the end of the cooking time, mix the topping ingredients together in a bowl, sprinkle over, and replace the lid. Ladle into warmed bowls and serve with crusty bread.

traditional method ⏱ PREP 15 MINS COOK 1¾ HRS

1 Preheat the oven to 180°C (350°F/Gas 4). Heat the oil in a large flameproof casserole over a medium heat, add the onion, and cook for 3–4 minutes until soft. Season with salt and pepper, add the garlic, cloves, carrots, celery, and bay leaf, and cook, stirring occasionally, on a very low heat for 8–10 minutes until it is all soft. Stir through the pumpkin and parsnip and cook for a few minutes more, then pour in the wine. Increase the heat, stir, and let it bubble for a minute or two. Then add the thyme, tomatoes, beans, and stock, and bring to the boil. Reduce to a simmer, season, cover with the lid, and put in the oven for 40 minutes.

2 Mix together the topping ingredients in a bowl, sprinkle it over the cassoulet and put back in the oven for 30 minutes. Then remove the lid and cook for about 10 minutes until the topping is golden. Ladle into warmed bowls and serve with crusty bread.

This is Brazil's national dish and is made with a variety of meats that mingle together for a delicious taste. Canned beans are used for ease but traditionally dried beans would be used.

Feijoada

SERVES 6

2 pig's trotters
250g (9oz) smoked pork ribs
175g (6oz) streaky bacon, left in 1 piece
200g can chopped tomatoes
1 tbsp tomato purée
1 bay leaf
salt and freshly ground black pepper
2 x 400g cans black-eyed beans, drained and rinsed

2 tbsp olive oil
300g (10oz) lean pork fillet, sliced, or steaks
1 small onion, finely chopped
2 garlic cloves, finely chopped
175g (6oz) chorizo, chopped into small chunks
1 green chilli, deseeded
1 orange, cut into wedges, to serve
3 spring onions, trimmed and chopped, to serve

in the slow cooker   ⏱ PREP 15 MINS   COOK 20 MINS PRECOOKING; AUTO/LOW 6–8 HRS OR HIGH 3–4 HRS

1 Preheat the slow cooker, if required. Place the pig's trotters, pork ribs, and streaky bacon in the slow cooker with the canned tomatoes and their juice, the tomato purée, bay leaf, salt and pepper, and beans. Cover with the lid and cook on auto/low for 6–8 hours or on high for 3–4 hours.

2 Heat 1 tbsp of the oil in a large flameproof casserole over a medium-high heat, and brown the pork fillet for about 5 minutes on each side. Remove and set aside. Add the remaining oil to the casserole and cook the onion and garlic over a medium heat for 3–4 minutes until soft. Add the chorizo and chilli and cook for a further 2 minutes. Transfer to the slow cooker, together with the pork fillet, for the last 45 minutes of cooking. To serve, remove the larger pieces of meat and cut into smaller pieces. Squash some of the beans with the back of a fork and remove the bay leaf. Transfer everything to a serving dish and garnish with orange wedges and spring onions. Serve with plain boiled rice, steamed or fried shredded kale, and a tomato salsa.

traditional method   ⏱ PREP 15 MINS   COOK 1¾ HRS

1 Place the pig's trotters, pork ribs, and streaky bacon in a large flameproof casserole with the canned tomatoes and their juice, the tomato purée, bay leaf, and salt and pepper. Add enough cold water to cover, bring to the boil, skim off any scum, cover, reduce the heat, and simmer for 50 minutes. Stir through the beans (reserving 3 tbsp) and top up with a little hot water, if needed, to just cover. Continue to cook, covered, over a low heat for a further 20 minutes.

2 Heat 1 tbsp of the oil in a heavy-based frying pan over a medium-high heat, and brown the pork fillet for about 5 minutes on each side. Add to the casserole and continue to cook for a further 10 minutes or until the meats are tender. Wipe out the frying pan, add the remaining oil, and cook the onion and garlic over a medium heat for 3–4 minutes until soft. Add the chorizo and chilli and cook for a further 2 minutes, stirring. Add the reserved beans to the frying pan and squash them with the back of a fork. Transfer everything to the casserole, stir, and cook for a further 10 minutes. To serve, remove the larger pieces of meat and cut into smaller pieces. Remove the bay leaf and transfer everything to a serving dish. Garnish with orange wedges and spring onions. Serve with plain boiled rice, steamed or fried shredded kale, and a tomato salsa.

This classic Spanish dish of brown lentils relies on salty bacon, spicy chorizo, and paprika for its flavour. The lentils benefit from slow cooking as they become soft, tender, and don't need soaking.

Spanish lentils

 SERVES 4

500g (1lb 2oz) brown lentils, rinsed and picked over
  for any stones
2 bay leaves
85g (3oz) chorizo, sliced
2 tbsp olive oil
2 garlic cloves, sliced
1 small slice of bread

salt
1 onion, finely chopped
75g (2½oz) thickly sliced tocino or streaky bacon,
  cut into strips
1 tbsp flour
1 tsp sweet paprika
90ml (3fl oz) hot vegetable stock, for both methods

 in the slow cooker ⏱ **PREP** 15 MINS   **COOK** 10 MINS PRECOOKING;
                                                       AUTO/LOW 5–6 HRS OR **HIGH** 3–4 HRS

1 Preheat the slow cooker, if required. Put the lentils in the slow cooker with just enough water to cover, plus an extra 100ml (3½fl oz). Stir in the the bay leaves and chorizo, cover with the lid, and cook on auto/low for 5–6 hours or on high for 3–4 hours.

2 Meanwhile, heat 1 tbsp of the oil in a heavy-based pan over a medium-low heat and cook the garlic, stirring, for about 30 seconds until softened but not browned. Remove and set aside. Add the bread to the pan and cook over a medium heat until lightly browned on both sides. Transfer to a food processor with the garlic and season with salt. Process into coarse crumbs, then set aside.

3 Add the remaining oil to the pan together with the onion and tocino or streaky bacon. Cook for 3–4 minutes until the onion is soft and the bacon is cooked. Stir in the flour and paprika and cook for 1 minute before adding the stock. Bring to the boil and simmer for 2 minutes, then stir into the lentils for the last 30 minutes of cooking. Stir through the crumb mixture for the last 15 minutes of cooking. Transfer to a warmed serving dish and serve with crusty bread.

traditional method ⏱ **PREP** 15 MINS   **COOK** 1 HR

1 Put the lentils into a large saucepan with 1 litre (1¾ pints) water, the bay leaves, and chorizo. Bring to the boil, then simmer for 35–40 minutes or until the lentils are tender.

2 Meanwhile, heat 1 tbsp of the oil in a heavy-based pan over a medium-low heat and cook the garlic, stirring, for about 30 seconds until softened but not browned. Remove and set aside. Add the bread to the pan and cook over a medium heat until lightly browned on both sides. Transfer to a food processor with the garlic and season with salt. Process into coarse crumbs, then set aside. When the lentils are cooked, drain, then return to the saucepan. Stir in the crumb mixture until combined.

3 Add the remaining oil to the heavy-based pan together with the onion and tocino or streaky bacon. Cook for 3–4 minutes until the onion is soft and the bacon is cooked. Stir in the flour and paprika and cook for 1 minute before adding the stock. Bring to the boil and simmer for 2 minutes, then stir into the lentils. If necessary, add a little more hot water to moisten the lentils. Transfer to a warmed serving dish and serve with crusty bread.

This is an intensely flavoured dish from France that is well worth the effort. The fat that the duck legs are cooked in – and this can be duck or goose fat – can be strained, left to cool, and re-used.

French-style duck and lentils

⊙ SERVES 4

4 duck legs
500g (1lb 2oz) duck fat
few sprigs of rosemary
1 tbsp olive oil
1 onion, finely chopped
salt and freshly ground black pepper
2 garlic cloves, finely chopped
few sprigs of thyme, leaves only
2 carrots, peeled and finely diced
1 bay leaf
1 tbsp dry sherry

250g (9oz) Puy lentils, rinsed and picked over for any stones
450ml (15fl oz) hot chicken stock, for both methods

FOR THE MARINADE
3 tbsp brandy
1 tbsp black peppercorns, crushed
3 garlic cloves, finely chopped
pinch of ground cinnamon
few sprigs of thyme
1 tbsp sea salt

in the slow cooker ⊙ **PREP** 15 MINS, PLUS MARINATING   **COOK HIGH** 50 MINS, THEN **AUTO/LOW** 3½–4 HRS

1 Put the duck legs in a shallow dish and add all the marinade ingredients. Cover with cling film, sit a weight on top, and put in the fridge overnight. Preheat the slow cooker, if required. Remove the duck from the marinade and set aside. Discard the liquid. Put the duck fat in the slow cooker with the rosemary, cover, and melt on high for about 50 minutes. Add the duck legs, cover with the lid, and cook on auto/low for 3½–4 hours until the meat is fork tender. Remove the legs and drain off excess fat.

2 Meanwhile, heat the oil in a large heavy-based pan over a medium heat, add the onion, and cook for 3–4 minutes until soft. Season, then stir through the garlic, thyme, carrots, and bay leaf. Cook on a low heat for 6–10 minutes, stirring, then increase the heat, add the sherry, and cook for 2 minutes. Stir through the lentils and then the stock. Bring to the boil, reduce to a simmer, and cook for about 40 minutes or until the lentils are tender. Top up with more hot water if the lentils start to dry out. Taste and season as needed, remove the bay leaf and thyme sprigs, and serve with the duck legs.

traditional method ⊙ **PREP** 15 MINS, PLUS MARINATING   **COOK** 3¾ HRS

1 Put the duck legs in a shallow dish and add all the marinade ingredients. Cover with cling film, sit a weight on top, and refrigerate overnight. Preheat the oven to 150°C (300°F/Gas 2), and melt the duck fat in a large flameproof casserole. Transfer the legs to the casserole (discard the liquid), ensuring they are covered in the fat. Throw in the rosemary, cover, and put in the oven for 3 hours or until the meat is fork tender and the skin crispy. Let the casserole cool, remove the legs, and drain off excess fat.

2 Meanwhile, heat the oil in a large heavy-based pan over a medium heat, add the onion, and cook for 3–4 minutes until soft. Season, then stir through the garlic, thyme, carrots, and bay leaf. Cook on a low heat for 6–10 minutes, stirring, then increase the heat, add the sherry, and cook for 2 minutes. Stir through the lentils and then the stock. Bring to the boil, reduce to a simmer, and cook for about 40 minutes or until the lentils are tender. Top up with more hot water if the lentils start to dry out. Taste and season as needed, remove the bay leaf and thyme sprigs, and serve with the duck legs.

This is a comforting dish that can be made with chicken or turkey. The cobbler topping makes it a substantial all-in-one dish that can be served without any other extras if there isn't enough time.

Chicken cobbler

 SERVES 4 ✳ **FREEZE** UP TO 3 MONTHS

3 tbsp olive oil
1 onion, finely chopped
salt and freshly ground black pepper
3 garlic cloves, finely chopped
3 parsnips, peeled and sliced
6 chicken thighs, with skin on
1 tbsp flour, seasoned with salt and pepper
120ml (4fl oz) Marsala wine, sherry, or white wine

few tarragon leaves
about 250ml (9fl oz) hot chicken stock for the slow cooker (450ml/15fl oz for the traditional method)
125g (4½oz) plain flour, sifted
50g (1¾oz) butter, softened
25g (scant 1oz) Cheddar cheese, grated
3–4 tbsp buttermilk

 in the slow cooker 🕐 **PREP** 20 MINS **COOK** 15 MINS PRECOOKING; **AUTO/LOW** 6–8 HRS OR **HIGH** 4 HRS

1 Preheat the slow cooker, if required. Heat 1 tbsp of the oil in a large flameproof casserole over a medium heat, add the onion, and cook for 3–4 minutes until soft. Season with salt and pepper, then stir in the garlic and parsnips and cook for a few more minutes until the parsnips take on some colour. Remove the vegetables and set aside. Heat the remaining oil in the casserole over a higher heat. Toss the chicken in the flour and cook, skin-side down, for 8–10 minutes or until golden all over. Pour in the Marsala and bring to the boil, then return the onion and parsnips to the casserole, add the tarragon, and transfer everything to the slow cooker. Pour over enough stock to cover, season, and cover with the lid. Cook on auto/low for 6–8 hours or on high for 4 hours.

3 Meanwhile, for the cobblers, put the sifted flour in a bowl, season, then rub in the butter until it resembles fine breadcrumbs. Stir in the cheese and add the buttermilk to form a dough. Roll out on a lightly floured surface to 2.5cm (1in) thick and cut out about ten 5cm (2in) diameter rounds. For the last hour of cooking, place them around the edge of the stew and re-cover.

 traditional method 🕐 **PREP** 20 MINS **COOK** 2¼ HRS

1 Preheat the oven to 150°C (300°F/Gas 2). Heat 1 tbsp of the oil in a large flameproof casserole over a medium heat, add the onion, and cook for 3–4 minutes until soft. Season with salt and pepper, then stir in the garlic and parsnips and cook for a few more minutes until the parsnips take on some colour. Remove the vegetables and set aside. Heat the remaining oil in the casserole over a higher heat.

2 Toss the chicken in the flour and cook, skin-side down, for 8–10 minutes, or until golden all over. Pour in the Marsala and bring to the boil, then return the onion and parsnips to the casserole, add the tarragon, and pour over the stock. Bring to the boil, reduce to a simmer, cover with the lid, and put in the oven for 2 hours. Check occasionally that it's not drying out, topping up with a little hot water if needed.

3 Meanwhile, for the cobblers, put the sifted flour into a bowl, season, then rub in the butter until it resembles fine breadcrumbs. Stir in the cheese and add the buttermilk to form a dough. Roll out onto a lightly floured surface to 2.5cm (1in) thick and cut out about ten 5cm (2in) diameter rounds. For the last 30 minutes of cooking, place them around the edge of the stew and return to the oven, uncovered.

Dried fruit works well with a fatty meat such as pork belly – it creates a delicious, sweet sauce that cuts through the richness. The earthiness of celeriac is a great addition.

Belly pork and prunes

SERVES 4–6

1 tbsp olive oil
1.1kg (2½lb) pork belly, cut into bite-sized pieces
salt and freshly ground black pepper
1 onion, finely sliced
3 garlic cloves, finely chopped
1 tbsp sherry vinegar
120ml (4fl oz) white wine

600ml (1 pint) hot vegetable stock for the slow cooker (900ml/1½ pints for the traditional method)
140g (5oz) soft prunes, finely chopped
6 sage leaves, finely shredded
600g (1lb 5oz) celeriac, peeled and chopped into bite-sized pieces

in the slow cooker   **PREP** 15 MINS   **COOK** 30 MINS PRECOOKING; **AUTO/LOW** 8 HRS

1 Preheat the slow cooker, if required. Heat half the oil in a large flameproof casserole over a high heat and season the pork belly with salt and pepper. Add the pork (in batches, if necessary), skin-side down, and cook until it turns golden and begins to crisp a little. Remove and sit the pork on kitchen paper to drain.

2 Heat the remaining oil in the casserole over a medium heat, add the onion, and cook for 3–4 minutes until soft. Then stir in the garlic and cook for a minute more. Increase the heat and add the sherry vinegar, letting it simmer for 2–3 minutes. Pour in the wine and continue to boil for a few more minutes until the alcohol evaporates.

3 Transfer everything to the slow cooker, including the pork. Pour over the stock and stir in the prunes, sage, and celeriac. Cover with the lid and cook on auto/low for 8 hours. Taste and season more if needed, and serve with creamy mashed potatoes.

traditional method   **PREP** 15 MINS   **COOK** 3–3½ HRS

1 Preheat the oven to 160°C (325°F/Gas 3). Heat half the oil in a large flameproof casserole over a high heat and season the pork belly with salt and pepper. Add the pork (in batches, if necessary), skin-side down, and cook until it turns golden and begins to crisp a little. Remove and sit the pork on kitchen paper to drain.

2 Heat the remaining oil in the casserole over a medium heat, add the onion, and cook for 3–4 minutes until soft. Then stir in the garlic and cook for a minute more. Increase the heat and add the sherry vinegar, letting it simmer for 2–3 minutes. Pour in the wine and continue to boil for a few more minutes until the alcohol evaporates.

3 Add the stock and stir to scrape up the bits from the bottom of the casserole. Return the pork to the casserole and stir in the prunes, sage, and celeriac. Bring back to the boil, cover, and put in the oven for 2½–3 hours. Check occasionally that it's not drying out, topping up with a little hot water if needed. Taste and season more if needed, and serve with creamy mashed potatoes.

Here are some hot and spicy melt-in-your-mouth meatballs all tumbled together and cooked slowly in a zingy tomato sauce. If you are a fan of spicy food, don't deseed the chillies.

Mexican meatballs

 SERVES 4–6 ❄ **FREEZE** UP TO 3 MONTHS

700g (1lb 9oz) minced beef
1 garlic clove, finely chopped
2 red chillies, deseeded and finely chopped
½ tsp ground cumin
salt and freshly ground black pepper
1 large egg, lightly beaten
2 tbsp fresh white breadcrumbs
bunch of coriander, finely chopped
2–3 tbsp plain flour
3 tbsp olive oil

FOR THE SAUCE
1 large onion, finely chopped
1 garlic clove, finely chopped
1 red pepper, deseeded and finely chopped
½ tsp ground coriander
1 cinnamon stick, broken
pinch of dried chilli flakes
splash of Tabasco sauce
½ tsp caster sugar
2 x 400g cans whole tomatoes
150ml (5fl oz) hot vegetable stock, for both methods

 in the slow cooker ⏱ PREP 20 MINS   COOK 20 MINS PRECOOKING; **AUTO/LOW** 6–8 HRS

1 Preheat the slow cooker, if required. Put the minced beef, garlic, chillies, and cumin into a bowl and season. Combine with your hands, then add the egg, breadcrumbs, and fresh coriander, and mix well again. Shape the mixture into about 20 small balls and toss lightly in the flour. Heat 1 tbsp of the oil in a large flameproof casserole over a medium-high heat and cook half the meatballs (in batches and with extra oil, if necessary) for 6–8 minutes until brown all over. Remove with a slotted spoon and sit on some kitchen paper to drain. Wipe the casserole out with kitchen paper.

2 To make the sauce, heat the remaining 1 tbsp of oil in the casserole over a medium heat, add the onion, and cook for 3–4 minutes until soft. Stir in the garlic and red pepper, and cook for 3 minutes. Transfer the cooked vegetables to the slow cooker along with the remaining ingredients. Add seasoning, cover with the lid, and cook on auto/low for 6–8 hours. Taste and add more Tabasco sauce, if needed. Serve with rice and a green salad.

 traditional method ⏱ PREP 20 MINS   COOK 1¾–2¼ HRS

1 Preheat the oven to 180°C (350°F/Gas 4). Put the minced beef, garlic, chillies, and cumin into a bowl and season. Combine with your hands, then add the egg, breadcrumbs, and fresh coriander, and mix well again. Shape the mixture into about 20 small balls and toss lightly in the flour. Heat 1 tbsp of the oil in a large flameproof casserole over a medium-high heat and cook half the meatballs (in batches and with extra oil, if necessary) for 6–8 minutes until brown all over. Remove with a slotted spoon and sit on some kitchen paper to drain. Wipe the casserole out with kitchen paper.

2 To make the sauce, heat the remaining 1 tbsp of oil in the casserole over a medium heat, add the onion, and cook for 3–4 minutes until soft. Stir in the garlic and red pepper and cook for 3 minutes, then add the remaining ingredients and bring to the boil. Reduce to a simmer and add the meatballs and stock, pushing the meatballs down so they are immersed in the liquid. Add seasoning, cover, and put in the oven for 1½–2 hours. Check occasionally that it's not drying out, topping up with a little hot water if needed. Taste and add more Tabasco sauce, if needed. Serve with rice and a green salad.

Legend has it that one of Louis XIV's mistresses created this dish in an attempt to stay in the king's good graces. It is delicious, with its succulent chops between layers of sliced potatoes and onions.

Lamb chops champvallon

 SERVES 4

1 tbsp olive oil
6–8 lamb loin chops, each 2.5cm (1in) thick, (total weight about 1kg/2¼lb), trimmed of any excess fat
4 onions, thinly sliced
1.1kg (2½lb) baking potatoes, peeled and very thinly sliced

small bunch of thyme, leaves chopped, plus a few sprigs, to serve
salt and freshly ground black pepper
3 garlic cloves, finely chopped
about 600ml (1 pint) hot vegetable stock for the slow cooker (about 1 litre/1¾ pints for the traditional method)

 in the slow cooker 🕒 **PREP** 20 MINS **COOK** 15 MINS PRECOOKING; **AUTO/LOW** 6–8 HRS

1 Preheat the slow cooker, if required. Heat the oil in a large flameproof casserole over a high heat. Add the chops and cook for 1–2 minutes on each side, until well browned. Remove from the casserole and set aside.

2 Pour off all but about 1 tbsp of fat from the casserole. Add the onions and cook over a medium heat for 3–4 minutes until soft. Transfer to a large bowl.

3 Gently stir the potato slices into the softened onions and thyme leaves and season with salt and pepper. Spread half the potato mixture at the bottom of the slow cooker, then sprinkle with the garlic. Arrange the chops on top. Cover with the remaining potato, arranging the slices neatly in rows. Pour over enough stock to come just to the top of the potatoes. Cover with the lid and cook on auto/low for 6–8 hours. Serve the chops, potatoes, and onion with a spoonful of the cooking liquid, garnished with sprigs of thyme.

traditional method 🕒 **PREP** 25 MINS **COOK** 2¼ HRS

1 Preheat the oven to 180°C (350°F/Gas 4). Heat the oil in a large flameproof casserole over a high heat. Add the chops and cook for 1–2 minutes on each side, until well browned. Remove from the casserole and set aside.

2 Pour off all but about 1 tbsp of fat from the casserole. Add the onions and cook over a medium heat for 3–4 minutes until soft. Transfer to a large bowl.

3 Gently stir the potato slices into the softened onions and thyme leaves and season with salt and pepper. Brush a 23 x 32cm (9 x 13in) baking dish with oil. Spread half the potato mixture on the dish, then sprinkle with the garlic. Arrange the chops on top. Cover with the remaining potato, arranging the slices neatly in rows. Pour over enough stock to come just to the top of the potatoes. Bake, uncovered, for 2 hours, or until the lamb and potatoes are tender when pierced. Serve the chops, potatoes, and onion with a spoonful of the cooking liquid, garnished with sprigs of thyme.

Full of festive flavours, you can make this stew using leftover turkey meat if you have some. If you can't find fresh or frozen cranberries, use a tablespoon or two of cranberry sauce instead.

Turkey and cranberry casserole

 SERVES 4–6 ❄ **FREEZE** UP TO 3 MONTHS

2 large turkey breasts
salt and freshly ground black pepper
2–3 tbsp olive oil
4 sausages, sliced
1 red onion, finely sliced
3 garlic cloves, finely chopped
250g (9oz) chestnut mushrooms, quartered

few sprigs of rosemary
1 tbsp Dijon mustard
250ml (9fl oz) red wine
450ml (15fl oz) hot chicken stock for the slow cooker
 (600ml/1 pint for the traditional method)
handful of fresh or frozen cranberries
250g (9oz) fine green beans, trimmed

 in the slow cooker 🕑 **PREP** 15 MINS   **COOK** 15 MINS PRECOOKING;
AUTO/LOW 6–8 HRS OR **HIGH** 4 HRS

1 Preheat the slow cooker, if required. Season the turkey breasts with salt and pepper, and heat half the oil in a large flameproof casserole over a medium-high heat. Add the turkey to the casserole and cook for 6–8 minutes until golden. Remove and set aside.

2 Heat the remaining oil in the casserole and cook the sausage slices for 3–4 minutes until beginning to colour. Push them to one side, add the onion, and cook for 2–3 minutes until soft. Stir through the garlic, mushrooms, rosemary, and mustard and cook for a minute, then increase the heat and add the wine. Let the sauce bubble for a minute, then add the stock and bring to the boil.

3 Transfer everything to the slow cooker, including the turkey and cranberries, followed by seasoning, and cover with the lid. Cook on auto/low for 6–8 hours or on high for 4 hours. Add the beans for the last 15 minutes of cooking. Remove the rosemary and the turkey breasts with a slotted spoon and shred the meat with a fork. Return the meat to the slow cooker and stir in. Serve with creamy mashed potatoes or boiled potatoes.

traditional method 🕑 **PREP** 15 MINS   **COOK** 1¼–1¾ HRS

1 Preheat the oven to 160°C (325°F/Gas 3). Season the turkey breasts with salt and pepper, and heat half the oil in a large flameproof casserole over a medium-high heat. Add the turkey to the casserole and cook for 6–8 minutes until golden. Remove and set aside.

2 Heat the remaining oil in the casserole and cook the sausage slices for 3–4 minutes until beginning to colour. Push them to one side, add the onion, and cook for 2–3 minutes until soft. Stir through the garlic, mushrooms, rosemary, and mustard and cook for a minute, then increase the heat and add the wine. Let the sauce bubble for a minute, then add the stock and bring to the boil.

3 Return the turkey to the casserole, add seasoning, and stir through the cranberries. Cover with the lid and put in the oven for 1–1½ hours. Check occasionally that it's not drying out, topping up with a little hot water if needed. Add the beans for the last 15 minutes of cooking. Remove the rosemary and the turkey breasts with a slotted spoon and shred the meat with a fork. Return the meat to the casserole and stir in. Serve with creamy mashed potatoes or boiled potatoes.

Pork teams wonderfully with fruit. Red cabbage can look very bulky when first added to the slow cooker or casserole, but it soon reduces and adds a sweet, distinctive flavour to the rest of the dish.

Pork with red cabbage, pears, and ginger

 SERVES 6 **HEALTHY**

1 tbsp olive oil
1 onion, sliced
3 garlic cloves, finely chopped
½ tsp caraway seeds
2 tsp paprika
grated zest of 1 lemon
few sprigs of thyme
1.1kg (2½lb) pork leg, cut into chunky pieces
1 tbsp plain flour, seasoned with salt and pepper

½ red cabbage, cored and shredded
250ml (9fl oz) white wine
300ml (10fl oz) hot vegetable stock for the slow cooker (600ml/1 pint for the traditional method)
3 sweet pears, quartered, cored, and peeled
5cm (2in) piece of fresh root ginger, peeled and finely sliced
salt and freshly ground black pepper

 in the slow cooker 🕐 **PREP** 20 MINS **COOK** 15 MINS PRECOOKING; **AUTO/LOW** 8 HRS OR **HIGH** 4 HRS

1 Preheat the slow cooker, if required. Heat the oil in a large flameproof casserole over a medium heat, add the onion, and cook for 3–4 minutes until soft. Stir in the garlic, caraway seeds, paprika, lemon zest, and thyme and cook for a minute more.

2 Toss the pork in the flour and add to the casserole. Turn to coat, then increase the heat and cook, stirring occasionally, for 5–8 minutes. Stir through the cabbage, increase the heat, and add the wine, letting it bubble for a minute.

3 Transfer everything to the slow cooker, add the stock, and stir in the pears and ginger. Cover with the lid, and cook on auto/low for 8 hours or on high for 4 hours. Taste and season as needed, remove the thyme, and serve with rice or mashed potatoes.

traditional method 🕐 **PREP** 20 MINS **COOK** 1¾ HRS

1 Preheat the oven to 180°C (350°F/Gas 4). Heat the oil in a large flameproof casserole over a medium heat, add the onion, and cook for 3–4 minutes until soft. Stir in the garlic, caraway seeds, paprika, lemon zest, and thyme and cook for a minute more.

2 Toss the pork in the flour and add to the casserole. Turn to coat, then increase the heat and cook, stirring occasionally, for 5–8 minutes. Stir through the cabbage, increase the heat, and add the wine, letting it bubble for a minute. Add the stock, bring to the boil, then reduce to a simmer and add the pears and ginger to the casserole.

3 Cover with the lid and put in the oven for 1½ hours. Check occasionally that it's not drying out, topping up with a little hot water if needed. Taste and season as needed, remove the thyme, and serve with rice or mashed potatoes.

There are numerous versions of the "daube", but all are cooked in red wine. Choose a robust wine that you would happily drink. Throw in a cinnamon stick, if you wish, for a touch of warm spice.

Provençal lamb daube with olives

⏱ **SERVES** 4–6 ❄ **FREEZE** UP TO 3 MONTHS

1 orange, zest peeled in wide strips
2 garlic cloves, finely chopped
500ml (16fl oz) red wine
2 bay leaves
3–4 sprigs each of rosemary, thyme, and parsley
10 peppercorns
900g (2lb) boned lamb shoulder, cut into large cubes
2 tbsp olive oil
salt and freshly ground black pepper

300g (10oz) piece of smoked streaky bacon, cut into 5mm (¼in) lardons
400g can chopped tomatoes
2 onions, sliced
2 carrots, peeled and sliced
175g (6oz) mushrooms, trimmed and sliced
140g (5oz) stoned green olives
200ml (7fl oz) hot beef stock for the slow cooker (250ml/9fl oz for the traditional method)

in the slow cooker
⏱ **PREP** 15 MINS, PLUS MARINATING **COOK** 10 MINS PRECOOKING; AUTO/LOW 6–8 HRS

1 To make the marinade, combine the orange zest, garlic, wine, bay leaves, herbs, and peppercorns in a bowl. Add the lamb and mix well. Pour the oil on top and add seasoning. Cover and refrigerate, turning occasionally, and leave to marinate for 2 hours or up to 12 hours if time permits.

2 Preheat the slow cooker, if required. Put the bacon in a large heavy-based pan of water, bring to the boil, and blanch for 5 minutes. Drain and rinse with cold water. Remove the lamb from the marinade and dry on kitchen paper. Strain the marinade, reserving the liquid, bay leaf, and zest.

3 Put the bacon on the bottom of the slow cooker and cover with the lamb. Layer the tomatoes and onions on top, then the carrots, mushrooms, and olives. Pour in the strained marinade and stock, season with pepper, and add the bay leaf and zest. Cover with the lid and cook on auto/low for 6–8 hours. Remove the bay leaf and zest, taste, and season if needed. Serve with mashed potatoes.

traditional method
⏱ **PREP** 45–50 MINS, PLUS MARINATING **COOK** 3¾–4¼ HRS

1 To make the marinade, combine the orange zest, garlic, wine, bay leaves, herbs, and peppercorns in a bowl. Add the lamb and mix well. Pour the oil on top and add seasoning. Cover and refrigerate, turning occasionally, and leave to marinate for 2 hours or up to 12 hours if time permits.

2 Preheat the oven to 150°C (300°F/Gas 2). Put the bacon in a large heavy-based pan of water, bring to the boil, and blanch for 5 minutes. Drain and rinse with cold water. Remove the lamb from the marinade and dry on kitchen paper. Strain the marinade, reserving the liquid, bay leaf, and zest.

3 Put the bacon on the bottom of a large casserole and cover with the lamb. Layer the tomatoes and onions on top, then the carrots, mushrooms, and olives. Pour in the strained marinade and stock, season with pepper, and add the bay leaf and zest. Bring to the boil, cover with the lid, and put in the oven for 3½–4 hours. Check occasionally that it's not drying out, topping up with a little hot water if needed. Remove the bay leaf and zest, taste, and season if needed. Serve with mashed potatoes.

Sweet Madeira wine adds a wonderful flavour to the sauce in this dish, and wide noodles are the perfect accompaniment. If you don't have any chicken stock to hand, use water instead.

Duck with turnips and apricots

SERVES 4 **FREEZE** UP TO 3 MONTHS

4 portions of duck
salt and freshly ground black pepper
1 tbsp vegetable oil
15g (½oz) butter
2 tbsp plain flour
175ml (6fl oz) dry white wine
500ml (16fl oz) hot chicken stock, plus more
  if needed, for both methods

1 bouquet garni, made with 5–6 parsley sprigs,
  2–3 thyme sprigs, and 1 bay leaf
2 shallots, finely chopped
12–16 pickling onions, peeled and left whole
500g (1lb 2oz) turnips, peeled and roughly chopped
1 tsp granulated sugar
4 tbsp Madeira wine
175g (6oz) ready-to-eat dried apricots

in the slow cooker **PREP** 20 MINS **COOK** 30 MINS PRECOOKING; AUTO/LOW 6–8 HRS OR **HIGH** 3–4 HRS

1 Preheat the slow cooker, if required. Season the duck. Heat the oil and butter in a large flameproof casserole over a low heat and add the duck, skin-side down. Cook for 20–25 minutes until browned and the fat has rendered. Turn over and cook for only about 5 minutes until browned. Remove and set aside, draining and reserving the duck fat. Heat 2–3 tbsp of the duck fat in the casserole. Add the flour and cook, stirring constantly, for 1–2 minutes until lightly browned but not burnt. Stir in the white wine, stock, bouquet garni, shallots, and seasoning, and bring to the boil. Transfer everything to the slow cooker, including the duck, cover with the lid, and cook on auto/low for 6–8 hours or on high for 3–4 hours.

2 Meanwhile, heat 1–2 tbsp duck fat in the casserole over a medium heat. Add the onions, turnips, sugar, and seasoning and cook, stirring occasionally, for 5–7 minutes, until the vegetables are browned and begin to caramelize. Add to the slow cooker together with the Madeira wine and apricots for the last 1½ hours of cooking. Skim off any fat from the surface, remove the bouquet garni, taste, and add seasoning, if needed. Serve on warmed plates on a bed of wide noodles.

traditional method **PREP** 20 MINS **COOK** 1½–2 HRS

1 Preheat the oven to 180°C (350°F/Gas 4). Season the duck. Heat the oil and butter in a large flameproof casserole over a low heat and add the duck, skin-side down. Cook for 20–25 minutes until browned and the fat has rendered. Turn over and cook for only about 5 minutes until browned. Remove and set aside, draining and reserving the duck fat. Heat 2–3 tbsp of the duck fat in the casserole. Add the flour and cook, stirring constantly, for 1–2 minutes until lightly browned but not burnt. Stir in the white wine, stock, bouquet garni, shallots, and seasoning, and bring to the boil. Return the duck, cover with the lid, and put in the oven for 40–45 minutes.

2 Meanwhile, heat 1–2 tbsp duck fat in a heavy-based pan over a medium heat. Add the onions, turnips, sugar, and seasoning and cook, stirring occasionally, for 5–7 minutes, until the vegetables are browned and begin to caramelize. Add to the casserole with the Madeira wine and apricots, and top up with hot water if necessary. Cover with the lid and return to the oven for 20–25 minutes, until the duck and vegetables are tender. Skim off any fat from the surface, remove the bouquet garni, taste, and add seasoning, if needed. Serve on warmed plates on a bed of wide noodles.

Everyday minced lamb is transformed into a Middle Eastern favourite, packed with herbs, spices, and zesty flavours and served in a colourful tomato and sweet pepper sauce.

Lebanese meatballs

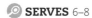 **SERVES** 6–8

675g (1½lb) lean lamb mince
2 onions, finely chopped
4 garlic cloves, finely chopped
handful of coriander, finely chopped
handful of flat-leaf parsley, finely chopped
2 tsp paprika
grated zest and juice of 1 lemon
2 tbsp tomato purée
4 tbsp pine nuts

2 eggs
6 tbsp plain flour
salt and freshly ground black pepper
4 tbsp olive oil
4 potatoes, peeled and chopped into bite-sized pieces
1 red pepper, deseeded and sliced
1 yellow pepper, deseeded and sliced
2 x 400g cans chopped tomatoes
1 tsp fennel seeds, crushed

 in the slow cooker 🕐 **PREP** 30 MINS   **COOK** 30 MINS PRECOOKING;
AUTO/LOW 6–8 HRS OR **HIGH** 3–4 HRS

1 Preheat the slow cooker, if required. Put the mince, onions, garlic, coriander, parsley, paprika, lemon zest and juice, tomato purée, pine nuts, eggs, and flour in a mixing bowl, and season well with salt and pepper. Mix thoroughly, then mash together with your hands to form a chunky paste. Roughly shape into small balls – you should get about 32 meatballs in all.

2 Heat 3 tbsp of the oil in a large flameproof casserole. Cook the meatballs in batches for 6–8 minutes each, turning frequently to ensure they brown all over. As each batch is cooked, remove and set aside. Wipe out the casserole with kitchen paper, add the potatoes and peppers together with the remaining oil, and cook over a high heat, turning frequently, for about 10 minutes until becoming golden brown. Add the tomatoes and fennel seeds, stir to combine, then season as needed. Transfer to the slow cooker, add the meatballs, and turn to coat with the sauce. Cover with the lid and cook on auto/low for 6–8 hours or on high for 3–4 hours. Serve with crusty bread and a green salad.

 traditional method 🕐 **PREP** 30 MINS   **COOK** 1 HR

1 Preheat the oven to 150°C (300°F/Gas 2). Put the mince, onions, garlic, coriander, parsley, paprika, lemon zest and juice, tomato purée, pine nuts, eggs, and flour in a mixing bowl, and season well with salt and pepper. Mix thoroughly, then mash together with your hands to form a chunky paste. Roughly shape into small balls – you should get about 32 meatballs in all.

2 Heat 3 tbsp of the oil in a large flameproof casserole. Cook the meatballs in batches for 6–8 minutes each, turning frequently to ensure they brown all over. As each batch is cooked, remove and set aside. Wipe out the casserole with kitchen paper, then add the potatoes and peppers together with the remaining oil, and cook over a high heat, turning frequently, for about 10 minutes until becoming golden brown. Add the tomatoes and fennel seeds, stir to combine, then season as needed. Return the meatballs to the casserole and stir well to coat with the sauce. Cover with the lid and put in the oven for 1 hour. Check occasionally that it's not drying out, topping up with a little hot water if needed. Serve with crusty bread and a green salad.

The meatballs impart all their wonderful flavours in a tomato sauce made smoky with paprika. Use fresh tomatoes if you prefer – roast or griddle them, then liquidize and add to the sauce.

Lamb meatballs in a tomato sauce

SERVES 4–6   **FREEZE** UP TO 3 MONTHS

½ onion, roughly chopped
1 chilli, deseeded and roughly chopped
2 garlic cloves, peeled and left whole
100g (3½oz) chorizo, roughly chopped
500g (1lb 2oz) minced lamb
pinch of sweet or hot smoked paprika
salt and freshly ground black pepper
2 tbsp plain flour
4 tbsp olive oil

FOR THE TOMATO SAUCE
1 onion, finely chopped
3 garlic cloves, finely chopped
120ml (4fl oz) red wine
2 x 400g cans whole tomatoes
1 tsp sweet or hot smoked paprika
1 tbsp chipotle sauce or a splash of
    smoked Tabasco sauce

in the slow cooker   ● PREP 30 MINS   **COOK** 25 MINS PRECOOKING;
                                                 AUTO/LOW 6–8 HRS OR **HIGH** 3 HRS

1 Preheat the slow cooker, if required. To make the meatballs, put the onion, chilli, and garlic into a food processor and whiz until finely chopped. Add the chorizo and pulse until combined. Tip the mixture into a bowl, stir in the lamb and paprika, and season with salt and pepper. Mix to a paste with your hands. Roll the mixture into small balls and dust each one with a little flour. Heat some of the oil in a large flameproof casserole and cook the meatballs (in batches and with extra oil, if necessary), until brown all over. Remove and set aside. Pour off all but about 2 tbsp of fat from the casserole.

2 To make the sauce, cook the onion in the casserole over a medium heat for 3–4 minutes until soft. Stir in the garlic and wine, and let the sauce bubble for a minute. Tip in the tomatoes, bring to the boil, then reduce to a simmer. Stir in the smoked paprika and chipotle or Tabasco sauce and add seasoning. Transfer everything to the slow cooker, including the meatballs. Cover with the lid and cook on auto/low for 6–8 hours or on high for 3 hours. Serve the meatballs and sauce piled over spaghetti.

traditional method   ● PREP 30 MINS   **COOK** 2½ HRS

1 Preheat the oven to 150°C (300°F/Gas 2). To make the meatballs, put the onion, chilli, and garlic into a food processor and whiz until finely chopped. Add the chorizo and pulse until combined. Tip the mixture into a bowl, stir in the lamb and paprika, and season with salt and pepper. Mix to a paste with your hands. Roll the mixture into small balls and dust each one with a little flour. Heat some of the oil in a large flameproof casserole and cook the meatballs (in batches and with extra oil, if necessary), until brown all over. Remove and set aside. Pour off all but about 2 tbsp of fat from the casserole.

2 To make the sauce, cook the onion in the casserole over a medium heat for 3–4 minutes until soft. Stir in the garlic and wine, and let the sauce bubble for a minute. Tip in the tomatoes, bring to the boil, then reduce to a simmer. Stir in the smoked paprika and chipotle or Tabasco sauce and add seasoning. Return the meatballs to the casserole and push them so they sit just under the sauce. Cover and put in the oven for 2 hours. Check occasionally that it's not drying out, topping up with a little hot water if needed. Serve the meatballs and sauce piled over spaghetti.

A hotpot is traditionally a filling supper dish that takes minimum preparation and uses foods from the storecupboard. Any sausages can be used for this dish – and they don't have to be spicy.

Red lentil and spicy sausage hotpot

⊘ **SERVES** 4　❄ **FREEZE** UP TO 1 MONTH

2 tbsp olive oil
8 spicy sausages, halved
1 onion, finely chopped
salt and freshly ground black pepper
1 tbsp paprika
2–3 garlic cloves, finely chopped
pinch of dried chilli flakes
few sprigs of rosemary, leaves finely chopped
2 celery sticks, finely chopped

2–3 red peppers, deseeded and finely chopped
200g (7oz) red lentils, rinsed and picked over
　for any stones
450ml (15fl oz) hot chicken stock for the
　slow cooker (750ml/1¼ pints for the
　traditional method)
handful of flat-leaf parsley, finely chopped
handful of coriander, finely chopped
chilli oil (optional)

in the slow cooker　🕑 **PREP** 35 MINS　**COOK** 20 MINS PRECOOKING;
AUTO/LOW 6–8 HRS OR **HIGH** 4 HRS

1 Preheat the slow cooker, if required. Heat half the oil in a large flameproof casserole over a medium-high heat, add the sausages, and cook for about 8 minutes, turning so they become golden on all sides. Remove and set aside.

2 Add the remaining oil and reduce the heat to medium. Add the onion and cook for 3–4 minutes until soft. Season with salt and pepper, stir through the paprika, garlic, chilli flakes, and rosemary, then add the celery and peppers and cook gently for about 5 minutes until softened.

3 Stir through the lentils until they are well coated, then add a little of the stock and increase the heat. Add the remaining stock and bring to the boil, reduce to a simmer, and transfer everything to the slow cooker, including the sausages and the remaining stock. Season, cover with the lid, and cook on auto/low for 6–8 hours or on high for 4 hours. Taste and season as needed, then stir through the herbs and serve with some crusty bread. A drizzle of chilli oil is also a tasty addition, if you like it.

traditional method　🕑 **PREP** 35 MINS　**COOK** 1¾ HRS

1 Preheat the oven to 160°C (325°F/Gas 3). Heat half the oil in a large flameproof casserole over a medium-high heat, add the sausages, and cook for about 8 minutes, turning so they become golden on all sides. Remove and set aside.

2 Add the remaining oil and reduce the heat to medium. Add the onion and cook for 3–4 minutes until soft. Season with salt and pepper, stir through the paprika, garlic, chilli flakes, and rosemary, then add the celery and peppers and cook gently for about 5 minutes until softened.

3 Stir through the lentils until they are well coated, then add a little of the stock and increase the heat. Add the remaining stock and bring to the boil, reduce to a simmer, and return the sausages to the casserole. Cover and put in the oven for 1½ hours. Check occasionally that it's not drying out, topping up with a little hot water if needed. Taste and season as needed, then stir through the herbs and serve with some crusty bread. A drizzle of chilli oil is also a tasty addition, if you like it.

Chicken and mustard is a classic combination – and in this recipe mustard is mixed with honey for a sweet marinade. If you have the time, let the chicken marinate for a few hours.

Mustard chicken casserole

 SERVES 4–6 ❄ **FREEZE** UP TO 1 MONTH

2 tbsp wholegrain mustard
1 tbsp English mustard
2 tbsp runny honey
8 chicken thighs, skin on
salt and freshly ground black pepper
2 tbsp olive oil
2 onions, roughly chopped

300g (10oz) parsnips, peeled and roughly chopped
few sprigs of thyme
600ml (1 pint) hot vegetable or chicken stock
 for the slow cooker (900ml/1½ pints for the
 traditional method)
bunch of flat-leaf parsley, finely chopped

 in the slow cooker 🕐 **PREP** 10 MINS, **COOK** 10–15 MINS PRECOOKING;
PLUS MARINATING **AUTO/LOW** 6–8 HRS OR **HIGH** 3–4 HRS

1 Mix together the mustards in a bowl and stir through the honey. Season the chicken thighs well with salt and pepper, then smother them with the mustard mixture. Cover and leave to marinate for 30 minutes, if time permits.

2 Preheat the slow cooker, if required. Heat half the oil in a large flameproof casserole over a medium-high heat and add the chicken pieces, a few at a time. Cook for 6–10 minutes until golden – be careful, as the honey may cause them to blacken quickly. Remove and set aside.

3 Heat the remaining oil in the casserole over a medium heat, add the onions, and toss them around in the casserole to coat in any juices. Stir to scrape up the sticky bits from the bottom, then add the parsnips and thyme. Transfer everything to the slow cooker, pour in the stock, and add the chicken pieces. Season, cover with the lid, and cook on auto/low for 6–8 hours or on high for 3–4 hours. Add the parsley, taste, and season, if necessary. Serve with steamed leeks or greens.

traditional method 🕐 **PREP** 10 MINS, PLUS MARINATING **COOK** 1¾ HRS

1 Preheat the oven to 160°C (325°F/Gas 3). Mix together the mustards in a bowl and stir through the honey. Season the chicken thighs well with salt and pepper, then smother them with the mustard mixture. Cover and leave to marinate for 30 minutes, if time permits.

2 Heat half the oil in a large flameproof casserole over a medium-high heat and add the chicken pieces, a few at a time. Cook for 6–10 minutes until golden – be careful, as the honey may cause them to blacken quickly. Remove and set aside.

3 Heat the remaining oil in the casserole over a medium heat, add the onions, and toss them around the casserole to coat in any juices. Stir to scrape up the sticky bits from the bottom, then add the parsnips and thyme. Pour in the stock, bring to the boil, and then reduce to a simmer. Return the chicken to the casserole together with any juices, nestling them in between the parsnips and making sure they are covered in liquid. Season, cover, and put in the oven for 1½ hours. Check occasionally that it's not drying out, topping up with a little hot water if needed. Add the parsley, taste, and season, if necessary. Serve with steamed leeks or greens.

The more mature the chicken, the better this dish will be – French cooks use a boiling fowl or, best of all, the traditional male cock bird. Mashed potatoes and peas are the perfect accompaniment.

Chicken in white wine

SERVES 4–6

1 onion, thinly sliced
1 celery stick, thinly sliced
1 carrot, peeled and thinly sliced
2 garlic cloves, 1 left whole, 1 chopped
6 black peppercorns
350ml (12fl oz) medium-dry white wine
2kg (4½lb) chicken, jointed into 8 pieces
2 tbsp olive oil
1 tbsp vegetable oil

15g (½oz) butter
18–20 baby onions, peeled
3 tbsp plain flour
2 shallots, chopped
500ml (16fl oz) hot chicken stock,
 for both methods
1 bouquet garni
salt and freshly ground black pepper
250g (9oz) mushrooms, quartered

 in the slow cooker ⏱ **PREP** 30 MINS, PLUS MARINATING   **COOK** 15 MINS PRECOOKING; **AUTO/LOW** 6–8 HRS OR **HIGH** 3–4 HRS

1 Put the onion, celery, carrot, whole garlic clove, and peppercorns in a pan with the wine and bring to the boil. Simmer for 5 minutes, then allow to cool. Put the chicken in a bowl, pour over the marinade, and add the olive oil. Cover and refrigerate for 8–12 hours, turning the pieces occasionally. Remove the chicken and dry on kitchen paper. Strain the marinade and reserve the liquid and vegetables.

2 Preheat the slow cooker, if required. Heat the vegetable oil and butter in a large flameproof casserole over a medium-high heat until foaming. Cook the chicken for about 5 minutes on each side, skin-side first, until brown. Remove and set aside. Cook the baby onions for 6–8 minutes until brown. Discard all but 2 tbsp of the fat, add the reserved vegetables, and cook for 4–5 minutes to soften. Sprinkle over the flour and cook, stirring, until lightly browned. Stir in the marinade, shallots, chopped garlic, stock, bouquet garni, and seasoning. Bring to the boil, then transfer to the slow cooker, add the chicken, cover with the lid, and cook on auto/low for 6–8 hours or on high for 3–4 hours. Stir through the mushrooms for the last 10 minutes of cooking.

 traditional method ⏱ **PREP** 30 MINS, PLUS MARINATING   **COOK** 1½–1¾ HRS

1 Put the onion, celery, carrot, whole garlic clove, and peppercorns in a pan with the wine and bring to the boil. Simmer for 5 minutes, then allow to cool. Put the chicken in a bowl, pour over the marinade, and add the olive oil. Cover and refrigerate for 8–12 hours, turning the pieces occasionally. Remove the chicken and dry on kitchen paper. Strain the marinade and reserve the liquid and vegetables.

2 Heat the vegetable oil and butter in a large flameproof casserole over a medium-high heat until foaming. Cook the chicken for about 5 minutes on each side, skin-side first, until brown. Remove and set aside. Cook the baby onions for 6–8 minutes until brown. Discard all but 2 tbsp of the fat, add the reserved vegetables, and cook for 4–5 minutes to soften. Sprinkle over the flour and cook, stirring, until lightly browned. Stir in the marinade, shallots, chopped garlic, stock, bouquet garni, and seasoning. Bring to the boil, return the chicken pieces, cover, and simmer for 45–60 minutes until the pieces are just tender when pierced with a fork. Stir through the mushrooms for the last 10 minutes of cooking.

Caraway seed dumplings are delicious with the chicken, as well as being an aid to the digestion. Steamed, crisp green beans or sugarsnap peas would provide the ideal crunch alongside.

Chicken paprika with dumplings

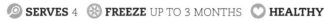 **SERVES** 4   **FREEZE** UP TO 3 MONTHS   **HEALTHY**

100g (3½oz) self-raising flour
½ tsp salt
60g (2oz) suet
2 tsp caraway seeds
4 chicken breasts on the bone
salt and freshly ground black pepper
2 tbsp vegetable oil
1 large onion, diced

2 garlic cloves, finely chopped
2 tbsp paprika, plus more to taste
1 tbsp plain flour
400g can chopped tomatoes
300ml (10fl oz) hot chicken stock for
   the slow cooker (500ml/16fl oz for
   the traditional method)
120ml (4fl oz) soured cream

 in the slow cooker   🕐 **PREP** 30 MINS   **COOK** 30 MINS PRECOOKING;
AUTO/LOW 6–8 HRS OR HIGH 3–4 HRS

1 Sift the flour and salt into a large bowl. Mix in the suet and caraway seeds and make a well in the centre. Add cold water, a little at a time, and draw in the flour, stirring to combine. Add more water until it is all combined; the dough should be moist but not soft or sticky. Roll into 2cm (¾in) balls, cover, and refrigerate.

2 Preheat the slow cooker, if required. Season the chicken. Heat the oil in a large flameproof casserole over a medium-high heat. Add the chicken skin-side down (in batches, if necessary) and cook for about 5 minutes on each side until brown. Remove and set aside. Add the onion and cook over a medium heat for 2–3 minutes until soft. Add the garlic and continue cooking for 3–5 minutes longer. Stir in the paprika. Cook gently, stirring occasionally, for about 5 minutes. Stir in the flour, add the tomatoes, stock, and seasoning, and bring to the boil. Transfer everything to the slow cooker, including the chicken, cover with the lid, and cook on auto/low for 6–8 hours or on high for 3–4 hours. Add the dumplings to the slow cooker for the last 40 minutes, pushing them down into the sauce. Stir through the soured cream to serve.

 traditional method   🕐 **PREP** 30 MINS   **COOK** 1½ HRS

1 Sift the flour and salt into a large bowl. Mix in the suet and caraway seeds and make a well in the centre. Add cold water, a little at a time, and draw in the flour, stirring to combine. Add more water until it is all combined; the dough should be moist but not soft or sticky. Roll into 2cm (¾in) balls, cover, and refrigerate.

2 Preheat the oven to 180°C (350°F/Gas 4). Season the chicken. Heat the oil in a large flameproof casserole over a medium-high heat. Add the chicken skin-side down (in batches, if necessary) and cook for about 5 minutes on each side until brown. Remove and set aside. Add the onion and cook over a medium heat for 2–3 minutes until soft. Add the garlic and continue cooking for 3–5 minutes longer. Stir in the paprika. Cook gently, stirring occasionally, for about 5 minutes. Stir in the flour, add the tomatoes, stock, and seasoning, and bring to the boil. Return the chicken, cover, and cook in the oven for 45–60 minutes until the pieces are just tender when pierced with a fork. Check occasionally that it's not drying out, topping up with a little hot water if needed. Add the dumplings to the casserole for the last 30 minutes, pushing them down into the sauce. Stir through the soured cream to serve.

Tagines

This dish is slow cooked in a casserole, but you could always use a tagine if you have one. Preserved lemons have a subtle and distinctive flavour and are available at larger supermarkets.

Chicken and green olive tagine

SERVES 4–6 **FREEZE** UP TO 1 MONTH

4 tbsp olive oil
1 tbsp ground ginger
2 tbsp paprika
pinch of cayenne pepper
1 tsp ground turmeric
salt and freshly ground black pepper
8 chicken drumsticks
4 onions, roughly chopped
4 garlic cloves, finely chopped
pinch of saffron threads
2.5cm (1in) piece of fresh root ginger,
 peeled and grated

4 large tomatoes, roughly chopped
juice of ½ lemon for the slow cooker
 (1 lemon for the traditional method)
600ml (1 pint) hot vegetable stock for
 the slow cooker (900ml/1½ pints for
 the traditional method)
150g (5½oz) green olives in brine, stoned
 and rinsed
2 preserved lemons, halved, flesh discarded,
 and rind shredded (optional)
handful of coriander, chopped
handful of flat-leaf parsley, chopped

 in the slow cooker **PREP** 20 MINS, PLUS MARINATING **COOK** 15 MINS PRECOOKING; **AUTO/LOW** 6–8 HRS OR **HIGH** 3–4 HRS

1 Preheat the slow cooker, if required. In a bowl, mix together half the oil with the spices and season with salt and pepper. Add the chicken drumsticks and toss until they are really well coated. Cover and leave overnight in the fridge, if time allows, or leave for 30 minutes. Heat a large flameproof casserole or tagine, add the chicken drumsticks (in batches and with extra oil, if necessary), and cook for 6–8 minutes until golden. Remove from the casserole and set aside.

2 Heat 1 tbsp of the oil in the casserole over a medium heat, add the onion, and cook for 3–4 minutes until soft. Then stir through the garlic, saffron, and grated ginger and cook for a minute more. Transfer everything to the slow cooker and add the tomatoes, chicken, lemon juice, stock, olives, and the preserved lemons, if using. Season, cover with the lid, and cook on auto/low for 6–8 hours or on high for 3–4 hours. Sprinkle over the herbs and serve with couscous.

 traditional method **PREP** 20 MINS, PLUS MARINATING **COOK** 2 HRS

1 In a bowl, mix together half the oil with the spices and season with salt and pepper. Add the chicken drumsticks and toss until they are really well coated. Cover and leave overnight in the fridge, if time allows, or leave for 30 minutes. Preheat the oven to 190°C (375°F/Gas 5). Heat a large flameproof casserole or tagine, add the chicken drumsticks (in batches and with extra oil, if necessary), and cook for 6–8 minutes until golden. Remove from the casserole and set aside.

2 Heat 1 tbsp of the oil in the casserole, add the onion, and cook for 3–4 minutes until soft. Then stir through the garlic, grated ginger, and saffron and cook for a minute more. Stir in the tomatoes and return the chicken to the casserole with any juices and the lemon juice. Season and pour in the stock. Bring to the boil, then reduce to a simmer, cover, and put in the oven for 1 hour. Add the olives and preserved lemons, if using, and cook for 30 minutes more. Check occasionally that it's not drying out, topping up with a little hot water if needed. Sprinkle over the herbs and serve with couscous.

Peppers add a fabulous sweetness to the dish – use a mixture of red, yellow, and orange peppers for maximum colour impact, and use green olives instead of black, if you prefer.

Chicken with olives and peppers

 SERVES 4 **HEALTHY**

3 tbsp olive oil
6 onions, 4 thinly sliced and 2 finely chopped
4 chicken pieces, skin on
500g (1lb 2oz) tomatoes, skinned and chopped
3 red peppers, deseeded and roughly chopped
1 lemon, cut into wedges
1 garlic clove, finely chopped

120ml (4fl oz) olive oil
2 tsp ground cumin
2 tsp ground coriander
salt and freshly ground black pepper
85g (3oz) stoned black olives
3–4 sprigs of fresh coriander, chopped

 in the slow cooker **PREP** 20 MINS **COOK** 10 MINS PRECOOKING;
AUTO/LOW 6–8 HRS OR **HIGH** 3–4 HRS

1 Preheat the slow cooker, if required. Heat the oil in a heavy-based pan over a medium heat, add the sliced onions, and cook for 5 minutes until soft. Remove and set aside. Put the chicken in the slow cooker and cover with the sliced onions, then with the chopped tomatoes, peppers, and one of the lemon wedges.

2 Put the chopped onions into the pan and cook for 5 minutes to soften. Transfer to a bowl and add the garlic, oil, ground cumin, and ground coriander, and add salt and pepper. Spoon the mixture over the chicken and sprinkle over the olives.

3 Cover with the lid and cook on auto/low for 6–8 hours or on high for 3–4 hours. Stir in the fresh coriander, taste the sauce for seasoning, and remove the lemon wedge. Serve the chicken with couscous or rice, and with the remaining lemon wedges on the side.

 traditional method **PREP** 20 MINS **COOK** 1½ HRS

1 Heat the oven to 180°C (350°F/Gas 4). Heat the oil in a heavy-based pan over a medium heat, add the sliced onions, and cook for 5 minutes until soft. Put the chicken in a large flameproof casserole or tagine and cover with the sliced onions, then with the chopped tomatoes, peppers, and one of the lemon wedges.

2 Put the chopped onions into the pan and cook for 5 minutes to soften. Transfer to a bowl and add the garlic, oil, ground cumin, and ground coriander, and add salt and pepper. Spoon the mixture over the chicken and sprinkle over the olives.

3 Cover with the lid and put in the oven for about 1½ hours until the chicken is tender when pierced with a fork. Stir in the fresh coriander, taste the sauce for seasoning, and remove the lemon wedge. Serve the chicken with couscous or rice, and with the remaining lemon wedges on the side.

Light, fresh, and zingy, this vegetarian version of a tagine is full of punchy flavours. It is a good dish to prepare ahead as the flavours improve with reheating.

Courgette, herb, and lemon tagine

 SERVES 4　♡ **HEALTHY**

2 tbsp olive oil
1 red onion, finely chopped
salt and freshly ground black pepper
3 garlic cloves, finely chopped
pinch of fennel seeds
pinch of ground cinnamon
1–2 tsp harissa paste, plus extra to serve

2 preserved lemons, quartered and flesh discarded
400g can whole tomatoes, chopped
1 head broccoli, broken into florets
3 courgettes, trimmed and sliced
juice of 1 lemon
handful of dill, finely chopped
handful of flat-leaf parsley, finely chopped

in the slow cooker　🕐 **PREP** 25 MINS　**COOK** 15 MINS PRECOOKING; **HIGH** 2–3 HRS

1 Preheat the slow cooker, if required. Heat half the oil in a large heavy-based pan or tagine over a low heat, add the onions, and cook for 8 minutes until soft and translucent. Season well with salt and pepper, then stir through the garlic, fennel seeds, cinnamon, harissa, and preserved lemons.

2 Add the tomatoes and stir well, crushing them with the back of a wooden spoon. Bring to the boil, then reduce to a simmer and transfer to the slow cooker. Cover with the lid and cook on high for 2–3 hours.

3 Cook the broccoli in a pan of boiling salted water for 3–5 minutes or until tender, then drain and refresh in cold water. Drain again and set aside. Heat the remaining oil in a frying pan over a low heat, add the courgettes and seasoning, and cook, stirring frequently, for 5 minutes or until they start to colour a little. Stir through the lemon juice and dill and transfer with the broccoli to the slow cooker, for the last 15 minutes of cooking. Taste and season as needed, then stir through the parsley. Serve on warmed plates with couscous, lemon wedges, and a spoonful of harissa on the side.

traditional method　🕐 **PREP** 25 MINS　**COOK** 45–55 MINS

1 Heat half the oil in a large heavy-based pan or tagine over a low heat, add the onions, and cook for 8 minutes until soft and translucent. Season well with salt and pepper, then stir through the garlic, fennel seeds, cinnamon, harissa, and preserved lemons.

2 Add the tomatoes and stir well, crushing them with the back of a wooden spoon. Bring to the boil, then reduce to a simmer and cook over a low heat for 30–40 minutes. If the sauce starts to dry out, top up with a little hot water.

3 Cook the broccoli in a pan of boiling salted water for 3–5 minutes or until tender, then drain and refresh in cold water. Drain again and set aside. Heat the remaining oil in a frying pan over a low heat, add the courgettes and seasoning, and cook, stirring frequently, for 5 minutes or until they start to colour a little. Add the lemon juice and stir through the dill. Add the broccoli and courgettes to the sauce and stir through the parsley. Serve on warmed plates with couscous, lemon wedges, and a spoonful of harissa on the side.

Chickpeas are a typical Middle Eastern ingredient. If you have the dried type, soak them in water for at least eight hours. Strain through a sieve, then rinse them under cold running water.

Middle Eastern lentils and peppers

SERVES 4–6 **HEALTHY**

100g (3½oz) brown or green lentils, rinsed
salt and freshly ground black pepper
1 tbsp olive oil
1 onion, finely chopped
3 garlic cloves, finely chopped
pinch of dried oregano
grated zest and juice of 1 lemon
½ tsp ground allspice

pinch of grated nutmeg
½ tsp ground cumin
2 red peppers, deseeded and sliced into strips
200g (7oz) rice
600ml (1 pint) hot vegetable stock for the slow
  cooker (900ml/1½ pints for the traditional method)
400g can chickpeas, drained and rinsed
bunch of parsley, finely chopped

in the slow cooker **PREP** 15 MINS **COOK** 20 MINS PRECOOKING; **HIGH** 1½–2 HRS

1 Put the lentils in a large heavy-based pan or tagine, season with salt and pepper, and cover with water. Bring to the boil, then simmer for about 30 minutes until they are beginning to soften, but don't let them turn mushy. Drain and set aside.

2 Preheat the slow cooker, if required. Heat the oil in the same heavy-based pan over a medium heat, add the onion, and cook for 3–4 minutes until soft. Add seasoning, then stir through the garlic, oregano, lemon zest, allspice, nutmeg, and cumin and cook for a minute. Add the peppers and cook for about 5 minutes, stirring to coat with the spices. Cook for 2–3 minutes until soft, then stir in the rice and a little stock, and bring to the boil. Transfer everything to the slow cooker with the chickpeas and just enough stock to cover. Add the lid and cook on high for 1½–2 hours.

3 About 5 minutes before the end of the cooking time, stir through the lentils, put the lid back on, and let the lentils warm through. Taste and season, then add the parsley and lemon juice. Serve with yogurt and pitta bread.

traditional method **PREP** 15 MINS **COOK** 45 MINS

1 Put the lentils in a large heavy-based pan or tagine, season with salt and pepper, and cover with water. Bring to the boil, then simmer for about 30 minutes until they are beginning to soften, but don't let them turn mushy. Drain and set aside.

2 Meanwhile, heat the oil in another heavy-based pan over a medium heat, add the onion, and cook for 3–4 minutes until soft. Add seasoning, then stir through the garlic, oregano, lemon zest, allspice, nutmeg, and cumin and cook for a minute.

3 Add the peppers and cook for about 5 minutes, stirring to coat with spices. Cook for 2–3 minutes until soft, then stir in the rice and little stock. Bring to the boil, add most of the stock, and boil for a minute. Reduce to a simmer, add the chickpeas, and cook on a very low heat for 15–20 minutes. Check occasionally that it's not drying out, topping up with a little hot stock if needed. Stir through the lentils, taste and season, then add the parsley and lemon juice. Serve with yogurt and pitta bread.

This is a version of the classic Moroccan tagine, a mixture of chicken, fruit, and spices baked in a conical earthenware dish. You can buy the chicken in four pieces instead of jointing it yourself.

Moroccan chicken baked with spices

 SERVES 4

1.5kg (3lb 3oz) chicken, jointed into 4 pieces
6 onions, 4 finely sliced and 2 finely chopped
500g (1lb 2oz) tomatoes, skinned and chopped
pinch of saffron threads, soaked in 3–4 tbsp
   boiling water
75g (2½oz) ready-to-eat dried apricots, chopped

2 tbsp runny honey
2 tsp ground cinnamon
1 tsp ground ginger
few sprigs of parsley, chopped
salt and freshly ground black pepper
120ml (4fl oz) olive oil

in the slow cooker   🕐 PREP 15 MINS   COOK AUTO/LOW 5–6 HRS OR HIGH 4 HRS

1 Preheat the slow cooker, if required. Put the chicken in the slow cooker, then cover with the sliced onions and chopped tomatoes.

2 Mix together the chopped onions, saffron and its liquid, apricots, honey, cinnamon, ginger, and chopped parsley in a bowl, and add seasoning and olive oil. Spoon the mixture over the chicken.

3 Cover with the lid and cook on auto/low for 5–6 hours or on high for 4 hours. Taste the sauce and add seasoning, if needed. Transfer the chicken and sauce straight from the slow cooker onto warmed plates. Serve with couscous.

traditional method   🕐 PREP 15 MINS   COOK 1½ HRS

1 Preheat the oven to 180°C (350°F/Gas 4). Put the chicken in a large flameproof casserole or a tagine. Cover with the sliced onions and chopped tomatoes.

2 Mix together the chopped onions, saffron and its liquid, apricots, honey, cinnamon, ginger, and chopped parsley in a bowl, and add seasoning and olive oil. Spoon the mixture over the chicken.

3 Cover with the lid and put in the oven for about 1½ hours until the chicken is tender when pierced with a fork. Check occasionally that it's not drying out, topping up with only 1 tbsp of water at a time to stop it from browning too much. Taste the sauce and add seasoning if needed. Transfer the chicken and sauce straight from the casserole onto warmed plates. Serve with couscous.

Dried apricots and chutney give an authentic sweetness to this fragrant tagine. The mint adds a freshness to temper the heat. You could use mutton instead, if your butcher has it.

Fiery lamb and chutney tagine

SERVES 4–6 **FREEZE** UP TO 1 MONTH

1 onion, thinly sliced
1 tsp ground coriander
1 tsp ground cumin
1 tsp ground ginger
1 tsp dried thyme
1–2 tsp cayenne pepper
2 tbsp sunflower oil
900g (2lb) boneless lamb, such as shoulder
  or chump steaks, cut into bite-sized pieces

2 tbsp plain flour
300ml (10fl oz) orange juice
450ml (15fl oz) hot chicken stock for the slow cooker
  (600ml/1 pint for the traditional method)
115g (4oz) ready-to-eat dried apricots
4 tbsp peach or apricot chutney, or any sweet and
  spicy fruit chutney
salt and freshly ground black pepper
mint leaves, to serve

in the slow cooker
PREP 10 MINS, PLUS MARINATING **COOK** 10 MINS PRECOOKING; **AUTO/LOW** 6–8 HRS OR **HIGH** 3–4 HRS

1 Put the onion, coriander, cumin, ginger, thyme, cayenne, and 1 tbsp of the oil in a large, non-metallic bowl, then mix in the lamb. Cover and refrigerate for at least 3 hours or overnight.

2 Preheat the slow cooker, if required. Put the flour in a small bowl and slowly stir in the orange juice until smooth, then set aside. Heat the remaining oil in a large flameproof casserole over a high heat. Add the lamb mixture and cook, stirring frequently, for about 5 minutes until browned.

3 Stir the flour mixture into the casserole with the stock, then stir in the apricots and chutney. Bring to the boil and transfer everything to the slow cooker. Cover with the lid and cook on auto/low for 6–8 hours or on high for 3–4 hours. Taste and add seasoning, if needed. Sprinkle with the mint leaves and serve with couscous.

traditional method
PREP 10 MINS, PLUS MARINATING **COOK** 1½ HRS

1 Put the onion, coriander, cumin, ginger, thyme, cayenne, and 1 tbsp of the oil in a large, non-metallic bowl, then mix in the lamb. Cover and refrigerate for at least 3 hours or overnight.

2 Preheat the oven to 160°C (325°F/Gas 3). Put the flour in a small bowl and slowly stir in the orange juice until smooth, then set aside. Heat the remaining oil in a large flameproof casserole over a high heat. Add the lamb mixture and cook, stirring frequently, for about 5 minutes until browned.

3 Stir the flour mixture into the casserole with the stock. Bring to the boil, stirring, then remove the casserole from the heat, cover, and put in the oven for 1 hour. Remove the casserole from the oven, stir in the apricots and chutney, re-cover, and return to the oven. Cook for a further 20 minutes or until the lamb is tender. Taste and add seasoning, if needed. Sprinkle with the mint leaves and serve with couscous.

One of the ingredients that gives a Moroccan tagine its unique flavour is preserved lemon. The lemons are pickled in salt water with lemon juice and are available at large supermarkets.

Mixed vegetable tagine

SERVES 4–6 ❄ **FREEZE** UP TO 3 MONTHS ♡ **HEALTHY**

1 tbsp olive oil
1 red onion, roughly chopped
salt and freshly ground black pepper
3 garlic cloves, finely chopped
5cm (2in) piece of fresh root ginger, peeled and grated
1 tsp ground turmeric
pinch of saffron threads
1 tsp coriander seeds, ground
½ tsp cumin seeds
4 large potatoes, peeled and chopped into chunky pieces

3 carrots, peeled and chopped into chunky pieces
1 fennel bulb, trimmed and chopped into chunky pieces
4 tomatoes, finely chopped
about 750ml (1¼ pints) hot vegetable stock, for both methods
handful of mixed olives, stoned and halved (optional)
2 preserved lemons, halved, flesh discarded and peel chopped (optional)
bunch of coriander leaves, roughly chopped

in the slow cooker ⏱ PREP 20–25 MINS   COOK 15 MINS PRECOOKING; HIGH 3 HRS

1 Preheat the slow cooker, if required. Heat the oil in a large heavy-based pan or tagine over a medium heat, add the onion, and cook for 3–4 minutes until soft. Season with salt and pepper, stir through the garlic, ginger, turmeric, saffron, coriander seeds, and cumin, and cook for 2 minutes.

2 Add the potatoes and toss to coat, then add the carrots and fennel and stir so everything is well combined. Cook for a few minutes, add the tomatoes, and transfer everything to the slow cooker.

3 Pour over enough stock to cover the vegetables, season, and cover with the lid. Cook on high for 3 hours. Taste and season, then stir through the olives and lemon, if using, and half the coriander leaves. Transfer to a serving dish and sprinkle over the remaining coriander leaves. Serve with couscous.

traditional method ⏱ PREP 20–25 MINS   COOK 50 MINS

1 Heat the oil in a large heavy-based pan or tagine over a medium heat, add the onion, and cook for 3–4 minutes until soft. Season with salt and pepper, stir through the garlic, ginger, turmeric, saffron, coriander seeds, and cumin, and cook for a couple of minutes.

2 Add the potatoes and toss to coat, then add the carrots and fennel and stir so everything is well combined. Cook for a few minutes, add the tomatoes, and pour over just enough stock to cover the vegetables.

3 Cover with the lid and simmer very gently for 30–40 minutes until the vegetables are soft and a lot of the liquid has evaporated. Top up with more hot stock if needed. Taste and season, then stir through the olives and lemon, if using, and half the coriander leaves. Transfer to a serving dish and sprinkle over the remaining coriander leaves. Serve with couscous.

The flavours in this tagine are a harmonious blend of citrus and spice. If you can't find the spice mix ras-el-hanout, use a pinch each of ground cinnamon and ground nutmeg instead.

Chicken and orange tagine

 SERVES 4 ❄ **FREEZE** UP TO 3 MONTHS

8 chicken thighs, skin on
1 tsp ras-el-hanout spice (optional)
salt and freshly ground black pepper
1–2 tbsp olive oil
1 red onion, finely chopped
2 tsp coriander seeds, half of them crushed
2 green chillies, deseeded and finely chopped

3 garlic cloves, finely chopped
2 oranges, segmented and juice reserved
4 large tomatoes, roughly chopped
600ml (1 pint) hot chicken or vegetable stock
for the slow cooker (900ml/1½ pints for the
traditional method)
handful of coriander, roughly chopped

 in the slow cooker 🕐 **PREP** 20 MINS **COOK** 15 MINS PRECOOKING;
AUTO/LOW 6–8 HRS OR **HIGH** 3–4 HRS

1 Preheat the slow cooker, if required. Smother the chicken with the ras-el-hanout spice mix, if using, and season with salt and pepper. Heat half the oil in a large flameproof casserole or tagine over a medium-high heat, and cook the chicken (in batches, if necessary) for 6–8 minutes until golden. Remove and set aside. Heat the remaining oil in the casserole over a medium heat, add the onion, and cook for 3–4 minutes until soft. Season with salt and pepper, stir through the coriander seeds, chillies, and garlic, and cook for a further minute.

2 Add the orange juice, increase the heat, and let the sauce bubble for a minute, then return the chicken to the casserole together with its juices. Add the tomatoes and a little of the stock and bring to the boil, then transfer everything to the slow cooker. Pour in the remaining stock, cover with the lid, and cook on auto/low for 6–8 hours or on high for 3–4 hours. Add the orange segments for the last 30 minutes of cooking. Stir in most of the coriander and serve with couscous, with the remaining coriander sprinkled over.

traditonal method 🕐 **PREP** 20 MINS **COOK** 1¾ HRS

1 Preheat the oven to 190°C (375°F/Gas 5). Smother the chicken with the ras-el-hanout spice mix, if using, and season well with salt and pepper. Heat half the oil in a large flameproof casserole or tagine over a medium-high heat, and cook the chicken (in batches, if necessary) for 6–8 minutes until golden. Remove and set aside.

2 Heat the remaining oil in the casserole over a medium heat, add the onion, and cook for 3–4 minutes until soft. Season with salt and pepper, stir through the coriander seeds, chillies, and garlic, and cook for a further minute. Add the orange juice, increase the heat, and let the sauce bubble for a minute, then return the chicken to the casserole together with its juices.

3 Add the tomatoes and a little of the stock and bring to the boil, then pour in the remaining stock and boil for 1–2 minutes. Reduce the heat, cover with the lid, and put in the oven for 1½ hours. Check occasionally that it's not drying out, topping up with a little hot water if needed. Add the orange segments for the last 30 minutes of cooking. Stir in most of the coriander and serve with couscous, with the remaining coriander sprinkled over.

Fig adds a sweet stickiness to this tagine and works well with lamb. Swap the walnuts for hazelnuts or pecans, if you prefer, and you could use fresh figs when they are in season.

Lamb tagine with walnuts and figs

SERVES 4–6   **FREEZE** UP TO 3 MONTHS

1–2 tbsp olive oil
900g (2lb) lean lamb, cut into bite-sized pieces
salt and freshly ground black pepper
2 onions, sliced
3 garlic cloves, peeled and finely chopped
grated zest and juice of 1 lemon
1 tsp ground cinnamon
½ tsp ground coriander
½ tsp ground ginger
2 tsp paprika

1 tbsp tomato purée
1 tbsp runny honey
200g (7oz) dried figs, roughly chopped
2 x 400g cans chickpeas, drained
about 300ml (10fl oz) hot vegetable stock for
  the slow cooker (900ml/1½ pints for the
  traditional method)
75g (2½oz) walnut halves, roughly chopped
large handful of flat-leaf parsley, roughly chopped

in the slow cooker   **PREP** 20 MINS   **COOK** 15 MINS PRECOOKING;
AUTO/LOW 6–8 HRS OR **HIGH** 3–4 HRS

1 Preheat the slow cooker, if required. Heat 1 tbsp of the oil in a large flameproof casserole or tagine over a medium-high heat, season the lamb with salt and pepper, and cook (in batches, if necessary) for 6–8 minutes until browned all over. Remove and set aside.

2 Cook the onions, garlic, and lemon zest and juice (together with a little more oil, if necessary) in the casserole over a medium heat for 2 minutes. Add seasoning, then stir though the spices and tomato purée.

3 Transfer everything to the slow cooker, including the lamb, add the honey, figs, and chickpeas, then pour over the stock until it just covers. Season and cover with the lid, and cook on auto/low for 6–8 hours or on high for 3–4 hours. Stir though the walnuts and most of the parsley for the last 30 minutes of cooking. Taste and season, if needed, and sprinkle with the remaining parsley. Serve with couscous.

traditional method   **PREP** 20 MINS   **COOK** 1¾–2¼ HRS

1 Preheat the oven to 150°C (300°F/Gas 2). Heat 1 tbsp of the oil in a large flameproof casserole or tagine over a medium-high heat, season the lamb with salt and pepper, and cook (in batches, if necessary) for 6–8 minutes until browned all over. Remove and set aside.

2 Cook the onions, garlic, and lemon zest and juice (together with a little more oil, if necessary) in the casserole over a medium heat for 2 minutes. Add seasoning, then stir though the spices and tomato purée.

3 Add the honey, figs, chickpeas, and stock. Bring to the boil, then reduce the heat to a simmer, return the meat, and add the walnuts and most of the parsley. Cover with the lid and put in the oven for 1½–2 hours. Check occasionally that it's not drying out, topping up with a little hot water if needed. Taste and season, if needed, and sprinkle with the remaining parsley. Serve with couscous.

Hearty chestnuts give substance to this otherwise traditional combination of lamb and orange. The tagine tastes even better reheated the next day as the flavours have melded together.

Slow-cooked lamb with orange and chestnuts

◎ **SERVES** 4–6 ❄ **FREEZE** UP TO 1 MONTH

½ tsp ground cinnamon
½ tsp ground cumin
½ tsp ground coriander
salt and freshly ground black pepper
900g (2lb) lean leg of lamb, diced
2–3 tbsp olive oil
1 onion, chopped

1 cinnamon stick
175g (6oz) ready-cooked chestnuts
150ml (5fl oz) fresh orange juice
600ml (1 pint) hot lamb stock for the slow cooker (900ml/1½ pints for the traditional method)
2 oranges, peeled and cut into thick slices
bunch of coriander, roughly chopped

in the slow cooker ⏱ **PREP** 15 MINS **COOK** 15–25 MINS PRECOOKING; **AUTO/LOW** 6–8 HRS

1 Preheat the slow cooker, if required. In a large bowl, mix together the spices and season with salt and pepper, then toss the meat in the mixture. Heat half the oil in a large flameproof casserole or tagine over a medium-high heat, add the lamb (in batches and with extra oil, if necessary), and cook for 6–8 minutes or until the lamb is browned on all sides. Remove and put in the slow cooker.

2 Heat the remaining oil in the casserole over a medium heat. Add the onion and cinnamon stick, and stir so the onion is coated in any residual lamb juices. Cook for 3–4 minutes until the onions are soft. Then stir in the chestnuts and pour in the orange juice. Increase the heat and let it bubble for a minute, stirring. Transfer everything to the slow cooker and pour in the stock. Cover and cook on auto/low for 6–8 hours. Add the orange slices for the last 30 minutes of cooking. Check for seasoning, stir through the coriander, and serve with couscous.

traditional method ⏱ **PREP** 15 MINS **COOK** 2¼ HRS

1 Preheat the oven to 160°C (325°F/Gas 3). In a large bowl, mix together the spices and season with salt and pepper, then toss the meat in the mixture. Heat half the oil in a large flameproof casserole or tagine over a medium-high heat, add the lamb (in batches and with extra oil, if necessary), and cook for 6–8 minutes or until the lamb is browned on all sides. Remove and set aside.

2 Heat the remaining oil in the casserole over a medium heat. Add the onion and cinnamon stick, and stir so the onion is coated in any residual lamb juices. Cook for 3–4 minutes until the onions are soft. Then stir in the chestnuts and pour in the orange juice. Increase the heat and let it bubble for a minute, stirring. Reduce the heat and return the lamb to the casserole along with any juices from the lamb.

3 Pour in the stock, bring to the boil, then reduce to a simmer, cover, and put in the oven for 2 hours. Check occasionally that it's not drying out, topping up with a little hot water, if needed. Add the orange slices for the last 30 minutes of cooking. Check for seasoning, stir through the coriander, and serve with couscous.

The beef in this tagine is slowly cooked in spices for maximum flavour. Silverside is the best cut for slow cooking; but if it isn't available top rump or topside are good alternatives.

Cumin beef tagine

SERVES 4–6 **FREEZE** UP TO 3 MONTHS

900g (2lb) lean beef, such as silverside, cut into
  2.5cm (1in) cubes
2 tsp ground cumin
2 tbsp plain flour, seasoned with salt and pepper
3 tbsp olive oil
1 large onion, chopped
4 garlic cloves, peeled and crushed
1 tsp ground ginger
1 tsp ground cinnamon

½ tsp cayenne pepper
450ml (15fl oz) hot chicken stock for the slow cooker
  (600ml/1 pint for the traditional method)
1 small butternut squash, peeled, deseeded,
  and diced
3 red peppers, deseeded and chopped into strips
handful of raisins (optional)
salt and freshly ground black pepper

in the slow cooker   PREP 20 MINS   COOK 15 MINS PRECOOKING;
AUTO/LOW 6–8 HRS OR **HIGH** 3–4 HRS

1 Preheat the slow cooker, if required. Toss the beef in the cumin so it is evenly coated, then do the same with the flour. Heat the oil in a large flameproof casserole or tagine over a medium-high heat, and cook the beef in batches for about 10 minutes until evenly browned.

2 Reduce the heat, then add the onion, garlic, and all the spices, stir well to coat, and cook for 2 minutes. Pour over the stock and bring to the boil. Reduce the heat and transfer everything to the slow cooker, season, cover with the lid, and cook on auto/low for 6–8 hours or on high for 3–4 hours.

3 Add the squash, peppers, and raisins, if using, for the last hour of cooking. Taste and season if needed. Serve with baby roast potatoes and couscous or rice.

traditional method   PREP 20 MINS   COOK 2½ HRS

1 Preheat the oven to 150°C (300°F/Gas 2). Toss the beef in the cumin so it is evenly coated, then do the same with the flour. Heat the oil in a large flameproof casserole or tagine over a medium-high heat, and cook the beef in batches for 10 minutes until evenly browned.

2 Reduce the heat, then add the onion, garlic, and all the spices, stir well to coat, and cook for 2 minutes. Pour over the stock and bring to the boil. Reduce the heat once more, season, cover with the lid, and put in the oven for 1½ hours.

3 Add the squash and then 15 minutes later, the peppers and raisins, if using, and cook everything for a further 30 minutes, or until tender. You may need to top up with a little hot water. Taste and season if needed. Serve with baby roast potatoes and couscous or rice.

This is a light dish of vegetables and fish cooked with a heady mix of herbs and spices. Charmoula is a north African marinade that infuses the fish still further with lemon and coriander.

Fish tagine

 SERVES 4–6 **HEALTHY**

900g (2lb) red snapper fillets, or use sea bass, cut into chunky pieces
1–2 tbsp olive oil
2 onions, sliced into rings
2 celery sticks, finely chopped
salt and freshly ground black pepper
3 garlic cloves, chopped
1 tsp ground ginger
1 preserved lemon, flesh only, finely chopped or use grated zest of ½ lemon
2 carrots, peeled and sliced
2 red peppers, deseeded and roughly chopped
6 new potatoes, halved
about 300ml (10fl oz) hot fish stock for the slow cooker (600ml/1pint for the traditional method)

3 tomatoes, deseeded and chopped into thin slices
squeeze of lemon juice
coriander leaves, to serve (optional)

FOR THE CHARMOULA
1 tsp coriander seeds, crushed in a mortar
1 tsp black peppercorns, crushed in a mortar
1 tsp ground cumin
1 tsp paprika
1 tsp ground turmeric
1 red chilli, deseeded and roughly chopped
4 tbsp extra virgin olive oil
juice of 1 lemon
bunch of coriander leaves
sea salt and freshly ground black pepper

 in the slow cooker **PREP** 20 MINS **COOK** 15 MINS PRECOOKING; AUTO/LOW 4-5 HRS

1 Preheat the slow cooker, if required. Put the charmoula ingredients in a food processor and whiz until smooth. Smother the fish with half the charmoula and set aside to marinate. Heat the oil in a large flameproof casserole or tagine over a medium heat, add the onions and celery, season, and cook for 5–6 minutes until soft. Stir in the garlic, ginger, lemon flesh or zest, and remaining charmoula and cook for a few minutes, then cook the carrots and peppers for 5 minutes.

2 Transfer everything to the slow cooker, add the potatoes, and pour over the stock so it just covers. Cover with the lid and cook on auto/low for 4–5 hours. Add the fish and layer the tomatoes over the top for the last 30 minutes of cooking. Taste and season, if needed, add a squeeze of lemon juice, and stir through the coriander leaves, if using. Serve with fluffy couscous and lemon wedges.

traditional method **PREP** 20 MINS **COOK** 1¼–1½ HRS

1 Put the charmoula ingredients in a food processor and whiz until smooth. Smother the fish with half the charmoula and set aside to marinate. Heat the oil in a large flameproof casserole or tagine over a medium heat, add the onions and celery, season, and cook for 5–6 minutes until soft. Stir in the garlic, ginger, lemon flesh or zest, and remaining charmoula and cook for a few minutes, then cook the carrots and peppers for 5 minutes.

2 Add the potatoes and stock, bring to the boil, cover with the lid, and cook at a very low simmer for about 45 minutes, topping up with a little hot water if needed. Add the fish and layer the tomatoes over the top, re-cover, and bring up to a simmer once again. Cook for a further 15–30 minutes until the fish is opaque and cooked through. Taste and season, if needed, add a squeeze of lemon juice, and stir through the coriander leaves, if using. Serve with fluffy couscous and lemon wedges.

One of the spices in this recipe is sumac, a Middle Eastern spice that is slightly tart in taste. It is found in most major supermarkets. Black olives are suggested, but use green if you prefer.

Red mullet with Middle Eastern spices

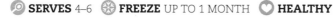 **SERVES** 4–6 **FREEZE** UP TO 1 MONTH **HEALTHY**

1 tbsp olive oil
6 shallots, finely chopped
1 fennel bulb, trimmed and finely chopped
1 carrot, peeled and finely chopped
½ tsp ground cumin
1 tsp of sumac or use a preserved lemon, flesh discarded and rind finely chopped (optional)
4 plum tomatoes, roughly chopped
600ml (1 pint) hot vegetable stock for the slow cooker (900ml/1½ pints for the traditional method)

salt and freshly ground black pepper
8 black olives, stoned
about 1.6kg (3½lb) red mullet, filleted (about 675g/1½lb filleted weight) and cut into chunky pieces
small handful of coriander, finely chopped
small handful of mint, finely chopped
1 preserved lemon, flesh discarded and rind sliced finely, to serve (optional)

 in the slow cooker **PREP** 15 MINS **COOK** 10 MINS PRECOOKING; **HIGH** 3–4 HRS

1 Preheat the slow cooker, if required. Heat the oil in a large heavy-based pan or tagine over a medium heat, add the shallots, fennel, and carrot, and cook for 5 minutes until soft. Stir through the cumin and sumac or preserved lemon, and cook for a further minute.

2 Transfer everything to the slow cooker, then stir through the tomatoes and just enough stock to cover the vegetables, and season with salt and pepper. Add the olives, cover with the lid, and cook on high for 3–4 hours, adding the fish for the last 30 minutes of cooking.

3 Stir through most of the coriander and mint, taste and season, if needed. Serve with couscous and scatter over the remaining fresh herbs and preserved lemon rind, if using.

 traditional method **PREP** 15 MINS **COOK** 1½ HRS

1 Heat the oil in a large heavy-based pan or tagine, add the shallots, fennel, and carrot, and cook for 5 minutes until soft. Stir through the cumin and sumac or preserved lemon, and cook for a further minute. Add the tomatoes and stock, season with salt and pepper, and bring to the boil, then reduce to a simmer.

2 Add the olives, partially cover with a lid, and simmer gently for about 1 hour, stirring occasionally and topping up with hot water, if needed. Sit the fish on top of the tomato mixture, cover with the lid, and cook for a further 10 minutes or until the fish is cooked through.

3 Stir through most of the coriander and mint, taste and season, if needed. Serve with couscous and scatter over the remaining fresh herbs and preserved lemon rind, if using.

Tender lamb is perfectly suited to oregano and lemon. Add the okra to the slow cooker halfway through the cooking time so that it holds its shape. The dish is topped with pine nuts and parsley.

Turkish lamb and lemon

⊙ SERVES 4   **❄ FREEZE** UP TO 3 MONTHS

8 lamb cutlets, trimmed of any fat
1 tsp paprika
1 tbsp olive oil
2 onions, sliced
salt and freshly ground black pepper
3 garlic cloves, finely chopped
grated zest of 1 lemon and juice of 2 lemons
½ tbsp dried oregano

6 tomatoes, roughly chopped
about 250ml (9fl oz) hot vegetable stock for
 the slow cooker (about 300ml/10fl oz for
 the traditional method)
250g (9oz) okra, trimmed and chopped
100g (3½oz) pine nuts, toasted
handful of flat-leaf parsley, finely chopped

in the slow cooker   🕐 **PREP** 15 MINS   **COOK** 15 MINS PRECOOKING;
AUTO/LOW 6–8 HRS OR **HIGH** 3–4 HRS

1 Preheat the slow cooker, if required. Toss the lamb cutlets in the paprika, then heat a tiny drizzle of the oil in a large flameproof casserole or tagine over a medium-high heat. Add the cutlets and cook for 2–3 minutes on each side or until golden. Remove and set aside.

2 Add the remaining oil to the casserole, if needed, reduce the heat, and cook the onions for 4–6 minutes until soft. Season with salt and pepper, stir through the garlic, lemon zest, and oregano, and cook for a minute.

3 Add the tomatoes and lemon juice, and cook for 5 minutes. Transfer everything to the slow cooker, including the lamb, and pour over the stock so it just covers. Cook on auto/low for 6–8 hours or on high for 3–4 hours, adding the okra halfway through. Taste and season, if needed, then stir through the pine nuts and parsley and serve with boiled potatoes.

traditional method   🕐 **PREP** 15 MINS   **COOK** 1¼–1¾ HRS

1 Preheat the oven to 160°C (325°F/Gas 3). Toss the lamb cutlets in the paprika, then heat a tiny drizzle of the oil in a large flameproof casserole or tagine over a medium-high heat. Add the cutlets and cook for 2–3 minutes on each side or until golden. Remove and set aside.

2 Add the remaining oil to the casserole, if needed, reduce the heat, and cook the onions for 4–6 minutes until soft. Season with salt and pepper, stir through the garlic, lemon zest, and oregano, and cook for a minute.

3 Add the okra and cook for 3–4 minutes, stirring, then add the tomatoes and lemon juice, and cook for a further 5 minutes. Return the meat to the casserole, and pour over the stock so it just covers. Cover with the lid and put in the oven for 1–1½ hours. Check occasionally that it's not drying out, topping up with a little hot water if needed. Taste and season, if needed, then stir through the pine nuts and parsley and serve with boiled potatoes.

Here is a full-flavoured, delightfully simple vegetarian dish with pulses and nuts added for protein and texture. Serve it with spoonfuls of brown rice or couscous for the complete meal.

Chickpea, tomato, and herb tagine

 SERVES 4–6   ❄ **FREEZE** UP TO 3 MONTHS   ♡ **HEALTHY**

2 tbsp olive oil
2 large onions, chopped into eighths
salt and freshly ground black pepper
3 garlic cloves, peeled and crushed
1 tbsp paprika
½ tsp dried chilli flakes
1 tsp ground cinnamon
1 tsp ground ginger
12 tomatoes, left whole

450ml (15fl oz) hot vegetable stock for the slow cooker (750ml/1¼ pints for the traditional method)
2 tbsp runny honey
75g (2½oz) flaked almonds
400g can chickpeas, drained
handful of flat-leaf parsley, roughly chopped
handful of coriander, roughly chopped
2 sprigs of thyme
small handful of oregano (optional)

 in the slow cooker   🕐 **PREP** 15 MINS   **COOK** 15 MINS PRECOOKING; AUTO/LOW 6–8 HRS OR **HIGH** 3–4 HRS

1 Preheat the slow cooker, if required. Heat the oil in a large flameproof casserole or tagine over a moderate heat, add the onions, and cook for 4–6 minutes until soft. Add seasoning and the garlic and cook for a further minute.

2 Add the paprika, chilli flakes, cinnamon, and ginger, and mix so the onions are coated. Then add the tomatoes, stock, and honey, combine well, and bring to the boil.

3 Transfer everything to the slow cooker, then add the almonds, chickpeas, and herbs. Season and cover with the lid, and cook on auto/low for 6–8 hours or on high for 3–4 hours. Remove the thyme sprigs and serve with couscous or brown rice.

traditional method   🕐 **PREP** 15 MINS   **COOK** 1¼ HRS

1 Preheat the oven to 160°C (325°F/Gas 3). Heat the oil in a large flameproof casserole or tagine over a moderate heat, add the onions, and cook for 4–6 minutes until soft. Add seasoning and the garlic and cook for a further minute.

2 Add the paprika, chilli flakes, cinnamon, and ginger, and mix so the onions are coated. Then add the tomatoes, stock, and honey, combine well, and bring to the boil.

3 Add the almonds, chickpeas, and herbs, then season, cover with the lid, and put in the oven for 1 hour. Remove the thyme sprigs and serve with couscous or brown rice.

Curries

This is a relatively dry curry, although if you like a curry with more sauce, you can top up the stock during cooking. Fresh ginger and bird's eye chillies make the dish more fragrant.

Karahi chicken

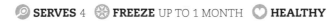

🔍 **SERVES** 4   ❄ **FREEZE** UP TO 1 MONTH   ♡ **HEALTHY**

1 tsp coriander seeds
2 green chillies, deseeded
3 garlic cloves, peeled
1 tsp ground turmeric
2 tbsp sunflower oil
8 chicken thighs, skin on, slashed a few
   times across each thigh
salt and freshly ground black pepper

1 onion, roughly chopped
6 tomatoes, roughly chopped
450ml (15fl oz) hot vegetable stock for the slow
   cooker (900ml/1½ pints for the traditional method)
5cm (2in) piece of fresh root ginger, peeled and
   finely chopped
3–4 green bird's eye chillies, left whole
bunch of coriander, finely chopped

in the slow cooker   ⏱ PREP 15 MINS   COOK 25 MINS PRECOOKING;
AUTO/LOW 6 HRS OR **HIGH** 3 HRS

1 Preheat the slow cooker, if required. Put the coriander seeds, chillies, garlic, turmeric, and half the oil into a food processor and blend until it becomes a paste. Season the chicken with salt and pepper and smother them with the paste, using your hands and pushing it into all the cuts. Heat half the remaining oil in a large flameproof casserole over a medium-high heat and add the chicken pieces. Cook for 5–6 minutes on each side or until beginning to colour, then remove and set aside.

2 Heat the remaining oil in the casserole over a medium heat, add the onion, and cook for 3–4 minutes until soft. Then add the tomatoes and cook for 5–10 minutes until they too are soft. Transfer everything to the slow cooker. Pour over the stock and add the ginger, bird's eye chillies, and chicken, pushing the chicken under the liquid as much as you can. Cover with the lid and cook on auto/low for 6 hours or on high for 3 hours. Remove the chillies, then taste and season as necessary, stirring through the coriander. Serve with rice, chapatis, and some minted yogurt on the side.

traditional method   ⏱ PREP 15 MINS   COOK 1 HR

1 Put the coriander seeds, chillies, garlic, turmeric, and half the oil into a food processor and blend until it becomes a paste. Season the chicken with salt and pepper and smother them with the paste, using your hands and pushing it into all the cuts. Heat half the remaining oil in a large flameproof casserole over a medium-high heat and add the chicken pieces. Cook for 5–6 minutes on each side or until beginning to colour, then remove and set aside.

2 Heat the remaining oil in the casserole over a medium heat, add the onion, and cook for 3–4 minutes until soft. Then add the tomatoes and cook for a further 5–10 minutes until they, too, are soft. Pour in the stock and bring to the boil. Reduce to a simmer, stir in the ginger and bird's eye chillies, and return the chicken to the casserole. Cover with the lid and cook gently for 30–40 minutes, keeping an eye on the sauce. You want it to be fairly dry, but if it is sticking, add a little hot water.

3 Remove the chillies, then taste and season, as necessary, stirring through the coriander. Serve with rice, chapatis, and some minted yogurt on the side.

This curry has an intense heat of chilli running though it, which cuts through the rich, creamy coconut and sweet pumpkin. Use butternut squash if you can't get hold of pumpkin.

Sri Lankan coconut pumpkin curry

SERVES 4–6

2 tbsp olive oil
900g (2lb) pumpkin or butternut squash, peeled, deseeded, and chopped into bite-sized pieces
2 red chillies, deseeded and finely chopped
4 shallots, finely chopped
5cm (2in) piece of fresh root ginger, peeled and grated
3 garlic cloves, grated
1 lemongrass stalk, trimmed, woody outer leaves removed, and finely chopped

juice of 1 lime
400ml can coconut milk
600ml (1 pint) hot vegetable stock for the slow cooker (900ml/1½ pints for the traditional method)
pinch of dried chilli flakes
200g (7oz) spinach leaves
salt and freshly ground black pepper

in the slow cooker 🕑 **PREP** 20 MINS **COOK** 15 MINS PRECOOKING; **HIGH** 3–4 HRS

1 Preheat the slow cooker, if required. Heat half the oil in a large heavy-based pan over a medium heat, add the pumpkin or butternut squash, and cook, stirring, for about 10 minutes until it begins to turn golden. Add the chillies and cook for a minute more.

2 Add the remaining oil and then stir in the shallots, ginger, garlic, and lemongrass. Add the lime juice and stir to scrape up any sticky bits from the bottom of the pan. Add a little coconut milk and let it bubble for a few minutes. Transfer everything to the slow cooker, then pour in the remaining coconut milk and stock together with the chilli flakes. Cover with the lid and cook on high for 3–4 hours.

3 Stir in the spinach and leave for a few minutes for it to wilt before serving. Taste and season, as necessary, and serve with rice.

traditional method 🕑 **PREP** 20 MINS **COOK** 1¼ HRS

1 Preheat the oven to 180°C (350°F/Gas 4). Heat half the oil in a large flameproof casserole over a medium heat, add the pumpkin or butternut squash, and cook, stirring, for about 10 minutes until it begins to turn golden. Add the chillies and cook for a minute more.

2 Add the remaining oil and then stir in the shallots, ginger, garlic, and lemongrass. Add the lime juice and stir to scrape up the bits from the bottom of the casserole. Add a little coconut milk and let it bubble for a few minutes.

3 Pour in the remaining coconut milk and the stock, and bring to the boil. Then reduce to a simmer, add the chilli flakes, cover with the lid, and put in the oven for 1 hour. Check occasionally that it's not drying out, topping up with a little hot water if needed. Remove from the oven and stir in the spinach. It will wilt in the heat. Taste and season, as necessary, and serve with rice.

This is much lighter in flavour than lots of other curries. Plenty of lime, ginger, and coriander make up its basis, and of course, you could always add some cooked chicken or fish if you wish.

Malaysian mango curry

SERVES 4

2 tsp ground turmeric
2 red chillies, deseeded
4 garlic cloves, peeled and left whole
5cm (2in) piece of fresh root ginger, peeled and roughly chopped
1 tbsp sunflower oil
8 shallots, very finely chopped
salt and freshly ground black pepper
400ml can coconut milk

100ml (3½fl oz) hot vegetable stock for the slow cooker (150ml/5fl oz for the traditional method)
juice of 1–2 limes
1 tbsp palm or demerara sugar (optional)
150g (5½ oz) vermicelli noodles, soaked in water and drained
2 ripe mangoes, peeled and cut into bite-sized pieces
bunch of coriander, finely chopped

in the slow cooker   **PREP** 20 MINS   **COOK** 10 MINS PRECOOKING; **HIGH** 3–4 HRS

1 Preheat the slow cooker, if required. Put the turmeric, chillies, garlic, and ginger in a food processor, whiz with half the oil to make a paste, and set aside. Alternatively, grind the ingredients with a pestle and mortar.

2 Heat the remaining oil in a large heavy-based pan, add the shallots, and cook for 3–4 minutes until soft. Season with salt and pepper, then add the paste and cook, stirring occasionally, for a few more minutes. Pour in the coconut milk and stock, and bring to the boil. Transfer everything to the slow cooker, cover with the lid, and cook on high for 3–4 hours.

3 Stir in the lime juice, to taste, and adjust the flavour with a little sugar and seasoning if needed. Stir through the noodles, mango, and coriander.

traditional method   **PREP** 20 MINS   **COOK** 1 HR

1 Put the turmeric, chilli, garlic, and ginger in a food processor, whiz with half the oil to make a paste, and set aside. Alternatively, grind the ingredients with a pestle and mortar.

2 Heat the remaining oil in a large heavy-based pan over a medium heat, add the shallots, and cook for 3–4 minutes until soft. Season with salt and pepper, then add the paste and cook, stirring occasionally, for a few more minutes. Pour in the coconut milk and stock and bring to the boil. Reduce the heat to low, partially cover with the lid, and leave to simmer for about 40 minutes until the sauce has thickened.

3 Stir in the lime juice, to taste, and adjust the flavour with a little sugar and seasoning, if needed. Stir through the noodles, mango, and coriander.

This is a great vegetarian dish, with distinctively sweet flavours of cinnamon and cardamom. The peanuts add a contrasting texture to the potatoes and aubergine. Make it as hot and fiery as you wish.

Aubergine massaman curry

SERVES 4–6

2 red chillies, deseeded
1 lemongrass stalk, tough outer leaves removed
5cm (2in) piece of fresh root ginger, peeled and roughly chopped
5 cardamom pods, crushed
1 tbsp sunflower oil
1 onion, finely chopped
salt and freshly ground black pepper
450ml (15fl oz) hot vegetable stock for the slow cooker (600ml/1 pint for the traditional method)
400ml can coconut milk

1 cinnamon stick, broken
splash of dark soy sauce
splash of fish sauce (nam pla) – omit if cooking for vegetarians
4 potatoes, peeled and chopped into bite-sized pieces
6 baby aubergines, halved lengthways, or use 2 large ones, roughly chopped
1 tbsp palm sugar or demerara sugar (optional)
85g (3oz) roasted unsalted peanuts, roughly chopped

in the slow cooker
PREP 15 MINS   **COOK** 15 MINS PRECOOKING; **AUTO/LOW** 8 HRS OR **HIGH** 3–4 HRS

1 Preheat the slow cooker, if required. Put the chillies, lemongrass, ginger, and cardamom in a food processor and whiz with a drop of the sunflower oil to make a paste.

2 Heat the remaining oil in a large heavy-based pan over a medium heat, add the onion, and cook for 3–4 minutes until soft. Then add the paste and some seasoning and cook for a few minutes more. Stir in the stock and coconut milk and bring to the boil, then add the cinnamon stick, soy sauce, and fish sauce, if using, and stir. Reduce to a simmer and leave uncovered for about 20 minutes, for the sauce to thicken slightly. Transfer everything to the slow cooker and add the potatoes and aubergines. Cover with the lid and cook on auto/low for 8 hours or on high for 3–4 hours.

3 Taste and season with the sugar, if using, and stir in half the peanuts. Ladle into warmed bowls and sprinkle with the remaining peanuts. Serve with rice and lime wedges.

traditional method
PREP 15 MINS   **COOK** 1 HR

1 Put the chillies, lemongrass, ginger, and cardamom in a food processor and whiz with a drop of the sunflower oil to make a paste.

2 Heat the remaining oil in a large heavy-based pan over a medium heat, add the onion, and cook for 3–4 minutes until soft. Then add the paste and some seasoning and cook for a few minutes more. Stir in the stock and coconut milk, and bring to the boil, then add the cinnamon stick, soy sauce, and fish sauce, if using, and cook on a low heat for about 20 minutes. Stir in the potatoes and aubergines and cook for a further 20 minutes.

3 Stir in half the peanuts, taste, and adjust the flavour by adding the sugar, if using, and more salt or fish sauce, also if using, as needed. Ladle into warmed bowls and sprinkle with the remaining peanuts. Serve with rice and lime wedges.

Prawns need minimum cooking, so they can simply be stirred through at the end. You could use ready-cooked ones instead, if you prefer, or you could stir though some cooked chicken.

Prawn makhani

 SERVES 4–6 **FREEZE** UP TO 3 MONTHS, WITHOUT THE CREAM

3 tbsp vegetable oil
3 garlic cloves, finely chopped
5cm (2in) piece of fresh root ginger, peeled and finely chopped
1 cinnamon stick, broken into pieces
2 red chillies, deseeded and finely chopped
4 cardamom pods, crushed
500g (1lb 2oz) tomatoes, chopped

700g (1lb 9oz) (shelled weight) uncooked prawns
salt and freshly ground black pepper
200ml (7fl oz) thick plain yogurt
1–2 tsp medium-hot chilli powder
75g (2½oz) cashew nuts, ground, plus a handful, roughly chopped, to serve
1–2 tsp ground fenugreek
100ml (3½fl oz) double cream

 in the slow cooker **PREP** 20 MINS, PLUS MARINATING **COOK** 10 MINS PRECOOKING; **AUTO/LOW** 4–5 HRS OR **HIGH** 3–4 HRS

1 Preheat the slow cooker, if required. Heat 2 tbsp of the oil in a large heavy-based pan over a low heat, add half the garlic, half the ginger, the cinnamon, chillies, and cardamom pods and cook, stirring occasionally, for 2 minutes. Stir in the tomatoes and 100ml (3½fl oz) of water. Transfer everything to the slow cooker, cover with the lid, and cook on auto/low for 4–5 hours or on high for 3–4 hours.

2 At the last hour of cooking, season the prawns with salt and pepper and toss with the rest of the garlic and ginger, the remaining oil, the yogurt, and chilli powder. Leave to marinate for 20 minutes. Meanwhile, use a stick blender to whiz the mixture in the slow cooker until smooth, stir in the ground cashews and fenugreek, and continue cooking.

3 Heat the pan over a high heat, then add the prawns and yogurt marinade and cook, tossing them all the time, for 5–8 minutes until no longer pink. For the last 5 minutes of cooking, add the prawns and cream to the slow cooker. Season if needed. Garnish with the chopped cashews and serve with rice.

 traditional method **PREP** 20 MINS, PLUS MARINATING **COOK** 40 MINS

1 Heat 2 tbsp of the oil in a large heavy-based pan over a low heat, add half the garlic, half the ginger, the cinnamon, chillies, and cardamom pods and cook, stirring occasionally, for 2 minutes. Stir in the tomatoes and cook for 10 minutes or until they start to reduce. Cover with a little hot water and simmer for a further 10 minutes or until puréed. Push the tomato mixture through a sieve into a food processor and whiz until smooth.

2 Season the prawns with salt and pepper and toss with the rest of the garlic and ginger, the remaining oil, the yogurt, and chilli powder. Leave to marinate for 20 minutes. Heat the pan over a high heat, then add the prawns and yogurt marinade and cook, tossing them all the time, for 5–8 minutes until no longer pink. Remove and set aside.

3 Return the tomatoes to the pan, stir in the ground cashews and fenugreek, and simmer for 10 minutes, adding a little hot water if the sauce looks too thick. For the last 5 minutes of cooking, add the prawns and cream. Season if needed. Garnish with the chopped cashews and serve with rice.

Traditionally, dhansak would be made with three different types of lentils and plenty of vegetables. This version is simpler, but no less tasty for that. It can be made two days ahead and reheated.

Lamb dhansak

 SERVES 6 ⊛ **FREEZE** UP TO 3 MONTHS

4 tbsp vegetable oil
750g (1lb 10oz) boned shoulder of lamb, cut into bite-sized pieces
salt and freshly ground black pepper
1 large aubergine, chopped into bite-sized pieces
1 large onion, finely chopped
2cm (¾in) piece of fresh root ginger, peeled and finely chopped

5 garlic cloves, finely chopped
2 tsp ground cumin
2 tsp ground coriander
2 tsp ground turmeric
pinch of cayenne pepper
1 tbsp plain flour
175g (6oz) green lentils
1 small cauliflower, chopped into florets

 in the slow cooker 🕒 **PREP** 20 MINS **COOK** 20 MINS PRECOOKING; AUTO/LOW 6–8 HRS OR **HIGH** 3–4 HRS

1 Preheat the slow cooker, if required. Heat two-thirds of the oil in a large flameproof casserole over a high heat. Season the lamb with salt and pepper and cook (in batches, if necessary), stirring, for 3–5 minutes until brown on all sides. Remove and set aside. Add the remaining oil to the casserole, then add the aubergine and cook over a medium heat, stirring occasionally, for 5–7 minutes until brown. Also remove and set aside, but in a separate bowl.

2 Add the onion to the casserole and cook for 7–10 minutes until golden brown. Stir in the ginger and garlic and cook for 2–3 minutes until softened and fragrant. Add the ground cumin, coriander, turmeric, and cayenne and cook for 1–2 minutes until thoroughly combined. Return the lamb with any juices, sprinkle with the flour, and cook, stirring, for about 1 minute. Stir in 450ml (15fl oz) of water and bring to the boil. Transfer everything to the slow cooker, then stir in the lentils. Cover with the lid and cook on auto/low for 6–8 hours or on high for 3–4 hours. Stir in the aubergine and cauliflower for the last 30 minutes of cooking, topping up with water if necessary. Serve with fluffy rice and a mango chutney.

 traditional method 🕒 **PREP** 20 MINS **COOK** 2 HRS

1 Heat two-thirds of the oil in a large flameproof casserole over a high heat. Season the lamb with salt and pepper and cook (in batches, if necessary), stirring, for 3–5 minutes until brown on all sides. Remove and set aside. Add the remaining oil to the casserole, then add the aubergine and cook over a medium heat, stirring occasionally, for 5–7 minutes until brown. Also remove and set aside, but in a separate bowl.

2 Add the onion to the casserole and cook for 7–10 minutes until golden brown. Stir in the ginger and garlic and cook for 2–3 minutes until softened and fragrant. Add the ground cumin, coriander, turmeric, and cayenne and cook for 1–2 minutes until thoroughly combined. Return the lamb with any juices, sprinkle with the flour, and cook, stirring, for about 1 minute. Stir in 1 litre (1¾ pints) of water and bring to the boil. Lower the heat, cover, and simmer gently, stirring occasionally, for 30 minutes. Stir in the lentils and cook for 15 minutes longer. Stir in the aubergine, cauliflower, and 500ml (16fl oz) more water; continue simmering, stirring often, for 50–60 minutes until completely tender. Add more water during cooking if the curry seems dry. Serve with fluffy rice and a mango chutney.

Vindaloo originates from Goa on the western coast of India, where the cooking combines Portuguese influences with fiery Indian flavours. This is an elaborate dish, but worth the effort.

Pork vindaloo

 SERVES 4 ✽ **FREEZE** UP TO 3 MONTHS ♡ **HEALTHY**

900g (2lb) boned pork, cut into 5cm (2in) cubes
4 tbsp vegetable oil
5 garlic cloves, finely chopped
2 onions, chopped
1 tsp ground turmeric
1–2 tsp chilli powder
½ tsp tomato purée
3 tomatoes, chopped
3 tbsp wine vinegar or cider vinegar
salt
pinch of crushed black peppercorns
1 tbsp chopped coriander leaves

FOR THE SPICE PASTE
1 tsp cumin seeds
4 cardamom pods
4 cloves
2.5cm (1in) cinnamon stick
5 black peppercorns
1–2 green chillies, chopped
2.5cm (1in) piece fresh root ginger, chopped
4 garlic cloves, peeled and left whole
3 tbsp lemon juice

 in the slow cooker 🕐 **PREP** 30 MINS, PLUS MARINATING   **COOK** 20 MINS PRECOOKING; **AUTO/LOW** 6–8 HRS OR **HIGH** 3–4 HRS

1 To make the spice paste, grind the cumin seeds, cardamom pods, cloves, cinnamon stick, and peppercorns in a clean coffee grinder or spice mill, into a fine powder. Then blend the spice powder with the green chilli, ginger, garlic and lemon juice in a food processor to make a paste. Mix the pork with the paste in a large bowl, cover with cling film, and put in the refrigerator for 1½ hours.

2 Preheat the slow cooker, if required. Heat the oil in a large flameproof casserole, add the garlic, and cook for 1 minute. Add the onions and cook for about 5 minutes, stirring occasionally, until they are golden. Stir in the turmeric, chilli powder, tomato purée, tomatoes, and vinegar. Add the marinated pork and some salt, and cook for 10 minutes, stirring occasionally. Transfer everything to the slow cooker and pour in 275ml (9½fl oz) hot water. Cover with the lid and cook on auto/low for 6–8 hours or on high for 3–4 hours. Add the crushed black pepper, garnish with the chopped coriander, and serve immediately.

 traditional method 🕐 **PREP** 30 MINS   **COOK** 1 HR

1 To make the spice paste, grind the cumin seeds, cardamom pods, cloves, cinnamon stick, and peppercorns in a clean coffee grinder or spice mill, into a fine powder. Then blend the spice powder with the green chilli, ginger, garlic and lemon juice in a food processor to make a paste. Mix the pork with the paste in a large bowl, cover with cling film, and put in the refrigerator for 1½ hours.

2 Heat the oil in a large flameproof casserole, add the garlic, and cook for 1 minute. Add the onions and cook for about 5 minutes, stirring occasionally, until they are golden. Stir in the turmeric, chilli powder, tomato purée, chopped tomatoes, and vinegar. Add the marinated pork and some salt, and cook for 10 minutes, stirring occasionally. Pour in 275ml (9½fl oz) water and bring to the boil, then reduce the heat and simmer on a really low heat for about 40 minutes, or until the meat is cooked through and the sauce is thick. Check occasionally that it's not drying out, topping up with a little hot water if needed. Add the crushed black pepper, garnish with the chopped coriander, and serve immediately.

Don't be shy with the garlic and ginger – this dish is big on bold flavours. For vegetarians, cut a block of paneer or tofu into large cubes and add the pieces to the sauce at the end of cooking.

Chicken tikka masala

SERVES 4 ❄ **FREEZE** UP TO 3 MONTHS, WITHOUT THE CREAM

juice of 2 limes
1 tsp paprika
6 skinless boneless chicken thighs, about 675g (1½lb) total weight, cut into bite-sized pieces
2 shallots, roughly chopped
4 large garlic cloves, roughly chopped
2 green chillies, deseeded and roughly chopped
7.5cm (3in) piece fresh root ginger, roughly chopped
125g (4½oz) plain Greek-style yogurt
½ tsp garam masala

½ tsp coriander seeds, dry-roasted and ground
1½ tsp cumin seeds, dry-roasted and ground
1 tbsp vegetable oil
400g can chopped tomatoes
1 rounded tsp tomato purée
handful of coriander leaves, roughly chopped
½ tsp caster sugar
50g (1¾oz) unsalted butter
120ml (4fl oz) single cream

in the slow cooker
🕐 **PREP** 20 MINS, PLUS MARINATING   **COOK** 15 MINS PRECOOKING; AUTO/LOW 4–5 HRS OR **HIGH** 2–3 HRS

1 In a bowl, mix together most of the lime juice, paprika, and chicken. Set aside. Put the shallots, garlic, chillies, and half the ginger into a food processor. Strain the lime juice and paprika from the chicken and add the liquid to the processor. Whiz until smooth. Tip into a bowl and stir in the yogurt, garam masala, and half the coriander and cumin powder. Pour the yogurt mixture over the chicken and turn to coat. Cover with cling film and refrigerate overnight, if time permits, or cook immediately.

2 Preheat the slow cooker, if required. Heat the oil in a large flameproof casserole until hot, add the chicken pieces, and cook for about 10 minutes until golden on each side. Remove and set aside. Combine the tomatoes, tomato purée, coriander leaves, sugar, and the remaining ginger, lime juice, cumin, and coriander powder in a food processor and whiz until smooth. Melt the butter in the casserole and stir in the tomato mixture. Pour into the slow cooker, add the chicken, cover, and cook on auto/low for 4–5 hours or on high for 2–3 hours. Stir through the cream and cook for 10 minutes. Serve with Indian breads.

traditional method
🕐 **PREP** 20 MINS, PLUS MARINATING   **COOK** 50 MINS

1 In a bowl, mix together most of the lime juice, paprika, and chicken. Set aside. Put the shallots, garlic, chillies, and half the ginger into a food processor. Strain the lime juice and paprika from the chicken and add the liquid to the processor. Whiz until smooth. Tip into a bowl and stir in the yogurt, garam masala, and half the coriander and cumin powder. Pour the spiced yogurt mixture over the chicken and turn to coat. Cover with cling film and refrigerate overnight, if time permits, or cook immediately.

2 Heat the oil in a large flameproof casserole until hot, add the chicken pieces, and cook for about 10 minutes until golden on each side. Remove and set aside. Combine the tomatoes, tomato purée, coriander leaves, sugar, and the remaining ginger, lime juice, cumin, and coriander powder in a food processor and whiz until smooth. Melt the butter in the casserole and stir in the tomato mixture and chicken. Cover and cook for about 30 minutes, topping up with a little hot water if needed. Stir through the cream and cook for 10 more minutes. Serve with Indian breads.

Sambar is made in hundreds of ways, using various vegetables and roasted spices. You can buy tamarind paste in most major supermarkets or look for it in an Asian store.

Vegetable sambar

 SERVES 4   **FREEZE** UP TO 3 MONTHS   **HEALTHY**

100g (3½oz) split yellow lentils
1 tsp ground turmeric
1 tsp chilli powder
2 onions, cut into small pieces
100g (3½oz) carrots, peeled and chopped
100g (3½oz) frozen or fresh green beans, chopped
3 tomatoes, quartered
100g (3½oz) potatoes, peeled and cut into cubes
1 tbsp tamarind paste mixed with 4 tbsp water
salt

FOR THE SPICE PASTE
100g (3½oz) desiccated coconut
2 tsp coriander seeds
1 dried red chilli

FOR TEMPERING
1 tbsp vegetable oil
1 tsp mustard seeds
10 curry leaves
3 dried red chillies

 in the slow cooker   **PREP** 20 MINS   **COOK** 15 MINS PRECOOKING; AUTO/LOW 4–6 HRS OR **HIGH** 2–3 HRS

1 Preheat the slow cooker, if required. For the spice paste, heat a small frying pan over medium heat, add the coconut and spices, and dry-roast until brown. Leave to cool, then put in a food processor and blend to a paste, gradually adding about 250ml (9fl oz) water.

2 Bring 300ml (10fl oz) of water to the boil in a large heavy-based pan and add the lentils, turmeric, chilli powder, and onions. Simmer for 10–15 minutes until the lentils soften. Transfer to the slow cooker and stir in the vegetables. Then add the tamarind water and salt, to taste, and stir in the spice paste. Cover with the lid and cook on auto/low for 4–6 hours or on high for 2–3 hours.

3 For tempering, heat the oil in a heavy-based frying pan and add the mustard seeds. As they begin to pop, add the curry leaves and dried red chillies. Pour this over the curry and gently stir through. Serve hot with some lime wedges and rice or dosas.

 traditional method   **PREP** 20 MINS   **COOK** 50 MINS

1 For the spice paste, heat a small frying pan over medium heat, add the coconut and spices, and dry-roast until brown. Leave to cool, then put in a food processor and blend to a paste, gradually adding about 250ml (9fl oz) water.

2 Bring 300ml (10fl oz) of water to the boil in a large heavy-based pan and add the lentils, turmeric, chilli powder, and onions. Simmer for 10–15 minutes until the lentils soften. Stir in the vegetables. Cover with the lid and cook for about 10 minutes until the vegetables are tender. Add the tamarind water and salt, to taste. Cover and cook for a further 5 minutes. Stir in the spice paste. Bring to the boil, then reduce the heat to moderate and cook, uncovered, for 5 minutes, stirring occasionally.

3 For tempering, heat the oil in a heavy-based frying pan and add the mustard seeds. As they begin to pop, add the curry leaves and dried red chillies. Pour this over the curry and gently stir through. Serve hot with some lime wedges and rice or dosas.

For this recipe, potatoes and cauliflower are tumbled in a tikka coconut sauce. This is a simple and economical dish to make, and can easily be made ahead and reheated when required.

Cauliflower curry

 SERVES 4–6

1 tbsp vegetable oil
1 onion, roughly chopped
salt and freshly ground black pepper
5cm (2in) piece of fresh root ginger,
  peeled and finely chopped
3 garlic cloves, finely chopped
2 green chillies, deseeded and finely chopped

2 tbsp medium-hot tikka curry paste
400g can chickpeas, drained and rinsed
400ml can coconut milk
450ml (15fl oz) hot vegetable stock for the slow
  cooker (600ml/1 pint for the traditional method)
3 potatoes, peeled and cut into bite-sized pieces
1 cauliflower, cut into bite-sized florets

 in the slow cooker   🕐 **PREP** 15 MINS   **COOK** 5 MINS PRECOOKING;
AUTO/LOW 8 HRS OR **HIGH** 4 HRS

1 Preheat the slow cooker, if required. Heat the oil in a large heavy-based pan over a medium heat, add the onion, and cook for 3–4 minutes until soft. Season with salt and pepper, stir through the ginger, garlic, and chillies, and cook for a couple of minutes. Stir in the tikka paste and chickpeas and transfer everything to the slow cooker.

2 Pour in the coconut milk and stock, then add the raw potatoes and cauliflower, and stir. Cover with the lid and cook on auto/low for 8 hours or on high for 4 hours. Serve with some rice and naan bread.

 traditional method   🕐 **PREP** 15 MINS   **COOK** 1 HR

1 Heat the oil in a large heavy-based pan over a medium heat, add the onion, and cook for 3–4 minutes until soft. Season with salt and pepper, stir through the ginger, garlic, and chillies, and cook for a couple of minutes. Stir in the tikka paste, chickpeas, coconut milk, and stock and bring to the boil. Reduce to a simmer and cook gently, partially covered with the lid and stirring occasionally, for 30 minutes.

2 Meanwhile, bring another large pan of salted water to the boil. Add the potatoes and cook for about 15 minutes or until just beginning to soften. Remove the potatoes with a slotted spoon and set aside. Put the cauliflower in the boiling water and cook for about 5 minutes, then drain well.

3 Tip the potato and cauliflower into the sauce and turn so they are well coated, then simmer very gently for a further 15 minutes or so, to allow all the flavours to mingle. Serve with some rice and naan bread.

Cashew nuts and sultanas enrich this lamb curry. Make it as hot as you desire as the yogurt will mellow it a little. The lamb becomes very tender when slow cooked and isn't at all fatty.

Balti lamb curry

⊘ **SERVES** 4–6 ❄ **FREEZE** UP TO 1 MONTH

1 tbsp vegetable oil
1 onion, finely chopped
salt and freshly ground black pepper
3 garlic cloves, finely chopped
5cm (2in) piece of fresh root ginger,
   peeled and finely chopped
1–2 red chillies, depending on your heat
   preference, deseeded and finely chopped

1 tbsp curry balti paste
900g (2lb) lamb leg, cut into bite-sized pieces
600ml (1 pint) hot vegetable stock for the slow
   cooker (750ml/1¼ pints for the traditional method)
125g (4½oz) sultanas
125g (4½oz) cashew nuts (half of them ground)
100g (3½oz) plain yogurt
small bunch of coriander, finely chopped

in the slow cooker ⏱ **PREP** 15 MINS **COOK** 20 MINS PRECOOKING; AUTO/LOW 6–8 HRS OR **HIGH** 3–4 HRS

1 Preheat the slow cooker, if required. Preheat the oven to 180°C (350°F/Gas 4). Heat the oil in a large flameproof casserole over a medium heat, add the onion, and cook for 3–4 minutes until soft. Season well with salt and pepper, stir through the garlic, ginger, and chillies, and cook for a few more minutes.

2 Stir through the curry paste, then add the lamb and toss to coat. Increase the heat a little and cook for 5–8 minutes until the lamb is no longer pink. Pour in a little stock and let it bubble for a few minutes, then transfer everything to the slow cooker.

3 Pour in the remaining stock and tip in the sultanas and ground cashew nuts. Cover with the lid and cook on auto/low for 6–8 hours or on high for 3–4 hours. Stir in the whole cashew nuts for the last 30 minutes of cooking. Stir through the yogurt and coriander and serve with rice, naan bread, and some lemon wedges on the side.

traditional method ⏱ **PREP** 15 MINS **COOK** 1½ HRS

1 Preheat the oven to 180°C (350°F/Gas 4). Heat the oil in a large flameproof casserole over a medium heat, add the onion, and cook for 3–4 minutes until soft. Season well with salt and pepper, stir through the garlic, ginger, and chillies, and cook for a few more minutes.

2 Stir through the curry paste, then add the lamb and toss to coat. Increase the heat a little and cook for 5–8 minutes until the lamb is no longer pink. Pour in a little stock and let it bubble for a few minutes, then add the remaining stock, bring back to the boil, and reduce to a simmer.

3 Tip in the sultanas and cashew nuts, both whole and ground, and stir. Cover with the lid and put in the oven for 1 hour. Check occasionally that it's not drying out, topping up with a little hot water if needed. Stir through the yogurt and coriander and serve with rice, naan bread, and some lemon wedges on the side.

Duck curry is extremely rich and has a great depth of flavour. If you like your curry hot, use two red chillies rather than the one specified – and leave the seeds in for an even greater kick.

Duck curry

 SERVES 4 ✳ **FREEZE** UP TO 1 MONTH

2 duck breasts
1 tbsp sunflower oil
1 onion, finely chopped
2 celery sticks, finely chopped
salt and freshly ground black pepper
3 garlic cloves, finely chopped
1 red chilli, deseeded and finely chopped
5cm (2in) piece of fresh root ginger, peeled
   and finely chopped

2 carrots, peeled and finely chopped
1 tbsp garam masala
1 tsp ground turmeric
1 tsp paprika
1 tbsp tomato purée
2 x 400g cans chopped tomatoes
600ml (1 pint) hot vegetable stock
   for the slow cooker (900ml/1½ pints
   for the traditional method)

 in the slow cooker 🕐 **PREP** 15 MINS **COOK** 25 MINS PRECOOKING; **AUTO/LOW** 8 HRS

1 Preheat the slow cooker, if required. Heat a heavy-based pan over a medium-high heat and add the duck breasts, skin-side down. Cook each side for 3–6 minutes until golden. Remove and set aside. Heat the oil in the pan over a medium heat, add the onion and celery, and cook for about 5 minutes until soft. Season with salt and pepper, stir in the garlic, chilli, and ginger, and cook for a couple more minutes. Add the carrots, turn to coat, and continue cooking for 5 more minutes, stirring occasionally. Stir through the spices and tomato purée and cook for 1–2 minutes.

2 Transfer everything to the slow cooker and then add the tomatoes and stock. Add the duck breasts and tuck them into the sauce. Cover with the lid and cook on auto/low for 8 hours. Remove the duck breasts, peel off the skin, and then shred the meat. Put the duck meat back into the slow cooker and stir, then taste and season, as required. Serve with rice and chapatis.

traditional method 🕐 **PREP** 15 MINS **COOK** 2 HRS

1 Preheat the oven to 180°C (350°F/Gas 4). Heat a large flameproof casserole over a medium-high heat and add the duck breasts, skin-side down. Cook each side for 3–6 minutes or until golden. Remove and set aside. Heat the oil in the casserole over a medium heat, add the onion and celery, and cook for about 5 minutes until soft. Season with salt and pepper, stir in the garlic, chilli, and ginger, and cook for a couple more minutes.

2 Add the carrots, turn to coat, and continue cooking for 5 more minutes, stirring occasionally. Stir through the spices and tomato purée and cook for 1–2 minutes, then tip in the tomatoes and stock. Bring to the boil, reduce to a simmer, and return the duck breasts to the casserole, tucking them into the sauce. Cover with the lid and put in the oven for 1½ hours. Check occasionally that it's not drying out, topping up with a little hot water if needed.

3 Remove from the oven and spoon out the duck breasts. Peel off the skin and then shred the meat. Put the duck meat back into the casserole and return it to the oven for another 30 minutes (if the sauce is too thin, remove the lid). Taste and season, if necessary. Serve with rice and chapatis.

This is a hot and sour curry that features chillies and pineapple in a thick sauce of lentils, which successfully temper the heat and add texture to the finished dish.

Prawn dhansak

⊘ SERVES 6 **❄ FREEZE** UP TO 3 MONTHS

250g (9oz) red lentils
salt and freshly ground black pepper
3 tbsp vegetable oil or 2 tbsp ghee
4 cardamom pods, crushed
2 tsp mustard seeds
2 tsp chilli powder
2 tsp ground turmeric
2 tsp ground cinnamon
2 onions, finely chopped

10cm (4in) piece fresh root ginger, peeled and
   finely chopped
4 garlic cloves, finely chopped
3–4 green chillies, deseeded and finely sliced
½ pineapple, peeled and cut into bite-sized pieces
6 tomatoes, skinned and roughly chopped
450g (1lb) (shelled weight) uncooked king prawns
handful of coriander, finely chopped

in the slow cooker 🕐 **PREP** 15 MINS **COOK** 10 MINS PRECOOKING;
AUTO/LOW 6–8 HRS OR **HIGH** 3–4 HRS

1 Preheat the slow cooker, if required. Put the lentils in the slow cooker, season well with salt and pepper, then pour in enough cold water to cover. Cover with the lid and cook on auto/low for 6–8 hours or on high for 3–4 hours.

2 Meanwhile, while the lentils are starting to cook in the slow cooker, heat 1 tbsp of the oil or ½ tbsp of the ghee in a large heavy-based pan, add the dried spices, and cook, stirring, for 2 minutes or until the seeds pop. Stir in the onions, ginger, garlic, and chillies, and cook for 5 minutes or until soft and fragrant. Transfer to the slow cooker with the lentils, re-cover with the lid, and continue cooking.

3 Heat 1 tbsp of the oil or ½ tbsp of ghee in the pan, stir through the pineapple and tomatoes, then stir these into the lentils for the last 30 minutes of cooking. When ready to serve, heat the remaining oil or ghee, add the prawns, and cook briefly until pink, then stir them into the lentils. Taste and season if needed, stir through the coriander, and serve with rice or naan bread.

traditional method 🕐 **PREP** 15 MINS **COOK** 50 MINS

1 Put the lentils in a large heavy-based pan, season well with salt and pepper, then pour in enough cold water to cover. Cover with the lid, bring to the boil, then reduce to a simmer, and cook for 20 minutes or until soft. Top up with hot water if they begin to dry out. Drain and set aside.

2 Meanwhile, heat 1 tbsp of the oil or ½ tbsp of the ghee in a large heavy-based pan, add the dried spices, and cook, stirring, for 2 minutes or until the seeds pop. Stir in the onions, ginger, garlic, and chillies, and cook for 5 minutes or until soft and fragrant.

3 Add 1 tbsp of the oil or ½ tbsp of ghee to the pan, stir through the pineapple, add the lentils and tomatoes, and a little hot water so the mixture is slightly sloppy, then simmer on a really low heat for about 15 minutes. Meanwhile, heat the remaining oil or ghee, add the prawns and cook briefly until pink, then stir them into the lentils. Taste and season if needed, stir through the coriander, and serve with rice or naan bread.

This is a mild vegetarian curry and the sweet peppers marry well with the paneer. This is an Indian cheese that won't melt upon cooking; you'll find it with the other cheeses at the supermarket.

Paneer and sweet pepper curry

 SERVES 4–6 **HEALTHY**

2 tbsp vegetable oil
1 x 230g packet paneer, cubed
10cm (4in) piece fresh root ginger, peeled and sliced
2 red chillies, deseeded and finely chopped
2 tbsp dried curry leaves, crushed
2 tsp cumin seeds

4 tsp garam masala
2 tsp ground turmeric
6 red peppers, deseeded and sliced
6 tomatoes, skinned and roughly chopped
salt and freshly ground black pepper
bunch of coriander, finely chopped

 in the slow cooker **PREP** 20 MINS **COOK** 15 MINS PRECOOKING;
AUTO/LOW 5–6 HRS OR HIGH 3–4 HRS

1 Preheat the slow cooker, if required. Heat half the oil in a heavy-based pan over a medium-high heat, add the paneer, and cook for 5–8 minutes, stirring, until golden all over. Remove and set aside.

2 Heat the remaining oil in the pan, add the ginger, chillies, curry leaves, cumin seeds, garam masala, and turmeric, and stir well to coat with the oil. Then add the peppers, tomatoes, and 100ml (3½fl oz) water and bring to the boil.

3 Transfer everything to the slow cooker, including the paneer, and season with salt and pepper. Cover with the lid and cook on auto/low for 5–6 hours or on high for 3–4 hours. Stir through the coriander and serve with rice, chapatis, or naan bread.

traditional method **PREP** 20 MINS **COOK** 1 HR

1 Heat half the oil in a heavy-based pan over a medium-high heat, add the paneer and cook for 5–8 minutes, stirring, until golden all over. Remove and set aside.

2 Heat the remaining oil in the pan, add the ginger, chillies, curry leaves, cumin seeds, garam masala, and turmeric, and stir well to coat with the oil. Then add the peppers and cook over a low heat for about 15 minutes until beginning to soften.

3 Add the tomatoes and 100ml (3½fl oz) water and cook on low for 15 minutes. Return the paneer to the pan, season with salt and pepper, then simmer gently for 15–20 minutes, topping up with a little hot water if needed. Stir through the coriander and serve with rice, chapatis, or naan bread.

Lots of spices enliven these red lentils, making them delicious enough to eat on their own with rice. Wash the lentils well before using and pick them over for any stones.

Red lentil dahl

 SERVES 4 ✸ **FREEZE** UP TO 3 MONTHS ♡ **HEALTHY**

1 tbsp sunflower oil
1 onion, finely chopped
salt and freshly ground black pepper
3 garlic cloves, finely chopped
1 red chilli, deseeded and finely chopped
5cm (2in) piece of fresh root ginger, peeled and grated
1 tsp ground cumin
1 tsp ground coriander
1 tsp ground turmeric

1 tsp paprika
6 curry leaves, crushed
175g (6oz) red lentils, rinsed and picked over for any stones
400g can chopped tomatoes
600ml (1 pint) hot vegetable stock for the slow cooker (900ml/1½ pints for the traditional method)
juice of ½ lemon (optional)
small bunch of coriander leaves, finely chopped

 in the slow cooker 🕐 **PREP** 15 MINS **COOK** 10 MINS PRECOOKING; **AUTO/LOW** 8 HRS OR **HIGH** 4 HRS

1 Preheat the slow cooker, if required. Heat the oil in a large heavy-based pan over a medium heat, add the onion, and cook for 3–4 minutes until soft. Season with salt and pepper, stir through the garlic, chilli, and ginger, and cook for a couple more minutes.

2 Add all the spices and curry leaves and stir well, then stir through the lentils so they get well coated with the spices. Tip in the tomatoes and transfer everything to the slow cooker. Pour in the stock, cover with the lid, and cook on auto/low for 8 hours or on high for 4 hours.

3 Taste and season as needed, adding the lemon juice, if using, and stir through the coriander. Serve with rice, chapatis, and a spoonful of yogurt on the side.

traditional method 🕐 **PREP** 15 MINS **COOK** 1¼ HRS

1 Heat the oil in a large heavy-based pan over a medium heat, add the onion, and cook for 3–4 minutes until soft. Season with salt and pepper, stir through the garlic, chilli, and ginger, and cook for a couple more minutes.

2 Add all the spices and curry leaves and stir well, then stir through the lentils so they are well coated with the spices. Tip in the tomatoes and 600ml (1 pint) of the stock. Bring to the boil, then reduce to a simmer, partially cover with the lid, and cook on a low heat for about 1 hour, stirring occasionally and topping up with the reserved stock when needed.

3 Taste and season as needed, adding the lemon juice, if using, and stir through the coriander. Serve with rice, chapatis, and a spoonful of yogurt on the side.

Okra is becoming more popular, and when chopped and cooked in this way it still remains firm. Lots of ginger is the key to this dish, it works really well with the acidity of the tomatoes.

Ginger and okra curry

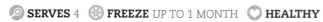 **SERVES** 4 ✽ **FREEZE** UP TO 1 MONTH ♡ **HEALTHY**

1 tbsp sunflower oil
6 shallots, finely chopped
salt and freshly ground black pepper
1–2 green chillies, depending on your heat
  preference, deseeded and finely chopped
3 garlic cloves, finely chopped
175g (6oz) okra, tops trimmed
10cm (4in) piece of fresh root ginger, peeled
  and finely chopped

1 tsp black onion seeds
4 tomatoes, finely chopped
400g can chopped tomatoes
300ml (10fl oz) hot vegetable stock for
  the slow cooker (600ml/1 pint for the
  traditional method)
lemon wedges, for serving

 ### in the slow cooker   ⏱ **PREP** 15 MINS   **COOK** 15 MINS PRECOOKING;
                                                 AUTO/LOW 8 HRS OR **HIGH** 4 HRS

1 Preheat the slow cooker, if required. Heat the oil in a large heavy-based pan over a medium heat, add the shallots, and cook for about 5 minutes until soft. Season with salt and pepper, stir through the chillies and garlic, and cook for a few more minutes.

2 Add the okra, increase the heat a little and fry them, stirring, until they take on some colour. Stir in the ginger and onion seeds, turning to coat. Transfer everything to the slow cooker. Stir in the fresh and canned tomatoes and the stock. Cover with the lid and cook on auto/low for 8 hours or on high for 4 hours. Taste and season, as necessary, and serve the curry with rice, chapatis, and lemon wedges on the side.

 ### traditional method   ⏱ **PREP** 15 MINS   **COOK** 1¼ HRS

1 Heat the oil in a large heavy-based pan over a medium heat, add the shallots, and cook for about 5 minutes until soft. Season with salt and pepper, then stir through the chillies and garlic, and cook for a few more minutes.

2 Add the okra, increase the heat a little and fry them, stirring, until they take on some colour. Stir in the ginger and onion seeds, turning to coat.

3 Add the fresh and canned tomatoes and bring to the boil, then pour in the stock and let the sauce bubble for a few minutes more. Reduce to a simmer, cover with the lid, and cook on a low heat for about 1 hour, stirring occasionally and topping up with hot water if needed. For the last 15 minutes or so, remove the lid and let the sauce simmer to thicken. Taste and season, as necessary, and serve the curry with rice, chapatis, and lemon wedges on the side.

This is a simple vegetarian curry centred on nutty chickpeas and spices. You could stir through some fresh spinach at the end and spice it up with chillies if you wish.

Chickpea curry with cardamom

SERVES 4   ❄ **FREEZE** UP TO 3 MONTHS   ♥ **HEALTHY**

1 tbsp vegetable oil
1 onion, finely chopped
salt and freshly ground black pepper
1 tsp cumin seeds
1 tsp ground turmeric
1 tsp ground coriander

6 cardamom pods, lightly crushed
400g can chickpeas, drained and rinsed
400g can chopped tomatoes
1–2 tsp garam masala
1 tsp chilli powder

 in the slow cooker   ⏱ **PREP** 10 MINS   **COOK** 10 MINS PRECOOKING;
AUTO/LOW 4–5 HRS OR **HIGH** 2–3 HRS

1 Preheat the slow cooker, if required. Heat the oil in a large heavy-based pan over a low heat, add the onion and a pinch of salt, and cook gently for about 5 minutes until soft. Stir in the cumin seeds, turmeric, coriander, and cardamom and continue cooking for about 5 minutes until fragrant.

2 Add the chickpeas to the pan and stir well, crushing them slightly with the back of a wooden spoon. Tip in the tomatoes, including any juices, then fill the can with water and add this also. Sprinkle in the garam masala and chilli powder and bring to the boil. Transfer everything to the slow cooker, cover with the lid, and cook on auto/low for 4–5 hours or on high for 2–3 hours. Taste and season if needed. Serve hot with a squeeze of lemon and topped with a spoonful of yogurt, together with naan bread and basmati rice.

 traditional method   ⏱ **PREP** 10 MINS   **COOK** 50 MINS

1 Heat the oil in a large heavy-based pan over a low heat, add the onion and a pinch of salt, and cook gently for about 5 minutes until soft. Stir in the cumin seeds, turmeric, coriander, and cardamom and continue cooking for about 5 minutes until fragrant.

2 Add the chickpeas to the pan and stir well, crushing them slightly with the back of a wooden spoon. Tip in the tomatoes, including any juices, then fill the can with water and add this also. Sprinkle in the garam masala and chilli powder and bring to the boil.

3 Reduce the heat to low and simmer gently for about 40 minutes, until the sauce begins to thicken slightly, and topping up with a little hot water if needed. Taste and season if needed. Serve hot with a squeeze of lemon and topped with a spoonful of yogurt, together with naan bread and basmati rice.

Korma refers to a fragrant Indian dish in which meat is gently cooked with spices and plain yogurt. Here, the korma is made with lamb, but you could also use chicken and prawns.

Lamb korma

 SERVES 6 ❄ **FREEZE** UP TO 3 MONTHS

120ml (4fl oz) vegetable oil
6 onions, total weight about 750g (1lb 10oz), sliced
2.5cm (1in) piece of fresh root ginger, peeled and grated
2 garlic cloves, finely chopped
1.4kg (3lb) boned lamb shoulder, excess fat trimmed, and cut into bite-sized pieces
250ml (9fl oz) plain yogurt
salt
250ml (9fl oz) double cream
3–5 sprigs of coriander, leaves chopped

FOR THE SPICE MIXTURE
2 dried red chillies, deseeded
5 cardamom pods, seeds extracted
1 cinnamon stick, crushed, or 2 tsp ground cinnamon
5 whole cloves
7 black peppercorns
2 tsp ground cumin
1 tsp ground mace
1 tsp paprika

in the slow cooker ⏱ PREP 25 MINS COOK 25 MINS PRECOOKING; AUTO/LOW 5–6 HRS OR HIGH 3–4 HRS

1 Preheat the slow cooker, if required. To make the spice mixture, put the chillies, cardamom seeds, crushed cinnamon, cloves, and peppercorns in a mortar or clean coffee grinder and grind them as finely as possible. Stir in the cumin, mace, paprika, and ground cinnamon, if using.

2 Heat the oil in a large flameproof casserole over a low heat, add the onions, and cook for about 20 minutes until soft and golden brown. Stir in the ginger and garlic and cook for about 2 minutes until soft and fragrant. Stir in the spice mixture and cook for 1–2 minutes until thoroughly combined. Add the lamb and cook for about 5 minutes, stirring and tossing constantly, so they absorb the flavour of the spices. Then add the yogurt and a little salt, and transfer everything to the slow cooker. Cover with the lid and cook on auto/low for 5–6 hours or on high for 3–4 hours. Stir through the cream for the last 20 minutes of cooking. Taste and season if needed, garnish with the coriander, and serve with rice.

traditional method ⏱ PREP 25 MINS COOK 2½–3 HRS

1 To make the spice mixture, put the chillies, cardamom seeds, crushed cinnamon, cloves, and peppercorns in a mortar or clean coffee grinder and grind them as finely as possible. Stir in the cumin, mace, paprika, and ground cinnamon, if using.

2 Heat the oil in a large flameproof casserole over a low heat, add the onions, and cook for about 20 minutes until soft and golden brown. Stir in the ginger and garlic and cook for about 2 minutes until soft and fragrant. Stir in the spice mixture and cook for 1–2 minutes until thoroughly combined. Add the lamb and cook for about 5 minutes, stirring and tossing constantly, so they absorb the flavour of the spices. Then add the yogurt and a little salt, and bring almost to the boil. Reduce the heat to very low, cover, and cook for 2–2½ hours until the lamb is tender enough to crush with your fingers. Stir occasionally during cooking so the meat does not stick. If the liquid evaporates too quickly, add a little hot water. Stir the cream into the lamb. Taste and season if needed, garnish with the coriander, and serve with rice.

Chillies &
gumbos

A blend of hot spices and dark chocolate combine in this famous Mexican dish. Turkey is a good lean meat, but use chicken if you prefer. Make sure you use the best quality dark chocolate.

Turkey mole

 SERVES 4–6 **HEALTHY**

900g (2lb) boneless turkey thighs
salt and freshly ground black pepper
3 tbsp vegetable oil
45g (1½oz) dark chocolate (70 per cent cocoa),
  broken into pieces

FOR THE MOLE MIXTURE
400g can chopped tomatoes
½ onion, quartered
3 garlic cloves, peeled and left whole

1 slice of stale white bread, torn into pieces
1 stale corn tortilla, torn into pieces
175g (6oz) blanched almonds
75g (2½oz) raisins
30g (1oz) chilli powder
1 tsp each of ground cloves, coriander, and cumin
¼ tsp ground aniseed
2 tsp ground cinnamon
30g (1oz) sesame seeds

 in the slow cooker ⏱ **PREP** 20 MINS **COOK** 15 MINS PRECOOKING;
AUTO/LOW 6–8 HRS OR **HIGH** 3–4 HRS

1 Preheat the slow cooker, if required. Season the turkey and heat half the oil in a large flameproof casserole over a medium heat. Add the turkey pieces, skin-side down, and cook for 10–15 minutes until browned all over. Set aside. For the mole mixture, put all the ingredients, except for half the sesame seeds, in a food processor and blend to a smooth paste.

2 Heat the remaining oil in the casserole over a moderate heat, add the mole mixture, and cook, stirring, for about 5 minutes, until it is thick. Add the chocolate and stir until it has melted, then slowly add 250ml (9fl oz) of hot water, stirring. Season with salt and bring to the boil. Transfer everything to the slow cooker, including the turkey. Cover with the lid and cook on auto/low for 6–8 hours or on high for 3–4 hours Remove the turkey and set aside until cool enough to handle. Remove the skin and any fat, and shred the meat with your fingers. Return to the sauce and stir. Taste for seasoning. Toast the remaining sesame seeds for 2–3 minutes in a dry frying pan until lightly golden. Serve with white rice and sprinkle with the sesame seeds.

 traditional method ⏱ **PREP** 45–50 MINS **COOK** 1¼–1¾ HRS

1 Season the turkey and heat half the oil in a large flameproof casserole over a medium heat. Add the turkey pieces, skin-side down, and cook for 10–15 minutes until browned all over. Add 900ml (1½ pints) water, bring to a boil, and cover. Simmer for 45–60 minutes, until the turkey is very tender when pierced with a fork. Set aside. Strain the cooking liquid into a bowl. For the mole mixture, put all the ingredients, except for half the sesame seeds, in a food processor and blend to a smooth paste.

2 Heat the remaining oil in the casserole over a moderate heat, add the mole mixture, and cook, stirring, for about 5 minutes, until it is thick. Add the chocolate and stir until it has melted. Pour in the cooking liquid, season with salt, and stir. Simmer for 25–30 minutes, to thicken. Toast the remaining sesame seeds for 2–3 minutes in a dry frying pan until lightly golden. Remove the skin and any fat from the turkey and shred the meat with your fingers. Return the turkey to the casserole and simmer for 10–15 minutes. Taste for seasoning. Serve with white rice and sprinkle with the sesame seeds.

In Texas, you will never find red beans in a chilli; they are served on the side, as in this authentic recipe. Do mix them in with the meat, if you prefer. For a real Texan touch, serve it with cornbread.

Chilli con carne

⊙ **SERVES** 6   ❄ **FREEZE** UP TO 3 MONTHS   ♡ **HEALTHY**

3 tbsp vegetable oil, plus more if needed
1.35kg (3lb) braising steak, cut into bite-sized pieces
3 onions, chopped
3 garlic cloves, finely chopped
2 x 400g cans chopped tomatoes
2–4 dried red chillies, deseeded and finely chopped
  or crumbled
5–6 sprigs of oregano, leaves chopped or
  1 tbsp dried oregano

2 tbsp chilli powder
1 tbsp paprika
2 tsp ground cumin
1–2 tsp Tabasco sauce
salt and freshly ground black pepper
1 tbsp fine cornmeal (polenta)

in the slow cooker   ⏱ **PREP** 35 MINS   **COOK** 20 MINS PRECOOKING;
AUTO/LOW 6–8 HRS OR **HIGH** 3–4 HRS

1 Preheat the slow cooker, if required. Heat half the oil in a large flameproof casserole over a high heat, add the beef (in batches and with extra oil, if necessary), and cook, stirring, until browned. If the meat has been cooked in batches return it all to the casserole, then add the onions, garlic, and tomatoes, and cook, stirring, for 8–10 minutes until the onions are just soft.

2 Transfer everything to the slow cooker and pour in 300ml (10fl oz) water. Stir, then add the chillies, oregano, chilli powder, paprika, cumin, Tabasco sauce, and salt and pepper. Cover with the lid and cook on auto/low for 6–8 hours or on high for 3–4 hours. Stir though the cornmeal for the last hour of cooking. At the end of cooking, the chilli should be thick and rich. Taste for seasoning, and serve it with boiled, white long-grain rice and bowls of warmed red kidney beans.

traditional method   ⏱ **PREP** 35 MINS   **COOK** 2¼–2¾ HRS

1 Heat half the oil in a large flameproof casserole over a high heat, add the beef (in batches and with extra oil, if necessary), and cook, stirring, until browned. If the meat has been cooked in batches return it all to the casserole, then add the onions, garlic, and tomatoes, and cook, stirring, for 8–10 minutes until the onions are just soft.

2 Pour in 500ml (16fl oz) water and stir into the casserole with the chillies, oregano, chilli powder, paprika, cumin, Tabasco sauce, and salt and pepper. Bring just to the boil, cover, and simmer over a low heat, stirring occasionally, for about 2–2½ hours until the meat is very tender. About 30 minutes before the end of cooking, stir in the cornmeal. At the end of cooking, the chilli should be thick and rich. Taste for seasoning, and serve it with boiled, white long-grain rice and bowls of warmed red kidney beans.

In Louisiana, gumbo can be made from any number of ingredients. Best of all is prawn gumbo bolstered, as here, with oysters. It is thickened with a dark roux of flour toasted slowly in oil.

Prawn and okra gumbo

 SERVES 4–6

1 bay leaf
3–5 sprigs of thyme
1½ tsp allspice berries
1 tsp crushed chillies
75ml (2½fl oz) vegetable oil
60g (2oz) plain flour
1 large onion, finely chopped
3 garlic cloves, finely chopped
2 green peppers, deseeded and diced
salt and freshly ground black pepper
350g (12oz) tomatoes, skinned and coarsely chopped

150g (5½oz) smoked sausage, such as
  kielbasa, outer casing removed, if necessary,
  and cut into 1cm (½in) slices
250g (9oz) okra, chopped into 1cm (½in) slices
450g (1lb) raw medium prawns, peeled
  and deveined
12 shelled oysters
small bunch of spring onions, trimmed and
  sliced diagonally
small bunch of parsley, leaves finely chopped
½ tsp Tabasco sauce, plus more to taste

in the slow cooker   PREP 45 MINS   COOK 25 MINS PRECOOKING; AUTO/LOW 6–8 HRS OR HIGH 3–4 HRS

1 Preheat the slow cooker, if required. Put the bay leaf, thyme, allspice, and crushed chillies in a muslin bag and tie the top. To make a roux, heat the oil in a large flameproof casserole over a low heat, stir in the flour, and cook for about 5 minutes, stirring constantly, until the roux is medium brown. Stir the onion, garlic, peppers, and seasoning into the roux and cook for 7–10 minutes, stirring, until they are softened and lightly browned. Add the tomatoes and sausage and cook, stirring occasionally, for a further 10–12 minutes. Add the okra, spice bag, and 450ml (15fl oz) water.

2 Transfer everything to the slow cooker, cover with the lid, and cook on auto/low for 6–8 hours or on high for 3–4 hours. Add the prawns for the last 10 minutes of cooking, until they start to turn pink. Add the oysters and spring onions for the last 5 minutes of cooking, until the edges of the oysters start to curl. Discard the spice bag. Stir in the parsley and Tabasco sauce. Taste for seasoning, adding more Tabasco sauce, if you like. To serve, spoon the gumbo into warmed soup bowls.

traditional method   PREP 45 MINS   COOK 1¼ HRS

1 Put the bay leaf, thyme, allspice, and crushed chillies in a muslin bag and tie the top. To make a roux, heat the oil in a large flameproof casserole over a low heat, stir in the flour, and cook for about 5 minutes, stirring constantly, until the roux is medium brown. Stir the onion, garlic, peppers, and seasoning into the roux and cook for 7–10 minutes, stirring, until they are softened and lightly browned. Add the tomatoes and sausage and cook, stirring occasionally, for a further 10–12 minutes. Add the okra, spice bag, and 450ml (15fl oz) water. Partially cover the casserole and let it simmer for 40–50 minutes until the okra is very tender and the gumbo is thick and rich.

2 Just before serving, add the prawns to the gumbo and simmer gently for 3–5 minutes until they begin to turn pink. Add the oysters and spring onions and cook for 1–2 minutes, until the edges of the oysters start to curl. Discard the spice bag. Stir in the parsley and Tabasco sauce. Taste for seasoning, adding more Tabasco sauce, if you like. To serve, spoon the gumbo into warmed soup bowls.

Pinto beans are creamy pink and, when mashed, are the common base filling of burritos. If you can't find them, use the same amount of black or kidney beans instead. They will taste just as good.

Pinto bean chilli

 SERVES 4–6 **FREEZE** UP TO 3 MONTHS **HEALTHY**

1 tbsp olive oil
2 red onions, finely chopped
salt and freshly ground black pepper
3 garlic cloves, finely chopped
2–3 red chillies, depending on your heat
   preference, deseeded and finely chopped
1 tsp ground allspice
pinch of ground cumin
1 large cinnamon stick
1 tsp dried oregano

2 bay leaves
1 tbsp cider vinegar
2 x 400g cans chopped tomatoes
1 tbsp tomato purée
1 tbsp dark brown sugar
2 x 400g cans pinto beans, drained
   and rinsed
450ml (15fl oz) hot vegetable stock
   for the slow cooker (900ml/1½ pints
   for the traditional method)

 in the slow cooker **PREP** 15 MINS **COOK** 5 MINS PRECOOKING;
                                                    AUTO/LOW 6–8 HRS OR **HIGH** 4–5 HRS

1 Preheat the slow cooker, if required. Heat the oil in a large heavy-based pan over a medium heat, add the onions, and cook for 3–4 minutes until soft. Season with salt and pepper, stir in the garlic, chillies, ground spices, and herbs, and cook for 2 minutes.

2 Transfer everything to the slow cooker, then stir in the vinegar, tomatoes, tomato purée, sugar, beans, and stock. Cover with the lid and cook on auto/low for 6–8 hours or on high for 4–5 hours.

3 Taste and season as needed, removing the bay leaves and cinnamon stick, and serve with bowls of grated cheese and soured cream, if you like.

 traditional method **PREP** 15 MINS **COOK** 1½ HRS

1 Heat the oil in a large heavy-based pan over a medium heat, add the onions, and cook for 3–4 minutes until soft. Season with salt and pepper, stir in the garlic, chillies, ground spices, and herbs, and cook for 2 minutes.

2 Add the vinegar, tomatoes, tomato purée, sugar, beans, and stock and bring to the boil. Reduce to a simmer, partially cover with the lid, and cook gently for 1–1½ hours until thickened.

3 Taste and season as needed, removing the bay leaves and cinnamon stick, and serve with bowls of grated cheese and soured cream, if you like.

A much-loved favourite with plenty of chilli heat, this particular version is cooked in beer. You might want to add a few more bird's eye chillies to the dish depending on how hot you like it.

Hot and fiery chilli with beer

⊙ **SERVES** 4–6   ❄ **FREEZE** UP TO 3 MONTHS

1.1kg (2½lb) skirt beef, braising steak, or lean minced beef
1 tbsp olive oil
1 onion, finely chopped
salt and freshly ground black pepper
3 garlic cloves, finely chopped
1 tsp ground cumin
1 tsp dried chilli flakes
300ml (10fl oz) light ale
1 tsp English mustard

2 tbsp tomato purée
400g can chopped tomatoes
400g can red kidney beans, drained
4–6 red bird's eye chillies, left whole
about 300ml (10fl oz) hot vegetable stock for the slow cooker (600ml/1 pint for the traditional method)
splash of Tabasco sauce
handful of coriander, finely chopped

in the slow cooker   🕐 **PREP** 15 MINS   **COOK** 15 MINS PRECOOKING; **AUTO/LOW** 6–8 HRS OR **HIGH** 3–4 HRS

1 Preheat the slow cooker, if required. If using the skirt beef or braising steak rather than the lean minced beef, put the meat in the food processor and whiz until minced. Heat the oil in a large flameproof casserole over a medium heat, add the onion, and cook for 3–4 minutes until soft. Season with salt and pepper, stir through the garlic, cumin, and chilli flakes, and cook for a minute more. Add the beef, increase the heat a little, and stir. Cook for about 8 minutes or until it is all browned, then increase the heat further, add the beer, and let it bubble for a few minutes. Reduce the heat and add the mustard, tomato purée, and tomatoes.

2 Transfer everything to the slow cooker. Add the beans and chillies and pour over the stock just to cover. Season, cover with the lid, and cook on auto/low for 6–8 hours or on high for 3–4 hours. Taste and season, if necessary, then stir through the Tabasco sauce and coriander, and remove the whole chillies. Serve with fluffy rice, topped with chopped avocado and soured cream, if you like.

traditional method   🕐 **PREP** 15 MINS   **COOK** 1¾ HRS

1 Preheat the oven to 180°C (350°F/Gas 4). If using the skirt beef or braising steak rather than the lean minced beef, put the meat in the food processor and whiz until minced. Heat the oil in a large flameproof casserole over a medium heat, add the onion, and cook for 3–4 minutes until soft. Season with salt and pepper, stir through the garlic, cumin, and chilli flakes, and cook for a minute more. Add the beef, increase the heat a little, and stir. Cook for about 8 minutes or until it is all browned, then increase the heat further, add the beer, and let it bubble for a few minutes. Reduce the heat, stir through the mustard and tomato purée, and tip in the tomatoes and stock. Bring to the boil, then reduce to a simmer, add the kidney beans, and throw in the chillies.

2 Season and cover with the lid and put in the oven for 1½ hours. Check occasionally that it's not drying out, topping up with a little hot water if needed. Taste and season, if necessary, then stir through the Tabasco sauce and coriander and remove the whole chillies. Serve with fluffy rice, topped with chopped avocado and soured cream, if you like.

This Cajun-style gumbo is a mixture of vegetables, sausages, and chicken. You could also add some shellfish to the dish at the end of cooking for extra variety. Enjoy it spooned over some rice.

Sausage and chicken gumbo

🅟 **SERVES** 4–6 ❄ **FREEZE** UP TO 1 MONTH

1 tbsp olive oil
1 onion, finely chopped
salt and freshly ground black pepper
3 celery sticks, finely diced
2 red peppers, deseeded and finely chopped
2 garlic cloves, finely chopped

400g (14oz) pork sausages, each sliced into 3 pieces
2 tbsp plain flour
2–3 tsp Cajun seasoning
400g (14oz) chicken breast, cut into bite-sized pieces
450ml (15fl oz) hot chicken stock for the slow cooker
  (900ml/1½ pints for the traditional method)

in the slow cooker 🕑 **PREP** 20 MINS **COOK** 30 MINS PRECOOKING;
AUTO/LOW 6–8 HRS OR **HIGH** 3–4 HRS

1 Preheat the slow cooker, if required. Heat the oil in a large flameproof casserole over a medium heat, add the onion, and cook for 3–4 minutes until soft. Season with salt and pepper, stir through the celery, peppers, and garlic, and cook for a further 5–8 minutes until very soft. Add the sausages to the casserole and cook for 5–8 minutes until no longer pink.

2 Mix the flour and Cajun seasoning on a plate and toss the chicken in the spicy flour. Add to the casserole and cook, stirring, for 5–8 minutes, then add a little stock and bring to the boil.

3 Transfer everything to the slow cooker and pour over the remaining stock. Season, cover with the lid, and cook on auto/low for 6–8 hours or on high for 3–4 hours. Taste and season, if necessary, then ladle out over warmed bowls of rice.

traditional method 🕑 **PREP** 20 MINS **COOK** 2 HRS

1 Preheat the oven to 160°C (325°F/Gas 3). Heat the oil in a large flameproof casserole over a medium heat, add the onion, and cook for 3–4 minutes until soft. Season with salt and pepper, stir through the celery, peppers, and garlic, and cook for a further 5–8 minutes until very soft. Add the sausages to the casserole and cook for 5–8 minutes until no longer pink.

2 Mix the flour and Cajun seasoning on a plate and toss the chicken in the spicy flour. Add to the casserole and cook, stirring, for 5–8 minutes, then add a little stock and bring to the boil. Pour over the remaining stock and continue boiling for a minute. Reduce to a simmer and add the seasoning.

3 Cover the casserole with the lid and put in the oven for 1½ hours. Check occasionally that it's not drying out, topping up with a little hot water if needed. Taste and season, if necessary, then ladle out over warmed bowls of rice.

Lamb with sweet squash is the perfect combination and the minced meat benefits from long, slow cooking. Stirring mint and oregano leaves into the dish adds a distinct freshness.

Lamb mince and squash with green chillies

SERVES 4–6 ✳ **FREEZE** UP TO 1 MONTH

2 tbsp olive oil
1 butternut squash, peeled, deseeded, and chopped into bite-sized pieces
salt and freshly ground black pepper
1 onion, finely chopped
handful of fresh oregano, leaves only, or 1 tsp dried oregano
handful of thyme, leaves only
3 garlic cloves, finely chopped

1 green chilli, deseeded and finely chopped
450g (1lb) lamb mince
600ml (1 pint) hot vegetable stock for the slow cooker (900ml/1½ pints for the traditional method)
400g can chopped tomatoes
60g (2oz) sultanas
bunch of mint leaves, finely chopped
1–2 tsp harissa paste, depending on how spicy you like it

in the slow cooker 🕐 PREP 25 MINS COOK 25 MINS PRECOOKING; **AUTO/LOW** 8 HRS

1 Preheat the slow cooker, if required. Heat half the oil in a large flameproof casserole over a medium heat and add the squash. Season with salt and pepper and cook for 5–8 minutes, stirring, until it starts to turn golden. Remove the squash from the casserole and set aside.

2 Heat the remaining oil in the casserole, add the onion, and cook for 3–4 minutes until soft. Stir through the oregano, thyme, garlic, and chilli and cook for a few more minutes. Add the mince, increase the heat a little, and cook, stirring, for 5–8 minutes until it is no longer pink. Reduce the heat, return the squash to the casserole, add the stock and tomatoes, and bring to the boil. Transfer everything to the slow cooker and stir in the sultanas. Cover with the lid and cook on auto/low for 8 hours.

3 Taste and season, if necessary, then stir through the mint and harissa paste. Serve with rice or warmed pitta bread and a lightly dressed crisp green salad.

traditional method 🕐 PREP 25 MINS COOK 1½–2 HRS

1 Preheat the oven to 180°C (350°F/Gas 4). Heat half the oil in a large flameproof casserole over a medium heat and add the squash. Season with salt and pepper and cook for 5–8 minutes, stirring, until it starts to turn golden. Remove the squash from the casserole and set aside.

2 Heat the remaining oil in the casserole, add the onion, and cook for 3–4 minutes until soft. Stir through the oregano, thyme, garlic, and chilli and cook for a few more minutes. Add the mince, increase the heat a little, and cook, stirring, for 5–8 minutes until it is no longer pink. Reduce the heat, return the squash to the casserole, add the stock and tomatoes, and bring to the boil. Reduce to a simmer, stir through the sultanas, cover with the lid, and put in the oven for 1–1½ hours. Check occasionally that it's not drying out, topping up with a little hot water if needed.

3 Taste and season, if necessary, then stir through the mint and harissa paste. Serve with rice or warmed pitta bread and a lightly dressed crisp green salad.

The black beans in this recipe become fabulously tender when cooked in the coconut milk. Add lots of chilli and garlic and the result is a tasty vegetarian dish.

Spicy black beans and coconut

SERVES 4–6

175g (6oz) black beans, soaked overnight
and drained
1 tbsp olive oil
1 onion, very finely chopped
salt and freshly ground black pepper

5 garlic cloves, finely chopped
2 red chillies, deseeded and finely chopped
2 x 400ml cans coconut milk
450ml (15fl oz) hot vegetable stock, for
both methods

in the slow cooker   **PREP** 10 MINS, PLUS SOAKING   **COOK** 20 MINS PRECOOKING;
AUTO/LOW 8 HRS

1 Preheat the slow cooker, if required. Put the black beans in a large heavy-based pan and cover with plenty of water. Bring to the boil, cover with the lid, and cook for 10 minutes. Drain and set the beans aside in a bowl. Heat the oil in the pan over a medium heat, add the onion, and cook for 3–4 minutes until soft. Season with salt and pepper, then stir in the garlic and chilli. Return the beans to the pan and turn until well coated.

2 Tip in the coconut milk and stock, season again, and bring the sauce to the boil. Transfer everything to the slow cooker, cover with the lid, and cook on auto/low for 8 hours. Taste and season as required and serve with warm bowls of rice.

traditional method   **PREP** 10 MINS, PLUS SOAKING   **COOK** 1¾–2¼ HRS

1 Preheat the oven to 160°C (325°F/Gas 3). Put the black beans in a large heavy-based pan and cover with plenty of water. Bring to the boil, cover with the lid, and cook for 10 minutes. Drain and set the beans aside in a bowl. Heat the oil in the pan over a medium heat, add the onion, and cook for 3–4 minutes until soft. Season with salt and pepper, then stir in the garlic and chilli. Return the beans to the pan and turn until well coated.

2 Tip in the coconut milk and stock, season again, and bring the sauce to the boil. Cover with the lid and put in the oven for 1½–2 hours or until the beans are soft. Check occasionally that it's not drying out, topping up with a little hot water if needed. Taste and season as required and serve with warm bowls of rice.

This highly flavoured, gutsy dish is guaranteed to make the taste buds tingle. To make the most of its flavours, enjoy the jambalaya on its own with a simple salad and crusty bread.

Sausage and shrimp jambalaya

SERVES 6 ❄ **FREEZE** UP TO 3 MONTHS

1–2 tbsp olive oil
250g (9oz) smoked sausage, cut into bite-sized pieces
250g (9oz) chorizo, chopped into thick slices
2 onions, diced
1 green pepper, deseeded and diced
1 red pepper, deseeded and diced
salt and freshly ground black pepper
3 garlic cloves, peeled and finely chopped
2 tsp Cajun seasoning

1 tbsp plain flour
about 450ml (15fl oz) hot chicken stock for the slow cooker (900ml/1½ pints for the traditional method)
2 tbsp Worcestershire sauce
300g (10oz) easy-cook rice
2 bay leaves
250g (9oz) shrimps or small prawns
250g (9oz) okra, sliced
handful of flat-leaf parsley, finely chopped

in the slow cooker 🕐 PREP 15 MINS   COOK 15 MINS PRECOOKING; AUTO/LOW 3–4 HRS OR HIGH 1–2 HRS

1 Preheat the slow cooker, if required. Heat the oil in a large flameproof casserole over a medium-high heat, add the sausage and chorizo, and cook for 5–8 minutes until golden. Remove and set aside.

2 Reduce the heat to medium, add the onions, and cook for 3–4 minutes until soft. Then stir through the peppers and cook for a few more minutes, until beginning to soften. Add seasoning, stir though the garlic and Cajun seasoning, and cook for 1 minute. Stir through the flour to combine and ladle in a little stock. Return the sausages and chorizo and add the Worcestershire sauce.

3 Transfer everything to the slow cooker, stir through the rice and bay leaves, then pour over just enough stock to cover. Cover with the lid and cook on auto/low for 3–4 hours or on high for 1–2 hours. Add the shrimps or prawns and okra for the last hour of cooking. Remove the bay leaves, taste and season if needed, then stir through the parsley. Serve with a salad and some crusty bread.

traditional method 🕐 PREP 15 MINS   COOK 2¼ HRS

1 Preheat the oven to 150°C (300°F/Gas 2). Heat the oil in a large flameproof casserole over a medium-high heat, add the sausage and chorizo, and cook for 5–8 minutes until golden. Remove and set aside.

2 Reduce the heat to medium, add the onions, and cook for 3–4 minutes until soft. Then stir through the pepper and cook for a few more minutes, until beginning to soften. Add seasoning, stir though the garlic and Cajun seasoning, and cook for 1 minute. Stir through the flour to combine and ladle in a little stock. Return the sausages, chorizo, and peppers and add the Worcestershire sauce.

3 Stir through the rice and bay leaves, then pour over the stock. Mix well, cover with the lid, and put in the oven for 1½ hours. Check occasionally that it's not drying out, topping up with a little hot water if needed. Stir in the shrimps or prawns and okra, re-cover, and cook for a further 30 minutes. Remove the bay leaves, taste and season if needed, then stir through the parsley. Serve with a salad and some crusty bread.

This is a Mexican-inspired dish with lots of gutsy heat provided by the chipotle sauce, a key ingredient in many Mexican recipes. You could use pork in place of the stewing steak, cooking until tender.

Beef chilli mole

⊘ **SERVES** 4 ❄ **FREEZE** UP TO 3 MONTHS

700g (1lb 9oz) stewing beef, cut into bite-sized pieces
1 tbsp chipotle sauce or salsa
3 tbsp olive oil
30g (1oz) sesame seeds, toasted
60g (2oz) almonds, skin on, toasted
1 red pepper, deseeded and roughly chopped
4 tomatoes, roughly chopped
2 flour tortillas, roughly torn

450ml (15fl oz) hot vegetable stock for the slow cooker (600ml/1 pint for the traditional method)
3 garlic cloves, finely chopped
1 red chilli, deseeded and finely chopped
1 green chilli, deseeded and finely chopped
salt and freshly ground black pepper
small bunch of coriander, leaves chopped
1 red onion, finely chopped

in the slow cooker   🕑 **PREP** 15 MINS   **COOK** 15 MINS PRECOOKING; **AUTO/LOW** 6–8 HRS

1 Preheat the slow cooker, if required. Toss the beef in the chipotle sauce. Heat 1 tbsp of the oil in a large flameproof casserole over a high heat and cook the beef for 5–8 minutes (in batches, if necessary), turning it until browned all over. Remove and set aside.

2 Put the sesame seeds and almonds in a food processor and whiz until ground. Leave in the food processor and set aside. Heat 1 tbsp of the oil in the casserole over a medium heat, add the pepper and tomatoes, and cook for 2–3 minutes until soft. Add to the food processor and blend to a paste. Then add the tortillas and a couple of ladlefuls of stock and whiz until it is a sauce-like consistency. Set aside.

3 Heat the remaining oil, add the garlic and chillies, and cook for 1 minute, taking care not to burn them. Add the tomato and pepper sauce, the remaining stock, and season well. Bring to the boil, then reduce to a simmer, add the beef, and transfer everything to the slow cooker. Cover with the lid and cook on auto/low for 6–8 hours. Stir through the coriander and serve scattered with the red onion and some warmed tortillas on the side.

traditional method   🕑 **PREP** 15 MINS   **COOK** 2¼–2¾ HRS

1 Preheat the oven to 160°C (325°F/Gas 3). Toss the beef in the chipotle sauce. Heat 1 tbsp of the oil in a large flameproof casserole over a high heat and cook the beef for 5–8 minutes (in batches, if necessary), turning it until browned all over. Remove and set aside.

2 Put the sesame seeds and almonds in a food processor and whiz until ground. Leave in the food processor and set aside. Heat 1 tbsp of the oil in the casserole over a medium heat, add the pepper and tomatoes, and cook for 2–3 minutes until soft. Add to the food processor and blend to a paste. Then add the tortillas and a couple of ladlefuls of stock and whiz until it is a sauce-like consistency. Set aside.

3 Heat the remaining oil, add the garlic and chillies, and cook for 1 minute, taking care not to burn them. Add the tomato and pepper sauce, the remaining stock, and season well. Bring to the boil, then reduce to a simmer, add the beef, cover with the lid, and put in the oven for 2–2½ hours. Check occasionally that it's not drying out, topping up with a little hot water if needed. Stir through the coriander and serve scattered with the red onion and some warmed tortillas on the side.

Kidney beans become very tender and soft when they are gently cooked for a long time. Swap the sweet potatoes for squash, if you wish, and add some chopped yam if it is available.

Chilean pork and beans

⊘ **SERVES** 6 ✱ **FREEZE** UP TO 3 MONTHS ♡ **HEALTHY**

200g (7oz) dried red kidney beans, soaked in
  cold water overnight, drained, and rinsed
2 tbsp olive oil
900g (2lb) boned loin of pork, cut into
  bite-sized pieces
1 large onion, finely sliced
2 garlic cloves, finely chopped
salt and freshly ground black pepper
400g can chopped tomatoes

1 tbsp tomato purée
few sprigs each of parsley, coriander, and
  oregano, leaves stripped and chopped
1 green chilli, deseeded and diced
2 green peppers, deseeded and diced
500g (1lb 2oz) sweet potatoes, peeled and
  chopped into 2.5cm (1in) cubes
2 tbsp red wine vinegar

in the slow cooker 🕑 **PREP** 20 MINS, PLUS SOAKING **COOK** 30 MINS PRECOOKING;
AUTO/LOW 6–8 HRS

1 Preheat the slow cooker, if required. Put the beans in a saucepan, cover with fresh water, and boil for 10 minutes, then drain and set aside.

2 Heat the oil in a large flameproof casserole over a medium-high heat, add the pork, and cook for about 10 minutes (in batches, if necessary) until brown on all sides. Remove and set aside. Reduce the heat and add the onion, garlic, and seasoning. Cover and cook very gently for about 15 minutes until the onion is very soft and brown.

3 Return the pork to the casserole, stir in the tomatoes, tomato purée, and herbs, and bring to the boil. Transfer everything to the slow cooker and add the beans, vegetables, and red wine vinegar, together with 450ml (15fl oz) water to cover. Cover with the lid and cook on auto/low for 6–8 hours. Taste and add seasoning, if needed. Serve with rice or flour tortillas.

traditional method 🕑 **PREP** 20 MINS, PLUS SOAKING **COOK** 3–3½ HRS

1 Put the beans in a saucepan, cover with fresh water, and boil for 10 minutes. Reduce the heat, cover, and simmer for 1 hour or until almost tender but still slightly firm. Drain well.

2 Preheat the oven to 180°C (350°F/Gas 4). Heat the oil in a large flameproof casserole over a medium-high heat, add the pork, and cook for about 10 minutes (in batches, if necessary) until brown on all sides. Remove and set aside. Reduce the heat and add the onion, garlic, and seasoning. Cover and cook very gently for about 15 minutes until the onion is very soft and brown. Return the pork to the casserole and add the tomatoes, tomato purée, and herbs, together with 500ml (16fl oz) hot water. Cover and put in the oven for 1¼–1½ hours until the pork is just tender.

3 Add the beans and vegetables and top up with enough water to cover. Put back in the oven and cook for a further 45–60 minutes, then remove and sit on the hob. Stir in the red wine vinegar and simmer, uncovered, for 5 minutes. Taste and add seasoning, if needed. Serve with rice or flour tortillas.

Jambalaya is a traditional southern American dish from Louisiana. Variations include spiced sausages in place of the chicken, and shrimps, which are added towards the end of the cooking time.

Chicken jambalaya

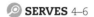 **SERVES** 4–6

2 tbsp olive oil
6 boneless chicken pieces (thigh and breast), cut into large chunky pieces
salt and freshly ground black pepper
2 tsp dried oregano
2 tsp cayenne pepper
1 red onion, finely chopped
3 garlic cloves, finely chopped
1 green pepper, deseeded and finely chopped

1 red pepper, deseeded and finely chopped
200g (7oz) thick slices ready-cooked ham, roughly chopped
600ml (1 pint) hot chicken stock for the slow cooker (900ml/1½ pints for the traditional method), plus extra if necessary
175g (6oz) easy-cook long-grain rice
140g (5oz) frozen or fresh peas
small handful of coriander, finely chopped (optional)

 in the slow cooker 🕐 **PREP** 15–20 MINS **COOK** 20 MINS PRECOOKING; **AUTO/LOW** 2–3 HRS

1 Preheat the slow cooker, if required. Heat half the oil in a large flameproof casserole over a medium-high heat. Season the chicken pieces with salt and pepper, toss in the oregano and cayenne pepper, then add to the casserole (in batches, if necessary) and cook for 6–10 minutes until golden brown. Remove and set aside.

2 Heat the remaining oil in the casserole over a medium heat, add the onion, garlic, and peppers, and cook for 5–8 minutes, stirring. Transfer everything to the slow cooker, including the chicken. Add the ham and pour in enough stock to just cover the meat. Stir in the rice and peas, then season, cover with the lid, and cook on auto/low for 2–3 hours or until all the liquid has been absorbed, stirring after an hour of cooking.

3 Taste and add seasoning, if needed, and stir in the coriander, if using. Try serving with a green salad, green beans, plain yogurt or soured cream, and some crusty bread.

 traditional method 🕐 **PREP** 15–20 MINS **COOK** 1½ HRS

1 Heat half the oil in a large flameproof casserole over a medium-high heat. Season the chicken pieces with salt and pepper, toss in the oregano and cayenne pepper, then add to the casserole (in batches, if necessary) and cook for 6–10 minutes until golden brown. Remove and set aside.

2 Heat the remaining oil in the casserole over a medium heat, add the onion, garlic, and peppers and cook for 5–8 minutes, stirring. Return the chicken to the casserole and stir in the ham. Pour in the stock and bring to the boil, then reduce to a simmer, season well, partially cover with the lid, and cook gently for about 40 minutes. Check occasionally that it's not drying out, topping up with a little hot water if needed. Stir in the rice, turning so it absorbs all the stock, and cook for about 15 minutes or until the rice is cooked, topping up with more stock, if necessary. Add the peas for the last 5 minutes.

3 Taste and add seasoning, if needed, and stir in the coriander, if using. Try serving with a green salad, green beans, plain yogurt or soured cream, and some crusty bread.

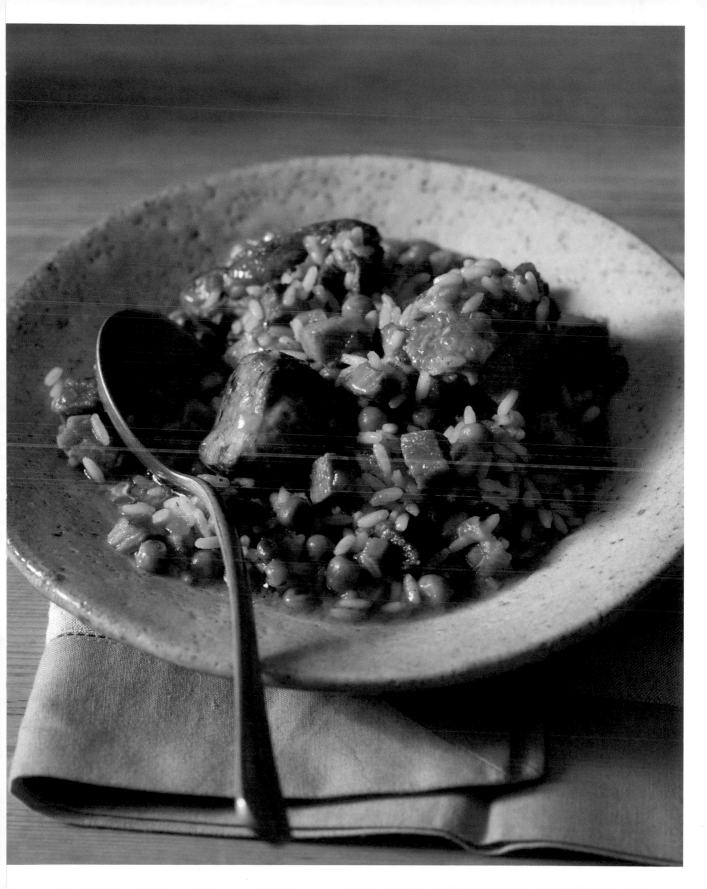

The basis of this tasty stew is sweetcorn. If you can't get hold of creamed sweetcorn, use a can of regular sweetcorn and blend it in the food processor. Omit the fish if you are cooking for vegetarians.

Creole fish and corn stew

SERVES 4–6 ✳ **FREEZE** UP TO 1 MONTH ♡ **HEALTHY**

2 tbsp olive oil
1 onion, finely chopped
3 garlic cloves, finely chopped
3 celery sticks, finely chopped
3 carrots, peeled and finely chopped
1 tsp dried oregano
few sprigs of thyme, leaves only
1 tsp cayenne pepper (use less if you
    don't like it too hot)
400g can creamed sweetcorn

400g can sweetcorn, drained
600ml (1 pint) hot vegetable stock for the slow
    cooker (900ml/1½ pints for the traditional method)
salt and freshly ground black pepper
2 potatoes, peeled and diced into bite-sized pieces
200g (7oz) ready-cooked prawns, chopped
300g (10oz) white fish, skinned and cut into
    chunky pieces
splash of Tabasco sauce (optional)

in the slow cooker ⏱ **PREP** 15 MINS **COOK** 10 MINS PRECOOKING; **HIGH** 3–4 HRS

1 Preheat the slow cooker, if required. Heat the oil in a large heavy-based pan over a medium heat, add the onion, and cook for 3–4 minutes until soft. Then stir through the garlic, celery, and carrot and cook on a gentle heat for a further 5 minutes, or until the carrot is soft.

2 Stir through the herbs and cayenne pepper, then add both the cans of sweetcorn. Transfer everything to the slow cooker, pour in the stock, season with salt and pepper, and then add the potatoes.

3 Cover with the lid and cook on high for 3–4 hours. For the last 15 minutes of cooking, add the prawns and fish and cook until the fish is opaque and cooked through. Taste and season further, if necessary, and stir in the Tabasco sauce, if using. Ladle into warmed bowls and serve with crusty bread.

traditional method ⏱ **PREP** 15 MINS **COOK** 1¼ HRS

1 Heat the oil in a large heavy-based pan over a medium heat, add the onion, and cook for 3–4 minutes until soft. Then stir through the garlic, celery, and carrot and cook on a gentle heat for a further 5 minutes or until the carrot is soft.

2 Stir through the herbs and cayenne pepper, then add both the cans of sweetcorn and the stock. Season well with salt and pepper, bring to the boil, reduce to a simmer and cook gently, partially covered, for 30–40 minutes. Add the potatoes and cook for a further 15 minutes.

3 Add the prawns and fish to the casserole and simmer gently for 6–10 minutes, until the fish is opaque and cooked through. Taste and season further, if necessary, and stir in the Tabasco sauce, if using. Ladle into warmed bowls and serve with crusty bread.

A good barbecue sauce adds flavour and moisture to the meat. This one features tangy tomato spiked with vinegar, orange juice, and cloves to add a spicy-sweet twist to a classic sauce.

Shredded beef in barbecue sauce

SERVES 4–6 ❄ **FREEZE** UP TO 3 MONTHS

1 tbsp olive oil
1.1kg (2½lb) beef brisket

FOR THE BARBECUE SAUCE
1 onion, very finely chopped
3 garlic cloves, finely chopped
1 red chilli, deseeded and finely chopped
1 tbsp tomato purée
100ml (3½fl oz) white wine vinegar

juice of 1 orange
pinch of ground cloves
1 tbsp demerara sugar
1 tbsp runny honey
300ml (10fl oz) passata
150ml (5fl oz) hot vegetable stock for
   the slow cooker (300ml/10fl oz for the
   traditional method)
salt and freshly ground black pepper

in the slow cooker 🕐 PREP 15 MINS   COOK 15 MINS PRECOOKING; AUTO/LOW 8 HRS

1 Preheat the slow cooker, if required. In a bowl, mix together all the barbecue sauce ingredients and season well with salt and pepper.

2 Heat the oil in a large flameproof casserole over a medium-high heat. Season the beef with salt and pepper and cook in the casserole for 4–6 minutes on each side, including on its edge, until the meat is browned evenly all over. Add the barbecue sauce and bring to the boil, then transfer everything to the slow cooker. Cover with the lid and cook on auto/low for 8 hours.

3 Remove the brisket from the slow cooker, shred it with two forks, and stir it into the sauce. Serve with hot pitta bread and some crisp green salad leaves.

traditional method 🕐 PREP 15 MINS   COOK 3¼ HRS

1 Preheat the oven to 160°C (325°F/Gas 3). In a bowl, mix together all the barbecue sauce ingredients and season well with salt and pepper.

2 Heat the oil in a large flameproof casserole over a medium-high heat. Season the beef with salt and pepper and cook in the casserole for 4–6 minutes on each side, including on its edge, until the meat is browned evenly all over. Add the barbecue sauce and let it bubble for a minute, then cover and put in the oven for 3 hours. Check regularly that it's not drying out, topping up with a little hot water if needed. Don't add too much water, though, or it will dilute the taste – reduce the oven temperature a little instead.

3 Remove from the oven, shred the brisket with two forks, and stir it into the sauce. Serve with hot pitta bread and some crisp green salad leaves.

Pot roasts & ribs

This beef is slow cooked in sweet Madeira for maximum flavour. Buy the meat in one piece from your butcher and don't forget to soak the dried porcini mushrooms in water for 20 minutes.

Beef pot roast

SERVES 4–6   **FREEZE** UP TO 1 MONTH

2 tbsp olive oil
900g (2lb) whole piece of chuck beef
salt and freshly ground black pepper
1 large onion, chopped into eighths
1 tbsp wholegrain mustard
150ml (5fl oz) Madeira wine

30g (1oz) dried porcini mushrooms, soaked
    in 120ml (4fl oz) warm water for 20 mins,
    strained, and liquid reserved
600ml (1 pint) hot beef stock for the slow cooker
    (900ml/1½ pints for the traditional method)
handful of flat-leaf parsley, finely chopped

in the slow cooker   PREP 10 MINS, PLUS SOAKING   COOK 25 MINS PRECOOKING; AUTO/LOW 8 HRS

1 Preheat the slow cooker, if required. Heat half the oil in a large flameproof casserole over a medium-high heat. Season the beef with salt and pepper, add it to the casserole, and cook for 6–8 minutes on each side until golden. It is ready when it lifts away from the bottom of the casserole easily. Remove and set aside.

2 Heat the remaining oil in the casserole over a medium heat, add the onion, and cook for 3–4 minutes until soft. Stir through the mustard, increase the heat, and add the Madeira wine. Cook for a minute, then add the drained mushrooms.

3 Transfer everything to the slow cooker, including the beef. Add the stock and about 100ml (3½fl oz) of the strained mushroom liquid. Cover with the lid and cook on auto/low for 8 hours. Taste and season as necessary. Sprinkle with parsley and serve with mashed potatoes or baby cubed roast potatoes.

traditional method   PREP 10 MINS, PLUS SOAKING   COOK 2½ HRS

1 Preheat the oven to 160°C (325°F/Gas 3). Heat half the oil in a large flameproof casserole over a medium-high heat. Season the beef with salt and pepper, add it to the casserole, and cook for 6–8 minutes on each side until golden. It is ready when it lifts away from the bottom of the casserole easily. Remove and set aside.

2 Heat the remaining oil in the casserole over a medium heat, add the onion, and cook for 3–4 minutes until soft. Stir through the mustard, increase the heat, and add the Madeira wine. Cook for a minute, then add the drained mushrooms, beef stock, and about 100ml (3½fl oz) of the strained mushroom liquid. Bring to the boil and stir, then reduce to a simmer and return the beef to the casserole.

3 Cover with the lid and put in the oven for 2 hours. Check occasionally that it's not drying out, topping up with a little hot water if needed. Be careful not to add too much, however, or this will dilute the flavour. Taste and season as necessary. Sprinkle with parsley and serve with mashed potatoes or baby cubed roast potatoes.

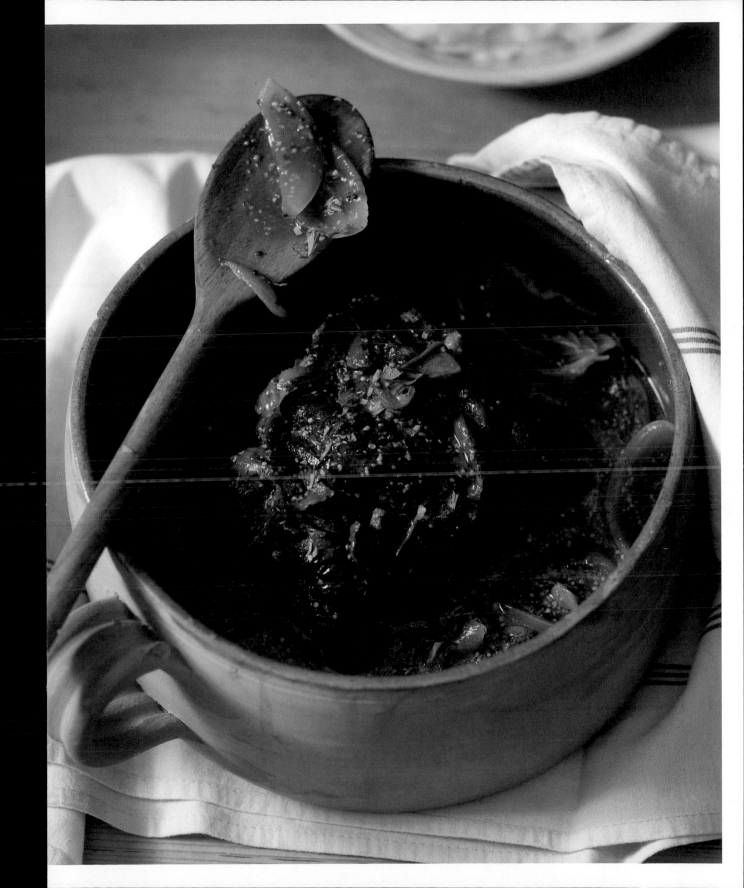

Chicken wings are cheap to buy and have lots of succulent meat on them. Serve these moreish, sticky charred chicken wings with a fiery hot dip or with something cool, such as a blue cheese dip.

Buffalo chicken wings

 SERVES 4

2 tbsp olive oil, plus extra for oiling
1 shallot, finely chopped
1 garlic clove, crushed
2 tbsp tomato purée
1 tbsp dried oregano

few drops of Tabasco sauce
2 tsp light soft brown sugar
salt and freshly ground black pepper
12 chicken wings, tips removed

 in the slow cooker 🕐 PREP 20 MINS, PLUS MARINATING **COOK** AUTO/LOW 5–6 HRS

1 Preheat the slow cooker, if required. Place the oil, shallot, garlic, tomato purée, oregano, Tabasco, and sugar in a food processor, season with salt and pepper, and blend to a paste. Spoon into a large food bag and add the chicken wings. Shake the bag until the meat is well coated with the marinade, then chill in the refrigerator for at least 30 minutes to marinate.

2 Put the chicken wings and marinade into the slow cooker, spreading them evenly across the bottom. Cover with the lid and cook on auto/low for 5–6 hours, turning them halfway through the cooking time, if you wish. Serve with a spicy chilli, tomato, and coriander dip or a blue cheese dip and some salad.

 traditional method 🕐 PREP 20 MINS, PLUS MARINATING **COOK** 40 MINS

1 Place the oil, shallot, garlic, tomato purée, oregano, Tabasco, and sugar in a food processor, season with salt and pepper, and blend to a paste. Spoon into a large food bag and add the chicken wings. Shake the bag until the meat is well coated with the marinade, then chill in the refrigerator for at least 30 minutes to marinate.

2 Preheat the oven to 160°C (325°F/Gas 3). Remove the chicken wings from the bag and lay them, skin-side down, on 2 lightly oiled baking trays. Put in the oven for 20 minutes. Turn the chicken wings over and cook for a further 20 minutes or until cooked through. Serve with a spicy chilli, tomato, and coriander dip or a blue cheese dip and some salad.

Gherkins, sea salt, and mustard are the classic accompaniments to a pot au feu. It can be served as two courses – first, the rich cooking broth, then the meat and vegetables to follow.

Pot au feu

SERVES 4–6

1kg (2¼lb) boneless beef shin, tied with string lengthways at 2.5cm (1in) intervals
675g (1½lb) beef blade steak
600ml (1 pint) hot chicken stock for the slow cooker (4 litres/7 pints for the traditional method)
1 onion, peeled and studded with 2 cloves
1 large bouquet garni, made with 12–15 sprigs of parsley, 4–5 sprigs of thyme, and 2 bay leaves
salt

10 peppercorns
500g (1lb 2oz) carrots, chopped into 7.5cm (3in) lengths
1 small head of celery, chopped into 7.5cm (3in) lengths
350g (12oz) leeks, chopped into 7.5cm (3in) lengths
about 1kg (2¼lb) marrow bones (optional)
½ French loaf, sliced diagonally and toasted

in the slow cooker **PREP** 40 MINS **COOK** 10 MINS PRECOOKING; **AUTO/LOW** 6–8 HRS

1 Preheat the slow cooker, if required. Put the shin, blade steak, and stock in the slow cooker and add the onion, bouquet garni, a pinch of salt, and the peppercorns. Cover with the lid and cook on auto/low for 6–8 hours. Tie the carrots, celery, leeks, and marrow bones, if using, each in a separate bundle of muslin and add to the slow cooker for the last 2 hours of cooking, along with salt for seasoning.

2 Remove the meat and marrow bones from the broth. Discard the strings from the beef shin and cut it into slices, then cut the blade steak into pieces, discarding any bones. Remove the vegetable bundles, unwrap, and arrange them on a serving platter with the meat. Cover with foil and keep warm.

3 Strain the broth into a clean pan and taste for seasoning. If necessary, boil it until reduced and well flavoured. If using the marrow bones, scoop out the marrow with a teaspoon and spread it on the toasts. Discard the bones. Place the toasts in warmed bowls, pour over the hot broth, and serve immediately with the meat and vegetables.

traditional method **PREP** 40 MINS **COOK** 3½–4 HRS

1 Put the shin, blade steak, and stock in a large flameproof casserole. Bring to the boil, skimming. Add the onion, bouquet garni, a pinch of salt, and the peppercorns. Simmer gently, uncovered, for 2 hours, skimming occasionally. Tie the carrots, celery, leeks, and marrow bones, if using, each in a separate bundle of muslin and add to the casserole. Season with salt. Simmer for 1½–2 hours until the meat and vegetables are very tender. Add more hot water if needed to ensure everything is always covered.

2 Remove the meat and marrow bones from the broth. Discard the strings from the beef shin and cut it into slices, then cut the blade steak into pieces, discarding any bones. Remove the vegetable bundles, unwrap, and arrange them on a serving platter with the meat. Cover with foil and keep warm.

3 Strain the broth into a clean pan and taste for seasoning. If necessary, boil it until reduced and well flavoured. If using the marrow bones, scoop out the marrow with a teaspoon and spread it on the toasts. Discard the bones. Place the toasts in warmed bowls, pour over the hot broth, and serve immediately with the meat and vegetables.

Knuckle or ham hock is amazing value, and tasty, too.
The Jerusulem artichokes add a nutty, creamy texture,
but if they're not available you can use parsnips instead.

Pot roast smoked ham

⊙ **SERVES** 4–6 ✳ **FREEZE** UP TO 1 MONTH

2 smoked ham hocks (knuckles), about
    1.35kg (3lb) each
1 bay leaf
1 tbsp olive oil
1 onion, finely chopped
salt and freshly ground black pepper
3 garlic cloves, finely chopped

few sprigs of thyme
3 carrots, peeled and chopped
225g (8oz) Jerusalem artichokes, peeled and sliced
125g (4½oz) yellow split peas
100ml (3½fl oz) dry cider
600ml (1 pint) hot vegetable stock for the slow
    cooker (900ml/1½ pints for the traditional method)

in the slow cooker ⏱ **PREP** 25 MINS **COOK** 15 MINS PRECOOKING; **AUTO/LOW** 8 HRS OR
HIGH 4 HRS, THEN **AUTO/LOW** 8 HRS OR **HIGH** 4 HRS

1 Preheat the slow cooker, if required. Put the ham hocks and bay leaf in the slow cooker and pour over 1.7 litres (3 pints) of water. Cook on auto/low for 8 hours or on high for 4 hours. Remove the hams and, when cool enough to handle, peel away the skins and discard. Set the hams aside. (You can reserve the stock and use it if you wish, but it can be salty.)

2 Heat the oil in a large heavy-based pan over a medium heat, add the onion, and cook for 3–4 minutes until soft. Season with salt and pepper, stir through the garlic, thyme, carrots, and artichokes, and cook for a few more minutes. Stir through the split peas to coat. Increase the heat and pour in the cider, let it bubble for a minute, then add the stock. Transfer everything to the slow cooker, including the hams, tucking them down as much as possible. Cover with the lid and cook on auto/low for 8 hours or on high for 4 hours. The ham meat should now slide off the bone, so remove it with a fork and stir into the slow cooker. Taste and season, if necessary, and serve with some crusty bread.

traditional method ⏱ **PREP** 25 MINS **COOK** 3¼ HRS

1 Put the ham hocks and bay leaf in a large heavy-based pan, cover with water, and cook for about 2 hours, skimming away any scum that comes to the top of the pan. Remove the hams and, when cool enough to handle, peel away the skins and discard. Set the hams aside. (You can reserve the stock and use it if you wish, but it can be salty.)

2 Preheat the oven to 180°C (350°F/Gas 4). Heat the oil in a large flameproof casserole over a medium heat, add the onion, and cook for 3–4 minutes until soft. Season with salt and pepper, stir through the garlic, thyme, carrots, and artichokes, and cook for a few more minutes. Stir through the split peas to coat. Increase the heat and pour in the cider, let it bubble for a minute, then add the stock and bring to the boil. Reduce to a simmer and return the hams, tucking them down as much as possible.

3 Cover and put in the oven for about 1 hour or until the split peas are soft. Check occasionally that it's not drying out too much, topping up with hot water if needed. The ham meat should now slide off the bone, so remove it with a fork and stir into the casserole. Taste and season, if necessary, and serve with some crusty bread.

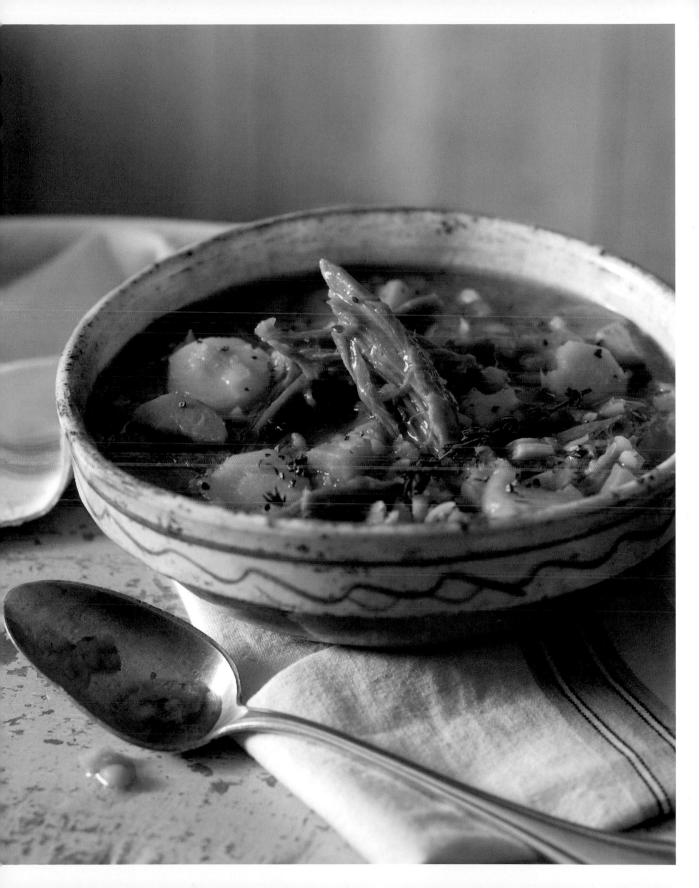

This slow-cooked whole chicken becomes meltingly tender and also results in no waste, as the chicken bones can be used to make stock for a soup. Swap the vegetables to match the seasons.

Pot roast chicken with turnips and fennel

 SERVES 4–6

2 tbsp olive oil
1 whole chicken, weighing about 1.35kg (3lb)
salt and freshly ground black pepper
6 pork sausages, roughly chopped
1 fennel, roughly chopped
1 bay leaf

2 sprigs of rosemary
250ml (9fl oz) white wine
250g (9oz) turnips, peeled and roughly chopped
600ml (1 pint) hot chicken stock for the slow cooker
 (900ml/1½ pints for the traditional method)

 in the slow cooker 🕐 **PREP** 15 MINS **COOK** 30 MINS PRECOOKING;
AUTO/LOW 8 HRS OR **HIGH** 4 HRS

1 Preheat the slow cooker, if required. Heat half the oil in a large flameproof casserole, season the chicken with salt and pepper, then add it to the casserole, breast-side down. Cook for about 10 minutes, then turn and cook the other side for about the same time. Remove and set aside.

2 Heat the remaining oil in the casserole on a high heat, add the sausages, and cook for 6–8 minutes until browned. Then reduce the heat, add the fennel, bay leaf, and rosemary, and cook for a further 5 minutes. Increase the heat, add the wine, and let it bubble for a minute, then add the turnips.

3 Transfer everything to the slow cooker. Add the chicken, breast-side down, and shuffle the vegetables around it. Pour over the stock, cover with the lid, and cook on auto/low for 8 hours or on high for 4 hours. Carefully remove the chicken from the casserole (together with the bay leaf and rosemary), peel off the skin, and pull off the meat, putting it back into the slow cooker. Serve immediately with steamed Savoy cabbage.

traditional method 🕐 **PREP** 15 MINS **COOK** 2–2½ HRS

1 Preheat the oven to 180°C (350°F/Gas 4). Heat half the oil in a large flameproof casserole, season the chicken with salt and pepper, then add it to the casserole, breast-side down. Cook for about 10 minutes, then turn and cook the other side for about the same time. Remove and set aside.

2 Heat the remaining oil in the casserole on a high heat, add the sausages, and cook for 6–8 minutes until browned. Then reduce the heat, add the fennel, bay leaf, and rosemary, and cook for a further 5 minutes. Increase the heat, add the wine, and let it bubble for a minute, then add the turnips.

3 Return the chicken to the casserole, breast-side down, and shuffle the vegetables around it. Pour over the stock, bring to the boil, then cover with the lid and put in the oven for 1½–2 hours. Check occasionally that it's not drying out, topping up with a little hot water if needed. Carefully remove the chicken from the casserole (together with the bay leaf and rosemary), peel off the skin, and pull off the meat, putting it back into the casserole. Serve immediately with steamed Savoy cabbage.

The rich tomato sauce on these ribs is made with fresh tomatoes and spiced with lots of fresh ginger. There's no need to deseed the red chillies, if you like really spicy food.

Ribs in a chilli and ginger tomato sauce

SERVES 4–6

rack of pork ribs, about 12 ribs (about 1.25kg /2¾lb)
salt and freshly ground black pepper
1 tsp black peppercorns
1 tbsp olive oil
1 onion, finely chopped
4 garlic cloves, finely chopped
5cm (2in) piece of fresh root ginger, peeled
    and finely chopped

2 red chillies, deseeded and finely chopped
grated zest and juice of 1 lime
1kg (2¼lb) tomatoes, roughly chopped
1 tsp ground cinnamon
1 tbsp tomato purée
1 tbsp demerara sugar

in the slow cooker ⏱ PREP 15 MINS COOK 15 MINS PRECOOKING; AUTO/LOW 6–8 HRS

1 Preheat the slow cooker, if required. Chop the rack into individual ribs and put in a bowl. Season with salt, add the peppercorns, cover, and set aside.

2 To make the tomato sauce, heat the oil in a large heavy-based pan over a medium heat, add the onion, garlic, ginger, chilli, and lime zest, and season well with salt and pepper. Cook for about 5 minutes until the vegetables begin to soften, then add the tomatoes, cinnamon, tomato purée, sugar, and lime juice, and cook on a very low heat, stirring occasionally, for about 10 minutes.

3 Transfer everything to the slow cooker, including the ribs, turning so they are coated. Cover with the lid and cook on auto/low for 6–8 hours. Serve with fluffy rice.

traditional method ⏱ PREP 15 MINS COOK 2–3 HRS

1 Preheat the oven to 160°C (325°F/Gas 3). Put the rack of ribs in a large pan and cover with water. Season with salt and add the peppercorns. Bring to the boil, then reduce to a simmer, partially cover with the lid, and cook for 1–1½ hours until the meat starts to come away from the bone. Remove and set aside until cool enough to handle.

2 To make the tomato sauce, heat the oil in a large heavy-based pan over a medium heat, add the onion, garlic, ginger, chilli, and lime zest, and season well with salt and pepper. Cook for about 5 minutes until the vegetables begin to soften, then add the tomatoes, cinnamon, tomato purée, sugar, and lime juice, and cook on a very low heat, stirring occasionally, for about 10 minutes.

3 Slice the rack into individual ribs and nestle them into the sauce in the casserole. Cover with the lid and put in the oven for 1–1½ hours. Check occasionally that it's not drying out, topping up with a little hot water if needed – the sauce should be fairly thick though. Serve with fluffy rice.

This dish can be made a day ahead and kept, covered, in the refrigerator. Reheat the birds with the cabbage, add the remaining plums, and thicken the sauce just before serving.

Poussins with plums and cabbage

 SERVES 4   **HEALTHY**

2–3 poussins, each weighing about 500g (1lb 2oz), trussed with string so wings and legs are neatly tucked in (your butcher can do this)
salt and freshly ground black pepper
2 tbsp vegetable oil
250g (9oz) streaky bacon rashers, sliced

½ Savoy cabbage, cored and coarsely shredded
400g (14oz) purple plums, halved and stoned
1 onion, peeled and studded with 1 clove
1 bouquet garni
250ml (9fl oz) dry white wine
500ml (16fl oz) hot chicken stock, for both methods

 ### in the slow cooker   **PREP** 15 MINS   **COOK** 30 MINS PRECOOKING; **AUTO/LOW** 6–8 HRS

1 Preheat the slow cooker, if required. Season the poussins inside and out. Heat the oil in a large flameproof casserole, add the birds, one or two at a time, and cook for 5–10 minutes until browned all over. Remove and set aside. Reduce the heat and cook the bacon, stirring, for 3–5 minutes until the fat has rendered. Spoon off all but 2 tbsp of fat and stir in the cabbage, then add half of this mixture to the slow cooker and set the rest aside. Top with the poussins and two-thirds of the plums. Add the clove-studded onion and bouquet garni. Pour over the wine and stock. Cover with the lid and cook on auto/low for 6–8 hours. Add the remaining cabbage and bacon for the last 30 minutes of cooking and the plums for the last 20 minutes of cooking.

2 Discard the onion and bouquet garni. Transfer the birds to a chopping board; remove the strings. Taste the cabbage for seasoning, then transfer the cabbage and plums to a serving dish. Set the birds on top, cover with foil, and keep warm. Strain the cooking liquid into a pan and boil for 10–15 minutes until reduced by about half. Taste, and season if needed. Serve the sauce with the poussins.

traditional method   **PREP** 15 MINS   **COOK** 1¾ HRS

1 Preheat the oven to 180°C (350°F/Gas 4). Season the poussins inside and out. Set aside. Put the cabbage in a pan of salted boiling water and cook for 2 minutes until beginning to soften. Drain and set aside. Heat the oil in a large flameproof casserole, add the birds, one or two at a time, and cook for 5–10 minutes until browned all over. Remove and set aside. Reduce the heat and cook the bacon, stirring, for 3–5 minutes until the fat has rendered. Spoon off all but 2 tbsp of fat and spread half the cabbage across the base of the casserole. Add the poussins and two-thirds of the plums. Add the clove-studded onion and bouquet garni. Cover with the remaining cabbage and pour over the wine and stock. Cover with the lid and put in the oven for 45–55 minutes, until the birds are cooked and the juices run clear when the thighs are pierced with a sharp knife.

2 Discard the onion and bouquet garni. Transfer the birds to a chopping board; remove the strings. Taste the cabbage for seasoning, then transfer to a serving dish. Set the birds on top, cover with foil, and keep warm. Add the remaining plums to the cooking liquid and simmer for 5–8 minutes until tender, then remove them and transfer to the serving dish. Boil the sauce for 10–15 minutes until reduced by about half. Taste, and season if needed. Serve the sauce with the poussins.

This simple recipe leaves the chicken incredibly moist and fragrant with lemon and fennel. It is served with a rich cheese and cream sauce. Good with crisply cooked vegetables.

Chicken en cocotte with Parmesan

SERVES 4

1 chicken, trussed with string so wings and legs
   are neatly tucked in (your butcher can do this)
salt and freshly ground black pepper
45g (1½oz) butter
1 onion, roughly chopped
1 fennel bulb, trimmed and roughly chopped
250ml (9fl oz) white wine
2 lemons, peeled, pith removed and zest cut
   into fine slices
handful of flat-leaf parsley, chopped

FOR THE CHEESE SAUCE
120ml (4fl oz) chicken stock
120ml (4fl oz) double cream
1 tsp cornflour or arrowroot
30g (1oz) Parmesan cheese, grated

in the slow cooker   🕐 **PREP** 15 MINS   **COOK** 10 MINS PRECOOKING; **AUTO/LOW** 6–8 HRS

1 Preheat the slow cooker, if required. Season the chicken inside and out. Melt the butter in a large flameproof casserole. Add the chicken and cook for about 10 minutes until browned all over. Put the onion and fennel in the slow cooker and sit the chicken on top. Pour over the wine, then add the lemon zest. Cover with the lid and cook on auto/low for 6–8 hours. Transfer the bird to a board, cover with foil, and keep warm. Discard the onion and fennel.

2 Meanwhile, make the sauce. Remove any excess fat from the casserole and add the stock. Bring to the boil, stirring to dissolve the pan juices. Boil for about 5 minutes, until well reduced, then strain it into a saucepan. Whisk in the cream and bring just to the boil. Mix the cornflour or arrowroot and 1 tbsp water together in a small bowl to form a smooth paste. Whisk in enough of the paste to thicken the sauce. It should lightly coat the back of a spoon. Take the sauce from the heat and whisk in the Parmesan cheese. Taste and add seasoning if needed. Set aside and reheat when required. Discard the trussing strings from the chicken, carve, and serve with the sauce and a scattering of chopped parsley.

traditional method   🕐 **PREP** 15 MINS   **COOK** 45 MINS

1 Preheat the oven to 190°C (375°F/Gas 5). Season the chicken inside and out. Melt the butter in a large flameproof casserole. Add the chicken and cook it for about 10 minutes until browned all over. Add the onion, fennel, wine, and lemon zest and cover. Cook in the oven for 30–40 minutes, turning occasionally, so it cooks evenly. The juices should run clear when pierced with a sharp knife. Transfer the bird to a board, cover with foil, and keep it warm. Discard the onion and fennel.

2 To make the sauce, remove any excess fat from the casserole and add the stock. Bring to the boil, stirring to dissolve the pan juices. Boil for about 5 minutes, until well reduced, then strain it into a saucepan. Whisk in the cream and bring just to the boil. Mix the cornflour or arrowroot and 1 tbsp water together in a small bowl to form a smooth paste. Whisk in enough of the paste to thicken the sauce. It should lightly coat the back of a spoon. Take the sauce from the heat and whisk in the Parmesan cheese. Taste and add seasoning if needed. Keep warm. Discard the trussing strings from the chicken, carve, and serve with the sauce and a scattering of chopped parsley.

Instead of the traditional Sunday roast, try this lamb recipe that renders the meat meltingly tender and boasts a delicious coating that mixes with the sauce as it cooks.

Lamb with parsley, tomato, and breadcrumbs

 SERVES 4–6

2kg (4½lb) leg of lamb
1 tbsp olive oil
3 large onions, sliced
handful of rosemary
about 600ml (1 pint) white wine,
   for both methods

FOR THE RUB
bunch of flat-leaf parsley
30g (1oz) sun-dried tomatoes
2 garlic cloves, peeled
85g (3oz) fine breadcrumbs, toasted
2 tbsp olive oil
salt and freshly ground black pepper

 in the slow cooker ⏱ **PREP** 20 MINS **COOK** 10 MINS PRECOOKING; **AUTO/LOW** 8 HRS

1 Preheat the slow cooker, if required. First make the rub by putting the ingredients into a food processor and pulsing until blended. Set aside.

2 Wipe the meat, season it well, then stab it all over with a sharp knife. Heat the oil in a large flameproof casserole over a medium-high heat, add the lamb, and fry for about 8 minutes, turning until it is evenly browned. Remove the meat from the casserole and rub the parsley mixture all over it and into all the cuts. Put it in the slow cooker together with the onions and rosemary and pour over enough wine to cover the meat. Cover with the lid and cook on auto/low for 8 hours.

3 Remove the lamb from the slow cooker, discard the rosemary, loosely cover the meat with foil, and leave it to rest for about 15 minutes. Serve with minted peas and new potatoes.

traditional method ⏱ **PREP** 20 MINS **COOK** 3¼ HRS

1 Preheat the oven to 160°C (325°F/Gas 3). First make the rub by putting the ingredients into a food processor and pulsing until blended. Set aside.

2 Wipe the meat, season it well, then stab it all over with a sharp knife. Heat the oil in a large flameproof casserole over a medium-high heat, add the lamb, and fry for about 8 minutes, turning until it is evenly browned. Remove the meat from the casserole and rub the parsley mixture all over it and into all the cuts. Set aside.

3 Add the onions to the casserole, reduce the heat to medium, and cook for about 10 minutes, until softened. Season with salt and pepper, then sit the lamb on top of the onions, add the rosemary, and pour over the wine. Cover with the lid and put in the oven for 3 hours. Check occasionally that it's not drying out, topping up with a little hot water if needed. Remove from the oven, discard the rosemary, loosely cover the meat with foil, and leave it to rest for about 15 minutes. Serve with minted peas and new potatoes.

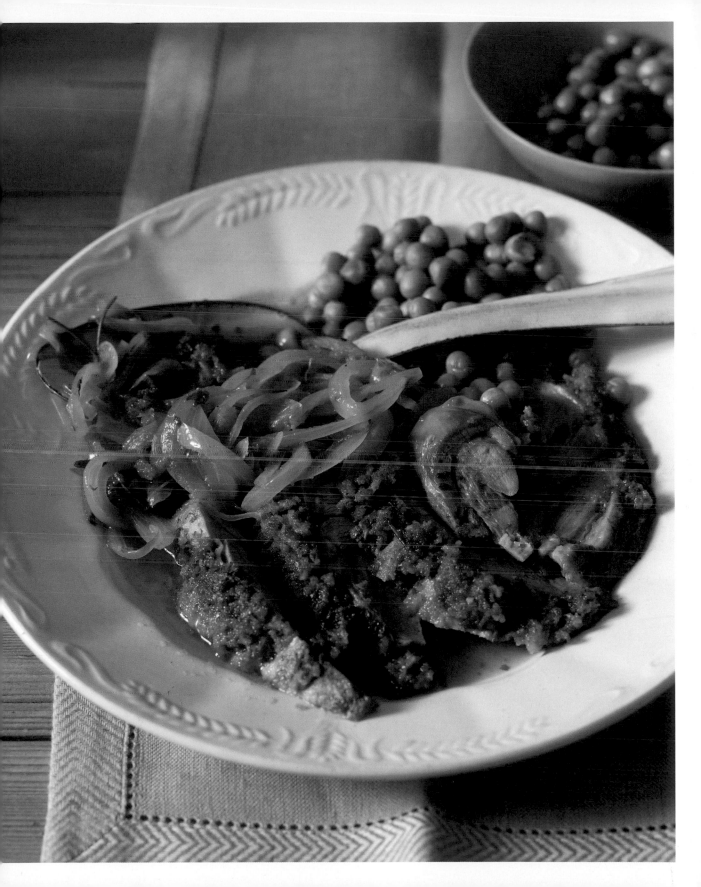

Pot-roasting a pheasant retains all its flavour and moistness. Choose a plump bird meaty enough for four. Otherwise, if your slow cooker will accommodate it, use two pheasants.

Pot-roast pheasant

 SERVES 4

2 tbsp olive oil
60g (2oz) butter, chilled
1 prepared pheasant, about 1kg (2¼lb)
salt and freshly ground black pepper
250g (9oz) chestnut mushrooms

2 tbsp chopped thyme
1 large onion, finely chopped
100g (3½oz) rindless streaky bacon, chopped
750ml (1¼ pints) red wine, for both methods

 in the slow cooker ⏱ **PREP** 40 MINS   **COOK** 20 MINS PRECOOKING; **AUTO/LOW** 6–8 HRS

1 Preheat the slow cooker, if required. Heat half the oil and half the butter in a large flameproof casserole. Brown the pheasant evenly for 6–8 minutes and season with salt and pepper. Remove and set aside. Add the mushrooms and thyme to the casserole and cook for 5 minutes, or until coloured. Also remove and set aside.

2 Heat the remaining oil in the casserole, add the onion and bacon, and cook for 4–5 minutes until the onion softens. Transfer to the slow cooker, together with the pheasant and mushrooms, and add the wine. Cover with the lid and cook on auto/low for 6–8 hours. Remove the pheasant to a serving platter, cover with foil, and keep warm.

3 Strain the liquid from the slow cooker into a heavy-based pan. Skim away any fat, then bring to the boil and simmer briskly for about 10 minutes until reduced by a third. Whisk in the remaining butter to make the sauce glossy. Carve the pheasant and serve with the hot gravy and some carrots, swede mash, and French beans.

traditional method ⏱ **PREP** 40 MINS   **COOK** 1¾ HRS

1 Preheat the oven to 190°C (375°F/Gas 5). Heat half the oil and half the butter in a large flameproof casserole. Brown the pheasant evenly for 6–8 minutes and season with salt and pepper. Remove and set aside. Add the mushrooms and thyme to the casserole and cook for 5 minutes or until coloured. Also remove and set aside.

2 Heat the remaining oil in the casserole, add the onion and bacon, and cook for 4–5 minutes until the onion softens. Add the pheasant and mushrooms and then the wine. Cover and put in the oven for 1½ hours, or until the pheasant is cooked and a leg pulls away from the bird easily. Remove the pheasant to a serving platter, cover with foil, and keep warm.

3 Strain the liquid from the casserole into a heavy-based pan. Skim away any fat, then bring to the boil and simmer briskly for about 10 minutes until reduced by a third. Whisk in the remaining butter to make the sauce glossy. Carve the pheasant and serve with the hot gravy and some carrots, swede mash, and French beans.

Pork belly is an ideal cut for slow cooking and it's great value, too. The pairing with cabbage is perfect for this dish and some mashed potatoes would be an excellent accompaniment.

Spicy pork with cabbage and caraway seeds

 SERVES 4–6

handful of thyme leaves
4 garlic cloves, roughly chopped
2 tbsp olive oil
2 tsp dried chilli flakes
1kg (2¼lb) piece pork belly, skin scored
2 tsp salt and freshly ground black pepper

300ml (10fl oz) dry cider for the slow cooker
(500ml/16fl oz for the traditional method)
1 Savoy cabbage, halved, cored, and shredded
1 tsp caraway seeds
knob of butter

 ### in the slow cooker 🕐 PREP 10 MINS COOK 15 MINS PRECOOKING; AUTO/LOW 6–8 HRS

1 Preheat the slow cooker, if required. Put the thyme, garlic, half the oil, and chilli flakes in a food processor and blend to a paste, then rub this all over the flesh of the pork. Rub the salt all over the skin-side of the pork, getting it into all the cracks.

2 Add the remaining oil to a large flameproof casserole, add the pork, skin-side down, and cook for about 15 minutes until golden and the skin is crispy. Add the cider and bring to the boil. Transfer everything to the slow cooker, cover with the lid, and cook on auto/low for 6–8 hours. Add the cabbage and caraway seeds for the last 30–40 minutes of cooking.

3 Transfer the cabbage to a warmed serving bowl and top with the butter and a pinch of pepper. Slice or cut the pork into bite-sized pieces and arrange on top of the cabbage along with the juices. Serve with creamy mashed potatoes and a spoonful of chilli jelly on the side.

traditional method 🕐 PREP 10 MINS COOK 2½ HRS

1 Preheat the oven to 220°C (425°F/Gas 7). Put the thyme, garlic, half the oil, and chilli flakes in a food processor and blend to a paste, then rub this all over the flesh of the pork. Sit the pork in a roasting tin, skin-side up, and rub with the salt, getting it into all the cracks. Cook in the oven for about 30 minutes or until the skin is golden.

2 Reduce the oven to 180°C (350°F/Gas 4). Pour the cider around the pork, cover with foil, securing it around the edges of the tin, and cook for 2 hours.

3 Just before the 2 hours are up, put the cabbage in a pan of boiling salted water and cook for 4–6 minutes until soft. Drain, then toss with the caraway seeds, butter, and a pinch of pepper. Transfer to a warmed serving bowl. Slice or cut the pork into bite-sized pieces and arrange on top of the cabbage along with the juices. Serve with creamy mashed potatoes and a spoonful of chilli jelly on the side.

No meat performs better when it is slow cooked than pork belly, as it becomes meltingly tender. It's a really economical cut, too. Use pumpkin instead of squash when it's in season.

Belly pork and squash

 SERVES 4–6

1 tbsp olive oil
700g (1lb 9oz) pork belly
salt and freshly ground black pepper
1 onion, finely chopped
3 garlic cloves, finely chopped
3 sage leaves, finely chopped

1 sprig of rosemary
1 butternut squash, peeled, deseeded, and cut into cubes
100ml (3½fl oz) dry sherry
900ml (1½ pints) hot vegetable stock for the slow cooker (1.2 litres/2 pints for the traditional method)

 in the slow cooker   🕐 **PREP** 30 MINS   **COOK** 15 MINS PRECOOKING; **AUTO/LOW** 8 HRS

1 Preheat the slow cooker, if required. Heat half the oil in a large flameproof casserole over a medium-high heat. Season the pork belly with salt and pepper and add it, skin-side down, to the casserole. Cook for about 10 minutes or until it begins to colour and become crispy. Remove from the casserole and set aside.

2 Heat the remaining oil in the casserole over a medium heat, add the onion and cook for 3–4 minutes until soft. Then stir in the garlic, sage, and rosemary, followed by the squash and turn to coat. Pour in the sherry, increase the heat, and let it bubble for a minute.

3 Transfer everything to the slow cooker, including the pork. Pour over the stock, cover with the lid, and cook on auto/low for 8 hours. Slice or cut the pork into bite-sized pieces and serve in warmed shallow bowls together with the squash and its juices. Serve with crusty bread.

 traditional method   🕐 **PREP** 30 MINS   **COOK** 2¼–2¾ HRS

1 Preheat the oven to 160°C (325°F/Gas 3). Heat half the oil in a large flameproof casserole over a medium-high heat. Season the pork belly with salt and pepper and add it, skin-side down, to the casserole. Cook for about 10 minutes or until it begins to colour and become crispy. Remove from the casserole and set aside.

2 Heat the remaining oil in the casserole over a medium heat, add the onion, and cook for 3–4 minutes until soft. Then stir in the garlic, sage, and rosemary, followed by the squash and turn to coat. Pour in the sherry, increase the heat, and let it bubble for a minute.

3 Return the pork belly to the casserole, add the stock, and bring to the boil. Reduce to a simmer, cover with the lid, and put in the oven for 2–2½ hours. Check occasionally that it's not drying out, topping up with a little hot water if needed. Slice or cut the pork into bite-sized pieces and serve in warmed shallow bowls together with the squash and its juices. Serve with crusty bread.

Slow cooking is the best way to transform brisket into tender, succulent meat that just falls into the sauce. The red onion adds a sweetness to balance the bitter Guiness in this dish.

Beef brisket and baby onions

SERVES 4–6

1 tbsp olive oil
1.1kg (2½lb) beef brisket
salt and freshly ground black pepper
2 red onions, roughly chopped
12 baby onions, peeled and left whole
2 celery sticks, roughly chopped
3 garlic cloves, finely chopped

1 bay leaf
6 juniper berries
200ml (7fl oz) Guinness
450ml (15fl oz) hot beef stock for the slow cooker
  (900ml/1½ pints for the traditional method)
3 carrots, peeled and roughly sliced
2 sprigs of rosemary

in the slow cooker   PREP 20 MINS   COOK 15 MINS PRECOOKING; **AUTO/LOW** 8 HRS

1 Preheat the slow cooker, if required. Heat the oil in a large flameproof casserole over a medium-high heat, season the brisket with salt and pepper, and add to the casserole. Cook for 6–8 minutes on each side, using tongs to turn it. It is ready when it comes away from the bottom of the pan easily. Remove from the casserole and set aside.

2 Add the red onions to the casserole and cook in the meat fat for about 10 minutes until they begin to soften. Add seasoning, then stir in the baby onions, pushing the red ones to one side a little so they get some colour. Cook for about 5 minutes, then add the celery and garlic, bay leaf, and juniper berries and cook for a further 5 minutes.

3 Pour in the Guinness and a little stock, and bring to the boil. Then add the carrots, rosemary, and the remaining stock and bring to the boil. Transfer everything to the slow cooker, including the brisket, cover with the lid, and cook on auto/low for 8 hours. To serve, slice or shred the brisket and spoon over the juices and vegetables, removing the rosemary stalks. Serve with mashed potatoes.

traditional method   PREP 20 MINS   COOK 2–2½ HRS

1 Preheat the oven to 180°C (350°F/Gas 4). Heat the oil in a large flameproof casserole over a medium-high heat, season the brisket with salt and pepper, and add to the casserole. Cook for 6–8 minutes on each side, using tongs to turn it. It is ready when it comes away from the bottom of the casserole easily. Remove and set aside.

2 Add the red onions to the casserole and cook in the meat fat for about 10 minutes until they begin to soften. Add seasoning, then stir in the baby onions, pushing the red ones to one side a little so they get some colour. Cook for about 5 minutes, then add the celery and garlic, bay leaf, and juniper berries and cook for a further 5 minutes.

3 Pour in the Guinness and a little stock, increase the heat, and let it bubble for few minutes. Then add the carrots, rosemary, and the remaining stock and bring to the boil. Reduce to a simmer, return the brisket to the casserole, cover with the lid, and put in the oven for 1½–2 hours. Spoon over the juices halfway through to keep it moist. To serve, slice or shred the brisket and spoon over the juices and vegetables, removing the rosemary stalks. Serve with mashed potatoes.

Pork ribs are cheap, full of succulent meat, and extremely filling. You can buy them in packs or, for the best value, get them as a rack of ribs from your butcher and chop them up yourself.

Pork ribs Oriental

⊘ SERVES 4

1 rack of pork ribs, about 12 ribs
  (about 700g/1lb 9oz)
salt
2 tsp black peppercorns
1–2 spring onions, green parts
  finely sliced, to serve

FOR THE MARINADE
2 tbsp sesame oil
4 tbsp dark soy sauce
4 tbsp runny honey
6 tbsp teriyaki sauce
1 tsp five-spice powder
juice of 2 limes
pinch of dried chilli flakes

in the slow cooker   🕐 **PREP** 5 MINS   **COOK** AUTO/LOW 8 HRS

1 Preheat the slow cooker, if required. Chop the rack into ribs and put them in the slow cooker. Season with salt and add the peppercorns. In a bowl, mix together all the marinade ingredients, add to the slow cooker, and turn the ribs to coat.

2 Cover the slow cooker with the lid and cook on auto/low for 8 hours. Remove the ribs from the slow cooker and serve with rice or on their own while piping hot. Garnish with the spring onions.

traditional method   🕐 **PREP** 5 MINS   **COOK** 2–2½ HRS

1 Put the rack of ribs in a large heavy-based pan and cover with water. Season with salt and add the peppercorns. Bring to the boil, then reduce to a simmer, partially cover with the lid, and cook for 1–1½ hours until the meat starts to come away from the bone. Remove the ribs from the pan with tongs and set aside in a baking tin until they are cool enough to handle.

2 Preheat the oven to 160°C (325°F/Gas 3). In a bowl, mix together all the marinade ingredients. Chop the rack into ribs and put them in a large flameproof casserole. Pour over the marinade and turn the ribs to coat. Cover with the lid and put in the oven for about 1 hour, keeping an eye on them to check they don't dry out completely – they may need turning in the marinade. Remove and serve with rice or on their own while piping hot. Garnish with the spring onions.

Rather than using ground pepper to season the ribs, use black peppercorns to give it more of a spicy hit. The marinade cooks to a lovely, thick, sticky coating – you'll need napkins to hand.

Spicy devilled pork ribs

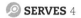 **SERVES** 4

rack of pork ribs, about 12 ribs
  (about 700g/1lb 9oz)
salt
2 tsp black peppercorns

FOR THE MARINADE
2 tbsp tomato ketchup
1 tbsp English mustard
1 tbsp Worcestershire sauce
3 garlic cloves, finely chopped
2 tbsp runny honey
2 tbsp soy sauce
splash of smoked Tabasco sauce
small bunch of coriander, very finely chopped

 in the slow cooker ⏱ **PREP** 5 MINS **COOK** AUTO/LOW 6–8 HRS

1 Preheat the slow cooker, if required. Chop the rack into ribs and put in the slow cooker. Season with salt and add the peppercorns. Mix all the marinade ingredients together in a bowl, add to the slow cooker, and turn the ribs to coat. Cover with the lid and cook on auto/low for 6–8 hours, turning them halfway through the cooking time. Remove from the slow cooker and serve while piping hot.

 traditional method ⏱ **PREP** 5 MINS **COOK** 2–2½ HRS

1 Put the rack of ribs in a large heavy-based pan and cover with water. Season with salt and add the peppercorns. Bring to the boil, then reduce to a simmer, partially cover with the lid, and cook for 1–1½ hours until the meat starts to come away from the bone. Remove from the pan and set aside until cool enough to handle.

2 Preheat the oven to 160°C (325°F/Gas 3). Mix all the marinade ingredients together in a bowl. Chop the rack into ribs, then sit them in a large flameproof casserole. Pour over the marinade and turn the ribs to coat. Cover with the lid and put in the oven for about 1 hour, keeping an eye on them so they don't dry out; they may need turning in the marinade to prevent this from happening. Remove from the casserole and serve while piping hot.

Shanks are ideal for slow cooking as the meat melts off the bone into the sauce to create the most gorgeous tasting dish. Tart vinegar and tomato purée counteract the fattiness of the lamb.

Sweet and sour lamb

SERVES 4–6

4–6 lamb shanks (allow 1 per person)
salt and freshly ground black pepper
1–2 tbsp olive oil
1 onion, cut into eighths
2 tbsp tomato purée
4 tbsp red wine vinegar

2 tbsp demerara brown sugar
300ml (½ pint) hot vegetable stock for the slow cooker (450ml/15fl oz for the traditional method)
1 cinnamon stick
1 Savoy cabbage or dark green cabbage, trimmed and shredded

in the slow cooker   **PREP** 15 MINS   **COOK** 20 MINS PRECOOKING; **AUTO/LOW** 6–8 HRS

1 Preheat the slow cooker, if required. Season the lamb with salt and pepper. Heat the oil in a large flameproof casserole over a medium-high heat, add the meat, and cook (in batches, if necessary) for 10–15 minutes, turning several times, until browned all over. Reduce the heat to medium, add the onion, and cook for 3–4 minutes until soft.

2 Add the tomato purée, vinegar, and sugar and pour over 300ml (10fl oz) of water. Bring to the boil, then transfer everything to the slow cooker. Add the stock and cinnamon stick, cover with the lid, and cook on auto/low for 6–8 hours. Add the cabbage for the last 30 minutes of cooking. Taste and season as required and serve on a bed of fluffy rice.

traditional method   **PREP** 15 MINS   **COOK** 2 HRS

1 Preheat the oven to 160°C (325°F/Gas 3). Season the lamb with salt and pepper. Heat the oil in a large flameproof casserole over a medium-high heat, add the meat, and cook (in batches, if necessary) for 10–15 minutes, turning several times, until browned all over. Reduce the heat to medium, add the onion, and cook for 3–4 minutes until soft.

2 Add the tomato purée, vinegar, and sugar and pour over 300ml (10fl oz) of water. Bring to the boil, then add the stock and cinnamon stick, cover with the lid, and put in the oven for about 1½ hours. Check occasionally that it's not drying out, topping up with a little hot water if needed. Add the cabbage for the last 20 minutes of cooking. Taste and season as required and serve on a bed of fluffy rice.

This is a substantial vegetarian dish. The artichokes and butter beans give it a wonderful creamy finish and breadcrumbs are stirred through at the last minute to add some texture.

Artichokes, butter beans, and peas

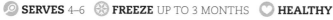 **SERVES** 4–6 **FREEZE** UP TO 3 MONTHS **HEALTHY**

1 tbsp olive oil
1 onion, finely chopped
3 garlic cloves, finely chopped
250g (9oz) small button mushrooms, larger
  ones halved
200g (7oz) dried butter beans, soaked overnight
  and drained, or use 2 x 400g cans butter beans,
  drained and rinsed
pinch of ground nutmeg

juice of ½ lemon
salt and freshly ground black pepper
600ml (1 pint) hot vegetable stock for the slow
  cooker (900ml/1½ pints for the traditional method)
125g (4½oz) frozen or fresh garden peas
675g (1½lb) antipasti artichoke hearts, drained
60g (2oz) breadcrumbs, toasted
few sprigs of flat-leaf parsley, finely chopped,
  to serve

 in the slow cooker **PREP** 15 MINS **COOK** 20 MINS PRECOOKING;
AUTO/LOW 4–6 HRS OR **HIGH** 2–3 HRS

1 Preheat the slow cooker, if required. Heat the oil in a large heavy-based pan over a medium heat, add the onion, and cook for 3–4 minutes until soft. Then stir in the garlic and mushrooms and cook for about 5 minutes until the mushrooms are tender. Meanwhile, if using the dried butter beans rather than canned beans, put them in a pan, cover with water, and boil on high for 10 minutes. Drain and set aside.

2 Transfer the mushroom mixture to the slow cooker, then stir in the butter beans, add the nutmeg and lemon juice, and season with salt and pepper. Pour over the stock, add the peas and artichokes, cover with the lid, and cook on auto/low for 4–6 hours or on high for 2–3 hours.

3 Spoon over the breadcrumbs and carefully fold some in, then top with the parsley. Serve with some freshly baked crusty bread.

traditional method **PREP** 15 MINS **COOK** 1½ HRS

1 Heat the oil in a large heavy-based pan over a medium heat, add the onion, and cook for 3–4 minutes until soft. Then stir in the garlic and mushrooms and cook for about 5 minutes until the mushrooms are tender.

2 Stir in the butter beans, add the nutmeg and lemon juice, and season with salt and pepper. Pour over the stock and bring to the boil. Boil for about 10 minutes, then reduce to a simmer, partially cover with the lid, and cook for 45 minutes. Check occasionally that it's not drying out, topping up with a little hot water if needed.

3 Stir in the peas and artichokes and cook gently for a further 15–20 minutes or until the butter beans are completely soft. Spoon over the breadcrumbs and carefully fold some in, then top with the parsley. Serve with some freshly baked crusty bread.

Risottos, pilafs, & paellas

Full of spring flavours – you can mix and match vegetables, such as French beans or broccoli, depending on what you have to hand. You could use chicken stock, if you aren't cooking for vegetarians.

Risotto primavera

 SERVES 4–6

2 tbsp olive oil
50g (1¾oz) butter
1 onion, finely chopped
salt and freshly ground black pepper
3 garlic cloves, finely chopped
300g (10oz) arborio rice or carnaroli rice
250ml (9fl oz) white wine
600ml (1 pint) hot vegetable stock for the slow
  cooker (900ml/1½ pints for the traditional method)

125g (4½oz) fresh or frozen broad beans
bunch of asparagus spears, trimmed and
  chopped into bite-sized pieces
2 small courgettes, diced
30g (1oz) grated Parmesan cheese, plus
  extra for serving

 in the slow cooker ⏱ **PREP** 15 MINS   **COOK** 10 MINS PRECOOKING; **AUTO/LOW** 1½–2 HRS

1 Preheat the slow cooker, if required. Heat the oil and half the butter in a large heavy-based pan over a medium heat, add the onion, and cook for 3–4 minutes until soft. Season with salt and pepper, then add the garlic and cook for a minute.

2 Stir through the rice and turn it in the oily butter so all the grains are coated. Cook for a few seconds. Increase the heat, add the wine, and let it bubble for 1–2 minutes until it has been absorbed. Transfer everything to the slow cooker, then pour in the stock and add the broad beans, asparagus, and courgettes. Cover with the lid and cook on auto/low for 1½–2 hours.

3 Stir though the remaining butter together with the Parmesan cheese, taste, and season if needed. Serve with more Parmesan and a lightly dressed wild rocket and tomato salad on the side.

🔲 **traditional method** ⏱ **PREP** 15 MINS   **COOK** 1 HR

1 Heat the oil and half the butter in a large heavy-based pan over a medium heat, add the onion, and cook for 3–4 minutes until soft. Season with salt and pepper, then add the garlic and cook for a minute.

2 Stir through the rice and turn it in the oily butter so all the grains are coated. Cook for a few seconds. Increase the heat, add the wine, and let it bubble for 1–2 minutes until it has been absorbed. Then add a ladleful of the hot stock at a time (keeping the rest simmering in a saucepan) and stir, cooking until it has been absorbed. Continue doing this for 30–40 minutes or until the rice is cooked to al dente and is creamy. You may not use all the stock or you may need a little more.

3 While that's cooking, add the broad beans to a large pan of boiling salted water, and cook for 3–4 minutes, then drain well and set aside. Heat the remaining oil in another frying pan over a medium heat, add the asparagus and courgettes, and cook for a few minutes until they just begin to colour. Stir all the vegetables into the risotto, dot the remaining butter all over, and stir it in. Then stir in the Parmesan cheese, taste and season, if needed. Serve with more Parmesan and a lightly dressed wild rocket and tomato salad on the side.

Aubergine and paprika work together really well, as the aubergine absorbs the flavour of this pungent spice. The chickpeas make this a substantial supper dish. Serve it alone or with lamb cutlets.

Paprika rice and aubergine

 SERVES 4–6 **HEALTHY**

3–4 tbsp olive oil
2 aubergines, chopped into bite-sized pieces
1 tbsp paprika
1 onion, finely chopped
1 tsp dried mint
salt and freshly ground black pepper
3 garlic cloves, finely chopped
2 green chillies, deseeded and finely chopped

grated zest of 1 lemon and juice of 2 lemons
350g (12oz) easy-cook basmati rice
400g can chickpeas, drained
about 750ml (1¼ pints) hot vegetable stock
   for the slow cooker (900ml/1½ pints for the
   traditional method)
small bunch of coriander leaves, roughly chopped
small bunch of flat-leaf parsley, roughly chopped

 in the slow cooker **PREP** 20 MINS **COOK** 15 MINS PRECOOKING; **AUTO/LOW** 3 HRS

1 Preheat the slow cooker, if required. Heat half the oil in a large heavy-based pan over a medium heat. Toss the aubergines in the paprika, add to the pan, and cook for 6–8 minutes, adding more oil if needed. Remove and set aside.

2 Heat the remaining oil, if necessary, and reduce the heat to low. Add the onion and mint, season with salt and pepper, and cook for 3–4 minutes until soft. Stir through the garlic, chillies, and lemon zest and cook for a further 2 minutes.

3 Stir through the rice and turn it in the oil, so all the grains are coated, and cook for a few seconds. Add the lemon juice and chickpeas, and return the aubergines to the pan. Transfer everything to the slow cooker, pour over the stock to just cover, season again, then cover with the lid and cook on auto/low for 3 hours. Stir through the herbs. Serve with a spoonful of Greek-style yogurt on top, a lightly dressed leaf and tomato salad, and some lamb cutlets.

 traditional method **PREP** 20 MINS **COOK** 45–55 MINS

1 Heat half the oil in a large heavy-based pan over a medium heat. Toss the aubergines in the paprika, add to the pan, and cook for 6–8 minutes, adding more oil if needed. Remove and set aside.

2 Heat the remaining oil, if necessary, and reduce the heat to low. Add the onion and mint, season with salt and pepper, and cook for 3–4 minutes until soft. Stir through the garlic, chillies, and lemon zest and cook for a further 2 minutes.

3 Stir through the rice and turn it in the oil, so all the grains are coated, and cook for a few seconds. Add the lemon juice and chickpeas, and return the aubergines to the pan. Pour in the stock, season again, then partially cover with the lid and leave to cook for 30–40 minutes, topping up with a little hot water if needed, and stirring occasionally so it doesn't stick. Stir through the herbs. Serve with a spoonful of Greek-style yogurt on top, a lightly dressed leaf and tomato salad, and some lamb cutlets.

In this recipe, the rice slowly steams on top of the meat and yogurt mixture. The cardamom pods also release their aromatic flavour during the long cooking time – but don't eat them!

Saffron and lamb biryani

SERVES 4–6

1 tsp saffron threads, ground with a pestle and mortar
100ml (3½fl oz) hot milk
200g (7oz) unsalted butter
1 tsp ground cinnamon
10 cardamom pods, split
10 whole cloves
20 black peppercorns
3 bay leaves
2 large onions, diced

8 garlic cloves, peeled and chopped
1 tsp ground ginger
1 tsp ground cumin
2 tsp medium hot chilli powder
2 tsp ground coriander
350ml (12fl oz) plain yogurt
1kg (2¼lb) lean lamb, cut into bite-sized pieces
500g (1lb 2oz) easy-cook basmati rice
100g (3½oz) toasted flaked almonds

in the slow cooker **PREP** 20 MINS **COOK** 15 MINS PRECOOKING; **AUTO/LOW** 6–8 HRS OR **HIGH** 3–4 HRS

1 Preheat the slow cooker, if required. Put the saffron into the hot milk and set aside. Melt the butter in a large flameproof casserole, then stir in the cinnamon, cardamom, cloves, and peppercorns and cook for 5 minutes. Add the bay leaves and onions and cook for 2–3 minutes until soft.

2 Add the garlic, ginger, cumin, chilli powder, coriander, and yogurt and stir to combine, then add the lamb and half the saffron milk. Mix thoroughly and turn off the heat.

3 Bring a large pan of salted water to the boil and add the rice. Cook for about 2 minutes and drain well. Add the lamb mixture to the slow cooker and top with the rice and the remaining saffron milk. Cover with the lid and cook on auto/low for 6–8 hours or on high for 3–4 hours until the rice is tender and the lamb is cooked. Discard the cardamom pods. Stir through the toasted almonds, combine gently with a fork, and serve with chutney and chapatis.

traditional method **PREP** 20 MINS **COOK** 1¾ HRS, PLUS STEAMING

1 Put the saffron into the hot milk and set aside. Melt the butter in a large flameproof casserole, then stir in the cinnamon, cardamom, cloves, and peppercorns and cook for 5 minutes. Add the bay leaves and onions and cook for 2–3 minutes until soft.

2 Add the garlic, ginger, cumin, chilli powder, coriander, and yogurt and stir to combine, then add the lamb and half the saffron milk. Mix thoroughly and turn off the heat.

3 Bring a large pan of salted water to the boil and add the rice. Cook for about 2 minutes and drain well, then tip the rice on top of the lamb mixture and pour over the remaining saffron milk. Cover the casserole tightly with foil to create a good seal, then cover it with the lid. Cook over a very low heat for 1½ hours until the rice is tender and the lamb is cooked. Check occasionally that it's not drying out, topping up with a little hot water if needed. Remove from the heat and stand for 15 minutes without opening. Uncover and discard the cardamom pods, then add the toasted almonds, combine gently with a fork, and serve with chutney and chapatis.

This delightfully simple dish is made extra tasty with a blend of parsley, thyme, and sage, which would be extra flavourful if picked freshly from the garden or pots on the windowsills.

Pork with rice and tomatoes

SERVES 4–6 **FREEZE** UP TO 3 MONTHS **HEALTHY**

4 tbsp olive oil
2 onions, diced
900g (2lb) lean pork, cut into 5cm (2in) chunks
3 garlic cloves, finely chopped
handful of flat-leaf parsley, chopped
1 tbsp thyme leaves

1 tbsp chopped sage leaves
1 tsp paprika
150ml (5fl oz) dry white wine
225g (8oz) long-grain rice
2 x 400g cans chopped tomatoes
salt and freshly ground black pepper

in the slow cooker **PREP** 30 MINS **COOK** 15 MINS PRECOOKING; **AUTO/LOW** 1–1½ HRS

1 Preheat the slow cooker, if required. Heat the oil in a large flameproof casserole over a medium heat, add the onions, and cook for 4–5 minutes until soft. Add the pork and cook, stirring occasionally, for about 5 minutes until no longer pink. Add the garlic, parsley, thyme, sage, and paprika and combine well, then add the wine and cook for 5 minutes. Add the rice and tomatoes, stir to combine, then season well with salt and black pepper.

2 Transfer everything to the slow cooker, cover with the lid, and cook on auto/low for 1–1½ hours. Stir halfway through, if you wish. Serve with a lightly dressed salad and crusty bread.

traditional method **PREP** 30 MINS **COOK** 1 HR

1 Preheat the oven to 150°C (300°F/Gas 2). Heat the oil in a large flameproof casserole over a medium heat, add the onions, and cook for 4–5 minutes until soft. Add the pork and cook, stirring occasionally, for about 5 minutes until no longer pink. Add the garlic, parsley, thyme, sage, and paprika and combine well, then add the wine and cook for 5 minutes. Add the rice and tomatoes, stir to combine, then season well with salt and black pepper.

2 Cover with the lid and put in the oven for 1 hour. Check occasionally that it's not drying out, topping up with a little hot water if needed. Remove from the oven and allow to stand for 10 minutes with the lid on before serving. Serve with a lightly dressed salad and crusty bread.

Choose an authentic Italian short-grain rice, such as arborio or carnaroli, to ensure the risotto has a creamy consistency. Shape any leftovers into patties, coat with breadcrumbs, and pan-fry.

Mushroom risotto

 SERVES 6 **HEALTHY**

3 tbsp sunflower oil
1 onion, chopped
400g (14oz) arborio rice or carnaroli rice
about 600ml (1 pint) hot vegetable stock for
  the slow cooker (1.5 litres/2¾ pints for the
  traditional method)

60g (2oz) butter, diced
450g (1lb) chestnut mushrooms, sliced
45g (1½oz) Parmesan cheese, grated, plus
  extra shavings to serve

 ### in the slow cooker **PREP** 10 MINS **COOK** 20 MINS PRECOOKING; **AUTO/LOW** 2–3 HRS

1 Preheat the slow cooker, if required. Heat the oil in a large heavy-based pan over a medium heat, add the onion, and cook for 4–5 minutes until soft. Add the rice and stir through so all the grains are well coated and cook for 2 minutes. Transfer to the slow cooker and pour over just enough stock to cover. Cover with the lid and cook on auto/low for 2–3 hours, giving it a stir halfway through.

2 Meanwhile, melt the butter in the pan over a medium heat. Add the mushrooms and cook for about 10 minutes, stirring frequently, until the mushrooms have browned and their liquid evaporates. Stir into the rice and continue cooking for the full length of time. Stir in the Parmesan cheese, then leave to rest, covered, for 5 minutes. Serve in warmed serving bowls with the Parmesan shavings on top.

traditional method **PREP** 10 MINS **COOK** 40 MINS

1 Heat the oil in a large heavy-based pan over a medium heat, add the onion, and cook for 4–5 minutes until soft. Add the rice and stir through so all the grains are well coated and cook for 2 minutes. Slowly add a ladleful of the hot stock at a time (keeping the rest simmering in a saucepan) and stir, cooking, until it has been absorbed. Continue doing this for about 20 minutes until the rice is cooked to al dente.

2 Meanwhile, melt the butter in another pan over a medium heat. Add the mushrooms and cook for about 10 minutes, stirring frequently, until the mushrooms have browned and their liquid evaporates. Stir the mushrooms into the rice and turn off the heat. Stir in the Parmesan cheese, then leave to rest, covered, for 5 minutes. Serve in warmed serving bowls with the Parmesan shavings on top.

Fragrant and full of colour, this pilaf has lots of layers of flavour. Swap in different dried fruits and nuts for variety. Dates and apricots are often used in Turkish dishes, as are almonds.

Turkish lamb and pomegranate pilaf

 SERVES 4–6

2 tbsp olive oil, plus extra for drizzling
675g (1½lb) lamb leg, cut into bite-sized pieces
1 onion, finely chopped
salt and freshly ground black pepper
3 garlic cloves, finely chopped
1 green chilli, deseeded and finely sliced
1 tsp dried mint
1 tsp ground cinnamon
60g (2oz) golden sultanas or use regular sultanas

350g (12oz) easy-cook basmati rice
600ml (1 pint) hot lamb stock for the slow cooker
(900ml/1½ pints for the traditional method)
60g (2oz) hazelnuts, toasted and roughly chopped
small handful of dill, finely chopped
100g (3½oz) pomegranate seeds (about 1 pomegranate)
75g (2½oz) feta cheese, crumbled (optional)

 in the slow cooker   🕐 **PREP** 15 MINS   **COOK** 15–20 MINS PRECOOKING; **AUTO/LOW** 2–3 HRS

1 Preheat the slow cooker, if required. Heat the oil in a large flameproof casserole over a medium-high heat, add the lamb (in batches, if necessary), and cook for 6–8 minutes until browned on all sides. Remove and set aside. Add the onion to the casserole and cook over a medium heat for 3–4 minutes until soft. Season with salt and pepper, stir in the garlic, chilli, mint, and cinnamon, and cook for another 2 minutes. Stir in the sultanas.

2 Stir through the rice and turn it, so all the grains are coated and the juices soaked up. Return the lamb to the casserole, pour over the stock, and bring to the boil. Transfer everything to the slow cooker, cover with the lid, and cook on auto/low for 2–3 hours, stirring halfway through, or until the rice is tender and the liquid has been absorbed. Taste and season, then stir through the hazelnuts and dill, and scatter with the pomegranate seeds. Top with crumbled feta, if using, and serve with warm pitta bread and a lightly dressed crisp green salad.

traditional method   🕐 **PREP** 15 MINS   **COOK** 1 HR

1 Heat the oil in a large flameproof casserole over a medium-high heat, add the lamb (in batches, if necessary) and cook for 6–8 minutes until browned on all sides. Remove and set aside.

2 Add the onion to the casserole and cook over a medium heat for 3–4 minutes until soft. Season with salt and pepper, stir in the garlic, chilli, mint, and cinnamon, and cook for another 2 minutes. Stir in the sultanas.

3 Stir through the rice and turn it, so all the grains are coated and the juices soaked up. Return the lamb to the casserole, pour over the stock, and reduce to a simmer. Partially cover and cook for 30–40 minutes, topping up with a little more hot stock if it begins to dry out. Taste and season, then stir through the hazelnuts and dill, and scatter with the pomegranate seeds. Top with crumbled feta, if using, and serve with warm pitta bread and a lightly dressed crisp green salad.

This is a traditional dish from the American South. You could cook the ham a day in advance, then chill the meat until ready to use. Dark cabbage or kale would make an ideal accompaniment.

Hoppin' John

SERVES 4–6

1 smoked ham hock, weighing about 1.1kg (2½lb)
1 bouquet garni, made with celery, thyme sprigs, and 1 bay leaf
2 large onions, chopped
1 dried red chilli, chopped (optional)

1 tbsp groundnut oil or sunflower oil
200g (7oz) long-grain rice
2 x 400g cans black-eyed beans, drained and rinsed
salt and freshly ground black pepper

in the slow cooker **PREP** 15 MINS **COOK** 5 MINS PRECOOKING; **AUTO/LOW** 4–6 HRS, THEN **AUTO/LOW** 2 HRS

1 Preheat the slow cooker, if required. Sit the ham hock in the slow cooker and pour in enough cold water to cover. Add the bouquet garni, half the onions, and the chilli, if using, then cover with the lid and cook on auto/low for 4–6 hours until you can pierce the ham easily with a knife. Remove the ham and set aside. Turn off the slow cooker and strain and reserve the stock. Discard the bouquet garni, onions, and chilli. Turn the slow cooker back on to auto/low.

2 Heat the oil in a heavy-based pan over a medium heat, add the remaining onion, and cook for 4–5 minutes until soft. Add the rice and stir, then transfer to the slow cooker. Add the black-eyed beans and pour over enough of the reserved stock to cover, adding a little hot water if needed. Return the ham to the slow cooker, cover with the lid, and continue cooking on auto/low for 2 hours. Stir the rice halfway through the cooking time.

3 Lift out the ham, then remove the meat from the bone and cut it into large chunks. Return the meat back to the slow cooker and stir through. Serve with steamed dark cabbage or kale and a splash of Tabasco sauce.

traditional method **PREP** 15 MINS **COOK** 3–3½ HRS

1 Put the ham hock in a heavy-based pan, pour in enough cold water to cover, and set over a high heat. Slowly bring to the boil, skimming the surface as necessary. Reduce the heat to low, add the bouquet garni, half the onions, and the chilli, if using, then re-cover the pan and leave to simmer for 2½–3 hours or until the meat is very tender when pierced with a knife. Remove the ham and set aside. Strain the stock and reserve.

2 Heat the oil in the pan over a medium heat, add the remaining onion, and cook for 4–5 minutes until soft. Add the rice and stir. Stir in 450ml (15fl oz) of the reserved stock and the black-eyed beans. Taste and add seasoning if needed. Bring to the boil, then reduce the heat to low, cover tightly, and simmer for 20 minutes without lifting the lid.

3 Meanwhile, remove the meat from the bone and cut it into large chunks. Remove the casserole from the heat and leave to stand for 5 minutes without lifting the lid. Using a fork, stir in the ham. Serve with steamed dark cabbage or kale and a splash of Tabasco sauce.

You could swap the chicken in this one-pot dish for ready-cooked prawns, stirring them in at the end of cooking. Apricots, dates, or figs would be worthy replacements for the sultanas.

Chicken and chickpea pilaf

 SERVES 4 **HEALTHY**

2 tsp vegetable oil
6 skinless boneless chicken thighs, cut into
  bite-sized pieces
2 tsp ground coriander
1 tsp ground cumin
1 onion, sliced
1 red pepper, deseeded and chopped
2 garlic cloves, crushed
225g (8oz) long-grain rice

450ml (15fl oz) hot chicken stock for the slow cooker
  (750ml/1¼ pints for the traditional method)
2 bay leaves
pinch of saffron threads, soaked in 100ml (3½fl oz)
  hot water for 10 minutes
400g can chickpeas, drained and rinsed
60g (2oz) sultanas
60g (2oz) flaked almonds or pine nuts, toasted
3 tbsp chopped flat-leaf parsley

 in the slow cooker **PREP** 20 MINS **COOK** 20 MINS PRECOOKING; **AUTO/LOW** 2–3 HRS

1 Preheat the slow cooker, if required. Heat half the oil in a large flameproof casserole over a medium heat, add the chicken, coriander, and cumin, and cook for about 10 minutes, stirring frequently. Remove and set aside. Reduce the heat, add the rest of the oil together with the onion, red pepper, and garlic, and cook for about 10 minutes until soft.

2 Stir in the rice so all the grains are coated, then transfer everything to the slow cooker, including the chicken. Pour in the stock, or just enough to cover, and add the bay leaves and saffron with its soaking water. Stir in the chickpeas, cover with the lid, and cook on auto/low for 2–3 hours, giving it a stir halfway though. Add the sultanas for the last 30 minutes of cooking. Transfer to a warmed platter and serve hot, sprinkled with the toasted nuts and chopped parsley.

traditional method **PREP** 20 MINS **COOK** 45 MINS

1 Heat half the oil in a large flameproof casserole over a medium heat, add the chicken, coriander, and cumin, and cook for about 10 minutes, stirring frequently. Remove and set aside. Reduce the heat, add the rest of the oil together with the onion, red pepper, and garlic, and cook for about 10 minutes until soft.

2 Stir in the rice so all the grains are coated, return the chicken to the casserole, and pour in about three-quarters of the stock (keeping the rest simmering in a saucepan). Add the bay leaves and saffron with its soaking water, and bring to the boil. Simmer for about 20 minutes or until the rice is almost cooked, adding more stock as needed. Stir in the chickpeas and sultanas and continue cooking the pilaf on a gentle heat for about 15 minutes, stirring occasionally so it doesn't stick. Transfer to a warmed platter and serve hot, sprinkled with the toasted nuts and chopped parsley.

Vibrant and robust, this is a simple supper dish that will satisfy the hungriest diners and requires little more than a leaf and tomato salad and some fresh crusty bread to accompany it.

Sausage and mixed pepper savoury rice

 SERVES 4–6

2 tbsp olive oil
1 large onion, finely chopped
salt and freshly ground black pepper
400g (14oz) pork sausages, skinned and
   mashed with a fork
2 green peppers, deseeded and diced
2 red peppers, deseeded and diced
2 yellow peppers, deseeded and diced

4 garlic cloves, finely chopped
1–2 tsp smoked paprika
1 tsp coriander seeds, crushed
300g (10oz) long-grain rice
about 450ml (15fl oz) hot chicken stock for the slow
   cooker (750ml/1¼ pints for the traditional method)
handful of flat-leaf parsley, finely chopped
small handful of coriander, finely chopped

in the slow cooker   ⏱ **PREP** 20 MINS   **COOK** 15 MINS PRECOOKING; **AUTO/LOW** 2–3 HRS

1 Preheat the slow cooker, if required. Heat the oil in a large flameproof casserole over a medium heat, add the onion, and cook for 3–4 minutes until soft. Season with salt and pepper, add the sausagemeat, and cook for 5–8 minutes until it is no longer pink.

2 Add the peppers and garlic and cook for a further 3 minutes, stirring so it all combines, then stir through the paprika, coriander seeds, and rice. Transfer everything to the slow cooker, then pour over enough stock to cover the contents. Season, cover with the lid, and cook on auto/low for 2–3 hours, stirring halfway through to prevent the rice from sticking. Stir through the herbs and serve with a leaf and tomato salad and some crusty bread.

traditional method   ⏱ **PREP** 20 MINS   **COOK** 1 HR

1 Preheat the oven to 160°C (325°F/Gas 3). Heat the oil in a large flameproof casserole over a medium heat, add the onion, and cook for 3–4 minutes until soft. Season with salt and pepper, add the sausagemeat, and cook for 5–8 minutes until it is no longer pink.

2 Add the peppers and garlic and cook for a further 3 minutes, stirring so it all combines, then stir through the paprika, coriander seeds, and rice. Pour in the stock and stir well, let it bubble for a minute, then season, cover with the lid, and put in the oven for about 40 minutes until cooked and the stock has been absorbed. Stir halfway through to prevent the rice from sticking to the casserole. Stir through the herbs and serve with a leaf and tomato salad and some crusty bread.

This is a fragrant mix of storecupboard staples – rice and lentils. Dukkah is an Egyptian mix of spices, roasted nuts, and ground sesame seeds. Add toasted almonds or hazelnuts, if you wish.

Egyptian rice

⊚ **SERVES** 4   ♡ **HEALTHY**

2 tbsp olive oil
2 large onions, sliced
salt and freshly ground black pepper
3 garlic cloves, grated
1 tsp cumin
3 tsp Dukkah spice (optional)
200g (7oz) easy-cook basmati rice
600ml (1 pint) hot vegetable stock for the
  slow cooker (900ml/1½ pints for the
  traditional method)

200g (7oz) Puy lentils, rinsed and picked over
  for any stones
1 bay leaf
juice of 1 lemon
small handful of flat-leaf parsley, finely chopped
small handful of mint leaves, finely chopped
small handful of coriander, finely chopped
200g (7oz) feta cheese, crumbled

in the slow cooker   🕐 **PREP** 15 MINS   **COOK** 10 MINS PRECOOKING; **AUTO/LOW** 2–2½ HRS

1 Preheat the slow cooker, if required. Heat the oil in a large heavy-based pan over a medium heat, add the onions, and cook for 8–10 minutes until they just begin to crisp slightly. Add seasoning, stir though the garlic, cumin, and dukkah spice, if using, and cook for a minute.

2 Add the rice and stir well so all the grains are coated, then transfer everything to the slow cooker. Pour the stock over the rice and stir in the lentils and bay leaf. Cover with the lid and cook on auto/low for 2–2½ hours, stirring the rice halfway through. Add the lemon juice and most of the herbs, remembering to remove the bay leaf. Serve topped with the feta or spoon over a tomato-based sauce or plain yogurt. Sprinkle over the remaining fresh herbs to garnish.

traditional method   🕐 **PREP** 15 MINS   **COOK** 1¼ HRS

1 Put the lentils and bay leaf in a heavy-based pan and pour over the stock. Season with salt and pepper, then bring to the boil, reduce the heat to a simmer, cover with the lid, and cook for about 20 minutes (depending on the packet's instructions). Remove the lid and cook for a further 10 minutes or so until the lentils are beginning to soften. Turn off the heat, put the lid back on, and set aside.

2 Put the rice in a separate pan, cover with water so it just skims the top of the rice, and bring to the boil. Reduce to a simmer and cook gently, partially covered with the lid, for about 10 minutes or until the rice is cooked through – you may need to top up the hot water if it the rice is becoming dry. Turn off the heat, cover with the lid, and set aside – the rice will continue to steam.

3 Heat the oil in a large flameproof casserole over a medium heat, add the onions, and cook for 8–10 minutes until they just begin to crisp slightly. Add seasoning, stir though the garlic, cumin, and dukkah spice, if using, and cook for a minute. Drain the lentils, then add to the rice, stirring well so all the grains and lentils are coated and everything is heated through. Add the lemon juice and most of the herbs, remembering to remove the bay leaf. Serve topped with the feta or spoon over a tomato-based sauce or plain yogurt. Sprinkle over the remaining fresh herbs to garnish.

This light and delicately flavoured pilaf requires gentle cooking, with fresh, fragrant ingredients added just before serving.
It makes a perfect summer dish – just right for outdoor dining.

Coconut, mango, and lime pilaf

SERVES 4–6

1 tbsp olive oil
1 onion, finely chopped
3 garlic cloves, finely chopped
2 red chillies, finely chopped
grated zest of 1 lime and juice of 2 limes
pinch of ground allspice
salt and freshly ground black pepper
350g (12oz) easy-cook basmati rice

60g (2oz) desiccated coconut
900ml (1½ pints) hot vegetable stock for
   the slow cooker (1.2 litres/2 pints for the
   traditional method)
1 mango, stoned, peeled, and chopped into
   bite-sized pieces
small bunch of coriander, leaves roughly chopped

in the slow cooker   **PREP** 15 MINS   **COOK** 10 MINS PRECOOKING; **AUTO/LOW** 2–3 HRS

1 Preheat the slow cooker, if required. Heat the oil in a large heavy-based pan over a medium heat, add the onion, and cook on a low heat for 3–4 minutes until soft. Season with salt and pepper, stir through the garlic, chillies, lime zest, and allspice, and cook for a further 2 minutes.

2 Stir through the rice, turning it until the grains are thoroughly coated, then stir through half the lime juice and the coconut. Pour in the stock, season again, and bring to the boil.

3 Transfer everything to the slow cooker, cover with the lid, cook on auto/low for 2–3 hours or until the rice is tender and the liquid has all been absorbed. Stir through the mango and coriander and add the remaining lime juice. Serve with a crisp green salad.

traditional method   **PREP** 15 MINS   **COOK** 45 MINS

1 Heat the oil in a large heavy-based pan over a medium heat, add the onion, and cook on a low heat for 3–4 minutes until soft. Season with salt and pepper, stir through the garlic, chillies, lime zest, and allspice, and cook for a further 2 minutes.

2 Stir through the rice, turning it until the grains are thoroughly coated, then stir through half the lime juice and the coconut. Pour in the stock, season again, and bring to a simmer. Partially cover with the lid and leave to cook for 30–40 minutes, stirring occasionally, and topping up with hot stock if needed. Stir through the mango and coriander and add the remaining lime juice. Serve with a crisp green salad.

This Spanish recipe of saffron-flavoured rice with chicken, prawns, mussels, and chorizo is named after the paellera in which it is traditionally cooked. It remains a firm favourite across the world.

Paella

⊙ **SERVES** 4–6   ♡ **HEALTHY**

3 tbsp olive oil
400g (14oz) skinless boneless chicken thighs, cut into bite-sized pieces
salt and freshly ground black pepper
150g (5½oz) chorizo, sliced
1 large onion, diced
1 large red pepper, deseeded and sliced
400g (14oz) paella rice or other short-grain rice
3 garlic cloves, finely chopped

2 large pinches of saffron threads, soaked in 100ml (3½fl oz) hot water for 10 minutes
400g can chopped tomatoes
125g (4½oz) French beans, cut into 1cm (½in) slices
300g (10oz) small mussels, scrubbed and debearded (discard any that do not close when tapped)
300g (10oz) raw, unpeeled king prawns, deveined and legs removed
1–2 tbsp chopped flat-leaf parsley

in the slow cooker   ⏱ **PREP** 20 MINS   **COOK** 20 MINS PRECOOKING; **AUTO/LOW** 2 HRS, THEN **HIGH** 40 MINS

1 Preheat the slow cooker, if required. Heat the oil in a wide heavy-based frying pan over a medium heat, add the chicken and seasoning, and cook for 10–12 minutes until browned all over. Remove and set aside. Cook the chorizo for 1–2 minutes on each side until browned. Also remove and set aside. Add the onion and red pepper to the pan and cook for 5–7 minutes until soft. Add the rice and stir, so all the grains are coated, and cook for 2–3 minutes. Transfer the rice to the slow cooker, add the chicken and chorizo, then add the garlic, saffron with its soaking liquid, and seasoning. Push the chicken down into the rice, add the tomatoes, and pour over 200ml (7fl oz) water, or just enough to cover.

2 Cover with the lid and cook on auto/low for 2 hours, adding the beans after 1 hour of cooking. Then turn the slow cooker to high, pour in 100ml (3½fl oz) boiling water, add the mussels and prawns, and continue cooking for 40 minutes. Remove the lid, cover with a tea towel, and let it stand for 5 minutes. Discard any mussels that haven't opened. Sprinkle with the parsley and serve.

traditional method   ⏱ **PREP** 20 MINS   **COOK** 1 HR

1 Heat the oil in a wide heavy-based frying pan over a medium heat, add the chicken and seasoning, and cook for 10–12 minutes until browned all over. Remove and set aside. Cook the chorizo for 1–2 minutes on each side until browned. Also remove and set aside. Add the onion and red pepper to the pan and cook for 5–7 minutes until soft. Add the rice and stir, so all the grains are coated, and cook for 2–3 minutes. Stir in 900ml (1½ pints) water, then the garlic, saffron with its soaking liquid, and plenty of seasoning. Push the chicken pieces down into the rice. Scatter the chorizo slices over, followed by the tomatoes and beans, and bring to the boil.

2 Simmer on a low heat, uncovered, for about 30 minutes until all the liquid has evaporated and the rice is al dente. Do not stir or the rice will become sticky. If the rice is undercooked or starts to stick to the pan, add a little more hot water and simmer for a few minutes longer. Add the mussels and prawns to the pan for the last 15 minutes of cooking, cover, and cook until the mussels open and the prawns turn pink. Remove from the heat and discard any mussels that have not opened. Cover with a tea towel and let it stand for 5 minutes. Sprinkle with the parsley and serve.

Vary this colourful dish to suit your mood or your storecupboard – use chilli powder instead of paprika, or carrots instead of peas. Stir through herbs, such as parsley or coriander, at the end.

Arroz con pollo

⊙ SERVES 4   **♡ HEALTHY**

2 tbsp olive oil
8 chicken thighs on the bone
1 Spanish onion or large onion, finely sliced
1 green pepper, deseeded and chopped
1 red pepper, deseeded and chopped
2 garlic cloves, finely chopped
1 tsp smoked paprika
1 bay leaf
200g can chopped tomatoes
1 tsp thyme leaves

1 tsp dried oregano
175g (6oz) long-grain rice
pinch of saffron threads, soaked in 100ml (3½fl oz)
   hot water for 10 minutes
350ml (12fl oz) hot chicken stock for the slow cooker
   (750ml/1¼ pints for the traditional method)
2 tbsp tomato purée
juice of ½ lemon
salt and freshly ground black pepper
100g (3½oz) frozen peas

in the slow cooker   🕒 **PREP** 20 MINS   **COOK** 20 MINS PRECOOKING; **AUTO/LOW** 3–3½ HRS

1 Preheat the slow cooker, if required. Heat half the oil in a large flameproof casserole over a high heat, add the chicken thighs (in batches, if necessary), and cook for about 15 minutes until browned all over. Remove and set aside.

2 Add the remaining oil, reduce the heat, and cook the onion for 4–5 minutes until soft. Add the peppers and garlic and cook for about 5 minutes until they start to soften. Add the paprika, bay leaf, tomatoes, thyme, and oregano, and stir in the rice. Fry for 1–2 minutes, stirring constantly. Transfer to the slow cooker and add the saffron with its soaking liquid, stock to cover, tomato purée, lemon juice, and seasoning.

3 Add the chicken thighs, pushing them down into the rice, cover with the lid, and cook on auto/low for 3–3½ hours. Add the peas for the last 10 minutes of cooking. Remove the bay leaf and serve hot.

traditional method   🕒 **PREP** 20 MINS   **COOK** 45 MINS

1 Preheat the oven to 180°C (350°F/Gas 4). Heat half the oil in a large flameproof casserole over a high heat, add the chicken thighs (in batches, if necessary), and cook for about 15 minutes until browned all over. Remove and set aside.

2 Add the remaining oil, reduce the heat, and cook the onion for 4–5 minutes until soft. Add the peppers and garlic and cook for about 5 minutes until they start to soften. Add the paprika, bay leaf, tomatoes, thyme, and oregano, and stir in the rice. Fry for 1–2 minutes, stirring constantly. Add the saffron with its soaking liquid, stock, tomato purée, lemon juice, and seasoning.

3 Return the chicken thighs to the casserole, pushing them down into the rice, cover with the lid, and put in the oven for 15 minutes. Add the peas and return to the oven for a further 10 minutes, or until the rice is tender and has absorbed the cooking liquid. Remove the bay leaf and serve hot.

Sweet squash combines with salty pecorino in this delicious, creamy risotto. For vegetarian fare, you could omit the sausage. Use Parmesan cheese rather than the pecorino if it's easier to find.

Squash, sausage, and pecorino risotto

SERVES 4–6

2 tbsp olive oil
25g (scant 1oz) butter
1 large onion, finely chopped
salt and freshly ground black pepper
3 garlic cloves, finely chopped
2–3 sprigs of thyme
400g (14oz) pork sausages, skinned

250ml (9fl oz) white wine
1 butternut squash, peeled, deseeded, and chopped into 1cm (½in) cubes
350g (12oz) arborio rice or carnaroli rice
about 600ml (1 pint) hot chicken stock, for both methods
200g (7oz) pecorino cheese, grated

in the slow cooker 🕐 **PREP** 20 MINS **COOK** 15 MINS PRECOOKING; **AUTO/LOW** 1½–2 HRS

1 Preheat the slow cooker, if required. Heat the oil and butter in a large flameproof casserole, add the onion, and cook for 3–4 minutes until soft. Season with salt and pepper and stir through the garlic and thyme. Add the sausagemeat and cook for 3–5 minutes until no longer pink, mashing them with the back of a wooden spoon to break it up. Add the wine and cook for a couple more minutes, then stir through the squash and combine so everything is coated.

2 Stir through the rice and turn it in the juices so all the grains are coated, and cook for a few seconds. Transfer everything to the slow cooker and pour over the stock so it just covers. Cover with the lid and cook on auto/low for 1½–2 hours. You may need to stir it halfway through. Stir through the pecorino (removing the thyme at the same time), taste, and add some pepper if needed. Serve with a crisp green salad.

traditional method 🕐 **PREP** 20 MINS **COOK** 50–60 MINS

1 Heat the oil and butter in a large flameproof casserole, add the onion, and cook for 3–4 minutes until soft. Season with salt and pepper and stir through the garlic and thyme.

2 Add the sausagemeat and cook for 3–5 minutes until no longer pink, mashing them with the back of a wooden spoon to break it up. Add the wine and cook for a couple more minutes, then stir through the squash and combine so everything is coated. Cook on a low heat for 5–10 minutes for the squash to soften slightly.

3 Stir through the rice and turn it in the juices so all the grains are coated, and cook for a few seconds. Increase the heat, add a ladleful of the hot stock at a time (keeping the rest simmering in a saucepan) and stir, cooking, until it has been absorbed. Continue doing this for 30–35 minutes until the rice is cooked to al dente and is creamy. You may not need all the stock or you may need a little more. Stir through the pecorino (removing the thyme at the same time), taste, and add some pepper if needed. Serve with a crisp green salad.

Creamy and light, this is a perfect supper for vegetarians, although you could stir through some pancetta, for something a little more substantial, and fresh herbs at the end of cooking.

Artichoke risotto

 SERVES 4

1 tbsp olive oil
50g (1¾oz) butter
1 onion, finely chopped
salt and freshly ground black pepper
3 garlic cloves, finely chopped
300g (10oz) arborio rice or carnaroli rice
250ml (9fl oz) white wine

about 700ml (1 pint 3½ fl oz) hot chicken stock
  for the slow cooker (about 1 litre/1¾ pints
  for the traditional method)
2 x 280g jars antipasti artichokes, drained
  and large ones halved
25g (scant 1oz) Parmesan cheese, grated,
  plus extra to serve

 in the slow cooker 🕐 **PREP** 20 MINS   **COOK** 15 MINS PRECOOKING; **AUTO/LOW** 1–1¼ HRS

1 Preheat the slow cooker, if required. Heat the oil and half the butter in a large heavy-based pan over a medium heat, add the onion, and cook for 3–4 minutes until soft. Season with salt and pepper, stir through the garlic, and cook for about a minute.

2 Stir through the rice and turn it in the oily butter so all the grains are coated, and cook for a few seconds. Increase the heat, add the wine, and let it bubble for 1–2 minutes or until it has been absorbed. Then pour in the stock, bring to the boil, and transfer everything to the slow cooker. Add the artichokes, cover with the lid, and cook on auto/low for 1–1¼ hours.

3 Stir though the remaining butter and Parmesan cheese, taste, and season, if needed. Serve with more Parmesan and some lightly dressed wild rocket and tomato salad on the side.

traditional method 🕐 **PREP** 20 MINS   **COOK** 45–50 MINS

1 Heat the oil and half the butter in a large heavy-based pan over a medium heat, add the onion, and cook for 3–4 minutes until soft. Season with salt and pepper, stir through the garlic, and cook for about a minute.

2 Stir through the rice and turn it in the oily butter so all the grains are coated, and cook for a few seconds. Increase the heat, add the wine, and let it bubble for 1–2 minutes or until it has been absorbed. Then add a ladleful of the hot stock at a time (keeping the rest simmering in a saucepan) and stir, cooking, until it has been absorbed. Continue doing this for 30–35 minutes until the rice is cooked to al dente and is creamy. You may not need all the stock or you may need a little more.

3 Add the artichokes to the risotto for the last 10 minutes of cooking and carefully stir them through. Dot with the remaining butter and stir it in together with the Parmesan cheese, taste, and season, if needed. Serve with more Parmesan and some lightly dressed wild rocket and tomato salad on the side.

You can serve this nutty, gingery pilaf on its own or with grilled lamb or fish. Grated root ginger freezes well, so wrap small quantities in cling film and you'll always have some to hand.

Cashew and courgette rice

SERVES 4   **HEALTHY**

1–2 tbsp olive oil
1 onion, finely chopped
salt and freshly ground black pepper
10cm (4in) piece of fresh root ginger, peeled and grated
4 courgettes, sliced into quarters lengthways and chopped into bite-sized pieces
3 garlic cloves, finely chopped
1 tbsp cider vinegar

pinch of cayenne pepper
200g (7oz) easy-cook basmati rice
250ml (9fl oz) hot vegetable stock for the slow cooker (about 900ml/1½ pints for the traditional method)
75g (2½oz) cashew nuts, roughly chopped
bunch of spring onions, green part only, thinly sliced
bunch of coriander, leaves only, chopped

in the slow cooker   **PREP** 15 MINS   **COOK** 10 MINS PRECOOKING; **HIGH** 2–2½ HRS

1 Preheat the slow cooker, if required. Heat 1 tbsp of oil in a large heavy-based pan over a medium heat, add the onion, and cook for 3–4 minutes until soft. Season with salt and pepper, increase the heat, and stir through the ginger and courgettes. Cook for 2–5 minutes until the courgette is lightly golden (adding more oil, if necessary), and then add the garlic and cook for a further 3 minutes.

2 Increase the heat, add the vinegar, and let it cook for a minute, then stir through the cayenne pepper and rice. Add a little stock and turn it so all the grains are coated. Transfer to the slow cooker, pour in enough stock just to cover, then cover with the lid, and cook on high for 2–2½ hours, stirring halfway through.

3 Stir through the cashew nuts, spring onions, and half the coriander, taste, and season as needed. Sprinkle with the remaining coriander to serve.

traditional method   **PREP** 15 MINS   **COOK** 40 MINS

1 Heat 1 tbsp of oil in a large heavy-based pan over a medium heat, add the onion, and cook for 3–4 minutes until soft. Season with salt and pepper, increase the heat, and stir through the ginger and courgettes. Cook for 2–5 minutes until the courgette is lightly golden (adding more oil, if necessary), and then add the garlic and cook for a further 3 minutes.

2 Increase the heat, add the vinegar, and let it cook for a minute, then stir through the cayenne pepper and rice. Add a little stock and turn it so all the grains are coated. Bring to the boil, add enough stock to cover, cover with a lid, and simmer gently for about 20 minutes or until the rice is tender. Top it up with more stock when needed.

3 Stir through the cashew nuts, spring onions, and half the coriander, taste, and season as needed. Sprinkle with the remaining coriander to serve.

Taleggio is a mellow Italian cheese with a slight tang that melts into the rice, making it deliciously creamy. Pair it with asparagus when in season, or try broccoli or peas when not available.

Asparagus and Taleggio risotto

SERVES 4

1 tbsp olive oil
25g (scant 1oz) butter
1 onion, finely chopped
3 garlic cloves, finely chopped
salt and freshly ground black pepper
300g (10oz) arborio rice or carnaroli rice

250ml (9fl oz) white wine
600ml (1 pint) hot chicken stock for the slow cooker
  (about 900ml/1½ pints for the traditional method)
bunch of asparagus, trimmed
75g (2½oz) Taleggio cheese, roughly sliced

in the slow cooker ⏱ **PREP** 20 MINS **COOK** 15 MINS PRECOOKING; **AUTO/LOW** 1–1¼ HRS

1 Preheat the slow cooker, if required. Heat the oil and butter in a large heavy-based pan over a medium heat, add the onion, and cook for 3–4 minutes until soft, then stir through the garlic and cook for a further minute. Season with salt and pepper.

2 Stir through the rice and turn it in the oily butter so all the grains are coated, and cook for a few seconds. Increase the heat, add the wine, and let it bubble for 1–2 minutes or until it has been absorbed. Then pour in the stock and bring to the boil. Transfer everything to the slow cooker, cover with the lid, and cook on auto/low for 1–1¼ hours.

3 Meanwhile, add the asparagus to a pan of boiling salted water and cook for 4–6 minutes, then drain, slice each spear into three and add to the rice along with the Taleggio cheese. Taste and season, if needed, and serve with a tomato and red onion salad.

traditional method ⏱ **PREP** 20 MINS **COOK** 45–55 MINS

1 Heat the oil and butter in a large heavy-based pan over a medium heat, add the onion, and cook for 3–4 minutes until soft, then stir through the garlic and cook for a further minute. Season with salt and pepper.

2 Stir through the rice and turn it in the oily butter so all the grains are coated, and cook for a few seconds. Increase the heat, add the wine, and let it bubble for 1–2 minutes or until it has been absorbed. Then add a ladleful of the hot stock at a time (keeping the rest simmering in a saucepan) and stir, cooking, until it has been absorbed. Continue doing this for 30–40 minutes until the rice is cooked to al dente and is creamy. You may not need all the stock or you may need a little more.

3 Meanwhile, add the asparagus to a pan of boiling salted water and cook for 4–6 minutes, then drain, slice each spear into three and add to the rice along with the Taleggio cheese. Taste and season, if needed, and serve with a tomato and red onion salad.

This is a rich seafood rice dish with lots of flavour. For even more variety, add a handful of prawns and clams towards the end of the cooking time, together with the mussels.

Risotto with mussels

 SERVES 4–6

1 tbsp olive oil
25g (scant 1oz) butter
1 onion, finely chopped
salt and freshly ground black pepper
3 garlic cloves, finely chopped
pinch of chilli flakes
1 fennel bulb, trimmed and finely chopped
300g (10oz) arborio rice or carnaroli rice
120ml (4fl oz) white wine

600ml (1 pint) hot vegetable stock for the
 slow cooker (about 900ml/1½ pints for the
 traditional method)
900g (2lb) mussels, scrubbed and debearded
 (discard any that do not close when tapped)
bunch of flat-leaf parsley, finely chopped
few sprigs of dill, finely chopped
juice of 1 lemon, to serve (optional)

 in the slow cooker   🕐 **PREP** 20 MINS   **COOK** 15 MINS PRECOOKING; **AUTO/LOW** 1 HR

1 Preheat the slow cooker, if required. Heat the oil and butter in a large heavy-based pan over a medium heat, add the onion, and cook for 3–4 minutes until soft. Season with salt and pepper, stir in the garlic and chilli flakes, and cook for 1 minute.

2 Add the fennel and cook for about 5 minutes until soft, then stir through the rice, turning well so the grains are coated. Increase the heat, add the wine, and let it bubble for 1–2 minutes until it has been absorbed. Then add the hot stock and bring to the boil.

3 Transfer everything to the slow cooker, season, and cover with the lid. Cook on auto/low for 1 hour or until the rice is cooked and the liquid has been absorbed. Add the mussels for the last 10 minutes of cooking, then stir through the parsley and dill, and add a squeeze of lemon juice, if using. Taste and season with some pepper if needed. Serve immediately, discarding any mussels that haven't opened when cooked.

traditional method   🕐 **PREP** 20 MINS   **COOK** 45–55 MINS

1 Heat the oil and butter in a large heavy-based pan over a medium heat, add the onion, and cook for 3–4 minutes until soft. Season with salt and pepper, stir in the garlic and chilli flakes, and cook for 1 minute.

2 Add the fennel and cook for about 5 minutes until soft, then stir through the rice, turning well so the grains are coated. Increase the heat, add the wine, and let it bubble for 1–2 minutes until it has been absorbed. Then add a ladleful of the hot stock at a time (keeping the rest simmering in a saucepan) and stir, cooking, until it has been absorbed. Continue doing this for 30–40 minutes or until the rice is cooked to al dente and is creamy. You may not need all the stock or you may need a little more.

3 Stir in the mussels, cover with the lid, and leave for a few minutes until all the mussels have opened (discard any that do not open). Stir through the parsley and dill, and add a squeeze of lemon juice, if using. Taste and season with some pepper if needed. Serve immediately.

For a successful risotto, keep checking the rice – it should be creamy but still have some bite. Stirring risotto rice releases starch from its grains, giving it its smooth texture.

Prawn risotto

 SERVES 6 **HEALTHY**

90ml (3fl oz) olive oil
500g (1lb 2oz) small or medium raw prawns
2 garlic cloves, finely chopped
small bunch of flat-leaf parsley, leaves chopped
salt and freshly ground black pepper

4 tbsp dry white wine
450ml (15fl oz) hot fish or chicken stock for the slow
   cooker (1 litre/1¾ pints for the traditional method)
1 onion, finely chopped
420g (15oz) arborio rice

 in the slow cooker **PREP** 15 MINS **COOK** 10 MINS PRECOOKING; **AUTO/LOW** 2–3 HRS

1 Preheat the slow cooker, if required. Heat a third of the oil in a large heavy-based pan over a medium heat, add the prawns, garlic, parsley, and seasoning, and cook for 1–2 minutes, stirring, until the prawns turn pink. Pour in the wine and stir thoroughly. Transfer the prawns to a bowl, set aside, and when cool, cover and chill. Simmer the liquid in the pan for 2–3 minutes until reduced by three-quarters. Add the stock, bring to the boil, and then reduce to a simmer.

2 Heat half the remaining oil in a second heavy-based pan over a medium heat, add the onion, and cook for 3–4 minutes until soft. Add the rice and stir until all the grains are coated with oil. Transfer to the slow cooker and pour in the simmering liquid or just enough to cover the rice. Cover with the lid and cook on auto/low for 2–3 hours or until the rice is cooked to al dente, giving it a stir halfway through. About an hour before the end of the cooking time, stir in the cooked prawns and the remaining olive oil. Taste and add seasoning if needed (you may not need much salt). Spoon the risotto into warmed bowls and serve immediately.

 traditional method **PREP** 15 MINS **COOK** 50 MINS

1 Heat a third of the oil in a large heavy-based pan over a medium heat, add the prawns, garlic, parsley, and seasoning, and cook for 1–2 minutes, stirring, until the prawns turn pink. Pour in the wine and stir thoroughly. Transfer the prawns to a bowl and set aside. Simmer the liquid in the pan for 2–3 minutes until reduced by three-quarters. Add the stock and 250ml (9fl oz) water and bring to the boil, then reduce to a simmer.

2 Heat half the remaining oil in a second heavy-based pan over a medium heat, add the onion, and cook for 3–4 minutes until soft. Add the rice and stir until all the grains are coated with oil. Then add a ladleful of the hot stock at a time, stirring constantly, until all the liquid is absorbed. Continue doing this for 30–40 minutes until the rice is cooked to al dente and creamy.

3 At the end of the cooking time, stir in the prawns and the remaining olive oil and cook until pink. Taste and add seasoning if needed (you may not need much salt). Spoon the risotto into warmed bowls and serve immediately.

In this dish, the rice is cooked first and then is gently steamed in the spiced vegetable mixture. Adjust the vegetable list to suit your refrigerator, adding more or less varieties as you wish.

Vegetable biryani

 SERVES 6 **HEALTHY**

350g (12oz) basmati rice
1 large carrot, peeled and sliced
2 potatoes, peeled and chopped into small pieces
½ cauliflower, chopped into small florets
3 tbsp vegetable oil
1 red onion, chopped
1 red pepper, deseeded and chopped
1 green pepper, deseeded and chopped
1 courgette, chopped

85g (3oz) frozen peas
1 tsp ground turmeric
1 tsp mild chilli powder
2 tsp ground coriander
2 tsp mild curry paste
1 tsp cumin seeds
150ml (5fl oz) hot vegetable stock, for both methods
60g (2oz) cashew nuts, lightly toasted

 ### in the slow cooker   **PREP** 30 MINS   **COOK** 30 MINS PRECOOKING; **AUTO/LOW** 2–3 HRS

1 Preheat the slow cooker, if required. In a pan of simmering water, cook the rice for 10 minutes or until just tender. Drain and set aside. Cook the carrot and potatoes in a pan of boiling water for about 5 minutes until almost tender. Then add the cauliflower and cook for a further 6–8 minutes until all the vegetables are tender. Drain and set aside.

2 Heat the oil in a large heavy-based pan over a medium heat, add the onion, and cook for 4–5 minutes until soft. Add the red and green peppers and the courgette, and cook for 5 minutes, stirring occasionally. Add the boiled vegetables and frozen peas, then stir in the turmeric, chilli powder, coriander, curry paste, and cumin seeds. Cook for a further 5 minutes, then transfer half the rice to the slow cooker and top with the vegetable mixture. Pour over the stock and top with the remaining rice. Cover with the lid and cook on auto/low for 2–3 hours, stirring halfway through. Scatter over the cashews and serve with naan bread, mango chutney, lime pickle, or raita.

traditional method   **PREP** 30 MINS   **COOK** 1¼ HRS

1 Preheat the oven to 180°C (350°F/Gas 4). In a pan of simmering water, cook the rice for 10 minutes or until just tender. Drain and set aside. Cook the carrot and potatoes in a pan of boiling water for about 5 minutes until almost tender. Then add the cauliflower and cook for a further 6–8 minutes until all the vegetables are tender. Drain and set aside.

2 Heat the oil in a large heavy-based pan over a medium heat, add the onion, and cook for 4–5 minutes until soft. Add the red and green peppers and the courgette, and cook for 5 minutes, stirring occasionally. Add the boiled vegetables and frozen peas, then stir in the turmeric, chilli powder, coriander, curry paste, and cumin seeds. Cook for a further 5 minutes, then stir in the stock.

3 Spoon half the rice into an ovenproof dish and top with the vegetable mixture. Top with the remaining rice, cover with foil, and bake for about 30 minutes until hot. Scatter over the cashews and serve with naan bread, mango chutney, lime pickle, or raita.

In this Caribbean dish, the "peas" are known as gungo peas in Jamaica and pigeon peas in Trinidad. It is particularly good served with grilled or roasted meat and poultry or fried fish.

Rice and peas

 SERVES 4 **HEALTHY**

400g can gungo peas or black-eyed beans,
  drained and rinsed
400ml can coconut milk
1 large onion, finely chopped

1 green pepper, deseeded and chopped
125g (4½oz) long-grain rice
salt and freshly ground black pepper
chilli powder, to serve

 in the slow cooker 🕑 **PREP** 10 MINS **COOK** AUTO/LOW 2–3 HRS

1 Preheat the slow cooker, if required. Put the peas, coconut milk, onion, green pepper, and rice in the slow cooker. Season with salt and pepper. Cover with the lid and cook on auto/low for 2–3 hours. Serve sprinkled with chilli powder.

 traditional method 🕑 **PREP** 10 MINS **COOK** 45 MINS

1 Put the peas, coconut milk, onion, and green pepper in a large heavy-based pan, and simmer over a low heat for 5 minutes. Stir in the rice and season with salt and pepper. Cover with the lid and cook gently for 35 minutes, or until the rice is tender, stirring occasionally. Serve sprinkled with chilli powder.

Traditional flavourings of coconut and kaffir lime leaves are used in this popular Asian dish. It's an easy dish to put together as most of the ingredients will be in the storecupboard or fridge.

Thai coconut rice

 SERVES 4–6

2 tbsp olive oil
25g (scant 1oz) butter
1 red chilli, deseeded and chopped
2 shallots, finely chopped
75g (2½oz) Thai red curry paste
grated zest of 1 lime
1 tsp chopped coriander stalks

400g (14oz) Thai jasmine rice
1 tsp salt
400ml can coconut milk
large pinch of shredded kaffir lime leaves
2 spring onions, trimmed and thinly sliced
1 tsp chopped coriander leaves

 in the slow cooker ◷ **PREP** 10 MINS **COOK** 10 MINS PRECOOKING; **AUTO/LOW** 2½–3 HRS

1 Preheat the slow cooker, if required. Heat the oil and butter in a large heavy-based pan over a low heat, add the chilli and shallots, and cook, stirring, for about 5 minutes until they start to turn golden. Stir in the curry paste and cook for 30 seconds. Add the lime zest, coriander stalks, rice, and salt, and stir until the grains of rice are coated in the curry paste.

2 Transfer everything to the slow cooker, then pour over the coconut milk and 200ml (7fl oz) water. Scatter in the lime leaves, cover with the lid, and cook on auto/low for 2½–3 hours. Stir the rice halfway through.

3 When ready to serve, stir in the spring onions and sprinkle over the coriander leaves. Serve on its own or with some soy-marinated roast fish or stir-fried chicken.

traditional method ◷ **PREP** 10 MINS **COOK** 40 MINS

1 Heat the oil and butter in a large heavy-based pan over a low heat, add the chilli and shallots, and cook, stirring, for about 5 minutes until they start to turn golden. Stir in the curry paste and cook for 30 seconds. Add the lime zest, coriander stalks, rice, and salt, and stir until the grains of rice are coated in the curry paste.

2 Pour in the coconut milk and 400ml (14fl oz) water and stir well. Bring to simmering point over a medium heat, stirring occasionally, so the rice doesn't stick. Scatter in the lime leaves and simmer, uncovered, for 5 minutes.

3 Give the rice a thorough stir, cover, and leave over a very low heat for 15 minutes or until the rice is tender. If the liquid has been absorbed but the rice is still not ready, add a little extra hot water. When ready to serve, stir in the spring onions and sprinkle over the coriander leaves. Serve on its own or with some soy-marinated roast fish or stir-fried chicken.

Puddings

Rich and decadent, these mini puddings are delicious served hot with some vanilla ice cream. To cook the puddings in one batch, use a slow cooker that is a minimum of 4.5 litres in size.

Chocolate and prune sponge puddings

MAKES 6

125g (4½oz) butter, softened
125g (4½oz) caster sugar
2 eggs, beaten

125g (4½oz) self-raising flour, sifted
30g (1oz) cocoa powder, mixed with 2 tbsp milk
125g (4½oz) prunes, stoned and chopped

in the slow cooker PREP 30–40 MINS   COOK HIGH 45 MINS

1 Preheat the slow cooker, if required. Grease six 150ml (5fl oz) metal pudding moulds. Put the butter and sugar into a mixing bowl and beat together until creamy and pale. Add the eggs slowly, beating as you go and adding a little flour to prevent any curdling. Then fold in the remaining flour until it is thoroughly combined, and stir through the cocoa mixture and prunes.

2 Divide the mixture between the moulds and cover each one with a pleated piece of greased greaseproof paper and a sheet of foil kept in place with string.

3 Sit the pudding moulds in the slow cooker and pour in enough boiling water to come halfway up the sides of the pudding moulds. Cover with the lid and cook on high for 45 minutes. Carefully lift the moulds out of the slow cooker, remove the string, foil, and paper, and turn out onto warmed plates. Serve hot with ice cream, cream, custard, or chocolate sauce.

traditional method PREP 30–40 MINS   COOK 45 MINS

1 Grease six 150ml (5fl oz) metal pudding moulds. Put the butter and sugar into a mixing bowl and beat together until creamy and pale. Add the eggs slowly, beating as you go and adding a little flour to prevent any curdling. Then fold in the remaining flour until it is thoroughly combined, and stir through the cocoa mixture and prunes.

2 Divide the mixture between the moulds and cover each one with a pleated piece of greased greaseproof paper and a sheet of foil kept in place with string.

3 Sit the moulds in a large heavy-based pan and pour in enough boiling water to come halfway up the sides of the pudding moulds. Cover with the lid and leave to simmer gently for about 45 minutes, topping up with more boiling water as and when needed. Carefully lift the moulds out of the pan, remove the string, foil, and paper, and turn out onto warmed plates. Serve hot with ice cream, cream, custard, or chocolate sauce.

Also known as *Arroz doce*, this is a traditional Portuguese dessert. Use full-fat milk as it will work far better. The eggs will cook in the residual heat. It is also good sprinkled with ground cinnamon.

Chocolate rice pudding

 SERVES 4–6

500g (1lb 2oz) short-grain rice
1 tsp salt
1.2 litres (2 pints) full-fat milk
1 tbsp cocoa powder
250g (9oz) caster sugar
6 egg yolks
4 tbsp grated dark chocolate

 in the slow cooker 🕐 **PREP** 10 MINS **COOK** AUTO/LOW 2½–3 HRS

1 Preheat the slow cooker, if required. Put the rice and salt into the slow cooker. Stir in the milk and cocoa powder, then add sugar, and stir again. Cover with the lid and cook on auto/low for 2½–3 hours. Turn off the slow cooker, beat in the eggs yolks, and leave to sit, unheated, for a few minutes.

2 Divide the rice between individual serving dishes, level the tops, and sprinkle with grated chocolate. Leave to cool, then serve.

 traditional method 🕐 **PREP** 10 MINS **COOK** 40 MINS

1 Bring 2 litres (3½ pints) water to the boil in a large saucepan. Add the rice and salt and bring back to the boil. Reduce the heat, cover, and cook for 10 minutes, then drain.

2 Pour the milk into a saucepan and add the cocoa. Bring to the boil, then add the rice. Reduce the heat and cook, uncovered, for 30 minutes or until the rice is soft. Add the sugar and stir until dissolved, then remove from the heat and quickly beat in the egg yolks.

3 Divide the rice between individual serving dishes, level the tops, and sprinkle with grated chocolate. Leave to cool, then serve.

This sweet, creamy, and very rich dessert is a popular party dish in Brazil where it is known as *Quindim*. It needs to be made ahead so it has plenty of time to chill in the refrigerator.

Brazilian baked custards with coconut

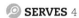 **SERVES** 4

100g (3½oz) caster sugar
4 egg yolks
2 tbsp grated fresh coconut or dessicated coconut,
  plus extra, toasted, to serve
60ml (2fl oz) coconut milk

 in the slow cooker   🕐 **PREP** 15 MINS, PLUS CHILLING   **COOK AUTO/LOW** 1 2 HRS

1 Preheat the slow cooker, if required. Whisk the sugar and egg yolks in a bowl until light and creamy. Add the grated or dessicated coconut and coconut milk and stir until evenly combined. Spoon into four 150ml (5fl oz) ramekins and cover each one with foil.

2 Stand the ramekins in the slow cooker, stacking if necessary (but not directly on top of each other), and pour in enough warm water to come halfway up the sides of the ramekins on the bottom.

3 Cover with the lid and cook on auto/low for 1–2 hours until the custards are set. Carefully lift the ramekins out of the slow cooker, leave to cool, and then chill for at least 3–4 hours. Serve with the toasted coconut sprinkled on top.

 traditional method   🕐 **PREP** 15 MINS, PLUS CHILLING   **COOK** 25–30 MINS

1 Preheat the oven to 180°C (350°F/Gas 4). Whisk the sugar and egg yolks in a bowl until light and creamy. Add the grated or dessicated coconut and coconut milk and stir until evenly combined. Spoon into four 150ml (5fl oz) ramekins and cover each one with foil.

2 Stand the ramekins in a roasting tin and pour in enough warm water to come halfway up the sides of the dishes. Put in the oven for 25–30 minutes until the custards are set. Carefully lift the dishes out of the tin, leave to cool, and then chill for at least 3–4 hours. Serve with the toasted coconut sprinkled on top.

Here is a light citrussy pudding that is best enjoyed with plenty of custard. You could add a small handful of chopped almonds to the mixture for added texture.

Lemon sponge pudding

SERVES 4–6

grated zest and juice of 2 lemons
juice of ½ large orange
60g (2oz) light soft brown sugar
115g (4oz) unsalted butter, softened

60g (2oz) caster sugar
1 tbsp golden syrup
2 eggs
175g (6oz) self-raising flour, sifted

in the slow cooker **PREP** 30–40 MINS **COOK** HIGH 2–3 HRS

1 Preheat the slow cooker, if required. Grease a 1-litre (1¾-pint) pudding basin. Stir together the juice of 1 lemon with the orange juice and brown sugar in a bowl, and pour this into the pudding basin. Put the butter, caster sugar, and golden syrup into a mixing bowl along with the lemon zest and beat together until creamy and pale. Add the eggs slowly, beating as you go and adding a little flour to prevent any curdling. Then fold in the remaining flour until it is thoroughly combined and stir through the remaining lemon juice.

2 Pour the mixture into the basin and cover with a pleated piece of greased greaseproof paper and a sheet of foil. Secure with string, looping it around the basin to form a handle.

3 Sit the pudding in the slow cooker and pour in enough boiling water to come halfway up the side of the basin. Cover with the lid and cook on high for 2–3 hours. Carefully lift the basin out of the slow cooker, remove the string, foil, and paper, and turn the pudding out onto a plate. Serve piping hot with custard or cream.

traditional method **PREP** 30–40 MINS **COOK** 1½ HRS

1 Grease a 1-litre (1¾-pint) pudding basin. Stir together the juice of 1 lemon with the orange juice and brown sugar in a bowl, and pour this into the pudding basin. Put the butter, caster sugar, and golden syrup into a mixing bowl along with the lemon zest and beat together until creamy and pale. Add the eggs slowly, beating as you go and adding a little flour to prevent any curdling. Then fold in the remaining flour until it is thoroughly combined, and stir through the remaining lemon juice.

2 Pour the mixture into the basin and cover with a pleated piece of greased greaseproof paper and a sheet of foil. Secure with string, looping it around the basin to form a handle.

3 Sit the pudding bowl in a large heavy-based pan and pour in enough boiling water to come halfway up the side of the basin. Cover with the lid and leave to simmer gently for about 1½ hours, topping up with more boiling water as and when needed. Carefully lift the basin out of the pan, remove the string, foil, and paper, and turn the pudding out onto a plate. Serve piping hot with custard or cream.

Steamed puddings do not have to be stodgy – this light version is a case in point and it's full of dried fruit and spices. For something a little simpler, use sultanas in place of the mixed dried fruit.

Mixed fruit pudding

SERVES 4–6 **FREEZE** UP TO 3 MONTHS

60g (2oz) butter, softened
60g (2oz) golden caster sugar
2 eggs, lightly beaten
85g (3oz) self-raising flour, sifted
100g (3½oz) mixed dried fruit

pinch of ground cinnamon
pinch of mixed spice
1 tbsp milk
1–2 tbsp golden syrup

in the slow cooker **PREP** 15 MINS **COOK** 10 MINS PRECOOKING; **HIGH** 3–4 HRS

1 Preheat the slow cooker, if required, and lightly grease a 600ml (1 pint) pudding basin. Put the butter and sugar in a food mixer and beat until pale and creamy, or use a hand-held electric mixer.

2 Add the eggs, a little at a time, with a little of the flour, beating gently as you go. Then add the remaining flour together with the fruit and spices and beat lightly. Finally, add the milk and stir until everything is combined.

3 Put 1–2 tbsp of the golden syrup (depending on how sweet you like it) in the bottom of the pudding basin, then spoon the mixture into the basin. Cover with a pleated piece of greaseproof paper and a sheet of foil. Secure with string, looping it around the basin to form a handle. Sit the pudding basin in the slow cooker and pour in enough boiling water to come halfway up the sides of the basin. Cover with the lid and cook on high for 3–4 hours. Carefully remove the basin from the slow cooker, remove the string, foil, and paper, and turn the pudding out onto a plate. Serve with cream or custard.

traditional method **PREP** 15 MINS **COOK** 1¾ HRS

1 Lightly grease a 600ml (1 pint) pudding basin. Put the butter and sugar in a food mixer and beat until pale and creamy, or use a hand-held electric mixer.

2 Add the eggs, a little at a time, with a little of the flour, beating gently as you go. Then add the remaining flour together with the fruit and spices and beat lightly. Finally, add the milk and stir until everything is combined.

3 Put 1–2 tbsp of the golden syrup (depending on how sweet you like it) in the bottom of the pudding basin, then spoon the mixture into the basin. Cover with a pleated piece of greaseproof paper and a sheet of foil. Secure with string, looping it around the basin to form a handle. Sit the pudding basin in a large heavy-based pan and pour in enough boiling water to come halfway up the side of the basin. Cover with the lid and simmer gently for about 1½ hours, topping up with more boiling water if needed. Carefully remove the basin from the pan, remove the string, foil, and paper, and turn the pudding out onto a plate. Serve with cream or custard.

For an even richer experience, consider using flavoured mint, ginger, or coffee chocolate. To cook the puddings in one batch, use a slow cooker that is a minimum of 4.5 litres in size.

Chocolate mousses

 MAKES 6

2 eggs
3 egg yolks
100g (3½oz) caster sugar

100g (3½oz) dark chocolate (70 per cent cocoa solids), broken into pieces
300ml (10fl oz) double cream

 in the slow cooker 🕐 **PREP** 20 MINS, PLUS CHILLING **COOK** 10 MINS PRECOOKING; **AUTO/LOW** 2½–3 HRS

1 Preheat the slow cooker, if required, and grease six 100ml (3½fl oz) ramekins or metal pudding basins. Put the eggs, egg yolks, and sugar in a mixing bowl and whisk until creamy. Set aside.

2 Put the chocolate in a heatproof bowl and sit it over a pan of barely simmering water. Stir occasionally until melted, remove from the heat, and set aside. Heat the cream in a pan so it is warm, but do not boil, then slowly add the egg mixture, whisking as you go. Stir through the chocolate until it is very well combined.

3 Pour the mixture into the prepared ramekins or basins and cover each one with foil. Pour 3cm (1¼in) hot water into the slow cooker and carefully place the mousses in the slow cooker, stacking them, if necessary, to fit (but not sitting directly on top of each other). Cover with the lid and cook on auto/low for 2½–3 hours; they should still have a wobble in them when they are ready. Remove the ramekins or basins from the slow cooker and leave to cool, then transfer to the refrigerator for a couple of hours to chill. Turn out each mousse onto a bowl and serve with ice cream or shortbread biscuits.

 traditional method 🕐 **PREP** 20 MINS **COOK** 30 MINS

1 Preheat the oven to 160°C (325°F/Gas 3) and grease six 100ml (3½fl oz) ramekins or metal pudding basins. Put the eggs, egg yolks, and sugar in a mixing bowl and whisk until creamy. Set aside.

2 Put the chocolate in a heatproof bowl and sit it over a pan of barely simmering water. Stir occasionally until melted, remove from the heat, and set aside. Heat the cream in a pan so it is warm, but do not boil, then slowly add the egg mixture, whisking as you go. Stir through the chocolate until it is very well combined.

3 Pour the mixture into the prepared ramekins or basins, then sit them in a roasting tin and carefully pour hot water into the tin so it comes halfway up the sides of the ramekins. Sit in the oven and cook for 15–20 minutes; they should still have a wobble in them when they are ready. Remove from the oven and leave to cool, then transfer to the refrigerator for a couple of hours to chill. Turn out each mousse onto a bowl and serve with ice cream or shortbread biscuits.

This is a delicious classic infused with the taste of vanilla. In this recipe, the seeds are discarded, but for something more aromatic, deseed the pod and add the seeds to the milk at the same time.

Classic crème caramel

 MAKES 6

600ml (1 pint) full-fat milk
1 vanilla pod, split lengthways and deseeded
225g (8oz) golden caster sugar

2 whole eggs
4 egg yolks

 in the slow cooker 🕐 **PREP** 15 MINS, PLUS INFUSING AND CHILLING   **COOK** 25 MINS PRECOOKING; **AUTO/LOW** 3–4 HRS

1 Preheat the slow cooker, if required. Pour the milk into a heavy-based pan, add the vanilla pod, and very gently bring almost to the boil. Turn off the heat, cover the pan with the lid, and leave for 20 minutes. This is to give the vanilla pod time to infuse the milk while it cools.

2 Add half of the sugar to another heavy-based pan, then pour in 75ml (2½fl oz) of cold water. Slowly bring to the boil, swirling it around the pan occasionally to ensure all the sugar has dissolved, then boil for about 15 minutes, until the liquid turns a dark golden caramel. Pour this into six 150ml (5fl oz) ramekins, or use larger ones if making fewer crème caramels.

3 Put the remaining sugar with the eggs and egg yolks into a bowl and whisk until well combined and the sugar has dissolved. Discard the vanilla pod and pour the cooled milk into the egg mixture, then briefly whisk again and pour through a sieve into the ramekins. Cover each ramekin with foil and sit them in the slow cooker. Pour in enough boiling water to come halfway up the sides of the ramekins. Cover with the lid and cook on low for 3–4 hours. Lift the slow cooker dish out and leave them to cool in it, then remove the ramekins and chill them overnight in the fridge. Turn out to serve.

traditional method 🕐 **PREP** 15 MINS, PLUS INFUSING AND CHILLING   **COOK** 1½ HRS

1 Preheat the oven to 150°C (300°F/Gas 2). Pour the milk into a heavy-based pan, add the vanilla pod, and very gently bring almost to the boil. Turn off the heat, cover the pan with the lid, and leave for 20 minutes. This is to give the vanilla pod time to infuse the milk while it cools.

2 Add half of the sugar to another heavy-based pan, then pour in 75ml (2½fl oz) of cold water. Slowly bring to the boil, swirling it around the pan occasionally to ensure the sugar has dissolved, then boil for about 15 minutes, until the liquid turns a dark golden caramel. Pour this into six 150ml (5fl oz) ramekins, or use larger ones if making fewer crème caramels.

3 Put the remaining sugar with the eggs and egg yolks into a bowl and whisk until well combined and the sugar has dissolved. Discard the vanilla pod and pour the cooled milk into the egg mixture, then briefly whisk again and pour through a sieve into the ramekins. Sit the ramekins in a deep ovenproof dish, pour in boiling water to come two-thirds of the way up the sides of the ramekins, and cook for 1 hour. Remove the dish from the oven, leaving the ramekins in the hot water for 30 minutes to continue setting. Then leave to cool and chill overnight in the fridge. Turn out to serve.

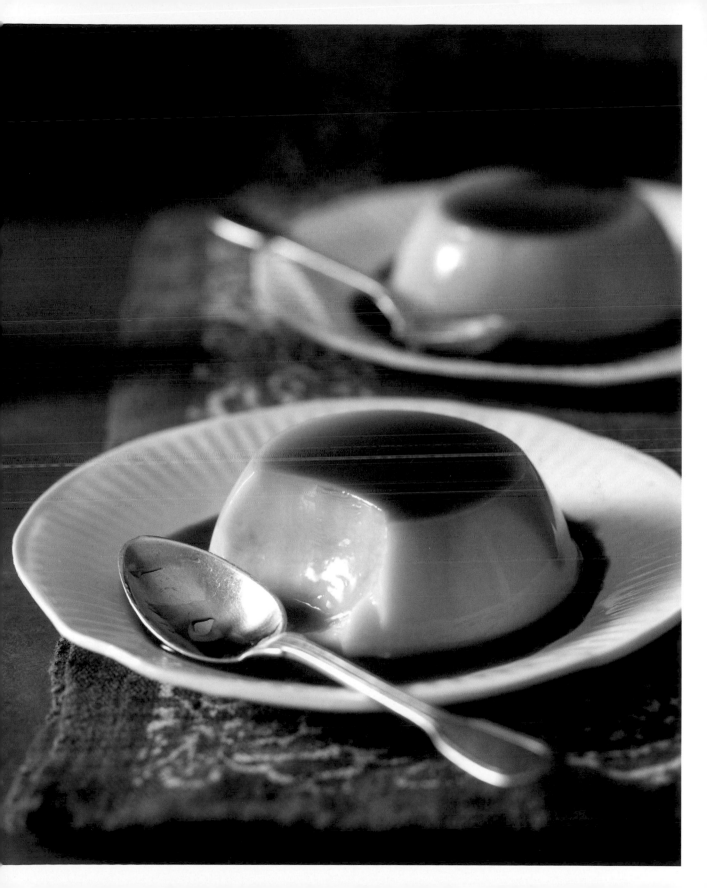

Careful cooking at a low temperature will produce a pudding with a smooth, velvety texture – a perfect use for leftover white bread. For extra decadence, you could use brioche or croissants.

Bread and butter pudding

SERVES 4

30g (1oz) butter, plus extra to grease
5–6 slices of day-old bread, crusts removed,
  about 175g (6oz) total weight
60g (2oz) raisins
3 eggs
300ml (10fl oz) full-fat milk

200ml (7fl oz) single cream
60g (2oz) caster sugar
1 tsp pure vanilla extract
4 tbsp apricot jam
2–3 tsp lemon juice

in the slow cooker   **PREP** 15 MINS, PLUS SOAKING   **COOK** AUTO/LOW 4–5 HRS

1 Lightly grease an ovenproof dish with a little butter (one that will fit in the slow cooker, a soufflé dish would be good). Spread the remaining butter on the slices of bread. Cut each slice in half diagonally, then in half again to form 4 triangles.

2 Place the raisins in the bottom of the dish and arrange overlapping slices of bread across the top. Beat together the eggs, milk, cream, sugar, and vanilla extract. Carefully pour the mixture over the bread, cover with foil, and leave to soak for at least 30 minutes.

3 Preheat the slow cooker, if required. Place the dish in the slow cooker and pour in enough boiling water to come halfway up the side of the dish. Cover with the lid and cook on auto/low for 4–5 hours or until still slightly moist in the centre, but not runny.

4 Meanwhile, put the jam in a small pan with the lemon juice and 1 tbsp water. Bring to the boil, then push the melted jam through a sieve. Carefully brush or spoon the sieved jam over the surface of the hot pudding to glaze. Serve with cream or custard.

traditional method   **PREP** 15 MINS, PLUS SOAKING   **COOK** 40 MINS

1 Lightly grease an ovenproof dish with a little butter. Spread the remaining butter on the slices of bread. Cut each slice in half diagonally, then in half again to form 4 triangles.

2 Place the raisins in the bottom of the dish and arrange overlapping slices of bread across the top. Beat together the eggs, milk, cream, sugar, and vanilla extract. Carefully pour the mixture over the bread, cover with foil, and leave to soak for at least 30 minutes.

3 Preheat the oven to 180°C (350°F/Gas 4). Place the dish in a deep roasting tin and pour boiling water into the tin to a depth of 2.5cm (1in). Bake in the oven for 30–40 minutes, until still slightly moist in the centre, but not runny.

4 Meanwhile, put the jam in a small pan with the lemon juice and 1 tbsp water. Bring to the boil, then push the melted jam through a sieve. Carefully brush or spoon the sieved jam over the surface of the hot pudding to glaze. Serve with cream or custard.

Both the rice and the peaches can be prepared one day ahead and kept covered in the refrigerator. Let the rice come to room temperature, or warm it in a low oven, before serving.

Creamy rice pudding with peaches

SERVES 4–6

65g (2¼oz) short-grain rice
1 litre (1¾ pints) milk, plus more if needed
5cm (2in) cinnamon stick
50g (1¾oz) caster sugar
salt

FOR THE PEACHES

4 ripe peaches, peeled, halved, stoned, and
  cut into wedges
60g (2oz) caster sugar, plus more if needed
250ml (9fl oz) dry red wine, plus more if needed

in the slow cooker ⏱ PREP 15–20 MINS, PLUS MACERATING AND STANDING COOK HIGH 3–4 HRS

1 To prepare the peaches, put them in a non-metallic bowl and sprinkle with sugar; they may need more or less sugar than specified, depending on their sweetness. Pour over enough red wine to cover the fruit completely. Set a plate on top and leave to macerate in the refrigerator for at least 2 hours and up to 24 hours. Strain the liquid into a saucepan, bring to the boil, and simmer for 2 minutes until syrupy. Stir it back into the peaches.

2 Preheat the slow cooker, if required. Put the rice, milk, cinnamon stick, sugar, and a pinch of salt into the slow cooker and stir. Cover with the lid and cook on high for 3–4 hours, giving it a stir halfway through if needed. Let it stand for 1 hour. Discard the cinnamon stick, ladle into serving bowls, and serve with the peaches and wine syrup, which can be either warmed or cold.

traditional method ⏱ PREP 15–20 MINS, PLUS MACERATING AND STANDING COOK 3 HRS

1 To prepare the peaches, put them in a non-metallic bowl and sprinkle with sugar; they may need more or less sugar than specified, depending on their sweetness. Pour over enough red wine to cover the fruit completely. Set a plate on top and leave to macerate in the refrigerator for at least 2 hours and up to 24 hours. Strain the liquid into a saucepan, bring to the boil, and simmer for 2 minutes until syrupy. Stir it back into the peaches.

2 Preheat the oven to 150°C (300°F/Gas 2). Put the rice, milk, cinnamon stick, sugar, and a pinch of salt into an ovenproof dish and stir. Put it in the oven for 3 hours, uncovered, and stirring gently every 30 minutes until the pudding is thick and creamy. Cover the dish with foil if it starts to brown too much.

3 Remove the pudding from the oven. Carefully slip a spoon down the side and stir from the bottom. Let it stand for 1 hour. Discard the cinnamon stick, ladle into serving bowls, and serve with the peaches and wine syrup, which can be either warmed or cold.

You could change the cinnamon in these dumplings for grated nutmeg or mixed spice, and use orange zest instead of lemon for a slightly sweeter finish.

Apple dumplings

SERVES 4

225g (8oz) self-raising flour, sifted
115g (4oz) vegetable suet
1 tsp ground cinnamon, plus extra to serve
grated zest of 1 lemon

4 cooking apples, peeled and cored
1 tbsp demerara sugar
60g (2oz) golden sultanas
icing sugar, to serve

in the slow cooker   **PREP** 20 MINS   **COOK** HIGH 3–4 HRS

1 Preheat the slow cooker, if required. To make the suet pastry, put the flour, suet, cinnamon, and lemon zest into a bowl. Then slowly trickle in about 100ml (3½fl oz) of cold water and mix together until it forms a dough.

2 Roll out the pastry and cut out 4 circles, large enough for each apple. Sit an apple on each round, sprinkle the demerara sugar into the apple holes, and add the sultanas to each. Brush the edges of the pastry with water and bring them together at the top, pinching to secure.

3 Turn the apples over so the sealed side is face down. If you have any pastry left over, you could fashion leaves and stalks for the dumplings. Loosely wrap foil around each and seal. Sit the dumplings in the slow cooker and add boiling water so it is about 2.5cm (1in) deep. Cover with the lid and cook on high for 3–4 hours. Lift the dumplings out of the slow cooker and remove the foil – be careful as they will be very hot. Sprinkle the dumplings with icing sugar and ground cinnamon and serve with cream, custard, or ice cream.

traditional method   **PREP** 20 MINS   **COOK** 30–40 MINS

1 Preheat the oven to 180°C (350°F/Gas 4) and lightly grease a baking sheet. To make the suet pastry, put the flour, suet, cinnamon, and lemon zest into a bowl. Then slowly trickle in about 100ml (3½fl oz) of cold water and mix together until it forms a dough.

2 Roll out the pastry and cut out 4 circles, large enough for each apple. Sit an apple on each round, sprinkle the demerara sugar into the apple holes, and add the sultanas to each. Brush the edges of the pastry with water and bring them together at the top, pinching to secure.

3 Turn the apples over so the sealed side is face down. If you have any pastry left over, you could fashion leaves and stalks for the dumplings. Sit them on the baking sheet. Cook in the oven for 30–40 minutes until golden. Sprinkle the dumplings with icing sugar and ground cinnamon and serve with cream, custard, or ice cream.

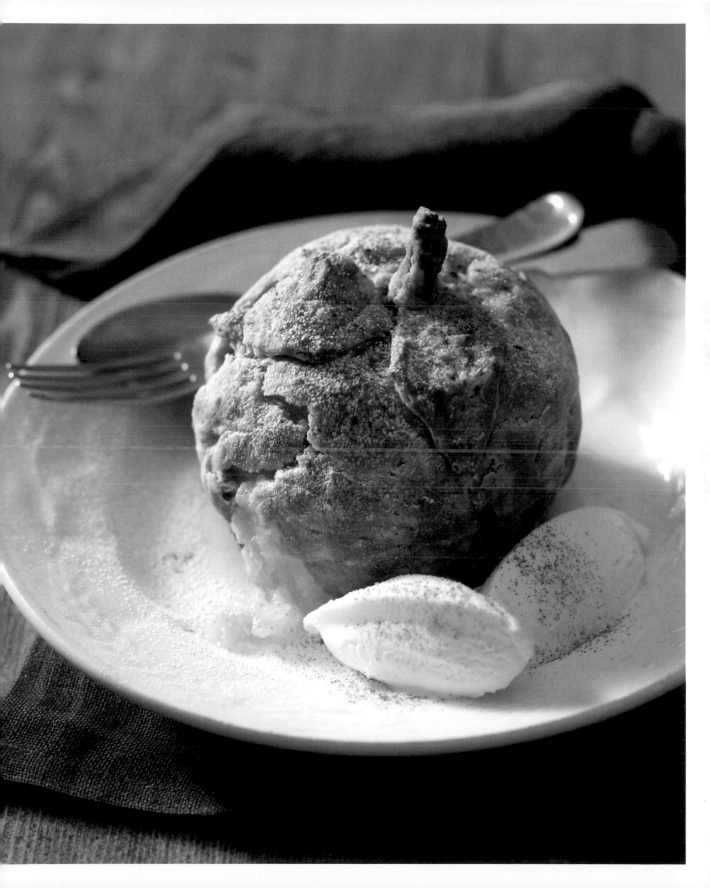

Tapioca is a starchy substance derived from the cassava plant. It is usually simmered in milk or coconut milk, but fruit juice is used here, which turns this dish into something far more lively.

Tapioca pudding

SERVES 4–6

300g can mandarin oranges in natural juice
220g can pineapple slices in natural juice
450–600ml (15fl oz–1 pint) orange juice
75g (2½oz) tapioca
4 tbsp caster sugar, or to taste

100g (3½oz) plain Greek-style yogurt or
  lightly whipped cream (optional)
freshly grated nutmeg or ground
  cinnamon (optional)

in the slow cooker   **PREP** 10 MINS   **COOK** HIGH 1½–2 HRS

1 Preheat the slow cooker, if required. Strain the juice from the oranges and pineapple and make up to 450ml (15fl oz) with orange juice. Set aside. Chop the pineapple into small pieces and set aside with the mandarin segments.

2 Put the tapioca in the slow cooker and stir in the juice. Cover with the lid and cook on high for 1½–2 hours until the tapioca "pearls" become translucent and the mixture is thick and glossy.

3 Stir in sugar to taste, then stir the fruit into the pudding and serve hot. Top with a spoonful of plain yogurt or whipped cream, if desired, and sprinkle with a little nutmeg or cinnamon, if using.

traditional method   **PREP** 10 MINS   **COOK** 50 MINS

1 Strain the juice from the oranges and pineapple and make up to 600ml (1 pint) with orange juice. Set aside. Chop the pineapple into small pieces and set aside with the mandarin segments.

2 Put the tapioca and juice in a heavy-based pan over a high heat and bring to the boil, stirring. The liquid will be very cloudy as it comes up to the boil, but will then clear. Boil gently for 30–50 minutes (or as directed on the packet), stirring often, and brushing down the side of the pan with a pastry brush, until the small "pearls" become translucent and the mixture is thick and glossy.

3 Remove the pan from the heat and stir in sugar to taste, then stir the fruit into the pudding and serve hot. Top with a spoonful of plain yogurt or whipped cream, if desired, and sprinkle with a little nutmeg or cinnamon, if using.

This traditional English pudding was originally steamed in a cloth or shirt sleeve. Here it is cooked as a roll with a layer of jam running through it. Raspberry jam works particularly well.

Hot jam roll

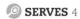 **SERVES** 4

225g (8oz) self-raising flour, sifted
115g (4oz) shredded suet
4–5 tbsp jam

 ### in the slow cooker 🕐 PREP 15 MINS COOK HIGH 3–4 HRS

1 Preheat the slow cooker, if required. Put the flour and suet into a mixing bowl and add 100ml (3½fl oz) water. Using a round-bladed knife, mix to a soft, but not wet dough. Add more water, if necessary. Put the dough onto a floured work surface and roll it out to a rectangle measuring about 18 x 25cm (7 x 10in), ensuring it is no wider than the dimension of the slow cooker.

2 Gently warm the jam in a small pan, but do not allow it to get too hot or it will burn. Spread the pastry with the jam, ensuring there is a narrow border of pastry around the edge so the jam doesn't ooze out when the pastry is rolled up. Roll it up loosely and wrap in greaseproof paper and foil, making a pleat in each to allow for the pudding to expand. Pinch the foil at the edges to secure it tightly so no moisture can get in. Secure with string, looping it around the pudding to form a handle.

3 Sit the pudding in the slow cooker, seam-side up, and pour in just enough hot water to come halfway up the side of the pudding, cover with the lid, and cook on high for 3–4 hours. Remove and leave for 10 minutes, then carefully remove the string, foil, and greaseproof paper, being careful as it will be incredibly hot. Serve sliced with custard or cream.

 ### traditional method 🕐 PREP 15 MINS COOK 30–40 MINS

1 Put the flour and suet into a mixing bowl and add 100ml (3½fl oz) water. Using a round-bladed knife, mix to a soft, but not wet dough. Add more water, if necessary. Put the dough onto a floured work surface and roll it out to a rectangle measuring about 18 x 25cm (7 x 10in), ensuring it is not wider than the dimension of a steaming pan.

2 Gently warm the jam in a small pan, but do not allow it to get too hot or it will burn. Spread the pastry with the jam, ensuring there is a narrow border of pastry around the edge so the jam doesn't ooze out when the pastry is rolled up. Roll it up loosely and wrap in greaseproof paper and foil, making a pleat in each to allow for the pudding to expand. Pinch the foil at the edges to secure it tightly so no moisture can get in.

3 Put the roll in the steaming pan and place it over a pan three-quarters filled with simmering water. Cover and steam for 1½–2 hours or until firm to the touch. Top up with water if it gets too low. Rest for 10 minutes then unwrap. Serve sliced with custard or cream.

Index

Entries in *italics* indicate references
to techniques.

Author

Heather Whinney is an experienced food writer and home economist. She has been the food editor of *Family Circle* and *Prima* magazines and freelance food editor at *BBC Good Food* magazine, as well as working freelance for several publications such as *Good Housekeeping* and *Woman and Home*. She is now the contributing food editor for *Prima*. As a working mother bringing up a family, she understands the issues families and busy households face when it comes to putting good food on the table. Her style and food philosophy has always remained constant – to keep it simple, and write easy recipes for the everyday cook. She is the author of *Cook Express* (2009) and co-author of *The Diabetes Cooking Book* (2010).

Acknowledgments

Heather Whinney would like to thank:

Emma Callery for excellent recipe editing and Tia Sarkar at DK for sterling hard work – what a good team we've made. Thanks to my husband Jos who is my ever-reliable recipe taster and critic and to my daughters Kim and Lorna for having healthy appetites!

Dorling Kindersley would like to thank:
Photography art direction: Luis Peral, Sara Robin
Food stylists: Katie Giovanni, Bridget Sargeson
Prop stylist: Rob Merret
Recipe testers: Jane Bamforth, Rebecca Blackstone, Louisa Carter, Sonja Edridge, Jan Fullwood, Katy Greenwood, Sylvain Jamois, Ann Reynolds, Natalie Seldon
Image retouching: Steve Crozier
Indexer: Hilary Bird
Thanks also to Kajal Mistry and David Fentiman for editorial assistance; and to Danaya Bunnag for design assistance.